Protection of Foreign Investment in India and Investment Treaty Arbitration

Protection of Foreign Investment in India and Investment Treaty Arbitration

Aniruddha Rajput

Published by:
Kluwer Law International B.V.
PO Box 316
2400 AH Alphen aan den Rijn
The Netherlands
Website: www.wolterskluwerlr.com

Sold and distributed in North, Central and South America by:
Wolters Kluwer Legal & Regulatory U.S.
7201 McKinney Circle
Frederick, MD 21704
United States of America
Email: customer.service@wolterskluwer.com

Sold and distributed in all other countries by:
Quadrant
Rockwood House
Haywards Heath
West Sussex
RH16 3DH
United Kingdom
Email: international-customerservice@wolterskluwer.com

Printed on acid-free paper.

ISBN 978-90-411-8231-9

e-Book: ISBN 978-90-411-8614-0
web-PDF: ISBN 978-90-411-8615-7

© 2018 Kluwer Law International BV, The Netherlands

All rights reserved. No part of this publication may be reproduced, stored in a retrieval system, or transmitted in any form or by any means, electronic, mechanical, photocopying, recording, or otherwise, without written permission from the publisher.

Permission to use this content must be obtained from the copyright owner. Please apply to: Permissions Department, Wolters Kluwer Legal & Regulatory U.S., 76 Ninth Avenue, 7th Floor, New York, NY 10011-5201, USA. Website: www.wolterskluwerlr.com

Printed in the United Kingdom.

MIX
FSC® C103993

Table of Contents

Foreword	ix
List of Abbreviations	xi
Acknowledgements	xiii

CHAPTER 1
Introduction — 1

CHAPTER 2
Historical Background of Investment Protection — 9
§2.01 The First Phase (1947-1991) — 9
    [A] The Role of Foreign Investment at the Time of Independence — 10
    [B] Domestic Policy Towards Foreign Investment — 11
    [C] Protection of Foreign Investment and International Law — 16
§2.02 The Second Phase (1991-2011) — 26
§2.03 The Third Phase (2011 Onwards) — 31

CHAPTER 3
Conditions of Entry, Operation and Consequences of Violations (Doctrine of Illegality) — 35
§3.01 Indian Arbitral Practice — 36
§3.02 Regulatory Framework in India for Entry and Operations — 39
§3.03 Consequences of Violation of Entry and Operation: The Doctrine of Illegality — 46
    [A] Doctrine of Illegality — 46
    [B] Investments Should Be Made in Good Faith to Gain Protection of Investment Treaties — 48
    [C] Extent of Violation of Domestic Law Necessary to Constitute Illegality — 52

Table of Contents

	[D]	Situations Where Defence of Illegality Would Be Unavailable to States	53
	[E]	Stage for Deciding Illegality	56

CHAPTER 4
Applicable Laws and Jurisdiction 59
§4.01 Applicable Laws 59
§4.02 Jurisdiction 69
    [A] Investment 69
    [B] Investor 78

CHAPTER 5
Treatment Standards 87
§5.01 Expropriation 88
    [A] Expropriation Provisions in Investment Treaties 89
    [B] Expropriation under Domestic Law of India 98
§5.02 FET and FPS 102
    [A] Treaty Practice 102
    [B] Analysis of Domestic Law 109
    [C] Legitimate Expectations 110
§5.03 MFN Treatment and NT 115

CHAPTER 6
Dispute Resolution and Enforcement of Investment Awards 127
§6.01 Dispute Resolution Provisions 127
§6.02 Enforcement of Investment Awards 135
§6.03 Proceedings under Indian Arbitration Act 139

CHAPTER 7
Indian Judiciary and Investment Treaty Arbitration 147
§7.01 The Structure and Nature of the Indian Judiciary 147
§7.02 Indian Judiciary and Protection of Foreign Investment 149
§7.03 The Responsibility of India for the Acts of Judiciary 155
    [A] Judicial Activism and Other Problems 158
    [B] Denial of Justice 160
    [C] FET 167
    [D] Expropriation 168
§7.04 Conclusions 169

CHAPTER 8
India and ICSID 171
§8.01 Reasons, Background and Negotiating History of ICSID 171
    [A] Reasons and Background 172
    [B] Negotiating History 177
§8.02 The Structure and Working of ICSID 179

| §8.03 | Why Did India Not Join ICSID? | 181 |
| §8.04 | Pros and Cons of Joining ICSID | 184 |

CHAPTER 9
Conclusion 195

Bibliography 199

Table of Cases 207

Table of Statutes 219

Table of Treaties and Other Legal Instruments 221

Index 225

Foreword

This book fulfils the expectations which are raised by its title, and it goes beyond. It provides a well-structured and comprehensive account of the law relating to the protection of foreign investment in India. But it is not merely a treatise which faithfully records this country's law and the practice regarding investment protection. This book also offers a historically informed and politically sensitive analysis of the Indian experience with investment protection from the time of independence to the complex situation today.

The author, Dr Aniruddha Rajput, is particularly qualified to write this book. After getting deeply acquainted with the topic academically, he was called, by the Government of India, to contribute to developing the new Indian Model BIT 2015. This unique combination of experience has enabled Dr Rajput to offer a meticulous description of the Indian practice over time, with an emphasis on the present situation, as well as an authentic articulation of the spirit of the current Indian policy. This spirit is self-confident and ambitious. One of its characteristics is the apparent tension between a perceived 'progress' in investment protection in India and a simultaneous 'regress' in the possibility of investors to bring claims before international investment tribunals. Dr Rajput, who, as an Advocate at the Supreme Court of India, has a strong basis in national law, can credibly describe the important protections which Indian Law, and in particular the Indian judiciary, provide for investors. At the same time, Dr Rajput, who is now also a member of the UN International Law Commission, displays a keen sense of the international political and legal situation in the area of investment protection more generally situates the Indian law and policy within this general framework. This entails the credible ambition of India to change from being a norm-taker to that of a norm maker.

This book is an important read, not only for those who wish to get a reliable sense of the state of investment protection in India, but also for those want to become familiar with the political dynamics and motivations in this context. Investment protection in

Foreword

India is an important element of investment protection law more generally, and its development. Dr Rajput's book gives us a missing piece in the development of investment law, and international law more generally.

Georg Nolte
Professor of Law, Humboldt University Berlin
Member and Chair of the International Law Commission
Berlin, September 2017

List of Abbreviations

BIPAs	Bilateral Investment Promotion and Protection Agreements
BIT	Bilateral Investment Treaty
CCEA	Cabinet Committee on Economic Affairs
CPC	Code of Civil Procedure, 1908
DPC	Dabhol Power Company
DTH	Direct to home
EU	European Union
FCN	Friendship Commerce and Navigation
FDI	Foreign Direct Investment
FEMA	Foreign Exchange Management Act
FERA	Foreign Exchange Regulation Act
FET	Fair and Equitable Treatment
FIB	Foreign Investment Board
FIPB	Foreign Investment Promotion Board
FPS	Full Protection and Security
FTA	Free Trade Agreement
G77	Group of 77
GATT	General Agreement on Tariff and Trade
GE	General Electric
IBA	International Bar Association
IBRD	International Bank for Reconstruction and Development
ICC	International Chamber of Commerce
ICC	International Criminal Court
ICJ	International Court of Justice
ICSID	International Center for Settlement of Investment Disputes

List of Abbreviations

IFAD	International Fund for Agriculture Development
IIAs	International Investment Agreements
ILC	International Law Commission
IMF	International Monetary Fund
ISA	International Seabed Authority
ITA	Investment treaty arbitration
LCIA	London Court of International Arbitration
LDCs	least developed countries
LIBOR	London Interbank Offered Rate
LLP	Limited Liability Partnership
MAI	Multilateral Agreement on Investments
MFN	Most Favoured Nation
MIGA	Multilateral Investment Guarantee Agreement
MNCs	Multinational Corporations
MSEB	Maharashtra State Electricity Board
NAFTA	North American Free Trade Agreement
NIEO	New International Economic Order
NT	National Treatment
OECD	Organization for Economic Cooperation and Development
OPIC	Overseas Private Investment Corporation
PCIJ	Permanent Court of International Justice
RBI	Reserve Bank of India
SEBI	Securities and Exchange Board of India
TRIM	Trade Related Investment Measures
UN	United Nations
UNCITRAL	The United Nations Commission on International Trade Law
UNCTAD	United Nations Conference on Trade and Development
US	United States
USA	United States of America
USD	United States Dollars
VCFs	Venture Capital Funds
VCLT	Vienna Convention on Law of Treaties, 1969
WTO	World Trade Organization

Acknowledgements

I take this opportunity to thank various persons and institutions that have contributed immensely for the successful completion of this book. Most portions of the book were written during my stay at Berlin with the KFG International Rule of Law Rise or Decline? My sojourn in Berlin was possible due to the generous invitation extended by Professor Georg Nolte – an invitation supported by his colleagues Professor Heike Krieger and Professor Andreas Zimmermann. The intellectual environment there was robust and gratifying, which facilitated the work on this book. Researchers at the research group were helpful to find books and other material from time to time.

I must also thank students that assisted me at various stages of the project. They are Sarthak Malhotra, Vikhyat Oberoi, Rouble Sorkkar, Debaranjan Goswami, Karthik Tayur, Vaishali Movva, Gayathree Devi K.T., Vishakha Choudhary, Nirmal Mathew and Pradyumna Duwarah.

Equally crucial has been the role of the publishers: Kluwer International. The professional and experienced team allowed, facilitated and expedited the preparation of the book; and its presentation in the form in which the readers have it before them.

My parents Dr Dhananjay Rajput and Mrs Vasundhara Rajput have always been a source of inspiration. Despite all my failings and drawbacks they always believed in me and persuaded me to undertake and continue in an uninterrupted manner, an 'intellectual journey' – of which, the present book is a part.

CHAPTER 1
Introduction

India is described as the 'bright spot' in the global economic landscape.[1] It is one of the fastest growing economies in the world, with the potential of becoming the largest in the future.[2] It has a burgeoning service sector and a rapidly expanding manufacturing sector. The demand for economic growth is high because that would alleviate the population below the poverty line and keep the global growth going.

India is rich with natural and economic resources. To satisfy its developmental needs, capital investment is crucial. There is domestic capital flow, but limited to certain sectors of the economy. Foreign capital is necessary for bolstering and maintaining the economic growth. Foreign investment in manufacturing and other labour intensive sectors has the potential to generate employment. Employment results into absorption of the workforce in the formal sectors and raises the standard of living. Employment in the sectors where foreign investors invest would involve skill and technical know-how thereby enhancing the skill set of the population. Foreign investment could also result in technology and skill transfer. The extent of benefits from technology transfer is limited since the technology is protected by intellectual property rights. But the imparting of skills to the labour force is long term and beneficial. Due care has to be taken while dealing with foreign investments. They need to be properly channelized in labour intensive and priority sectors. Otherwise, they tend to crowd in areas where large investments already exist or excessively exploit natural resources, without making a substantial contribution to the domestic economy. The challenge while dealing with foreign investment is to ensure that there is an appropriate balance

---

1. International Monetary Fund, *For India, Strong Growth Persists Despite New Challenges* (22 Feb. 2017) http://www.imf.org/en/News/Articles/2017/02/21/NA022217-For-India-strong-growth-persists-despite-new-challenges (accessed 1 Jul. 2017).
2. The Economic Times, *With $85 Trillion, How India Can Become World's Largest Economy* (12 Nov. 2011) http://economictimes.indiatimes.com/opinion/et-commentary/with-85-trillion-how-india-can-become-worlds-largest-economy/articleshow/10699821.cms (accessed 1 Jul. 2017). According to PwC Indian economy will be second largest, but the gap between the India and other economies will be large, PwC, *The world in 2050*, 2, https://www.pwc.com/gx/en/issues/the-economy/assets/world-in-2050-february-2015.pdf (accessed 1 Jul. 2017).

between the needs of the economy and the potential contribution that foreign investment can make.

Realizing the importance of foreign investment, the Government of India has undertaken various steps to encourage foreign investment and make India a favoured destination for foreign investments. The Foreign Direct Investment Policy (FDI Policy) is an important announcement made each year by the Government of India, under which the sectors in which investments are allowed, the extent to which investments can be made and other conditions of investment are set out. A survey of the FDI Policies over the years shows that more and more sectors have been opened to foreign investment and the extent of investment that can be made in these sectors has been enhanced from time to time. The prominent sectors to be opened in the recent times are media and entertainment, retail, 100% opening of aviation sectors, 100% opening in the defence manufacturing sectors, etc.[3] It is only natural that the gradual opening up of sectors and the extent of permissible investment has only grown over time and would also continue in the future depending on the needs and priorities of the economy. The gradual opening of the economy for foreign investments is a part of the larger goal of pushing the manufacturing sector in India – under the Make in India campaign.[4] The Make in India is a flagship programme that attempts to integrate all the departments of the government in order to attract foreign investments in certain important areas. During April-December 2015, nearly 40% increase in investment inflows has been attributed to the Make in India campaign.[5] The foreign investment attracted under Make in India continued to increase during 2016.[6] While working on FDI Policy and the Make in India campaign, the Government of India has been working consistently to improve India's position in the 'ease of doing business' ranking of the World Bank. India has made some upward progress in the ranking, yet a lot remains to be achieved.

In light of these measures, India is rapidly emerging as one of the favourite destinations for foreign investment. During 2015 and 2016, it was the ninth largest recipient of foreign investment and received USD 44 billion in each of those years.[7] For 2017, it is projected by United Nations Conference on Trade and Development (UNCTAD) that it is the third most favourite destination for foreign investment after the United States (US) and China.[8] The outflow of investments is also rising. But the rate of inflow outpaces outflow vastly. According to the Reserve Bank of India (RBI), during 2016-2017, the net foreign investment that came into India was USD 41,956 million and

---

3. Detailed discussion in Chapter 3.
4. About Us, http://www.makeinindia.com/about (accessed 1 Jul. 2017).
5. The Economic Times, *FDI up 40% to $29.44 bn in Apr-Dec FY16*, http://economictimes.indiatimes.com/news/economy/foreign-trade/fdi-up-40-to-29-44-bn-in-apr-dec-fy16/articleshow/51175467.cms (accessed 1 Jul. 2017).
6. Live Mint referring Nagesh Kumar, *South & South-West Asia Office of the United Nations Economic and Social Commission for Asia and the Pacific (UNESCAP)*, http://www.livemint.com/Money/K1BnZ0ZQV6FhJKsZWcMHVL/India-ranks-10th-in-FDI-inflows-UNCTAD-report.html (accessed 1 Jul. 2017).
7. UNCTAD, *World Investment Report*, 12, http://unctad.org/en/PublicationsLibrary/wir2017_en.pdf (accessed 1 Jul. 2017).
8. *Ibid.*, at 8, 9.

Chapter 1: Introduction

the total outflow of investments was USD 6,974 million. The inflow of foreign investment is more than six times the outflow of foreign investment in India. Therefore, India is still a predominantly capital-importing country.[9]

Various legal issues, and primarily issues of international law, emerge in situations where foreign investors enter a country. There are various challenges that a foreign investor faces. The first legal question is whether the foreign investor has made an investment. The International Monetary Fund (IMF) and the Organization for Economic Cooperation and Development (OECD) have defined 'FDI' as cross-border investment made by a resident enterprise in one economy (the 'direct investor' or 'multinational enterprise') with the objective of establishing a lasting interest in an enterprise resident in an economy other than that of the direct investor (the 'foreign affiliate').[10] Lasting interest implies the existence of a long-term relationship.[11] The foreign investor creates a presence in the host State by acquiring assets in the host State, which may take the form of a manufacturing plant, office space, etc. and employing persons. There is a commitment of capital, credit taken and expenses incurred in making and a continuous presence in the host State. There is a presence as well as a risk. The foreign investor has to face a different culture, local conditions, the legal system, approach of the administration (which may change over time), especially local administration and the approach of the courts towards foreigners. There is always a threat of change in the policy of administration towards foreign investment and hostility of national courts. Not in all countries that such situations exist, but there is no assurance that situations may not go wrong. Since a foreign investor has a permanent presence, the consequences of situations going wrong would be calamitous. International Investment Agreements (IIAs) aim at protecting foreign investors from arbitrary and unreasonable decisions of the government and the failure or the absence of the possibility of redress by the domestic courts. These agreements are entered between States, whereby they undertake obligations to treat foreign investors from other States, which are parties to the treaty, in the manner prescribed under the treaty. The treaties may take the form of a Bilateral Investment Treaty (BIT) or a Free Trade Agreement (FTA). BITs, as the name suggests, are treaties between two States for the protection of foreign investment. FTAs are treaties between two or more States that deal comprehensively with trade and investment issues. Thus, investment is one of the areas covered rather than the only area covered, as is the case with the BITs. Most of the IIAs (for convenience they have been referred to as BITs in this book) include a compulsory dispute resolution clause, whereby the foreign investor is capable of initiating international arbitration against the host State (i.e., the State where investment has been made). The arbitral tribunal consists of arbitrators of the choice of the parties to the dispute, i.e., the foreign investor and the host State. The arbitral tribunal issues binding decisions. The practice of entering into investment treaties started in 1959, when

---

9. OECD, *Detailed Benchmark Definition of Foreign Direct Investment*, 234 (4th ed., OECD 2008); IMF, *Balance of Payments Manual*, 278 (6th ed., IMF 2008).
10. OECD, *supra* n. 9, at p. 234; IMF, *Balance of Payments Manual*, 278 (6th ed., IMF 2008).
11. Lisa Sachs and Karp Sauvant, *BITs, DTTs, and FDI Flows: An Overview*, The Effect of Treaties on Foreign Direct Investment: Bilateral Investment Treaties, Double Taxation Treaties and Investment Flows, xxviii (Oxford University Press 2009).

Germany entered into the first two BITs with Pakistan and Dominican Republic in 1959. India joined in relatively late. India entered into its first BIT in 1994 and has been an active participant in treaty making since then.[12]

While BITs are aimed at protecting foreign investors from arbitrary actions of the host State, if the protection under the BITs is taken too far, investor protection may turn into an excessive restriction on regulatory exercises by the host State. The experience of investment treaty arbitration (ITA) for the last few decades has shown that actions were undertaken by the host State for public often get challenged before investment tribunals and States are found responsible for the adoption of such regulatory measures.[13] Even if the foreign investor does not resort to investment arbitration, the threat of an investment claim is also used to stop host States from undertaking regulations for public interest.[14] Investment treaties with dispute resolution clauses are said to be creating 'regulatory chill'.[15] Investment tribunals are capable of awarding compensation, which often runs in high amounts and concerns are being raised about the manner of adjudication of investment tribunals.[16]

Protection of foreign investors is unquestionably necessary but whether investment treaties and particularly those with mandatory dispute resolution clause are necessary is under question. While the BIT literature emphasizes the importance of strong investor protection as a stimulant for investment,[17] attributing a significant

---

12. See Chapter 2 for detailed discussion.
13. Asha Kaushal, *Revisiting History: How the Past Matters for the Present Backlash Against the Foreign Investment Regime*, 50 Harvard International Law Journal 491, 493-4 (2009); *Eastern Sugar B.V. v. Czech Republic*; SCC Case No. 088/2004 (27 Mar. 2007); See *Compañía de Aguas del Aconquija S.A. and Vivendi Universal S.A. v. Argentine Republic*, Award, ICSID Case No. ARB/97/3 (20 Aug. 2007); Refer to *Metalclad Corp v. Government of Mexico*, ICSID Case No. ARB (AF)/97/1; refer to *Ethyl Corporation v. Government of Canada* (NAFTA/UNCITRAL 1976) https://www.italaw.com/cases/409 (accessed 1 Jul. 2017) (Canada settled the claim and paid USD 13 million to the investor).
14. New Brunswick, Canada backed away from introducing public automobile insurance after being threatened by investors about a NAFTA arbitration; Indonesia was forced to allow open-pit mining in protected forest areas after investors threatened Indonesia about initiating arbitration; the notice of arbitration by Vattenfall to Germany forced the Federal Government of Hamburg to issue a modified and enforceable permit and absolve Vattenfall of prior responsibilities; Costa Rica paid the American investor Harken USD 11 Million after it sued Costa Rica for rejecting Harken Energy's Environment Impact Assessment for off shore oil explorations; Refer to *Eli Lilly v. Government of Canada*, ICSID Case No. UNCT/14/2 http://www.italaw.com/cases/1625 (accessed 1 Jul. 2017).
15. Leon E. Trakman, *Investor State Arbitration or Local Courts: Will Australia Set a New Trend?*, 46 Journal of World Trade 83, 95 (2012).
16. There is a lot of literature written in the field about inconsistent decision-making by investment tribunal and overstepping beyond its jurisdiction. See generally, Gus van Harten, *Investment Treaty Arbitration and Public Law*, 152-80 (Oxford University Press 2007); Susan Franck, *The Legitimacy Crisis in Investment Treaty Arbitration: Privatizing Public International Law through Inconsistent Decisions*, Fordham Law Review 73, 1521 (2004); Charles Brower, *A Crisis of Legitimacy*, 7 National Law Journal 1-3 (2002); Muthucumaraswamy Sornarajah, *A Coming Crisis: Expansionary Trends in Investment; Treaty Arbitration*, in Appeals Mechanism in International Investment Disputes 3 (Karl Sauvant with Michael Chiswick Patterson (eds), Oxford University Press, 2008).
17. For an example of an empirical study in support see: Eric Neumayer and Laura Spess, *Do Bilateral Investment Treaties Increase Foreign Direct Investment to Developing Countries?*, 33(10) World Development 1567-85 (October 2005).

Chapter 1: Introduction

inflow enhancement to the same, there has also been disagreement. For instance, examining the question of whether formally strongest BITs lead to greater investment flows, a study reported statistical analysis to present an unclear linkage.[18] Theoretical explanations relating to why BITs would strengthen inflows usually point towards risk mitigation as a factor – this is counterbalanced by the extraordinary complexity an investment decision entails. This coupled with the inconsistency of investment tribunals raises questions as to the impact of BITs in enhancing investment.

The World Bank has noted that many investors are unaware of the existence of a BIT when deciding the place of investment and remain oblivious until some issue arises which makes the BIT relevant.[19] It is at best, one of the multiple considerations – and a one that provides more of a psychological comfort. They could, therefore, be seen contributing towards a credible environment of good institutional quality but they do not encourage flow of investments.[20] There is a study suggesting that BITs may operate as a substitute for institutional quality in the host State and may result into higher flows of foreign investment.[21] It is difficult to firmly State the precise effect of BITs on FDI flows. The literature is divided and often convoluted between pro-investors and anti-investors debate. It may not be possible to provide decisive empirical or theoretical link between increase in foreign investment and present of investment treaties with compulsory dispute resolution clauses. From a business perspective, it is too much to expect that a foreign investor would make an investment in a country only because it is providing protection under an investment treaty and giving the option of investment claims. The priority of an investor is going to be the prospect of profits and absence of minimal presence of risks: including political and legal risks. Therefore, BITs with compulsory dispute resolution cannot be the sole or the crucial criterion in the decision of the foreign investor to investment in a country.[22]

Yet, States continue to enter into BITs, to give a signal to the investors that they are prepared to offer better investment protection framework under their domestic law.[23] If the investor perceives a certain jurisdiction to be conducive for business, the presence of a BIT is an added advantage rather than the underlying reason for deciding to invest in a country. BITs with dispute resolution clauses provide a psychological comfort to foreign investors while investing in a foreign country, which may not be the sole or the preponderant factor in the decision of investment.

Some States have expressed discomfort with investment treaties and particularly those with dispute resolution clauses. Australia was the first developed country to announce that it would not enter into any investment agreements with dispute

---

18. Jason Webb Yackee, *Bilateral Investment Treaties, Credible Commitment, and the Rule of (International) Law: Do BITs Promote Foreign Direct Investment?*, 42 4 Law and Society Review 805-32 (19 Nov. 2008).
19. World Bank, *World Development Report 2005*, World Bank, 177 (2005).
20. M. Hallward-Driemeier, 'Do Bilateral Investment Treaties Attract FDI? Only a Bit...and They Could Bite' World Bank Policy Research Papers, WPS 3121, 22-3.
21. Eric Neumayer and Laura Spess, *supra* n. 17, at 1567, 1582-3.
22. *Supra* n. 11, at 18-9.
23. *Ibid.*, at pp. 26-7.

resolution clauses;[24] Indonesia has terminated nearly twenty BITs, following it up with the strategy of allowing BITs to lapse upon their termination period.[25] Australia has negotiated the Trans Pacific Partnership with an investment chapter and a dispute resolution clause, albeit with a tobacco measures exception.[26] Ecuador has not signed any BITs since 2001[27] and terminated nine BITs in 2008.[28] Bolivia has announced its intention to withdraw from International Center for Settlement of Investment Disputes (ICSID)[29] and also announced to renegotiate a number of agreements.[30] South Africa seeks to replace its BIT model of investor protection with its domestic legislation which does not grant foreign investors the right to pursue international arbitration (unless the government consents to such arbitration).[31] Brazil has always stayed away from the system and not entered into BITs. India lost its first investment case in 2011 against an Australian investor White Industries. This led to a major reversal and subsequent alterations in the government policy on investment protection through investment treaties. The Government is keen on foreign investments but wants to be careful to see that frivolous or unnecessary investment claims are not filed. India brought out a new model BIT in December 2015, intending to replace its existing Bilateral Investment Promotion and Protection Agreements (BIPAs) and future investment treaties.[32] After issuing the Model BIT, the Government India unilaterally terminated all existing investment treaties on 31 March 2017, having given one year's time to countries to renegotiate the treaties based on the Model BIT passed by the cabinet. India has sent

---

24. During April 2011, the Labour-led Gilliard Government announced that it would omit ISDS clauses from investment treaties. However, subsequently, there has been much ambiguity about the stand of the Australian Government: Refer to http://kluwerarbitrationblog.com/2015/06/04/australias-conflicting-approach-to-isds-where-to-from-here/ (accessed 1 Jul. 2017); Kyla Tienhara and Patricia Ranald *Investment Treaty News* (12 Jul. 2011) http://www.iisd.org/itn/2011/07/12/australias-rejection-of-investor-state-dispute-settlement-four-potential-contributing-factors/ (accessed 1 Jul. 2017) (Note that the original Government of Australia page indicating the stance returns a 404 error, hence the references to blogs on the reportage.)
25. PanjiPrasetyo, *Protecting the Government in Investor-State Dispute*, The Jakarta Post (27 Jun. 2016) http://www.thejakartapost.com/news/2016/06/27/protecting-government-investor-state-dispute.html (accessed 3 Mar. 2017); The Economist, *The Arbitration Game* (11 Oct. 2014) http://www.economist.com/news/finance-and-economics/21623756-governments-are-souring-treaties-protect-foreign-investors-arbitration (accessed 1 Jul. 2017).
26. The Trans Pacific Partnership Agreement (TPP), Art. 29.5 (26 Jan. 2016) https://www.mfat.govt.nz/assets/_securedfiles/Trans-Pacific-Partnership/Text/29.-Exceptions-and-General-Provisions.pdf (accessed 1 Jul. 2017); for reportage, see The Sydney Morning Herald, (7 Oct. 2015) http://www.smh.com.au/comment/tobacco-carveout-highlights-risks-of-tpp-20151007-gk38os.html (accessed 1 Jul. 2017).
27. UNCTAD Investment Policy Hub, Ecuador Country Profile, http://investmentpolicyhub.unctad.org/IIA/CountryBits/61 (accessed 1 Jul. 2017).
28. UNCTAD, *Denunciation of the ICSID Convention and BITS: Impact on Investor-State Claims*, IIA Issues Note No. 2 (December 2010) http://unctad.org/en/Docs/webdiaeia20106_en.pdf (accessed 4 Mar. 2017).
29. IISD, *Bolivia Notifies World Bank of Withdrawal from ICSID, Pursues BIT Revisions* (4 May 2007) http://www.iisd.org/pdf/2007/itn_may9_2007.pdf (accessed 1 Jul. 2017).
30. Ibid.
31. Section 13, Protection of Investment Act 2015 https://www.thedti.gov.za/gazzettes/39514.pdf (accessed 1 Jul. 2017).
32. Asit Ranjan Mishra, *India Rejects EU, Canada's Bid for Global Investment Pact* http://www.livemint.com/Politics/3mD8bKW3Q6rSiyfQVFcgSM/India-rejects-EU-Canadas-bid-for-global-investment-pact.html (accessed 1 Jul. 2017).

Chapter 1: Introduction

notices to fifty-eight countries terminating and offering to negotiate the existing BITs.[33] The book discusses all these developments in detail. The past BITs have been terminated, and it is not clear what would be the precise contents of the BITs in the future. BIT negotiation is a long and arduous task. Therefore, at this stage, it would be useful to understand the contents of the past BITs that were recently terminated. That would help in understanding the reasons for changes in policy and specific contents of the BITs. As new BITs come into force the discussion of the old BITs will be of use in interpreting the future BITs, especially to understand the intention behind changing certain provisions.

India is a curious case for the study of the relationship and impact of foreign investment and ITA because it is an influential player in the cross-border movement of capital. In addition to the economic stature, India has been an active member at various international fora and has emerged as a leader in various negotiations. It is also in an influential position politically, which will only increase with its economic stature. Until now, India was mostly a rule taker in the field of international law. It has emerged as a rule maker by introducing innovative provisions in its Model BIT, which is bound to influence future treaty making of India and of other States.[34] These recent changes in foreign investment policy reflect that India is willing to think differently and have its relationship with foreign investment on its own terms.

Therefore, there are two related themes underlying this book: protection of foreign investment in India; and the present relationship with and the potential impact of ITA on India. This book will comprehensively discuss the legal position and policy towards investor protection in India and the impacts of ITA on the governance structures and regulatory framework of India. The extent to which ITA would be informed by the activities of the Indian state and to what extent would India be influenced by ITA. Questions of protection of foreign investors are also involved in State-to-State disputes and State contracts. In fact, a large area of disputes is covered by arbitration clauses in State contracts. In these cases, it is classically an entity of the State involved rather than the State itself. These disputes arise out of commercial contracts between State and the foreign corporate entity.[35] This book does not discuss

---

33. Government of India, Ministry of Commerce & Industry, Department of Industrial Policy & Promotion, Lok Sabha Unstarred Question No. 1290 (25 Jul. 2016), http://164.100.47.190/loksabhaquestions/annex/9/AU1290.pdf. (accessed 1 Jul. 2017).
34. Aniruddha Rajput, *India's Shifting Treaty Practice: A Comparative Analysis of the 2003 and 2015 Model BITs*, 7 Jindal Global Law Review 201, 224-6 (2016).
35. For a discussion on the law relating to State contracts *see* Robert Jennings, *State Contracts in International Law*, 37 British Yearbook of International Law 156 (1961); M. Sornarajah, *International Commercial Arbitration: The Problem of State Contracts* (Longman 1990); AFM Maniruzzaman, *State Contracts in Contemporary International Law: Monist vs Dualist Controversies*, 12 European Journal of International Law 309 (2001); Hop Dang, *The Applicability of International Law as Governing Law of State Contracts*, 17 Australian International Law Journal 133 (2010); Ivar Alvik, *Contracting with Sovereignty: State Contracts and International Arbitration* (Hart Publishing 2011); Michael Feit, *Responsibility of the State under International Law for the Breach of Contract Committed by a State-Owned Entity*, 28 Berkeley Journal of International Law 142 (2010); Andrea Giardina, *State Contracts: National versus International Law*, 5 Italian Yearbook of International Law 147 (1980); UNCTAD, *State Contracts: UNCTAD Series on Issues in International Investment Agreements* (2004).

State contracts or State-to-State disputes. It focuses only disputes arising out of investment treaties.

The book consists of nine chapters. The introductory chapter is followed by Chapter 2, which discusses the historical background of investor protection in India. The phases through which the attitude and policy of India regarding protection of foreign investment has undergone and the reasons for these changes are set out in detail.

Chapter 3 is about the requirement of valid entry and operation of foreign investment into India. The FDI Policy, domestic regulatory framework and the interpretation and application of entry requirements in ITA is discussed.

Chapter 4 is about the jurisdiction and applicable law in ITA. This chapter would reflect upon the treaty practice of India, jurisprudence of investment tribunals in relation to jurisdiction and applicable law and the role of the domestic law of India in investment arbitration proceedings where India is involved.

Chapter 5 discusses treatment standards in Indian BITs. The prominent treatment standards such as expropriation, fair and equitable treatment (FET), full protection and security (FPS), most favoured nation (MFN) and national treatment (NT) are discussed in detail, along with relevant arbitral jurisprudence. The interpretation of these legal principles and their relationship and impact on the domestic law of India is also elucidated.

Chapter 6 is on dispute resolution clauses and enforcement of investment arbitration awards. The provisions on dispute resolution in Indian BITs and various consequences that may follow once an investment tribunal delivers an award, *inter alia*, recognition and enforcement are discussed.

Chapter 7 explores the interaction of protection of foreign investment and the Indian judiciary. It is indeed a complex and ironical relationship. On the one hand, the Indian judiciary may protect the rights of foreign investors by controlling the actions of the Government of India, on the other hand, the very actions of Indian judiciary may constitute a basis for an investment claim. This tensed and conflicting relationship is elaborated in Chapter 7.

Chapter 8 is on India and ICSID. India is not a party to the ICSID Convention. The chapter explains the structure and working of ICSID, historical reasons for India not joining the ICSID Convention and lastly what could be the pros and cons of joining the ICSID system.

The last chapter concludes by bringing together the different themes discussed throughout the book.

CHAPTER 2
Historical Background of Investment Protection

Indian policy and outlook towards foreign investment and its protection have transformed overtime. It has oscillated from one approach to another in the past and now appears to have stabilized. There have been three phases. The first two phases represent oscillation from one approach to another, whereas the third represents maturity and stability. The first phase extended from the time of independence from the British rule, until the reluctant opening of the Indian economy in 1991. At this point, the second phase begins. The second period extends from the integration of the Indian economy with the world economy through regulatory reforms, including liberalization, allowing easier entry and operation of foreign investment and investors in India. This period ended with the first investment arbitration case that India lost in 2011 (*White Industries v. India*). This case marks an important policy shift in the policy and international legal framework for the protection of foreign investment.

§2.01 THE FIRST PHASE (1947-1991)

The first phase is long with some variations in the Indian policy. However, it would be appropriate to discuss the whole period of the first phase together, as there were no sudden policy shifts. The changes were mostly gradual. The approach of the Government of India could be understood better if the domestic and international law approaches are seen separately. However, before undertaking the discussion on the Indian approach to investor protection in domestic and international law, it would be informative to understand the nature of the Indian economy and the role of foreign investors at the time of independence from the British rule.

[A] The Role of Foreign Investment at the Time of Independence

Kidron starts his book on the history of foreign investment in India with the following instructive paragraph:

> With independence, India became host to a large body of foreign capital. It was three-quarters British, almost entirely privately-owned, and still fairly typical of business investment in a colonial economy. Characteristically, it concentrated on extractive industries and processing for export for international trade, and on ancillary services. At the first official count, less than a year after Independence, a little over one-quarter was in tea and jute which together made up half [of] India's exports; 17 percent in trading; finance and management accounted for just 8 percent; and utilities (electricity mainly) and transport (shipping mainly) for about 6 percent each. No more than one-fifth was invested in manufacturing jute.[1]

The reason for dominance of British private business was the policy of the British Government. In 1930, the bulk of British investments in India were in, 'tea, jute, cotton, mining, timber, leather, shipping, railways, agriculture, engineering, insurance, banking, and in general all forms of export and import trade.'[2] The British Government adopted a policy of encouraging investors from Britain, undertook steps for their promotion and protection and actively discouraged domestic Indian investments and investors. The Government gave aid to British companies in shipping, railway construction and made land and labour available for tree plantation. These British companies had lobbied for these benefits with their government.[3] The British funded and supported many industry associations. These associations were primarily meant to assist British businesses; they showed complete indifference to the needs of Indian businesses and expectations.[4] In the shipping industry, the authorities gave contracts to companies in which they had interests for a long duration without allowing any opportunity to Indian companies to compete. This kept the control of the shipping industry exclusively in British hands, and Indian competitors were driven out of business.[5] Moreover, during the Second World War, the Indian shipping industry was requisitioned and the control was handed over to those protecting British shipping interests.[6] There were various tariff benefits granted to British companies that were not extended to the Indian companies.[7]

In addition to the hostile regulatory framework towards Indian investors, the market conditions were maintained unfavourably through other means. Banks were inaccessible for Indian borrowers. The cost of borrowing was high and special privileges were granted to foreigners. Indian banks were discouraged and measures

---

1. Michael Kidron, *Foreign Investment in India*, 3 (Oxford University Press 1965).
2. *Ibid.* For a detailed discussion on the number of sectors under control of foreign investment, extent of control with individuals from England and development of an economic chain from financing, banking to import and export, *See ibid.*, at pp. 3-11.
3. *Ibid.*, at 112.
4. *Ibid.*, at 9.
5. Walchand Hirachand, *Why Indian Shipping Does Not Grow*, 4 Bombay Investors Yearbook 58-66 (1940) cited in Kidron, *supra* n. 1, at 16-7.
6. Kidron, *supra* n. 1, at 65.
7. *Ibid.*, at 12-4.

were taken to destroy their business by declining recognition and through unfavourable regulations.[8] The monetary policy, particularly the currency exchange rate, was structured to facilitate British investors. According to Jathar, 'the basis of the British Government and British business interests was towards a high rather than a low ratio for the rupee, in other words, towards making a certain number of rupees earned in India worth more and more in terms of pounds, shillings and pence in England'.[9] Kidron points out that 'there is substance in the charge of conscious and active discrimination'.[10] Despite these challenges, some Indian entrepreneurs emerged and survived the onslaught of British policies. The impact of the British policies on the Indian companies continued for years after independence, and the 'Indian capital bore the marks of having grown in the shadows of a powerful, tightly-knot foreign competitor, and an unsympathetic, frequently hostile state.'[11]

The situation in other newly independent countries was not very different. In some cases, it was dramatic as compared to India. The control of the economy was in the hands of companies and foreign investors from the colonizing State, and investments were mostly in non-priority sectors such as extraction and export of natural resources. There was no effort made by the colonial governments to adopt policies that would facilitate and ensure foreign investments in important sectors necessary for growth or the ones which were labour intensive. The focus was on protecting the business interests of the investors from the colonizing country.[12]

[B] Domestic Policy Towards Foreign Investment

Having faced discrimination at the hands of the British Government during the colonial times, there was resentment towards foreign investment from the domestic industry. The domestic industry was insisting that all foreign investments are bought and their control from foreign hands be taken away. The existing foreign investments were mostly in natural resource extraction; therefore, they were retarding the nation's development.[13]

The newly formed government of independent India did not accept this approach. During this time, especially in the 1950s and 1960s, the Government was receptive and welcoming towards foreign investment. The economic philosophy in this duration was to allow foreign investors to operate with the knowledge that eventually they would have to transfer technology, skill and finally control to nationals of the host State.[14] In the Industrial Policy Resolution of 1948, the Government gave an indication to that effect. It was unequivocally stated that whenever the control of the foreigner's property would be taken, it would be subject to the fundamental rights under the

---

8. *Ibid.*, at 9-10.
9. *Ibid.*, at 17.
10. *Ibid.*, at 9.
11. *Ibid.*, at 19.
12. *Ibid.*, at 300-5.
13. Jagdish Bhagwati and Padma Desai, *India: Planning for Industrialization*, 216-1 (Oxford University Press, 1970).
14. For a detailed discussion on import substitution policy, *see ibid.*

Indian Constitution, and, fair and equitable compensation. At that time, right to property was a fundamental right. The relevant part of the Resolution was:

> While the inherent right of the State to acquire any existing industrial undertaking will always remain, and will be exercised whenever the public interest requires it, Government has [sic]decided to let existing undertakings in these fields develop for a period of ten years, during which they will be allowed all facilities for efficient working and reasonable expansion. At the end of this period, the whole matter will be reviewed and a decision taken in the light of circumstances obtaining at the time. If it is decided that the State should acquire any unit, the fundamental rights guaranteed by the Constitution will be observed and compensation will be awarded on a fair and equitable basis.[15]

The insistence on the transfer of ownership within ten years was changed in the following year. There was a retreat from the Industrial Policy Statement of 1948,[16] and the Indian government adopted an open foreign investment regime.[17] The World Bank was influential in India's policy-making right from the early years of independence. In 1949, the Bank sent its first Mission to survey the potentialities of Indian economy. As a follow-up of the Industrial Policy of 1948, the Prime Minister, Jawaharlal Nehru submitted a special policy statement on foreign capital to the Parliament on 6 April 1949. It was declared that:

1. Existing foreign interests would be accorded 'national treatment': 'Government does not [sic]intend to place any restrictions or impose any conditions which are not applicable to similar Indian enterprise'.
2. New foreign capital would be encouraged: 'Government would so frame their policy as to enable further foreign capital to be invested in India on terms and conditions that are mutually advantageous.'
3. Profits and remittances abroad would be allowed, as would capital remittances of concerns 'compulsorily acquired'.
4. Fair compensation would be paid 'if and when foreign enterprises are compulsorily acquired'.
5. Although majority ownership by Indians was preferred, 'Government will not object to foreign capital having control of a concern for a limited period, if it is found to be in the national interest, and each individual case will be dealt with on its own merits'.
6. 'Vital importance' was still attached to rapid Industrialization of personnel, but 'Government would not object to the employment of non-Indians in posts requiring technical skills and experience when Indians of requisite qualifications are not available'.[18]

From the legal standpoint, two principles emerge from this policy and they remained the cornerstone of the Indian attitude towards foreign investment at the

---

15. Ministry of Micro, Small and Medium Enterprises, Government of India, *Industrial Policy Resolution (IPR)*, para. 4 (6 Apr. 1948) http://laghu-udyog.gov.in/policies/iip.htm (accessed 19 Mar. 2017).
16. N.K. Chandra, *Role of Foreign Capital in India*, 5(9) Social Scientist 3-20 (1977); G. Findlay Shirras, *Foreign Capital in India–A Rejoinder*, 43(171) The Economic Journal 532-4 (September 1933).
17. Arvind Panagariya, *India: The Emerging Giant*, 29-30 (Oxford University Press 2008).
18. Kidron, *supra* n. 1, at 101.

international level: national treatment (NT) (no higher treatment to foreign investors than domestic investors), and the right of nationalization, subject to the payment of fair compensation.

The Government gave many concessions to foreign firms including reduction in wealth tax and tax exemption to foreign personnel. In the budgets of 1959 and 1961, the government lowered taxes on corporate incomes and royalties of foreign firms. Double taxation treaties were signed in this period.[19] In 1961, the Government of India established the India Investment Centre with offices in major capital-exporting countries to disseminate information and advice on the profitability of investing in India. Officers from the Ministry of Commerce and Industry were appointed to guide foreign investors.[20] Local participation was encouraged but not insisted on, and foreign firms were welcome.[21] The response of MNCs was lukewarm in the early 1950s, and they did not show much interest in investing, except in oil refineries. After 1957, substantial investments came into various industries which were considered to be non-essential by the government. During this time there were some joint ventures of foreign investors with Indian companies, including setting up of manufacturing subsidiaries in India by drug companies.[22]

The peculiar characteristic of India was absence of mass scale nationalization of foreign business as was done in other newly independent countries. The post-independence era was marked by economic nationalism for many States. This was the time when the governments of the newly independent States took over control of major industries with strategic importance and high economic value from foreigners. These foreigners belonged mostly to the colonizing powers. The governments of the newly independent States nationalized or expropriated properties of foreigners. Whereas, targeted nationalization or expropriation of foreign property did not take place in India. There were no xenophobic tendencies, and the relations between India and its former colonizer England remained cordial and friendly. India continued to remain a part of Commonwealth while retaining its sovereignty and nationality. The last Viceroy sent to India by the British was requested to stay back as the Governor General of independent India.[23] However, Indians suffered effects of nationalization abroad, in Burma, Ethiopia, Mozambique, Portugal, Tanzania and Uganda. There were several problems but all of them were resolved peacefully.[24]

Nationalization was undertaken sector-wise in India, applicable without discrimination towards foreigners, and without the philosophy of taking back control from foreign corporations. In some cases, foreign investors were excluded from such measures. Air transport was nationalized in 1953, Imperial Bank was nationalized in

---

19. Panagariya, *supra* n. 17, at 30.
20. *Ibid.*
21. *Ibid.*
22. *Ibid.*, at 30-1.
23. There is a vivid description of how the Viceroy and his family were warmly received by Indians on streets at the time of independence. *See* Alex von Tunzelmann, *Indian Summer: The Secret History of the End of an Empire* (Henry Holt and Company 2007).
24. P.S. Rao, *Bilateral Investment Protection Agreements: A Legal Framework for the Protection of Foreign Investment*, 26 Commonwealth Law Bulletin 623-4 (2000).

1955, life insurance in January 1956 and Kolar Gold Fields in December 1956.[25] Each of these nationalizations was undertaken for specific and well-defined objectives, rather than as a part of an anti-private sector strategy. Air transport in India was weakly organized and incapable of being extended to other cities and abroad without government support. The Imperial Bank was nationalized to create structures for availability of credit in small towns to reduce the presence and influence of private money-lenders, and the overall unwillingness of banks to provide services in rural areas. This was an important area to be brought under financial inclusion. Life insurance was nationalized to clean up corruption and inefficiency in the sector. At no stage was there any hint or philosophy of confiscation, which normally underlines nationalization processes.[26] Nationalization in Europe took place in the same sectors to provide better public utility. In all cases, compensation was paid.[27]

The time during 1965-1981 was turbulent. This was a period of economic difficulty for India and economic disparity within India. In response, inward-looking protectionist policies were adopted, which made foreign investors lose faith in the economy. Relations with the US became difficult because India was unwilling to support the US in the Vietnam War. Food aid from the US was seen to be used as a lever to interfere in internal affairs.[28] It was at this time that the second wave of nationalizations took place. It targeted domestic companies and excluded foreign investors. Economic inclusion was one of the planks hailed by the then Prime Minister, Mrs. Gandhi. Privately owned commercial banks were unwilling to lend to crucial sectors such as agriculture and small-scale industry. These sectors had to be promoted because India was suffering from shortage of food grains and was dependent on the US for food aid and other imports of food grains. India started the programme of green revolution where the objective was to achieve self-sufficiency in food grains. To bolster this project, lending to the agricultural sector was necessary. Therefore, the Government decided to nationalize the banking sector. Consequently, the decision to nationalize banks was taken – however, foreign banks were excluded, to protect India's image abroad.[29]

Likewise, the nationalization of coal sector took place to control rampant and unregulated coal mining. In private coalmines, unscientific mining practices were adopted and poor labour conditions were maintained, which became matters of concern for the Government. The private coal sector had ignored safety, labour welfare and protection, lack of metallurgical output, etc. To address these problems, the Central Government took the decision to nationalize private coalmines.[30] The reasons

---

25. *Oxford Handbook on Indian Foreign Policy*, 291 (David M. Malone, C. Raja Mohan and Srinath Raghavan (eds), Oxford University Press, 2015).
26. Kidron, *supra* n. 1, at 133-5.
27. Rao, *supra* n. 24.
28. Panagariya, *supra* n. 17, at 49-51.
29. Panagariya, *supra* n. 17, at 53.
30. *See* Mohan Kumaramangalam, *Coal Industry in India: Nationalisation and Tasks Ahead* (Oxford & IBH Publishing Company 1973). It is natural that a more rational course would have been to regulate the coal mines rather than nationalize them, but this was the time of fervour for socialism.

were primarily domestic and did not have an element of taking away property of foreigners.[31]

The Foreign Investment Board (FIB) was setup in 1968 to regulate incoming foreign investment. Once the economic policy became protectionist and inward-looking in the 1970s, it became difficult to obtain permissions. The FIB conducted tougher scrutiny of investment proposals.[32] The rigid approach undertaken from 1973 through the enactment of Foreign Exchange Regulation Act (FERA), 1973 further antagonized the foreign investors. List of favoured sectors for setting up of industries was issued. The problem with the list was that the foreign investors were not interested in investing in those areas. And, where the foreign investors were interested in investing they had to have a domestic collaborator. In most situations, none existed. Shareholding of foreign firms in various sectors was strongly controlled.[33] These measures started choking foreign investment.

As per the Industrial Policy of 1977, foreign companies were required to dilute their equity up to 40% to get NT.[34] Companies in many sectors, such as airline, shipping and banking, were forced to incorporate under the Indian Companies Act. Multinational corporations that did not have manufacturing plants and were in the field of services or were monitoring the economy could not dilute to less than 40% and had to leave.[35] In 1977, Coca-Cola left the Indian market because the government insisted that it collaborate with an Indian entity. It came back in 1993, when the economy was liberalized.[36]

The low growth in the 1970s led to some changes in the policy in the mid-1980s. There was a somewhat receptive attitude towards foreign investment with the 40% cap of domestic ownership being removed.[37] Yet, the overall regulatory framework remained stringent and cumbersome, causing serious economic problems in the domestic economy and loss of faith of foreign investors in the potential for doing business and earning profits. There was a severe balance of payment crisis which led to the opening up of the Indian economy for foreign goods and investment in the 1990s. This is where the second phase of acceptability began.

These developments coincide with the resolution on the New International Economic Order (NIEO) and the Charter on Economic Rights and Duties of States, discussed below.

---

31. *Ibid. See* Rajiv Kumar, *Nationalisation by Default: The Case of Coal in India*, 16(18) Economic and Political Weekly 824-30 (2 May 1981).
32. Nagesh Kumar, *Liberalisation and Changing Patterns of Foreign Direct Investments*, 33(22) Economic and Political Weekly 1321, 1322 (1998).
33. Panagariya, *supra* n. 17, at 60-1.
34. Department of Industrial Development, Ministry of Industry, Government of India, *Industrial Policy Statement* http://www.dcmsme.gov.in/policies/iip.htm#Indus3 (accessed 19 Mar. 2017).
35. Panagariya, *supra* n. 17, at 14.
36. R. Nagaraj, *Foreign Direct Investment in India in 1990s: Trends and Issues*, 38(17) Economic and Political Weekly 1701, 1701 (2003); *see also* Arvind Virmani, *Policy Regimes, Growth and Poverty in India: Lessons of Government Failure and Entrepreneurial Success!* (ICRIER Working Paper No. 170 2005) http://icrier.org/pdf/WP170GrPov11.pdf (accessed 1 Jul. 2017).
37. Kumar, *supra* n. 32. A degree of flexibility was introduced in the policy concerning foreign ownership, and exceptions from the general ceiling of 40% on foreign equity were allowed on the merits of individual investment proposals.

[C] Protection of Foreign Investment and International Law

India has been an active participant at all international forum, including those regulating international economic relations, and the international policy towards economic relations with other States has been liberal. India concluded various bilateral treaties in relation to trade and participated in the negotiations for creating international organizations. Trade Agreements were concluded with Austria, Finland, Switzerland and West Germany in 1949, with Sweden in 1950 and with Norway in 1951. Difficulties were faced while negotiating a treaty for friendship, commerce and navigation with the United States of America (USA) – but practical arrangements were worked out to enhance commercial exchanges and facilitate industrial collaboration.[38] India naturally turned to other developing countries and its neighbours. A treaty was entered into with Nepal, Burma, Sri Lanka and Indonesia in 1950.[39] There were various cooperation arrangements with other States, including Afghanistan where India allowed imports despite restrictions on other imports due to balance of payment problems.[40]

India's participation in the making and working of international institutions was driven by the goal of protecting national interests, as well as providing leadership to the newly independent States that were also fighting for similar causes. India is a founding member of the United Nations (UN) and participated actively in the process of decolonization. India was involved in the process of creation of the General Agreement on Tariff and Trade (GATT), International Monetary Fund (IMF) and the World Bank. India's involvement in GATT was peripheral. Yet, soon India played an important role in protecting its own interests and interests of other developing countries.[41] During the formulation of the IMF's Articles, India was a vocal representative of the concerns of least developed countries (LDCs). The Indian delegation said that:

> Our experience in the past has shown that international organisations have tended to approach all problems from the point of view of the advanced countries of the West. We want to ensure that the new organization which we are trying to create will avoid this narrow outlook and give due consideration to the economic problems of countries like India.[42]

The Indian delegation proposed an amendment to the Fund's Articles that would have required the Fund to assist in the fuller utilization of the resources of economically underdeveloped countries. The proposal was supported by Ecuador, but was opposed

---

38. K.B. Lall, *India and the New International Economic Order*, 17 International Studies 435, 436 (1978).
39. *Ibid.*, at 437.
40. *Ibid.*, at 437-8.
41. *Ibid.*, at 435, 439-40.
42. Proceedings and Documents, Vol. 11, P.1G10, quoted in Gerald M. Meier, *Emerging from Poverty: The Economics that Really Matters*, 16 (Oxford University Press 1984); Anand Chandavarkar, Keynes and India: A Study in Economics and Biography, 122 (Macmillan Press Ltd. 1989); Lynge Nielsen, *Classifications of Countries Based on Their Level of Development: How It Is Done and How It Could Be Done*, WP/11/31, IMF Working Paper, 14 (2011).

by the United Kingdom and the US on the grounds that issues of development were a matter for the Bank rather than the Fund.[43]

The prominent forum where India profoundly contributed towards the shaping of international economic law, and specifically in relation to protection of foreign investors, was at the UN. India actively participated in supporting the right of self-determination of peoples under colonial rule and their subsequent struggle for economic independence and ending the monopoly of foreign rulers over economic resources. India associated itself with the cause of the countries under colonial rule. India was an active participant of the Non Aligned Movement and G77, where it was representing the vision and expectations of these countries.[44] Stating its reasons for joining and leading the movement, the Government of India declared that: 'India adopted a policy of non-alignment to promote peace and cooperation with all nations in order to devote its energy and resources to national development and social progress'.[45]

The crucial debate where India sided with the newly independent States from Asia and Africa and the Latin American countries in the UN was on protection of foreign investment in international law. The genesis of the debate was the already ongoing difference between Latin American countries and the Western European and North American countries.

In the nineteenth century, after the Latin American countries gained independence from their former Spanish colonisers, they allowed European and North American investors to invest in their countries.[46] The European and North American States were capital-exporting States and had interest in protecting investors from their countries investing in the Latin American countries. The points of difference about the contents of international law was on the standard of protection for foreign investors, invocation of diplomatic protection by the home State of the foreigner, and the standard of compensation in situations of nationalization, expropriation or other measures that affected the property of the foreign investor.

The capital-exporting countries insisted that the standard of protection of their investors in the host State was the international minimum standard, which in their view was customary international law standard for treatment of foreigners/aliens. According to the international minimum standard, States were free to have whatever judicial and legal system they wish to have in their jurisdiction and may treat their nationals in whichever manner they deem appropriate. But, the treatment of foreigners should not fall below a particular standard of justice.[47] The international minimum

---

43. *See* P. Subrahmanyam, *New International Economic Order and India* (1991), http://shodhganga.inflibnet.ac.in/handle/10603/74581 (accessed 19 Jul. 2017).
44. Rajen Harshe, *India's Non-Alignment, An Attempt at Conceptual Reconstruction*, 7(25) Economic and Political Weekly 399-405 (1990).
45. Government of India, *India 1987*, 252 (Annual Publications Division, 1988).
46. Alejandro Alvarez, *Latin America and International Law*, 3(2) American Journal of International Law 269-353 (1909).
47. Elihu Root, *The Basis of Protection of Citizen's Residing Abroad*, 4 American Journal of International Law 517, 521-2 (1910).

standard was set out in the *Neer*[48] case.[49] In response to the claim of international minimum standard, Argentine jurist, Carlos Calvo argued that international law did not entitle foreigners for a standard of treatment higher than that granted to nationals. The host State courts have exclusive jurisdiction over disputes involving foreign nationals.[50] This is the Calvo doctrine which insisted on NT and rejected the international minimum standard.

The Calvo doctrine was founded on the principle of equality of States and equality between foreigners and nationals of a State.[51] Although the substantive prescription of the Calvo doctrine was in favour of NT, this doctrine emerged in response to the doctrine of diplomatic protection.[52] Diplomatic protection grants the right to a State 'to protect its subjects, when injured by acts contrary to international law committed by another State, from whom they have been unable to obtain satisfaction through the ordinary channels'.[53] While 'taking up the case of one of its subjects and by resorting to diplomatic action or international judicial proceedings on his behalf, a State is in reality asserting its own rights – its right to ensure, in the person of its subjects, respect for the rules of international law'.[54] During the nineteenth and the first half of the twentieth century, diplomatic protection gained disrepute, because it was used to exert military, political or economic pressure by strong States against weaker States.[55] Whenever there was nationalization or failure to make payment on bonds by governmental authorities in Latin America, capital-exporting States would invoke the doctrine of diplomatic protection and resort to gun boat diplomacy to coerce the host State to make good the losses suffered by the foreign investor.

Three important conventions were concluded during the first half of the twentieth century for preventing forcible self-help of this kind. The first was the Convention Respecting the Limitation of the Employment of Force for the Recovery of Contractual Debts, also called the 'Porter Convention' – concluded at the Second Hague Conference, 1907. This treaty excluded use of forcible self-help in collection of contractual debts. The second was the General Treaty for the Renunciation of War of 1928, known as the 'Kellog-Brian Pact'. The third and the most important instrument was the UN Charter in 1945.[56] After the outlawing of the use of force by the Kellog-Brian Pact and

---

48. *L. Fay H. Neer (USA) v. United Mexican States*, USA – Mexico General Claims Commission (15 Oct. 1926) 4 RIAA 60.
49. According to Sornarajah, reliance on the *Neer* case to argue for the existence of the international minimum standard was incorrect because the observations by the arbitral tribunal were based on the need of physical protection of aliens entering a foreign State, rather than observations on the protection of property and other economic rights. M. Sornarajah, *International Law on Protection of Foreign Investment*, 122 (3rd ed., Cambridge University Press 2010).
50. Bernardo Cremades, *Resurgence of the Calvo Doctrine in Latin America*, 7 Bus. L. Int'l 53, 53-4 (2006).
51. Carlos Calvo, 1 *Derecho Internacional Teorico y Practico de Ruropa y America*, 393-7 (D'Amyot 1869) cited in Santiago Montt, *State Liability in Investment Treaty Arbitration: Global Constitutional and Administrative Law in the BIT Generation*, 38-9 (Hart Publishing 2009).
52. Santiago Montt, *supra* n. 51, at 35-8.
53. *Mavrommatis Palestine Concessions Case (Greece v. UK)* (1924) PCIJ Series A, No. 2, 12.
54. *Ibid*; see also *Panevezys-Saldutiskis Railway Case*, Judgment (1939) PCIJ Series A/B, No. 76, 14.
55. C. Wilfred Jenks, *The Prospects of International Adjudication*, 514-5 (Oceana Publications 1954).
56. Montt, *supra* n. 52, at 49-50.

the UN Charter, the possibility of force being used for exercising diplomatic protection was reduced. Calvo doctrine had originally emerged as a response to the possibility of use of force.[57]

These developments denuded the possibility of use of force accompanying diplomatic protection. The legal basis for taking up the claim of one's national was the breach of the international minimum standard, for which the host State allegedly attracted State responsibility. The need for insisting that the international minimum standard is a rule of customary law was that till the time the colonies were under control, no law for protection of their investments was required. The need of international rules for protection of foreign investment was required after States became independent from the foreign rule. Till the time they were rulers, the colonial powers controlled them, and the foreign investments originated in their States. They ensured that their investments are protected and even promoted to make substantial inroads into the economic life of the colonized countries. It was only after the colonies fought and achieved independence that the need of protecting foreign investment through external rules was felt.[58]

There was a fear that under the garb of State responsibility, the old practice of diplomatic protection would be 'used as a device for securing economic or political domination or supremacy in the life of another State'.[59] The arguments of absence of State responsibility for affecting aliens and lack of support in international law for diplomatic protection were pointed out by Indian scholars.[60] Foreigners are entitled to a treatment not higher than nationals.[61] India supported the NT principle, and Indian scholarship also supported this view.[62] At the International Law Commission (ILC), the Special Rapporteurs had narrowed the work on State responsibility only to the question of treatment of aliens. This focus remained despite the support for identification of substantive principles on State responsibility.[63] The narrow approach to State responsibility was also supported by the Latin American countries.[64] When it came to finding State responsibility, the Indian member at the ILC opposed the doctrine of State responsibility for injuries to aliens because this was 'a completely different ideology of social justice, involving completely different social and economic systems which endanger, among other things, the existing conception of private property.'[65] Ultimately, the ILC dropped any reference to protection of foreign investors or aliens in the final Draft Articles.[66]

---

57. *Ibid.*, at 31-3.
58. Sornarajah, *supra* n. 49, at 21-2.
59. S.N. Guha Roy, *Is the Law of Responsibility of States for Injuries to Aliens a Part of Universal International Law?*, 55(4) American Journal of International Law 886-7 (1961).
60. *Ibid.*, at 863, 872-5.
61. *Ibid.*, at 863, 884.
62. *See* generally *ibid.*
63. Philip Allott, *State Responsibility and the Unmaking of International Law*, 29 Harvard International Law Journal 1-26 (1988).
64. *The Pursuit of Nationalized Property*, 29-32 (M. Sornarajah (ed.), Martinus Nijhoff Publishers, 1986).
65. ILC, *Yearbook of the International Law Commission: Summary Records of the Ninth Session*, Vol. I, 158 (United Nations Publications 1957).
66. Montt, *supra* n. 52, at 59-60.

India rejected the argument that there was a customary international law on State responsibility for losses caused to aliens, and insisted that this area should be based on treaties. The discussion above has shown that in domestic policy, India had insisted on NT. India did not support absolute protection of private property. After independence, the urgent priority of India was social justice. Lands were concentrated in the hands of rulers of former princely states, aristocrats, land hoarders (called zamindars) and others close to the colonial administration. If steps for redistribution of land were not taken, the exploitation of the deprived would have continued and independence from colonial rule would have no real meaning or impact for the large majority. The domestic policies and the laws were shaped in a manner that redistribution of land would be upheld.

The Indian position can be summarized as follows: absence of State responsibility for economic losses caused to foreign investors due to actions of host State; the foreign investors are regulated by NT principle, whereby they should approach the domestic courts of the host State and should not claim higher protection than domestic investors and their home State should not grant them diplomatic protection; and third, the right of nationalization as an attribute of State sovereignty.

The final part of this debate between the capital-exporting countries and Latin American countries was played out in the UN General Assembly, with the participation of newly independent countries of Asia and Africa. India supported the views of the capital-importing countries in various *fora* of the UN. The post-World War II period was characterized by decolonization. The regions in Asia and Africa that were under colonial subjugation obtained political independence. It was realized that political independence would be incomplete without economic independence. In the colonies, the control of the economic activities was in the hands of former colonizers. The newly independent countries felt the need for recovering control over vital sectors of economies from foreign investors, which were owned mostly by the nationals of former colonial powers. The consequence was a wave of nationalization in these countries.[67] Nationalization was used as an instrument to claim back control of economic activity and natural resources. This was also the time when the Cold War was simmering. The States in Eastern Europe, Middle East, Asia, North Africa and Latin America resorted to nationalization, especially of oil industry. In many States, properties of former colonizers were nationalized.[68] For example, in Indonesia properties under Dutch control were nationalized.[69]

There were two aspects of the demands of these countries: control of natural resources and the control of their domestic economy with freedom from interference from other States, especially former colonial rulers. This was achieved through a string of resolutions. The first step was claiming control over natural resources, followed by declaration of an NIEO and finally a set of obligations and rights of States regarding economic relations. The principal resolutions were the Permanent Sovereignty over

---

67. Sornarajah, *supra* n. 49, at 21-2.
68. *See* generally *The Pursuit of Nationalized Property*, *supra* n. 64; Adeoye A. Akinsanya, *The Expropriation of Multinational Property in the Third World* (Praeger Publishers 1980).
69. Andreas F. Lowenfeld, *International Economic Law*, 405 (Oxford University Press 2002).

Chapter 2: Historical Background of Investment Protection §2.01[C]

Natural Resources, the NIEO and the Charter on Economic Rights and Duties of States. Although separated by a time gap, these resolutions represent continuity of thought. These resolutions were aimed at rejecting the international minimum standard and replacing it with the NT standard. The host State was not to attract State responsibility for violations of the rights of foreign investors, and the foreign investors were to approach national courts for redressal of their claims. The important element was the right of States to nationalize. The NIEO represented the philosophy of replacing the old economic order of colonial control with a new order of equality between States, cooperation between them as equals and greater integration of the world economy with free flow of goods with appropriate prices for raw materials and commodities produced mostly in the developing countries. The objective was the expectation of creation of an equitable international society where all States, irrespective of the past, have equal right of progress.[70] The movement for the NIEO was inspired by the thought that during colonial period inequitable and onerous arrangements were made to obtain greater benefit from the newly independent countries. The newly independent countries were seeking to undo these arrangements.[71]

These resolutions at the General Assembly represent this philosophy of the newly independent States, which Indian representatives spoke about at different discussions in the UN.

The movement in the direction of permanent sovereignty over natural resources started with the objective of promoting international cooperation for economic development in the developing countries. Prior to the resolutions on permanent sovereignty over natural resources, the General Assembly passed two resolutions that formed the basis of further actions: the resolution on integrated economic development and commercial agreements[72] and the resolution on right to exploit natural wealth and resources freely.[73]

Natural resources were important because they had the potential to act as engines of development for the newly independent States. A lot of the resources were already depleted during the colonial rule. The structure of the economies had become such due to the colonial rule that they were dependent on export of raw material or commodities.

---

70. The entire discussion on the NIEO is well-documented in academic discussions. See Georges Abi-Saab, 'Permanent Sovereignty Over Natural Resources and Economic Activities' in International Law: Achievements and Prospects (Mohammed Bedjaoui (ed.), UNESCO, 1991); M. Sornarajah, *The Pursuit of Nationalized Property*, 29-32 (Martinus Nijhoff Publishers 1986); Akinsanya, *supra* n. 68; Rosalyn Higgings, *The Taking of Property by the State: Recent Developments in International Law*, 176 Recueil des Cours 259 (1982); Rudolf Dolzer, *New Foundations of the Law of Expropriation of Alien Property*, 75 American Journal of International Law 553 (1981); Detlev Vagts, *Foreign Investment Risk Reconsidered: The View from the 1980's*, 2 Foreign Investment Law Journal 1 (1980); Ian Brownlie, *Legal Status of Natural Resources in International Law (Some Aspects)* 162 Recueil des Cours 244 (1980); Nico Schrijver, *Sovereignty Over Natural Resources: Balancing Rights and Duties* (Cambridge University Press 1977).
71. Kamal Hossain, *Permanent Sovereignty over Natural Resources: Principles and Practice*, 9-10 (Kamal Hossain and Subrata Roy Chowdhury (eds) Frances Printer, 1984).
72. Integrated Economic Development and Commercial Agreements, GA Res. 523, UN GAOR, 6th Sess., Supp. No. 20, at 20, UN Doc. A/2119(1952).
73. Right to Exploit Freely Natural Wealth and Resources, GA Res. 626, UN GAOR, 7th Sess., Supp. No. 20, at 18, UN Doc. A/2361(1952).

These commodities were sold at cheap rates as compared to the finished products. The technology and technical know-how was with the developed States. There was a lack of financial resources that would contribute towards setting up of industries and fostering research and development of technology. The newly developed countries needed capital as well as technology for which, they depended on the developed countries. While wanting foreign capital, these States wished to be careful that colonialism or interference in their economies does not return. There was a threat – whether perceived or real – of their return, if the control of economic resources and activities was under foreign control. Many saw that the first task to do was to take back control of the natural resources and economic activity from the foreign control and transfer it to the government or its nationals. The resolutions passed in the General Assembly tried to address these problems.

The newly independent States had the natural resources but did not have the necessary technical expertise to exploit and market them. The first step was to take back control from the former colonial powers and the next step was to enter into fair contractual engagements with corporations, which were mostly from the former colonial powers. The foreign investment that came into these countries was mostly in the field of exploitation of natural resources. The resolution on integrated economic development aimed at giving newly independent developing countries the freedom to exercise control over natural resources and use them for achieving economic development.[74] There was a need to ensure that these States could acquire machinery, equipment and industrial raw materials.[75] Appropriate agreements had to be entered into to ensure there was smooth movement of technical know-how and raw materials through agreements.[76]

Through Resolution 1314 of 12 December 1958, the Commission on Permanent Sovereignty over Natural Resources was established, which had to conduct 'survey of the status of the permanent sovereignty of peoples and nations over their natural wealth and resources, due regard should be paid to the rights and duties of States under international law and to the importance of encouraging international co-operation in the economic development of developing countries'.[77]

Permanent sovereignty over natural resources was declared through Resolution 1803 by the General Assembly. The focus of the GA resolution on Permanent Sovereignty over Natural Resources was of economic independence of the States. The Preamble stated:

> Attaching particular importance to the question of promoting the economic development of developing countries and securing their economic independence,
>
> Noting that the creation and strengthening of the inalienable sovereignty of States over their natural wealth and resources reinforces their economic independence,

---

74. Integrated Economic Development and Commercial Agreements, GA Res. 523, *supra* n. 72, at Preamble.
75. *Ibid*.
76. Integrated Economic Development and Commercial Agreements, GA Res. 523, *supra* n. 72, at Art. 1(b).
77. Preamble, GA Res. 1803, UN GAOR, 17th Sess., Supp. No. 17, at 15, UN Doc. A/5217 (1962).

Desiring that there should be further consideration by the United Nations of the subject of permanent sovereignty over natural resources in the spirit of international co-operation in the field of economic development, particularly that of the developing countries.[78]

The relationship between all States, especially the newly independent States and their former colonizers, 'must be based on the principles of equality and of the right of peoples and nations to self-determination.'[79] The idea was that even if foreign investment came into a developing State it did not conflict with the interest of the recipient States.[80] Yet, at the same time, it was necessary to ensure that there was exchange of technical and scientific information for promoting development.[81] The resolution declined preferential treatment to foreign investors and affirmed the right of States to regulate foreign investments as per their own economic objectives.[82] These resolutions apply to all agreements: including those between States, and between States and foreign investors.[83]

The follow-up on the resolution on Permanent Sovereignty over Natural Resources was the resolution establishing the NIEO. The General Assembly Resolution 3201 declared that:

Solemnly proclaim our united determination to work urgently for the Establishment of a New International Economic Order based on equity, sovereign equality, interdependence, common interest and cooperation among all States, irrespective of their economic and social systems which shall correct inequalities and redress existing injustices, make it possible to eliminate the widening gap between the developed and the developing countries and ensure steadily accelerating economic and social development and peace and justice for present and future generations, and, to that end, declare... .[84]

The resolution recognized the need of full participation of all States in resolving world economic problems on the basis of equality of States.[85] The resolution recognized that the States have 'full permanent sovereignty' over 'natural resources and all economic activities', 'including the right to nationalization or transfer of ownership to its nationals, this right being an expression of the full permanent sovereignty of the State'.[86] The concern of obtaining proper price for commodities was also focused – a point that was introduced and emphasized by India.[87]

Very soon, the Charter on Economic Rights and Duties of States was declared, which set out obligations of States. The Charter which focused on the need of

---

78. *Ibid.*
79. *Ibid.*
80. *Ibid.*
81. *Ibid.*
82. Georges Abi-Saab, *supra* n. 70, at 605.
83. *Ibid.*, at 606.
84. Declaration on the Establishment of a New International Economic Order, Preamble, GA Res. 3201, UN GAOR, 6th Spl. Sess., Supp. No. 1, at 3, UN Doc. A/RES/S-6/3201 (1974).
85. *Ibid.*, at para. c.
86. *Ibid.*, at para. e.
87. *Ibid.*, at para. j.

expanding liberal world trade without obstructions was postulated[88] with removal of obstructive tariff barriers.[89] It spelt out the attitude towards foreign investment in the following words:

> Article 2
> 1. Every State has and shall freely exercise full permanent sovereignty, including possession, use and disposal, over all its wealth, natural resources and economic activities.
> 2. Each State has the right:
>   (a) To regulate and exercise authority over foreign investment within its national jurisdiction in accordance with its laws and regulations and in conformity with its national objectives and priorities. No State shall be compelled to grant preferential treatment to foreign investment;
>   (b) To regulate and supervise the activities of transnational corporations within its national jurisdiction and take measures to ensure that such activities comply with its laws, rules and regulations and conform with its economic and social policies. Transnational corporations shall not intervene in the internal affairs of a host State. Every State should, with full regard for its sovereign rights, cooperate with other States in the exercise of the right set forth in this subparagraph;
>   (c) To nationalize, expropriate or transfer ownership of foreign property, in which case appropriate compensation should be paid by the State adopting such measures, taking into account its relevant laws and regulations and all circumstances that the State considers pertinent. In any case where the question of compensation gives rise to a controversy, it shall be settled under the domestic law of the nationalizing State and by its tribunals, unless it is freely and mutually agreed by all States concerned that other peaceful means be sought on the basis of the sovereign equality of States and in accordance with the principle of free choice of means.

The newly developed countries stayed together on political as well as economic issues, and the NIEO was an outcome of this united stand taken at the UN.[90] In the discussions that took place in the General Assembly on the NIEO, the Indian representative highlighted the vast differences in the economic conditions of the developing countries vis-à-vis the developed countries. One of the major factors was the taking of raw material from developing countries at cheaper rates. Paying appropriate value to developing countries for the raw materials was necessary.[91] The objective for pushing for the NIEO was to achieve fairness and removal of obstacles in the development of the developing countries.[92] The role of foreign investment was supported in the following words:

> the role of external capital in the development process is crucial. The targets for development aid provided in the International Development Strategy should be

---

88. Charter on Economic Rights and Duties, GA Res. 3281, UN GAOR, 29th Sess., Supp. No. 31, at para. 14, UN Doc. A/RES/29/3281 (1974).
89. *Ibid.*, at Art. 18.
90. Harshe, *supra* n. 44, at 403-5.
91. United Nations General Assembly, 6th Special Session, 223rd Plenary Meeting, paras 86, 88-97 (19 Apr. 1974).
92. *Ibid.*, at paras 101, 124.

fulfilled and the current arrangements revised to provide for speedier disbursement on softer terms.[93]

The emphasis was on resolving economic disparities in an atmosphere of cooperation, rather than 'conditions of chaos or by a bitter confrontation between the rich and the poor'.[94] The Indian delegation participated actively in the deliberations of the time, emphasizing the point that the requirements of the developing countries should receive greater attention in the present situation.[95] India was an active participant at the discussions in United Nations Conference on Trade and Development (UNCTAD) on the Charter of Economic Rights and Duties of States.

The overwhelming support of States to the NIEO in the UN represented that the international minimum standard was replaced by NT. In order to get the international minimum standard of treatment for foreigners back on the agenda, capital-exporting States started entering into bilateral investment treaties (BITs) that introduced this standard as a treaty standard. There was uncertainty about the standard of protection of foreign investment in customary international law; BITs were a response to this uncertainty.[96] It was the relative success of NIEO that made BITs desirable.[97]

The General Assembly resolutions were used as a basis by the host State to expropriate or nationalize foreign property. While Eastern Europe had justified nationalizations without any compensation, other developing nations generally offered compensation. However, the amount of compensation offered was variable. From complying with the capital exporters norm of 'adequate compensation' to variations including instances like compensation limited to infrastructure developed on land to deductions of 'excess profits', a wide divergence arose, especially in the context of the circumstances leading to the NIEO.[98] The developed countries were insisting on compensation based on the Hull formula, which was payment of 'prompt, adequate and effective compensation'.[99] The objective of BITs was to ensure that the expropriation occurred as per proper procedures and the host State would be responsible for payment of complete compensation – equivalent to the market value, for the losses suffered due to expropriation or nationalization. BITs also introduced other treatment standards that granted robust protection to foreign investors. Moreover, for the first time, they allowed direct right to initiate arbitration without the need of diplomatic protection.[100] Germany entered into the first two BITs with Pakistan and Dominican

---

93. *Ibid.*, at para. 129.
94. *Ibid.*, at 134.
95. Ad hoc Committee of the Sixth Special Session, 8th meeting, para. 37 (17 Apr. 1974).
96. *Total SA v. Argentina Decision on Jurisdiction*, ICSID Case No. ARB/04/01, para. 78 (25 Aug. 2006).
97. Kenneth Vandevelde, *The Political Economy of a Bilateral Investment Treaty*, 92 American Journal of International Law 621, 628 (1998).
98. M. Sornarajah, *Compensation for Expropriation*, 12 Journal of World Trade Law 108-31 (1979).
99. The formula of 'prompt, adequate and effective compensation' was articulated by the Secretary of States of the United States, Cordell Hull in a note to the Mexican government. *See* Kenneth Vandevelde, *United States Investment Treaties: Policy and Practice*, 118 (Kluwer Law and Taxation 1992).
100. This idea was based on Abs-Shawcross Draft Convention on Investments Abroad of 1959. *See* Georg Schwarzenberger, *Foreign Investments and International Law*, 109-34 (Stevens 1969).

Republic in 1959.[101] Other western countries quickly followed.[102] The BITs were primarily entered into between the developed and developing countries with the underlying assumption that the investments of the developing countries would be protected.[103]

India did not participate in the BIT making process until it was forced into economic reforms due to a serious balance of payments crisis in the 1990s. At this point, the second phase, a dramatic shift in policy, took place.

§2.02 THE SECOND PHASE (1991-2011)

The second phase was of acceptance – but forced acceptance. The trigger point for giving up the protectionist domestic policy and heavy regulatory framework was the balance of payment crisis in 1990-1991, when India had to give up protectionist policies. The reforms were drastic, and the regulatory framework underwent dramatic changes overnight.[104] Various macroeconomic reforms were undertaken, including bringing down high import tariffs and encouragement of foreign institutional investment (FII) and foreign direct investment (FDI).[105] FDI up to 51% was permitted in crucial sectors and 100% in the energy sector. The Foreign Investment Promotion Board (FIPB) was setup and the FERA was amended to treat foreign companies with more than 40% of foreign equity at par with domestic industries.[106] Later FERA was repealed and replaced by the Foreign Exchange Management Act (FEMA). This was a shift in attitude towards control of foreign capital from 'regulation' to 'management'. The new Act introduced liberal provisions on movement of capital making it easier to bring foreign capital into India and take capital out of India.

In April 1992, India joined the Multilateral Investment Guarantee Agreement (MIGA). On 20 December 1993, the European Union (EU) and India signed third generation Cooperation Agreement on Partnership and Development. Article 11 contemplated 'encourage[ment] and increase in mutually beneficial investment by establishing a favorable climate for private investments including better conditions for the transfer of capital and exchange of information on investment opportunities'.

The ICSID Convention was soon negotiated thereafter in 1965, which provided a forum for resolution of investment disputes.
101. UNCTAD, *Bilateral Investment Treaties in the Mid-1990s*, 8, 177 (United Nations Publications 1998).
102. Kenneth Vandevelde, *A Brief History of International Investment Agreements*, 12 UC Davis Journal of International Law and Policy 157, 169 (2005).
103. UNCTAD, *supra* n. 101, at 8-19.
104. Panagariya, *supra* n. 17, at 103-5.
105. For a detailed discussion on reforms, *see* R. Nagaraj, *Foreign Direct Investment in India in the 1990s: Trends and Issues*, 38(17) Economic and Political Weekly 1701 (2003); C. Rangarajan, *Two Episodes in the Reform Process*, in India's Economy: Performance and Challenges, 100 (Shankar Acharya and Rakesh Mohan (eds) Oxford University Press, 2010); Arvind Panagariya, *Growth and Reforms During 1980s and 1990s*, 39(25) Economic and Political Weekly (2003); Montek Singh Ahluwalia, *Productivity and Growth in Indian Manufacturing*, 67 (Oxford University Press 1991).
106. Nirupam Bajpai and Jeffery Sachs, *Foreign Direct Investment in India: Issues and Problems*, HIID Development Discussion Paper No. 759/2001, 13 (2001); Nagaraj, *supra* n. 36, at 1701-2.

Chapter 2: Historical Background of Investment Protection §2.02

After these early steps for encouraging foreign investment, India started entering into BITs with many countries. India expressed its willingness to adhere to higher standards of protection for foreign investment and gave up the insistence on NT. Writing in 2000, the legal adviser of India stated that: 'in the current context of negotiation of investment protection agreements a less ideological and more pragmatic approach to these concepts has become possible'.[107]

It was at this point of time that India wholeheartedly joined the project of BITs. India started entering into BITs to attract foreign investment. The programme was called Bilateral Investment Promotion and Protection Agreements (BIPA).[108] The dominant thinking within the Government was that entering into BITs would result into greater inflow of foreign investment.[109] It first floated a model BIT[110] and entered into the first BIT with UK in 1994. The second Model BIT was released in 2003. This Model BIT had strong capital-exporting country features. A capital-exporting country feature means a model of a treaty that capital-exporting developed countries would prefer to protect their investments abroad. The jurisdiction and dispute resolution clauses in these treaties are broad. The foreign investor would have the right to initiate arbitration against the host State for violation of the BIT, without the need of going to domestic courts. The treatments standards were broad and would lean in favour of investor protection, rather than seeking a balance between investor protection and the protection of regulatory freedom of the host State.[111] These treaties obviously meant there was little space for the host States to exercise regulatory freedom. From 1994 to 2000, India entered into BITs with major European countries including France, Germany, Italy, Netherlands, Belgium, Denmark, Poland, Switzerland and Sweden. From 2000 onwards, India entered into BITs with many developing countries such as Argentina, Mexico, China, Thailand, Indonesia and Saudi Arabia, as well as with LDCs such as Bangladesh, Sudan and Mozambique.[112] There is little literature or any other record of the reasons behind the Government of India undertaking the BIT programme. There were disparities within the BITs and FTAs that were entered into during this time because the nodal ministries for negotiating them were different. The FTAs were more carefully drafted that the BITs. The FTAs ensured that regulatory freedom is protected.[113] No steps were taken to find out the extent to which these investment treaties

---

107. Rao, *supra* n. 24, at 623, 626.
108. Ministry of Finance, Government of India, *Bilateral Investment Promotion and Protection Agreements (BIPA)*, http://dea.gov.in/bipa (accessed 19 Mar. 2017).
109. *See* the 'Foreword' by Palainappan Chidambaram in *India's Bilateral Investment Promotion and Protection Agreements*, Vol. 1 (Government of India, Ministry of Finance (ed.) 1997); *See* the 'Foreword' by Yashwant Sinha in *India's Bilateral Investment Promotion and Protection Agreements*, Vol. 3 (Government of India, Ministry of Finance (ed.) 1999); *See* the 'Foreword' by Pranab Mukherjee in *India's Bilateral Investment Promotion and Protection Agreements*, Vol. 7 (Government of India, Ministry of Finance (ed.) 2009).
110. The first model BIT is not in public domain.
111. For a detailed discussion, *see* Aniruddha Rajput, *India's Shifting Treaty Practice: A Comparative Analysis of the 2003 and 2015 Model BITs*, 7 Jindal Global Law Review 201, 224-6 (2016).
112. Prabhash Ranjan, *India and Bilateral Investment Treaties: A Changing Landscape*, 29 ICSID Review 420 (2014).
113. Prabhash Ranjan, *Comparing Investment Provisions in India's FTAs with India's Stand-Alone BITs*, 16(5-6) The Journal of World Investment & Trade 899-930 (2015).

would affect the freedom to regulate. Despite these efforts, the amount of foreign investment India attracted in this period was much less as compared to China – despite the fact that India had vital points of democracy and the rule of law as highlights.[114] During this time, India did not face any investment claim, except a brief brush in the Dabhol Power Project.

Immediately after liberalization of the economy in 1991, India started encouraging foreign investors to invest in India and established fast track approval.[115] The Enron Corporation, General Electric (GE) Corporation and Bechtel Enterprises together formed a company called Dabhol Power Company (DPC) in Maharashtra, a western Indian state and entered into an agreement with the Maharashtra State Electricity Board (MSEB) (the Board) for a two-phase project. The project was the largest until that date, with over $2 billion secured in loans.[116] Through an agreement, the MSEB agreed to purchase power from the Dabhol Power Corporation and the government of Maharashtra state, and the Government of India gave payment guarantees. Disputes arose in 1995 after a new government came to power in Maharashtra. On the basis that there was corruption, irregularities and high cost of power, the MSEB cancelled the contract, leaving DPC without a customer, because MSEB was the only customer.[117] DPC commenced arbitration proceedings against the Government of Maharashtra, against which the State of Maharashtra filed a suit in the Bombay High Court, praying that the contract may be declared as void since it was based on fraud and misrepresentation. Parties reached a negotiated settlement and the arbitration and court proceedings were terminated.[118]

Five years later, DPC sought to invoke the guarantees of the Government of India and Maharashtra on the ground that the MSEB had defaulted in payment. In April 2001, the Corporation commenced arbitration proceedings against the Board, the State Government and the Central Government.[119] The MSEB commenced proceedings against DPC before the Maharashtra State Electricity Regulatory Commission (Commission) – a quasi-judicial body constitution under the domestic law regulating electricity. The Commission held that it had exclusive jurisdiction over the dispute between DPC and the MSEB. This was challenged in the Bombay High Court, which held that the Commission had the authority to decide upon its own jurisdiction. This decision was challenged before the Supreme Court, where the Court sent the matter back to the High Court, directing the Bombay High Court to make a finding whether the

---

114. For a discussion on the disparity in investments, *see* Nagaraj, *supra* n. 106, at 1705-6; For a comparative discussion and the reasons for this disparity, *see* M. Sornarajah, *India, China and Foreign Investment*, in China, India and the International Economic Order (M. Sornarajah and Jiangyu Wang (eds), Cambridge University Press, 2011).
115. Ronald Bettauer, *India and International Arbitration: The Dabhol Experience*, 41 George Washington International Law Review 381, 382 (2009-2010).
116. Preeti Kundra, *Looking Beyond the Dabhol Debacle: Examining Its Causes and Understanding Its Lessons*, 41 Vanderbilt Journal of Transnational Law 907, 908-14 (2008).
117. *Ibid.*, at 932-3.
118. Bettauer, *supra* n. 115, at 381, 383.
119. *Ibid.*

Chapter 2: Historical Background of Investment Protection §2.02

Commission had exclusive jurisdiction. The Bombay High Court held that the Commission had the jurisdiction and the matter was taken back to the Supreme Court and remained pending until 2005, when the dispute was settled.[120]

The Government of Maharashtra approached the Bombay High Court, and the Government of India approached the Delhi High Court seeking anti-arbitration injunction and relief against the invocation of guarantee. During 2003-2005, the American companies filed arbitration against Overseas Private Investment Corporation (OPIC), invoking political risk insurance on the ground that the Government of India and its courts had thwarted the remedy of arbitration available under the contract. The arbitral panel also found that the MSEB, the Commission and the Indian courts had enjoined and taken away the claimants' international arbitration remedies in violation of established principles of international law and in disregard of India's commitments under the New York Convention (NYC) and the Indian Arbitration Act. As a result, the panel ordered OPIC to pay the companies.[121] Thereafter, the US filed proceedings against India, subrogating for the OPIC under the US Investment Guarantee Agreement with India.[122]

Proceedings under the International Chamber of Commerce (ICC) resulted into an award against India in April 2005. India was found to be in breach of its obligations under the BIT.[123] The American companies initiated arbitration proceedings through Mauritian subsidies under the India-Mauritius BIT. Before the matter could be decided, the matter was settled.[124] The commencement of arbitration by the US under the Investment Incentive Agreement and the investment treaty arbitration (ITA) under the Mauritius BIT had a significant impact.[125] The parties reached an overall settlement, and the proceedings before courts and arbitral tribunals were terminated.[126]

The *Dabhol Power* case presents the factual, legal and political complications that could be associated with investment disputes. Although India managed to settle the dispute, its legacy has been criticized.[127]

In the period from 1991 to 2011, India never faced investment claims, except for the *Dabhol Power* case, which was soon settled. It may not be argued that the situation

---

120. Ibid.
121. *Bechtel Enterprises Int'l Ltd. v. Overseas Private Inv. Corp.*, AAA Case No. 50 T195 0050902, at 3-24 (2003).
122. *United States v. India*, Request for Arbitration (4 Nov. 2004) https://www.opic.gov/sites/default/files/docs/GOI110804.pdf (accessed 1 Jul. 2017).
123. *Capital India Power Mauritius I v. Maharashtra Power Dev. Corp. Ltd.*, ICC International Court of Arbitration, Case No. 12913/MS (2004), 30-1, https://www.italaw.com/documents/Dabhol_award_050305.pdf (accessed 1 Jul. 2017). The proceedings under the Dutch bilateral investment treaty (BIT) were still pending at the time the Dabhol matter was settled.
124. GE Settles Dabhol Issue, The Indian Express (3 Jul. 2005) http://www.indianexpress.com/oldStory/73760 (accessed 1 Jul. 2017).
125. Bettauer, *supra* n. 115, at 385, 383.
126. *See* Press Release, Bechtel, *Statement by Bechtel on Dabhol Settlement* (12 Jul. 2005) http://www.bechtel.com/newsroom/releases/2005/07/statement-bechtel-dabhol-settlement/ (accessed 1 Jul. 2017); Press Release, GE, *GE Announces Comprehensive Settlement on Dabhol Power Project* (2 Jul. 2005) http://stage.genewsroom.com/press-releases/ge-announces-comprehensive-settlement-dabhol-power-project-260068 (accessed 1 Jul. 2017).
127. *See* Gus Van Harten, *TWAIL and the Dabhol Arbitration*, 3 Trade, Law and Development 131 (2011).

of the regulatory framework from 1991 to 2011 was perfect and therefore investors had no occasions to complain. There may have been many situations where the foreign investor might have been unhappy with the regulatory framework and suffered losses. Yet no investment claims were filed. One of the reasons for this phenomenon is the efficient and independent judicial system. The actions of the State can be challenged before the higher judiciary in India (Supreme Court and High Court), where decisions are delivered relatively faster. The jurisprudence developed by the courts grants more rights to investors than those granted under a BIT. These proceedings do not antagonize the governments as compared to investment arbitration. After the *White Industries* case, this trend of approaching domestic courts is broken and the investors are and would be willing to file investment claims.

Serious rethinking of an overly liberal investment protection regime in the BITs started only when India lost the first investment case in *White Industries v. Australia* in 2011. There have been concerns about the expansive interpretation of investment treaties.[128] Some States have experienced wearisome consequences of investment arbitration.[129] This was the first time India had a first-hand experience of an investment claim. The experience was painful for various reasons. It exposed the possibility that the actions of the Supreme Court (which is the highest Court of Appeal in India and also serves as the constitutional court) could be challenged before an arbitral tribunal. The claim in *White Industries* was based on delays in the Indian judicial system. The Supreme Court of India has a special position in the psyche of the political establishment, legal community and the general public, has steadfastly protected its independence and has intervened in various public interest issues.[130] The other troubling issue in the case was that a commercial arbitration award, which would technically be enforced by an Indian court, was enforced by the investment tribunal, thereby replacing the function of Indian courts. The tribunal adopted an expansive approach by invoking India-Kuwait BIT to import more convenient treatment standards through the most favoured nation (MFN) clause in the India-Australia BIT.[131] This exposed the possibility that an investment tribunal could import any provision from any treaty to hold India liable even if the investment claim was not based on a treaty in which a convenient standard is present. Almost all Indian BITs contained an MFN clause.

After losing this case, many investment claims were filed against India and the third phase with a policy shift thus commenced.

---

128. Susan D. Franck, *The Legitimacy Crisis in Investment Treaty Arbitration: Privatizing Public International Law through Inconsistent Decisions*, 73 Fordham Law Review 1521, 1626 (2005).
129. Latin American States have faced most of the investment claims. Argentina has faced more than 50 arbitration claims, which arose out of the regulations that Argentina had to undertake at the time of financial crisis. José Alvarez and Gustavo Topalian, *The Paradoxical Argentina Cases*, 6 World Arbitration and Mediation Review 491 (2012).
130. The significance of the judiciary in India and its role in the overall investment arbitration process cannot be ignored. Therefore, a full chapter is dedicated for this discussion below. *See* M.P. Singh, *Securing the Independence of the Judiciary – The Indian Experience*, 10 Indiana International & Comparative Law Review 245, 292 (2000); U. Baxi, *Taking Suffering Seriously: Social Action Litigation in the Supreme Court of India*, 4(6) Third World Legal Studies 107, 132 (1985).
131. For a detailed discussion, *see* Chapter 7.

§2.03 THE THIRD PHASE (2011 ONWARDS)

The third era started with India losing the first investment case filed by an Australian investor White Industries in 2011. This case marked an important shift in the Indian policy towards foreign investment. The case exposed the vulnerability of India to investment claims.

There is a swathe of notices lodged against the Indian government for various actions. Some of them involve the decision of the Supreme Court. The Supreme Court had struck down spectrum allocation to cellular companies due to irregularities in the grant of licences. The spectrum licences were procured through corruption and at a huge cost to the public exchequer.[132] The foreign investors that have suffered losses as a consequence of the decision of the Supreme Court have initiated investment arbitration. The investment claims would again question the decision of the Supreme Court on an important point that involves questions of corruption and protection of public interest.

For the first time the Government of India, through the Ministry of Commerce (which is one of the concerned ministries on the BIT programme) prepared a paper analysing the Indian BIT programme critically. It concluded that there is a need to 'rethink the role of BITs in attracting foreign investment in India' and 'while IIAs may be a desirable objective, they are neither necessary nor sufficient for promoting FDI'.[133] On the need of maintaining balance between investor protection and protection of domestic regulatory space, the paper stated that 'when developing countries enter into BITs, a balance between investor's rights and domestic policy must be ensured' and 'other legitimate public concerns must not be subordinated to investment protection issues'. The paper acknowledged that the existing Indian BITs lack balance between investor protection and regulatory freedom of India. A need to review the BITs was expressed, to ensure that regulatory freedom is adequately protected.[134]

Due to numerous BIT claims brought against India, India decided to put all ongoing stand-alone BIT negotiations on hold. In 2015, a Model BIT was issued, which would become the basis of negotiations for future BITs, and all the existing BITs were cancelled in 2017.

The Model BIT is the basis on which India negotiates BITs. In early 2015, a draft Model BIT was issued and comments were invited from public.[135] The draft Model BIT was far reaching since it severely curtailed the treatment standards and the dispute resolution clause by introducing the requirement of exhaustion of local remedies. The Law Commission of India constituted a Study Group to comment upon the draft Model

---

132. *Centre for Public Interest Litigation v. Union of India*, 3 SCC 1 (2012).
133. The paper is not in public domain but for extracts, *see* Prabhash Ranjan, *supra* n. 112, at 419, 439-41.
134. *Ibid.*, at 419, 440.
135. The first version of the Model BIT – Ministry of Commerce and Industry, Government of India, *Model Text for Indian Bilateral Investment Treaty* https://www.mygov.in/sites/default/files/master_image/Model%20Text%20for%20the%20Indian%20Bilateral%20Investment%20Treaty.pdf (accessed 19 Mar. 2017).

BIT. The Study Group made extensive comments[136] based on which the draft was changed and a new Model BIT was announced.[137]

The Model BIT represents a major shift in approach of India towards investor protection through BITs – an instance of shifting State practice.[138] It has introduced the concept of sustainable development in the preamble for the first time and emphasized the need of conserving regulatory space for undertaking regulations for public interest.[139] It has narrowed the definitions of investor, investment and treatment standards. For the first time, an enterprise-based definition has been introduced to ensure that only those investors that have actual and real presence in the host State are protected.[140] Many controversial treatment standards such as fair and equitable treatment (FET), MFN treatment and umbrella clause have been removed. The provisions on expropriation, particularly indirect expropriation, have been set out in detail.[141] The NT standard is retained.[142] The distinguishing characteristic of the Model BIT is the introduction of exceptions aimed at protecting regulatory exercise.[143] The dispute resolution procedure has been made strict with the need to first exhaust local remedies unless they are unavailable or futile.[144] There are various other provisions in relation to the conduct of the arbitral proceedings and requirements of independence of arbitrators.[145] In substance, the Model BIT makes every effort towards conserving India's regulatory space while protecting investor interests.[146]

Investment treaties come with an opportunity cost.[147] The choice would depend on where the country stands in terms of the reception and exportation of foreign

---

136. Law Commission of India, Government of India, *Report No. 260: Analysis of the 2015 Model Indian Bilateral Investment Treaty* (August 2015) http://lawcommissionofindia.nic.in/reports/Report260.pdf (accessed 19 Mar. 2017).
137. The final text of the Model BIT is at Ministry of Commerce and Industry, Government of India, *Model Text for the Indian Bilateral Investment Treaty*, Art. 1.2 (28 Dec. 2015) http://www.finmin.nic.in/reports/ModelTextIndia_BIT.pdf (accessed 17 Jul. 2017).
138. Rajput, *supra* n. 111.
139. *Model Text for the Indian Bilateral Investment Treaty*, *supra* n. 137, at Preamble.
140. *Ibid.*, at Arts 1.3-1.5.
141. *Ibid.*, at Art. 5.
142. *Ibid.*, at Art. 4.
143. *Ibid.*, at Art. 32.
144. *Ibid.*, at Chapter 4.
145. Lise Johnson, Lisa Sachs and Jesse Coleman, *International Investment Agreements, 2014: A Review of Trends and New Approaches*, Yearbook on International Investment Law and Policy 2014-2015, 15, 25-7 (Andrea K. Bjorklund (ed.), Oxford University Press, 2016); Grant Hanessian and Kabir Duggal, *The 2015 Indian Model BIT: Is This Change the World Wishes to See?*, 30 ICSID Review – FILJ 729 (Fall 2015); Kabir Duggal, *The Changing Landscape of Investor-State Arbitration in India*, 7 Jindal Global Law Review (2016); *See also* Prabhash Ranjan, *Investment Protection and Host State's Right to Regulate in Indian Model Bilateral Investment Treaty 2015: Lessons for Asian Countries* in Investment Law Arbitration in the Asia Pacific Region – Current Practice, Emerging Issues, Future Prospects (Julian Chaisse and others (eds), Cambridge University Press, 2017) (forthcoming).
146. Aniruddha Rajput, *Protection of Foreign Investment in India and International Rule of Law: Rise or Decline?*, No. 10 KFG Working Paper Series, Berlin Potsdam Research Group, 27 (June 2017).
147. Lauge N. Skovgaard Poulsen, Jonathan Bonnitcha and Jason Webb Yackee, *An Analytical Framework for Assessing Costs and Benefits of Investment Protection Treaties*, LSE Enterprise (March 2013) http://discovery.ucl.ac.uk/1471852/1/bit%20framework.pdf (accessed 3 Mar. 2017).

investment. In the situation where the amount of outgoing foreign investment outpaces incoming investments with a large margin, there are incentives for that State to insist on higher standards of investment protection abroad. Investments of such a State are under threat of mistreatment abroad. The extent of compensation such a State would have to pay if sued by a foreign investor would be far lesser as compared to the extent of protection required for its investors abroad. If the incoming investments are as high as compared to the outgoing investments, then a large successful investment claim may wipe off benefits of the investment to a substantial degree. But then the challenge is how far the State can insist on a conservative BIT, and whether other States would agree. The overall international scenario today has changed from what it was when investment arbitration had emerged. The first situation suited traditional capital-exporting States such as the USA and the Western European States. After the rise of China, India, South Africa and other Asian economies, the inflow of investments into these countries increased, exposing them to the prospect of an investment claim. There have been many claims filed against these countries, for example, the USA has faced fifteen claims.[148] The traditional capital-exporting countries that have insisted on high standards of protection have started reducing the standards of protection in their investment treaties.[149] There may be divergence on the precise extent of protection that one State would wish but consensus is evident amongst States that the standards of protection under investment treaties should be removed. There is discomfort with the existing model of dispute resolution in the BITs. Efforts are being made to reform the dispute resolution structures – prominent amongst them is the introduction of a world investment court.[150]

---

148. European Commission, *Investor-to-State Dispute Settlement (ISDS): Some Facts and Figures* (12 Mar. 2015) 6 http://trade.ec.europa.eu/doclib/docs/2015/january/tradoc_153046.pdf (accessed 4 Mar. 2017).
149. For example, see the changes made to the US Model BIT and Canada Model BIT over time.
150. United Nations Convention on Transparency in Treaty-based Investor-State Arbitration (10 Dec. 2014), 54 ILM 747 (2015); Unified Agreement for the Investment of Arab Capital in the Arab States (26 Nov. 1980) Economic Documents, No. 3; The idea to establish a permanent multilateral investment court to decide investment disputes has been proposed by the European Commission. *See* European Commission, *Fact Sheet, A Future Multilateral Investment Court*, http://europa.eu/rapid/press-release_MEMO-16-4350_en.htm (accessed 1 Jul. 2017); *See also* European Union, *Draft Text Transatlantic Trade and Investment Partnership*, http://trade.ec.europa.eu/doclib/docs/2015/september/tradoc_153807.pdf (accessed 1 Jul. 2017); For further information on the formation of the world investment court refer to the UNCTAD, *Reform of Investor-State Dispute Settlement: In Search of a Roadmap, Special Issue for the Multilateral Dialogue on Investment*, IIA Issue Note No. 2, UNCTAD/WEB/DIAE/PCB/2013/4 (14 May 2013); Also *see* chapter titled 'The Challenges of Creating a Standing International Investment Court' in Eduardo Zuleta, *Reshaping the Investor-State Dispute Settlement System*, International Law E-Books Online Collection 402-23 (2015); Further *see* Nicolette Butler; *In Search of a Model for the Reform of International Investment Dispute Resolution: an Analysis of Existing International and Regional Dispute Settlement Mechanisms*, TDM 1 (2014); For problems with the formation of a world investment court, refer to chapter titled 'Making Impossible Investor-State Reform Possible' in Luis Gonzalez Garcia, *Reshaping the Investor-State Dispute Settlement System*, International Law E-Books Online Collection 424-36 (2015); For the options taken by countries in Latin America to set up a permanent investment court, refer to Omar E. Garcia-Bolivar, *Permanent Investment Tribunals: The Momentum is Building Up*, TDM 1 (2014).

India has negotiated a BIT with Cambodia on the basis of the present Model BIT.[151] India is negotiating new BITs with other States. The final texts of BITs that emerge from negotiations may be different from the original Model BIT, since it would depend on the points of negotiations and the matching of priorities with the negotiating counterparties. It is too early to write off the Model BIT. It is certainly an important shift, since India would remain a predominantly capital-importing country for at least a decade or even more, but not less. The approach of major States has undergone a change, and there is scepticism towards the role of investment treaties and investment arbitration in promoting movement of capital.

The progress of this period represents moderation in approach towards investment treaties and investment arbitration. Investments are welcome but rigid investment protection treaties with broad treatment standards that would intrude upon regular freedoms are unacceptable. Through an innovative Model BIT, India has assumed the position of a rule maker rather than simply a rule taker.[152] It remains to be seen how other States take these rules. There are challenges raised to the capacity of investment treaties with dispute resolution clauses to attract investments. Yet, investment treaties provide psychological comfort for investors.

---

151. Prime Minister's Office, *Cabinet Approves Bilateral Investment Treaty between India and Cambodia to Boost Investment*, http://www.pmindia.gov.in/en/news_updates/cabinet-approves-bilateral-investment-treaty-between-india-and-cambodia-to-boost-investment/ (accessed 19 Mar. 2017).
152. Rajput, *supra* n. 138, at 201, 225-6.

CHAPTER 3
Conditions of Entry, Operation and Consequences of Violations (Doctrine of Illegality)

The freedom of a host State to impose conditions of entry and operation arises from general international law. By virtue of territorial supremacy, each State has the discretion to decide whether to allow entry and conditions based upon which the entry may be allowed. A State is competent to exclude foreigners (called 'aliens' in general international law) from the whole or any part of its territory. A corollary of this principle in customary international law is that no State has a right to claim that its nationals can enter and reside on the territory of a foreign State.[1] Treaties perform the task of allowing entry to nationals of one State into another and even control the conditions of operation in the host State.

In past, Friendship Commerce and Navigation (FCN) treaties facilitated entry and conduct of trade and business activities by nationals of one State into another.[2] Presently, investment treaties perform the task of getting over the limitation of entering into another State and operating, for foreign investors and their investments. The access granted to economies by the FCN treaties was far more liberal than BITs.[3] BITs allow access to investors to the markets of host States. However, what should be the terms of access and operation are decided by the host State in their domestic regulatory framework. The reception of a foreign investor in a host State is based on the conditions the host State deems appropriate to impose.[4] During the period of presence in the host State, the foreigner has to comply with the domestic legal regime – including laws that

---

1. Robert Jennings and Arthur Watts, *Oppenheim's International Law*, 897-8 (9th ed., Oxford University Press 2008).
2. *Ibid.*, at 898-9.
3. Rudolph Dolzer and Margarete Stevens, *Bilateral Investment Treaties*, 10 (Martins Nijhoff 1995).
4. Jennings and Watts, *supra* n. 1, at 899-900.

restrict the right to property and the conditions subject to which property can be held.[5] A host State also possesses the right to expel the alien. The limitation on the right is customary international law. The right must not be abused by acting arbitrarily.[6]

In addition to this established position in international law, there is an element of practicality involved in allowing limited entry. Entry of foreign investment into an economy has significant impact on the national and regional economy. It is therefore obvious and practical for States to regulate the entry and conditions of operation of foreign investment.[7]

BITs, and particularly Indian BITs of the past and the 2015 Model BIT, insist that the entry and operation of foreign investors and investments shall take place 'in accordance with host State law'. Investments that violate the laws of entry and operation cannot claim protection under the BIT and are covered by the doctrine of 'illegality'. This chapter will commence with a discussion on conditions of entry and operation, regulated predominantly by the Foreign Direct Investment Policy (FDI Policy) and the consequences of failure to comply with them, in light of the jurisprudence of investment tribunals.

§3.01 INDIAN ARBITRAL PRACTICE

There are two prominent models of entry: 'liberalized entry model' and 'controlled entry model'. The liberalized entry model is based on the principle of national treatment (NT), which means the foreign investor is allowed to enter and operate, based on same rules as those applied to similarly placed investors belonging to the host State, and investing in their home State.[8] The discretion of host State to impose conditions of entry is severely curtailed or diminished.

Traditionally, capital-exporting States, such as the USA, have preferred unbridled entry and operation. Investors are free to enter and establish investments like domestic investors in the host State. For example, North American Free Trade Agreement (NAFTA) Article 1102.1 states that:

> Each Party shall accord to investors of another Party treatment no less favorable than that it accords, in like circumstances, to its own investors with respect to the establishment, acquisition, expansion, management, conduct, operation, and sale or other disposition of investments.

In a liberalized entry model, the foreign investor can freely take a decision to invest in a State based on purely economic grounds. The drawback is that the host State loses its control on the inflow of investments. The scope for the exercise of regulatory

---

5. *Ibid.*, at 910-27. As long as the laws do not slip under the international minimum standard discussed in Chapter 2.
6. Jennings and Watts, *supra* n. 1, at 940-1.
7. United Nations Conference on Trade and Development, *Admission and Establishment*, UNCTAD/ITE/IIT/10 (Vol. II), 11 (UNCTAD Series on Issues in International Investment Agreements, 2002) http://unctad.org/en/Docs/iteiit10v2_en.pdf (accessed 17 Jul. 2017).
8. Peter Muchlinski, Federico Ortino and Christoph Schreuer, *Oxford Handbook of International Investment Law*, 242-3 (Oxford University Press 2008).

discretion of State, as to whether an entry should be allowed or not, based on the requirements and overall benefit of the economy is obviated.

In a 'controlled entry model', foreign investors are allowed to enter limited and specifically mentioned sectors of the domestic economy. The 'liberalized entry model' is prevalent with the traditionally capital-exporting, developed countries, whereas the 'controlled entry model' is popular with capital-importing, developing countries. The 'controlled entry model' is famous with developing countries because the host States retain the discretion to focus on sectors where foreign investment is required. Foreign investors are not allowed to invest in some strategically important sectors. Some sectors need to be protected, especially those with infant industries. The choice of the sectors would also be made based on comparative advantage of the host State economy. This model excludes the possibility of over-exploitation of natural resources since the foreign investor makes the decision to invest, on purely commercial considerations. Excess investments may result into crowding out of domestic industry by large multinational corporations (MNCs).[9] The entry of foreign investors is conditional upon approval in accordance with laws and regulations of the host State. These laws are not at par with the laws applicable to domestic investors, thereby denying NT. India follows the controlled entry model.

Although the two models create different patterns of entry, post entry, the requirement to comply with domestic laws is applicable for both. Therefore, not just at the stage of entry, but the investor has to be vigilant that the investment is in compliance with the domestic regulatory framework of the host State, throughout the life of the foreign investment. Both these conditions are reflected in the treaty practice of India.

Almost all investment treaties entered into by India, which have now been cancelled, required that the entry and operation of the foreign investment are in accordance with the laws of the host State. However, the provision used to exist at different places. In the Australia-India BIT, it was in the Preamble.[10] In majority of the investment treaties, it was a part of the definition of investment.[11] For example, UK-India BIT provides that: '"investment" means every kind of asset established or acquired, including changes in the form of such investment, in accordance with the national laws of the Contracting Party in whose territory the investment is made... .'[12]

In Article 3.1 of the Austria-India BIT, the entry of foreign investor is made subject to laws and policies of the host State in the following words: 'Each Contracting Party shall admit such investments in accordance with its laws and investment policies applicable from time to time.'[13]

---

9. *Ibid.*, at 240-2.
10. Agreement between the Government of Australia and the Government of the Republic of India on the Promotion and Protection of Investments, Preamble (signed 26 Feb. 1999, entered into force 4 May 2000).
11. Chapter 4 has a detailed discussion in the definition of investment.
12. Agreement between the Government of the United Kingdom of Great Britain and Northern Ireland and the Government of the Republic of India for the Promotion and Protection of Investments, Art. 1(b) (signed 14 Mar. 1994, entered into force 6 Jan. 1995).
13. *See* Agreement between the Government of the Republic of Austria and the Government of the Republic of India for the Promotion and Protection of Investments, Art. 3.1 (signed 8 Nov. 1999,

The practice of India reflects that requirement of legality is associated with treatment standards. The Germany-India BIT states that: 'Each Contracting Party shall encourage and create favourable conditions for investors of the other Contracting Party and also admit investment in its territory in accordance with its laws and policy.'[14]

Other treatment standards such as full protection and security (FPS),[15] fair and equitable treatment (FET)[16] and NT[17] are subject to compliance with local laws. Changes made to the nature of investments have to be in accordance with the laws of the host State.[18] In some cases, the requirement to comply with local laws applies before and after the coming into force of the BIT.[19]

In some treaties, the requirement of the legality of investment is contained in the applicable law clause. The India-Malaysia BIT states that: 'This Agreement shall apply to Investments made in the territory of either Contracting Party in accordance with its laws, regulations or national policies by investors of the other Contracting Party prior to as well as after the entry into force of this Agreement.'[20]

The 2015 Model BIT has a reference to the requirement of compliance with domestic law at several places. The Preamble recognizes the right of the host States to regulate the operation of foreign investment in accordance with the laws and policy of the host State.[21] Investment is defined as an enterprise. For an investor to claim protection, the investment must be made through an enterprise and that enterprise shall be a 'legal entity constituted, organized [sic] and operated in compliance with the Law of the Host State'.[22] It is necessary that the business operations of the foreign investor are carried out in accordance with the laws of host State.[23] The enterprise

---

entered into force 1 Mar. 2001); Agreement between the Government of the United Mexican States and the Government of the Republic of India on the Promotion and Protection of Investments, Art. 2 (signed 21 May 2007, entered into force 23 Feb. 2008).

14. Agreement between the Federal Republic of Germany and the Republic of India for the Promotion and Protection of Investments, Art. 3.1 (signed 10 Jul. 1995, entered into force 13 Jul. 1998).
15. Agreement between the Government of Australia and the Government of the Republic of India on the Promotion and Protection of Investments, *supra* n. 10, at Art. 3.3.
16. Agreement between the Government of the Republic of Austria and the Government of the Republic of India for the Promotion and Protection of Investments, *supra* n. 13, at Art. 2.1.
17. Agreement between the Government of Australia and the Government of the Republic of India on the Promotion and Protection of Investments, *supra* n. 10, at Art. 4.1.
18. Agreement between the Government of the Republic of Austria and the Government of the Republic of India for the Promotion and Protection of Investments, *supra* n. 13, at Art. 2.2.
19. Agreement between the Government of the Republic of India and the Government of the People's Republic of China for the Promotion and Protection of Investments, Art. 2 (signed 21 Nov. 2006, entered into force 1 Sept. 2007); Agreement between the Government of the Republic of India and the Government of Mongolia for the Promotion and Protection of Investments, Art. 2 (signed 3 Jan. 2001, entered into force on 29 Apr. 2002).
20. Agreement between the Government of the Republic of India and the Government of Malaysia for the Promotion and Protection of Investments, Art. 10 (signed 3 Aug. 1995, entered into force 12 Apr. 1997).
21. The language employed is: 'Reaffirming the right of Parties to regulate Investments in their territory in accordance with their Law'.
22. Ministry of Commerce and Industry, Government of India, *Model Text for the Indian Bilateral Investment Treaty*, Art. 1.2 (28 Dec. 2015) http://www.finmin.nic.in/reports/ModelTextIndia_BIT.pdf (accessed 17 Jul. 2017).
23. *Ibid.*, at Art. 1.2.1(v).

through which an investment is conducted shall be constituted, organized and operated in compliance with the law of the host State.[24] The Model BIT claims that it would protect investments made in accordance with the laws of the host State.[25] The requirement for compliance with entry conditions and operation subject to laws of India has been repeatedly provided in the 2015 Indian Model BIT. The conduct management and operation of investor and investment has to be in accordance with the host State law.[26] In addition to the need to comply with general regulatory framework, the 2015 Model BIT refers specifically to compliance with certain specific laws. A non-exhaustive list of laws such as environment, minimum wages, labour standards, social security, etc. is stipulated.[27]

§3.02 REGULATORY FRAMEWORK IN INDIA FOR ENTRY AND OPERATIONS

The regulatory framework controlling entry and operations in India comprises of the FDI Policy, Foreign Exchange Regulation Act, 1973 (FERA), Reserve Bank of India Act, 1934 (RBI Act) and Securities and Exchange Board of India Act, 1992 (SEBI Act) and other laws concerned with the sector in which the foreign investor is investing and the place in India where the foreign investor is investing.

The FDI Policy mostly contains the conditions of entry. The framework set out by the FDI Policy continues to regulate some aspects of the operations of investments. In the beginning itself, the FDI Policy states that in addition to the FDI Policy, a foreign investor has to comply with the other regulations that affect the foreign investor directly or indirectly.[28] The FEMA regulates receiving, holding, transferring and other dealings with foreign currency. The RBI Act, 1934 created the Reserve Bank of India (RBI). The RBI is responsible for control of inflow and outflow of foreign currency. For any activity relating to foreign exchange, prior permission of the RBI is required. The SEBI Act, 1992 created the SEBI, which is responsible for regulation of stock exchanges and securities markets. All foreign investors have to inevitably deal with these institutions since they are part of the regulatory framework specified in the FDI Policy. Also, a foreign investment transaction would inevitably involve dealing with foreign exchange and procuring of equity or security. Thus, the laws discussed are generally applicable to a foreign investment transaction. Additionally, separate laws would regulate the activities of the investor depending on the sector of investment. There would be some general laws as well that would regulate the activity of the foreign investor, such as the laws on protection of environment and prevention of pollution, labour laws, purchase of land and machinery, local laws regulating water supply, etc.

---

24. *Ibid.*, at Art. 1.6.
25. *Ibid.*, at Art. 2.1.
26. *Ibid.*, at Art. 8.1.
27. *Ibid.*, at Art. 12.
28. The regulatory framework for foreign investment consists of Acts, Regulations, Press Notes, Press Releases, Clarifications, etc. *See* Ministry of Commerce and Industry, Government of India, *Consolidated FDI Policy Circular of 2016*, para. 1.1.2 (7 Jun. 2015) http://dipp.nic.in/sites/default/files/FDI_Circular_2016%282%29.pdf (accessed 18 Jul. 2017).

The foreign investor has to comply with the laws at the central (federal) level, state (provincial) level and local levels. Investment tribunals have time and again reiterated that a foreign investor has to comply with the general regulatory framework of the host State, as well, which would encompass all those laws.[29] It would be impossible to discuss all those laws in detail here. Since the principal legal instrument that regulates the entry and operation of foreign investment is the FDI Policy, it is discussed in detail.

The Government of India announces the FDI Policy each year. Many fundamental facets of the FDI Policy remain the same, except for changes in the sectors in which investment is permitted and the extent of investments. The recent FDI Policy of 2015 is used as the basis for the present discussion.

The title 'FDI Policy' may give the impression that it is merely a policy and not an obligatory document. That is not correct. It is mandatory, and non-compliance would attract penal provisions. The FDI Policy is not passed by the Legislature. It is a governmental order, issued by the Government of India. As per Article 73 of the Constitution of India, the Government of India can exercise powers on subjects that are within the power of the Parliament. The corresponding legislative power of the Parliament extends to the legislative list contained in the Constitution. Thus, the Government of India is within its powers to issue the FDI Policy. The Supreme Court of India has held that the Government of India (through the Department of Industry Policy and Promotion) has the power to issue FDI Policy, and RBI would be responsible for monitoring foreign investments.[30]

The FDI Policy distinguishes FDI from portfolio investment. For an investment to qualify as FDI under the FDI Policy there shall be an establishment of 'a "lasting interest" in an enterprise that is resident'.[31] The FDI Policy distinguishes FDI from portfolio investment. Portfolio investment is an equity investment: an investment in shares or related financial instruments. There are policy reasons for excluding portfolio investment from protection under the investment treaties. The investor does not intend to enter the domestic market or have any long-term commitment. Portfolio investments do not create a lasting interest of the foreign investor and the investor can exit the markets at any time of choice.[32] Therefore, the FDI Policy conscribes for the protection of FDI. According to the FDI Policy, FDI means 'investment by non-resident entity/person resident outside India in the capital of an Indian company' as per the prescribed regulations drafter under the FEMA Act.[33] Non-resident entity or a person is defined in FEMA. FEMA simply defines non-resident as 'a person who is not resident in India.'[34]

---

29. *Inceysa Vallisoletana S.L. v. Republic of El Salvador*, Award, ICSID Case No. ARB/03/26, para. 262 (2 Aug. 2006).
30. *Manohar Lal Sharma v. Union of India*, 6 SCC 616, para. 15 (2013).
31. *Consolidated FDI Policy Circular of 2016*, supra n. 28, at para. 1.1.1.
32. Aniruddha Rajput, *Defining Investments: A Developmental Perspective*, 2(1) Indian Journal of Arbitration Law 12, 19 (2013); M. Sornarajah, *Portfolio Investments and Definition of Investment*, 24 ICSID Review – Foreign Investment Law Journal 516 (2009).
33. *Consolidated FDI Policy Circular of 2016*, supra n. 28, at para. 2.1.12.
34. Section 2(w), Foreign Exchange Management Act, 1999.

Chapter 3: Conditions of Entry, Operation and Consequences §3.02

The objective of FDI Policy is to protect direct investments into India. If the investments are indirect or merely financial in nature – without actual presence – prior permission of the Government is required. The FDI Policy keeps a close vigil on entities created merely as an instrument for routing investments into India. If indirect investment is made by an eligible Indian entity into another eligible Indian company/Limited Liability Partnership (LLP), then it is called 'downstream investment'.[35] Foreign investment into an Indian company that is engaged only in investing in another Indian company always requires prior approval of the Government and the Foreign Investment Promotion Board (FIPB), irrespective of the amount of foreign investment.[36] Purely financial companies are also required to comply with the RBI regulations.[37] Furthermore, if foreign investment is to be made in an Indian company that does not have any assets or 'downstream' investments, approval of the Government is required irrespective of the sector and the extent of investment. Further, as and when such an Indian company, which does not have any operations or any downstream investment, commences actual business activity or makes a downstream investment, it will have to comply with sectoral requirements and conform to the caps on investment.[38] Through these provisions, the Government can screen the source of investments and decline entry to certain investments which are created for the sole purpose of availing protection of Indian investment treaties by creating mailbox companies in India. The FDI Policy excludes calculation of investments made by Indian companies from computation of FDI.[39] This ensures that Indian companies do not incorporate corporate vehicles in other countries to file investment claims against India.

FDI can take place in India only in the form of 'capital' investment. The FDI Policy defines capital as equity shares; fully, compulsorily and mandatorily convertible preference shares; fully, compulsorily and mandatorily convertible debentures.[40] In addition to the requirement that investments have to be made in one of the capital forms specified, a foreign investor can make investments only in specified legal entities. The legal entities in which investments can be made shall be Indian companies,[41] partnership firms/proprietary concern,[42] venture capital fund (VCF),[43] and LLP,[44] and investment vehicles,[45] subject to conditions imposed in the FDI Policy (the

---

35. *Consolidated FDI Policy Circular of 2016*, supra n. 28, at para. 3.8.2 (i).
36. *Ibid.*, at para. 3.8.3.1.
37. *Ibid.*, at para. 3.8.3.2.
38. *Ibid.*, at para. 3.8.3.3.
39. *Ibid.*, at para. 3.8.1, Annexure 5, at para. 1.2. This problem arose in the case of *Tokios Tokelés*, where 90% of the shares and two-third of the management was controlled by the nationals of the host State and they sued their host State by incorporating an entity in another State. This transaction was upheld by the Tribunal in that case. *Tokios Tokelés v. Ukraine*, Decision on Jurisdiction, ICSID Case No. ARB/02/18, para. 30 (29 Apr. 2004). *See Tokios Tokelés v. Ukraine*, Dissenting Opinion (Chairman Prosper Weil), ICSID Case No. ARB/02/18 (29 Apr. 2004).
40. *Consolidated FDI Policy Circular of 2016*, supra n. 28, at para. 2.1.5.
41. *Ibid.*, at para. 3.2.1.
42. *Ibid.*, at para. 3.2.2.
43. *Ibid.*, at para. 3.2.3.
44. *Ibid.*, at para. 3.2.4.
45. *Ibid.*, at para. 3.2.5.

conditions are in the nature of caps and sector limitations, discussed in following paragraphs). In the 2015 FDI Policy, investments in Trusts were specifically disallowed, whereas the 2016 FDI Policy only permits FDI in VCFs registered and regulated by SEBI and 'Investment vehicle'.[46] Except for these forms of legal entities, FDI cannot be made in any other entity.[47]

Likewise, the manner of legal instrument through which investment can be made is specified. Investment in Indian companies can be made through equity shares, fully compulsorily and mandatorily convertible debentures and fully, compulsorily and mandatorily convertible preference shares subject to pricing guidelines and valuation norms prescribed under FEMA Regulations.[48] Foreign investors can enter India by purchasing or acquiring shares from Indian shareholders or other non-resident shareholders. The purchase is subject to sectoral policy. The approval requirement would depend on whether the Government or Automatic Route covers the investment.[49]

Foreign investment can be made in India by a non-resident entity through the Automatic Route or Government Route. Under the Automatic Route, prior approval of the Government is not required, whereas, in the Government Route, prior approval of the Government is necessary. In both situations, the foreign investor has to act in conformity with the laws of the host State.[50] For investments concerning equity where Automatic Route is allowed, prior approval from Government for investment is not necessary;[51] but it is mandatory to intimate the RBI's regional office within thirty days from the receipt of the foreign capital.[52]

Under the Government Route, prior permission of specified agencies of Central Government is required.[53]

Earlier there were three agencies of the Government involved in the approval process: the FIPB; the Finance Minister heading the Finance Ministry; and the Cabinet Committee on Economic Affairs (CCEA). The FIPB does background preparation on the proposals for foreign investment and makes recommendations. The Finance Minister or the CCEA, depending on the value of the transaction, takes the decision to approve foreign investment. According to the existing rules, if the total foreign equity inflow is of INR 5,000 crore (USD 50 billion approx.) or below, the Finance Minister takes the decision based on the recommendations of the FIPB.[54] For foreign equity inflow of more than INR 5,000 crore (USD 50 billion approx.) approval of the CCEA is required.[55] Fresh approvals are not required if additional foreign investment is brought into entities which have already been granted permission and the level of investment allowed in those sectors has increased; or the investment is within the prescribed limit

---

46. *Ibid.*, at para. 3.2.3.
47. *Ibid.*, at para. 3.2.6.
48. *Ibid.*, at para. 3.3, Annexures 2 and 3.
49. *Ibid.*, at para. 3.4.
50. *Fraport AG Frankfurt Airport Services Worldwide v. The Republic of the Philippines*, Award, ICSID Case No. ARB/03/25, para. 343 (16 Aug. 2007).
51. *Consolidated FDI Policy Circular of 2016*, *supra* n. 28, at para. 3.4.1.
52. *Ibid.*, at para. 2.1(i).
53. *Ibid.*, at para. 2.1.18.
54. *Ibid.*, at para. 4.2.1.
55. *Ibid.*, at para. 4.2.2.

Chapter 3: Conditions of Entry, Operation and Consequences   §3.02

of the cap and the sector has been converted into automatic route, or prior approval of the Government or FIPB is not required for any other reason.[56]

On 5 June 2017, the Government of India abolished the FIPB, and the responsibility of approval for the respective sectors has been transferred to the concerned sectors.[57]

The FDI Policy stipulates the sectors in which foreign investment can be made and the extent to which foreign investment can be made. The limitations as to the sectors in which investments can be made are sectoral limitations. Except for the sectors specifically mentioned, investment in any other section is not permitted. If a State limits the access to the foreign investor only to some sectors of the economy, if the foreign investor disregards such restrictions then the investment would not be eligible for protection.[58] Within the sectors, investment can be made to the extent allowed by the FDI Policy. These are called 'cap' on investments. The sectoral limitations and caps are set out in detail in the FDI Policy.[59] If the foreign investor makes an investment in excess of the cap in a sector then the investment will be illegal and not protected under a BIT.[60]

Different combinations of sectoral limitations and caps are used in different sectors. In some sectors 100% FDI is allowed. Thereafter, investments up to a certain limit may be through automatic route and above that limit would have to be through the government route. For example, in the Agriculture and Animal Husbandry, mining and exploration of non-metal ores and coal for captive consumption, 100% FDI is permitted under the automatic route.[61] Publication in scientific magazines, journals and periodicals are permitted 100% through the government route.[62] Investment in FM Radio is permitted up to 49% through Government Route.[63] In broadcasting services of direct to home (DTH), Mobile TV the sectoral cap is 100%. Investment through automatic route is permitted up to 49% and beyond 49%, and up to 100% is through the Government route.[64] For private security agency up to 49% FDI is allowed and is through the Government Route.[65] One hundred per cent FDI through automatic route is allowed in railway infrastructure.[66]

---

56. *Ibid.*, at para. 4.3.
57. Ministry of Finance, Government of India, *Office Memorandum – Abolition of the Foreign Investment Promotion Board* (5 Jun. 2017) http://fipb.gov.in/Forms/OMabolitionFIPB.pdf (accessed 1 Jul. 2017).
58. *Phoenix Action, Ltd. v. The Czech Republic*, Award, ICSID Case No. ARB/06/5, para. 101 (15 Apr. 2009).
59. *Consolidated FDI Policy Circular of 2016*, *supra* n. 28, at para. 3.5.1, Chapter 5.
60. *Phoenix Action, Ltd. v. The Czech Republic*, *supra* n. 58, at para. 100.
61. *Consolidated FDI Policy Circular of 2016*, *supra* n. 28, at paras 5.2.1, 5.2.3.
62. *Ibid.*, at para. 5.2.8.3.
63. *Ibid.*, at para. 5.2.7.2.1.
64. *Ibid.*, at para. 5.2.7.1.1.
65. *Ibid.*, at para. 5.2.13.
66. *Ibid.*, at para. 5.2.1.16.

There are certain sectors of national, strategic and economic importance, such as defence industry,[67] air transport services,[68] ground handling services,[69] asset reconstruction companies,[70] private sector banking,[71] broadcasting,[72] commodity exchanges,[73] credit information companies,[74] insurance,[75] print media,[76] telecommunications[77] and satellites,[78] where each of these aforementioned sectors have a specific requirement. Government approval is required irrespective of the cap conditions.

If the Indian company established with foreign investment is not owned or controlled by resident entity; or the control of the existing Indian company, currently owned by Indian resident will be transferred to a non-resident entity as a consequence of the share transfer or fresh issue of shares – through amalgamation or if merger/demerger, acquisition, etc. takes place – then the permission of the Government is again required.[79]

The restrictions in the form of caps are crucial. If a foreign investor fails to comply with these conditions then protection under IIAs is unavailable. In the case of *Fraport v. Philippines*, the Claimant made an investment in a public sector company operating an airport, in excess of the allowed limits. The Constitution provided that a foreigner cannot own equity in a public utility company in excess of 40%. The Anti Dummy Law of Philippines provided that foreign nationals could not interfere with the management, operation and control of a company for public utility, and there was a need to get a certificate from the President of Philippines attesting to the authority of the government signatories to sign on behalf of the Philippines.[80] If an investor invests in a higher percentage than that allowed under domestic law, then the investment would become illegal. Also, if the investor does not follow the specific rules on entry into the concerned sector, then the investment becomes illegal and the foreign investor cannot claim protection under the investment treaty.[81]

In addition to the requirement of compliance with caps and sectoral requirements, the principle of legality of investment requires that the manner or mechanism employed for entry is also valid. The contract for creation of a joint venture or a legal entity to operate in India will have to comply with domestic law of India. For example, if the agreement through which the foreign investor enters into an engagement with Indian entity is void *ab initio* under laws of India or if the entity entering into that

---

67. *Ibid.*, at para. 5.2.6.1.
68. *Ibid.*, at para. 5.2.9.2.
69. *Ibid.*, at para. 5.2.9.3.
70. *Ibid.*, at para. 5.2.17.
71. *Ibid.*, at para. 5.2.18.
72. *Ibid.*, at para. 5.2.7.
73. *Ibid.*, at para. 5.2.21.
74. *Ibid.*, at para. 5.2.20.
75. *Ibid.*, at para. 5.2.22.
76. *Ibid.*, at para. 5.2.8.
77. *Ibid.*, at para. 5.2.14.
78. *Ibid.*, at para. 5.2.12.
79. *Ibid.*, at para. 3.5.2.(iii).
80. *Fraport v. Philippines*, *supra* n. 50, at para. 120.
81. *Ibid.*, at paras 353-6.

agreement was not permitted to enter into such an agreement by law, then the investment will lack illegality.

In addition to the above requirements, it is mandatory that every Indian company receiving foreign investment has to intimate the concerned regulatory authorities, especially RBI and SEBI (the regulator of securities market).[82] They perform a dominant role in the setting up and operations conducted thereafter by a foreign investor by issuing various circulars from time to time. This facilitates monitoring of the amount of foreign investment that enters the economy. It also earmarks and distinguishes foreign investment from domestic investment. In addition to the FDI Policy RBI Act, SEBI Act, and FEMA Act regulate the entry and operation of foreign investments. Prior to the Liberalization of 1991, due to lack of exports, the holding of US dollars by the Central Bank was insignificant, often raising the balance of payment issues. This was addressed through strict control on possession of foreign currency by private entities through the FERA. As the inflow of capital into India started, it became necessary to loosen the restrictions on free movement of foreign currency. This was achieved by replacing the FERA with FEMA. The dealing in foreign currency are monitored and regulated by RBI, and the activities in the securities exchange are within the domain of SEBI. In addition to the above-stated legal provisions, 'the investment/investors are required to comply with all relevant sectoral laws, regulations, rules, security conditions, and state/local laws/regulations.'[83] According to the Tribunal in *Plama v. Bulgaria*, if there is a material change in the shareholding of the investor which would have an effect on the approval of the investment, then the investor is required to inform the concerned authorities of the host State. Intentional withholding of information would be contrary to good faith.[84]

The FDI Policy is replete with compliance requirements. It normally imposes obligations on entities receiving foreign investment, of intimating the regulators. The entry into specified sectors is subject to entry conditions, and these conditions may include norms for minimum capitalization, lock in period, etc.[85] In most cases involving transfer of capital instruments, prior permission of RBI is required.[86] Existing foreign investors can also seek to enhance their shareholding by purchasing more shares and debentures, subject to sectoral caps.[87] This would happen in cases where a subsequent FDI Policy increases the sectoral cap or allows 100% FDI in a sector. Similar principles govern merger or demerger or amalgamation of two or more companies.[88]

Each year the Government of India issues the FDI Policy. Over the years, the Policy has been liberalized by opening new sectors of the economy for investment and enhancing the extent to which investments can be made in permitted sectors. The

---

82. *Consolidated FDI Policy Circular of 2016*, supra n. 28, at para. 2.
83. *Ibid.*, at para. 3.7.1.
84. *Plama Consortium Limited v. Republic of Bulgaria*, Award, ICSID Case No. ARB/03/24, para. 145 (27 Aug. 2008).
85. *Consolidated FDI Policy Circular of 2016*, supra n. 28, at para. 3.6.
86. *Ibid.*, at para. 5.
87. *Ibid.*, at para. 3, Annexure 4.
88. *Ibid.*, at para. 4, Annexure 4.

Policy, therefore, undergoes a change every year, but there is nothing to suggest in the FDI Policy that it would apply retrospectively. In future, if it is declared that the FDI Policy would operate retrospectively and is prejudicial for existing investors then it would create problems. The change in framework could be a ground for alleging violation of the FET. But since the 2015 Model BIT does not contain FET principle, it is doubtful if such a challenge could be maintainable. However, considering increasing acceptability of foreign investment in India such a measure may not be undertaken. Moreover, the government is keen on ensuring stability in the environment for investing in India. The Policy expressly assures that it aims to 'put in place a policy framework on Foreign Direct Investment, which is transparent, predictable and easily comprehensible'.[89]

§3.03 CONSEQUENCES OF VIOLATION OF ENTRY AND OPERATION: THE DOCTRINE OF ILLEGALITY

The question is what happens if a foreign investor fails to comply with these regulations: can there still be access to investment arbitration? This section is dedicated to the discussion on various aspects of violation of conditions of entry and operation; the doctrine of illegality; need of making investments in good faith to gain access to investment arbitration; extent of illegality necessary to disallow access to investment arbitration; when can the host State not rely on illegality degree to which such violations should exist and at what stage the decision on illegality would be made.

[A] Doctrine of Illegality

If the foreign investor does not comply with the conditions of entry and operation then the investor cannot access investment treaty arbitration (ITA) due to the 'doctrine of illegality'. The requirement of legality or absence of illegality is reflected in the standard: 'in accordance with host State law' contained in investment treaties.[90] The requirement of compliance with domestic laws is a prerequisite for obtaining access to 'the substantive provisions on the protection of the investor under the BIT.'[91] The importance of the need to comply with domestic law is such that whether or not the BIT contains a clause on 'in accordance with host State law' clause, a foreign investor has to comply with the laws of the host State. The clause is implied even if it does not exist in an investment treaty.[92] Investment treaties do not grant unlimited protection to

---

89. *Ibid.*, at para. 1.1.2.
90. *See* discussion above in Section §3.02.
91. *Phoenix Action, Ltd. v. The Czech Republic, supra* n. 58, at para. 104.
92. *Plama Consortium Limited v. Republic of Bulgaria, supra* n. 84, at paras 138-9, followed in *Phoenix Action, Ltd. v. The Czech Republic, supra* n. 58, at para. 101; *Fraport AG Frankfurt Airport Services Worldwide v. Republic of the Philippines [II]*, Award, ICSID Case No. ARB/11/12, para. 332 (10 Dec. 2014).

foreign investment. The conditions of entry and operation need not be stagnated, but the host State can 'formulate, modify, amend, apply or revoke its Law in good faith.'[93]

According to the Tribunal in *Kardassopoulos v. Georgia*:

> Protection of investments' under a BIT is obviously not without some limits. It does not extend, for instance, to an investor making an investment in breach of the local laws of the host State. A State thus retains a degree of control over foreign investments by denying BIT protection to those investments that do not comply with its laws.[94]

Investment treaties impose reciprocal obligations on States as well as foreign investors. While States are bound under the investment treaty to not to breach treatment standards, investors are bound not to violate the domestic law of the host State. Elaborating on the need for integrity of foreign investment a tribunal held that:

> It is arguable that even an investment which is not made in accordance with host State law may import economic value to the host State. But that is not the only goal of this sector of international law. Respect for the integrity of the law of the host State is also a critical part of development and a concern of international investment law. That said, the Tribunal's decision in this matter does not rest on policy. It is the language of the BIT which is dispositive and it is unequivocal in this matter.[95]

In *Salini v. Morocco*, explaining the purpose behind the illegality rule, the tribunal held that the purpose of the clause is 'to prevent the Bilateral Investment Treaty from protecting investment that should not be protected, particularly because they would be illegal.'[96]

The need to comply with the regulatory framework of the host State also arises from the principle governing applicable law in investment arbitration. Domestic law is applicable alongside international law in investment arbitration cases.[97] Therefore, a tribunal will look into domestic law to determine whether the investment treaty covers the investment.[98] A tribunal has to respect the choice of law by the parties and apply the municipal law as well in appropriate circumstances.[99] This principle is aptly summarized in Article 42(1) of the ICSID Convention, which defines applicable law as: 'The Tribunal shall decide a dispute in accordance with such rules of law as may be agreed by the parties. In the absence of such agreement, the Tribunal shall apply the law of the Contracting State party to the dispute (including its rules on the conflict of laws) and such rules of international law as may be applicable.'

---

93. *Model Text for the Indian Bilateral Investment Treaty, supra* n. 22, at Art. 2.4.
94. *Ioannis Kardassopoulos v. The Republic of Georgia*, Decision on Jurisdiction, ICSID Case No. ARB/05/18, para. 182 (6 Jul. 2007).
95. *Fraport AG Frankfurt Airport Services Worldwide v. The Republic of Philippines, supra* n. 50, at para. 402.
96. *Salini Costruttori S.p.A. and Italstrade S.p.A. v. Kingdom of Morocco*, Decision on Jurisdiction, ICSID Case No. ARB/00/4, para. 46 (23 Jul. 2001).
97. *See* Chapter 4 below.
98. *Ioannis Kardassopoulos v. The Republic of Georgia, supra* n. 94, at para. 146.
99. *Ibid.*, at para. 145.

Certainly, this provision is limited to ICSID cases, but even in non-ICSID arbitrations, municipal law continues to play a major role.[100]

[B] Investments Should Be Made in Good Faith to Gain Protection of Investment Treaties

Legality is implied in the absence of explicit language because it arises from the need of compliance with treaty provision in good faith. Rights granted under a treaty shall not be abused and 'every rule of law includes an implied clause that it should not be abused.'[101] Good faith is a part of most of the national systems of the world and also a part of international law. It thus has dual application (in domestic law as well as international law), and they both go hand in hand.[102] Tribunals have recognized the importance of good faith in domestic law as well as international law and have accordingly applied the principle to decide cases.[103] Good faith is an integral part of domestic law of India.[104] The requirement of an investment to be in compliance with the host State law, international law and good faith and non-protection of investments made by way of corruption, fraud or deceitful means is 'general principles that exist independently of specific language to this effect in the Treaty.'[105]

The purpose of international protection of foreign investment is to protect legal and bona fide investments. If an investment is made in violation of the host State's laws or not made in good faith – 'obtained for example through misrepresentations, concealment or corruption', or amounting to an abuse of the international ICSID arbitration system, then protection under the investment treaty would not be available.[106] In *Phoenix v. Czech Republic*, the tribunal held that the purpose of ICSID Convention is not to protect investments that are made in violation of the laws of the host State or investments not made in good faith. Therefore, an investment will not be entitled to protection if it is 'obtained for example through misrepresentations, concealments or corruption, or amount to the abuse of the international ICSID arbitration system. In other words, the purpose of international protection is to protect

---

100. See generally Monique Sasson, *Substantive Law in Investment Arbitration: The Unsettled Relationship Between International Law and Municipal Law* (Kluwer Law International 2010); Hege Elisabeth Kjos, *Applicable Law in Investor-State Arbitration: The Interplay Between National and International Law* (Oxford University Press 2013).
101. *Phoenix Action, Ltd. v. The Czech Republic*, supra n. 58, at para. 107. This award was made while interpreting the Energy Charter Treaty. An opposite view, without considering this award or giving reasons was taken in *Anatolie Stati, Gabriel Stati, Ascom Group S.A. and Terra Raf Trans Trading Ltd. v. Republic of Kazakhstan*, Award, SCC Case No. V116/2010, para. 812 (19 Dec. 2013).
102. *Phoenix Action, Ltd. v. The Czech Republic*, supra n. 58, at para. 109.
103. *Ibid.*, at paras 110-2 citing *Inceysa Vallisoletana S.L. v. Republic of El Salvador*, supra n. 29, at para. 230 and *Plama Consortium Limited v. Republic of Bulgaria*, supra n. 84, at para. 143-4.
104. Good faith is defined in Section 3(22) of the General Clauses Act, 1897 [India] as 'a thing shall be deemed to be done in "good faith", where it is in fact done honestly, whether it is done negligently or not'. See also *Brijendra Singh v. State of Uttar Pradesh*, 1 SCC 597, at pp. 602-4 (1981).
105. *Gustav FW Hamester GmbH & Co KG v. Republic of Ghana*, Award, ICSID Case No. ARB/07/24, para. 123-4 (18 Jun. 2010).
106. *Phoenix Action, Ltd. v. The Czech Republic*, supra n. 58, at paras 100, 106.

legal and *bona fide* investments.'[107] These observations may appear to have been made in relation to ICSID, but they are generally applicable as well. It cannot be that ICSID cannot be availed due to bad faith but ordinary arbitration could be initiated through a claim based on bad faith. The requirement of compliance with domestic laws is linked to international law. If the investor does not comply with domestic law then, in the context of ICSID, access to ICSID would not be available.[108] There is no separate requirement of legality under the ICSID system. It emanates from the BIT; hence these comments by ICSID tribunals would extend to ad hoc arbitrations as well.[109]

Good faith excludes protection to investments made through misrepresentation or fraud. If the permission to invest is obtained through misrepresentation or fraud then the investor cannot claim protection under the investment treaty.[110] In cases of investment through misrepresentation, a foreign investor cannot contend that it acted in good faith.[111]

If the foreign investment is an outcome of deliberate concealment amounting to fraud, calculated to induce the governmental authorities to authorize the transaction or grant permission, then that transaction would not be protected under the investment treaty. The investor would not be protected because it would be contrary to domestic law, as well as international law.[112]

In *Inceysa v. El Salvador*, the foreign investor had invested in the host State through a tender for service contract for stations for mechanical inspection of vehicles and emission control of contaminating gases. It was found that the tender was obtained through misrepresentations in the bid documents. The decision to award the contract was based on the bid presented by the foreign investor. There were misrepresentations made in the bid.[113] If the underlying transaction for investment is tainted by fraud or misrepresentation then protection under an investment treaty would not be available. The fundamental principle of law is that 'nobody can benefit from his own fraud', enunciated in the maxim: *nemo auditor turpitudinem allegans*.[114]

Likewise, an investment acquired through bribery will not be protected under an investment treaty. States have condemned bribery and undertaken obligations to stop and punish it through various international conventions.[115] The recently issued Model BIT of India eschews corruption and deprives protection to investors indulging in such an activity.[116]

In cases of fraud or bribery, defence of estoppel has been raised. The question arises whether a foreign investor can plead that the State was complacent in the act of taking bribery because it did not take steps within reasonable time. Or, whether the

---

107. *Ibid.*, at para. 100.
108. *Ibid.*, at para. 101.
109. *Inceysa Vallisoletana S.L. v. Republic of El Salvador*, *supra* n. 29, at paras 258-9.
110. *Ibid.*, at paras 111-3.
111. *Plama Consortium Limited v. Republic of Bulgaria*, *supra* n. 84, at para. 134.
112. *Ibid.*, at paras 134-5.
113. *Inceysa Vallisoletana S.L. v. Republic of El Salvador*, *supra* n. 29, at paras 104-10.
114. *Ibid.*, at paras 240-4.
115. *World Duty Free Company Limited v. Republic of Kenya*, Award, ICSID Case No. ARB/00/7, paras 146-7, 157 (4 Oct. 2006).
116. *Model Text for the Indian Bilateral Investment Treaty*, 2015, *supra* n. 22, Art. 9.

actions of a corrupt leader can be attributed to the State? In *World Duty Free v. Kenya*, the foreign investor had paid bribery to the President to procure a contract to construct, operate and maintain duty-free shops on the international airports of Nairobi and Mombassa. In that case, the applicable law was English law. Applying that law, the Tribunal held that the corrupt actions of an official of a State cannot be imputed to a State due to the following reasons:

> In the Tribunal's view, it is significant that in England, historically, the common law has traditionally abhorred the corruption by bribery of officers of State, ranking its offence next to high treason. Such corruption is more odious than theft, but it does not depend upon any financial loss and it requires no immediate victim. Corruption of a State officer by bribery is synonymous with the most heinous crimes because it can cause huge economic damage, and its long-term victims can be legion. The offence lies in bribing a person to exercise his public duty corruptly and not in accordance with what is right and proper for the State and its citizens. Like any other contract, a State contract procured by bribing a State officer is legally unenforceable, as an affront to the public conscience. The fact that the transaction is performed outside England or is subject to a law other than English law is immaterial.[117]

The Tribunal held that there could be no waiver and affirmation of the bribe because the knowledge of bribe of the President cannot be attributed to Kenya. Since the President was acting corruptly to the detriment of Kenya and in violation of its laws, there can be no attribution of knowledge to the State.[118]

The foreign investor may not have indulged into an illegal activity himself but may have invested through someone who has committed fraud or bribery. Thus, if the foreign investor has made an investment through someone who has committed illegality, then the investment also becomes illegal. Benefits derived from an illegality, whether direct or indirect are not protected. In *Alasdair Ross Anderson v. Costa Rica*, a bunch of foreign investors had invested in a Ponzischeme run by two Costa Rican nationals. The Costa Rican nationals, through whom investments were made, engaged in a money exchange business. The regulatory authorities in Costa Rica allowed only licensed and authorized entities to engage into the concerned business and the list of licences granted to authorized persons was updated from time to time. The depositors had to deposit a certain amount at the beginning and interest would be deposited in their account each month.[119] Incorporation 'in accordance with host State laws' has an important role in the findings of the tribunal. The assurance of legality of investment is crucial for the 'public welfare and economic well-being of any country.'[120] A regulation requiring only authorized entities to engage in a business to protect public from being defrauded is a perfectly legitimate regulation. If an investor invests into an activity which has been so restricted without ensuring that the person has an authorization then the investor is participating in an illegal activity. The investor may not have

---

117. *World Duty Free Company Limited v. Republic of Kenya*, supra n. 115, at para. 173.
118. *Ibid.*, at para. 185.
119. *Alasdair Ross Anderson et al v. Republic of Costa Rica*, Award, ICSID Case No. ARB(AF)/07/3, paras 17-9 (19 May 2010).
120. *Ibid.*, at para. 53.

committed a crime by investing in such an entity, but the fact that the investment or the ownership of assets was not in accordance with the host State law would result into depriving the protection of the investment treaty.[121] It would be too narrow to suggest that investment into a transaction which is in turn not in accordance with the laws of host State does not mean that the first transaction is illegal.[122] However, if the genesis of the transaction itself is illegal then any derivative rights would also be illegal. Schill criticizes the decision on the ground that the activity in which investments were made was illegal but not the action on investing in such a scheme. It did not amount to shareholding in an illegal business but a contractual claim for interest and principal in an illegal business. Therefore, the tribunal was incorrect in holding that the investment of foreign investors was itself illegal.[123] The argument suggests that although smuggling would be an illegal business, but investment and expecting returns from that investment would not. Tellingly, the Tribunal took a view that the manner of entering into the transaction has to be seen. According to the tribunal:

> In order to determine whether the ownership of a property is in accordance with the law of a particular country, one must of necessity examine how the possession or ownership of that property was acquired and in particular whether the process by which that possession or ownership was acquired complied with all of the prevailing laws.[124]

In foreign investment transactions, it is elementary to expect the foreign investor to be careful. If the investor can see that the transaction is 'high-risk high return' the investor should exercise care. The failure to exercise case could not be imputed on the host State. Therefore, for example, if the foreign investor is asked to invest in a company which has procured government licences at a price far too less than the market price, then it is the responsibility of the investor to be wary about these transactions. The investor cannot claim that the illegality of the transaction in which it has invested would not affect the legality of its own investments. Placing this responsibility on the investor, the Tribunal stated that 'prudent investment practice requires that any investor exercise due diligence before committing funds to any particular investment proposal. An important element of such due diligence is for investors to assure themselves that their investments comply with the law. Such due diligence obligation is neither overly onerous nor unreasonable'.[125]

Similar issues are pending before some investment tribunals, where the Supreme Court of India found that the foreign investors had purchased licences from those who had obtained those licences by fraud and bribery. The principles discussed above would apply in such cases.

---

121. *Ibid.*, at para. 55.
122. *Ibid.*, at para. 56.
123. Stephan Schill, *Illegal Investment in Investment Treaty Arbitration*, 11 The Law and Practice of International Courts and Tribunals 281, 306 (2012).
124. *Alasdair Ross Anderson et al v. Republic of Costa Rica, supra* n. 119, at para. 57.
125. *Ibid.*, at para. 58.

[C] Extent of Violation of Domestic Law Necessary to Constitute Illegality

Not all violations of domestic law would amount to illegality. A distinction has to be drawn between illegality and irregularity or a discrepancy. Illegality is attracted in cases of breaches of fundamental norms of domestic law. If the alleged violation of the municipal law is trivial, the overall investment activity may still be legal. A tribunal elucidated the requisite threshold for illegality in the following words:

> The Tribunal agrees with the view that not every trivial, minor contravention of the law should lead to a refusal of jurisdiction. It must strike a balance between two criteria. On the one hand, neither Claimant nor the Tribunal may presume that the host State waives its sovereignty and agrees to the arbitration of disputes when the investor made the investment in violation of its substantive or procedural legislation. On the other hand, States must not be allowed to abuse the process by scrutinizing the investment *post festum* with the intention of rooting out minor or trivial illegalities as a pretext to free themselves of an obligation. A State must act consistently with its obligations and not resist jurisdiction because it wants to escape the consequences of its standing agreement to arbitrate.[126]

The weighing factor is the significance of the norm in question.[127] The key factor is the gravity of infraction.[128] An investor would have to comply with the substantive laws of the host State: material norms regulating investments.[129] The gravity would depend on context. A minor flaw in registration may not appear to result into illegality. In the domestic law, that flaw is of grave consequence then that apparently minor discrepancy could be serious considering the context. For example, if specific authorization is necessary to do the business of banking for foreign companies and a foreign investor does not obtain that authorization then the so-called minor discrepancy has serious repercussions.

Illegality may also occur if the investor fails to comply with the procedural requirements of the regulations of the host State.[130] If the investment treaty stipulates a special procedure for registration, then that procedure must be satisfied. In *YCO v. Myanmar*, the ASEAN Investment Agreement required that the investment must be specifically approved in writing and registered in the host State. The investor, in that case, had commenced business operations but did not possess an approval in writing. The Tribunal held that it did not have jurisdiction over the dispute.[131]

---

126. *Mamidoil Jetoil Greek Petroleum Products Societe S.A. v. Republic of Albania*, Award, ICSID Case No. ARB/11/24, para. 483 (30 Mar. 2015).
127. Ursula Kriebaum, *Investment Arbitration – Illegal Investments*, Austrian Arbitration Yearbook 307, 319 (2010).
128. *Ibid.*, at 307, 334.
129. *Mamidoil Jetoil Greek Petroleum Products Societe S.A. v. Republic of Albania*, supra n. 126, at para. 372.
130. *Ibid.*, at para. 378.
131. *Yaung Chi Oo Trading Pte Ltd v. Government of the Union of Myanmar*, Award, ASEAN ID Case No. ARB/01/1, paras 62-3 (31 Mar. 2003).

Chapter 3: Conditions of Entry, Operation and Consequences §3.03[D]

Formal discrepancies in the documents do not constitute fraud.[132] If there are some defects in the registration paperwork, then the investment does not become illegal.[133] In *Tokios Tokelés v. Ukraine*, the Respondent State argued that the investments were illegal because the subsidiary was registered under a wrong name. The recognized form of name was different under domestic law. There were errors in the documents relating to asset procurement and transfer including absence of signatures or notarization in some cases.[134] The Tribunal found that the business activity in which the foreign investor was involved – advertising, printing and publishing – in this case – was not illegal. The discrepancies in documentation were 'minor errors' that would not be 'inconsistent with the object and purpose of the Treaty.'[135] Therefore, minor errors in compliance do not affect the overall validity of the investment. If the non-compliances of law can be cured under the domestic law then there is no reason for a tribunal to decline jurisdiction.[136]

If the host law provides for a certain punishment for timely registration then it would be disproportionate to punish the foreign investor under illegality for failure to register within statutory time.[137] Minor discrepancies do not result into illegality.[138] However, a discrepancy may appear minor but it may be fundamental in relation to the investment. In such a case, the investment would be illegal. The regulation covering the activity also has to be seen and analysed. If the regulations provide that the effect of non-registration would result into deprivation of certain taxation and other privileges then failure to register cannot become a reason for derecognizing the investment. Failure to register in and thus comply with technicalities that do not affect the investment as such does not amount to illegality.[139]

[D] Situations Where Defence of Illegality Would Be Unavailable to States

The objection of illegality will not be available in some situations. An investment would be illegal if the law is not clear and the mistake by the foreign investor was made in good faith. An example of good faith would be where a competent local lawyer did the due diligence and failed to flag the issue, or the illegality is not central to the profitability of the investment and the investment would have been made without

---

132. *Alpha Projektholding GmbH v. Ukraine*, Award, ICSID Case No. ARB/07/16, paras 190-1 (8 Nov. 2010).
133. *Ibid.*, at para. 297.
134. *Tokios Tokelés v. Ukraine*, supra n. 39, at para. 83.
135. *Ibid.*, at para. 86; *Mytilineos Holdings SA v. The State Union of Serbia & Montenegro and Republic of Serbia*, Partial Award on Jurisdiction, UNCITRAL, paras 154, 157 (8 Sept. 2006).
136. *Mamidoil Jetoil Greek Petroleum Products Societe S.A. v. Republic of Albania*, supra n. 126, at para. 494.
137. Kriebaum, *supra* n. 127, at 307, 322, citing *Metalpar S.A. and Buen Aire S.A. v. The Argentine Republic*, Award on Merits, ICSID Case No. ARB/03/5, para. 84 (6 Jun. 2008).
138. *Achmea B.V. (formerly Eureko B.V.) v. Slovak Republic [I]*, Final Award, PCA Case No. 2008-13, para. 173-6 (7 Dec. 2012); *Hochtief AG v. The Argentine Republic*, Decision on Liability, ICSID Case No. ARB/07/31, para. 199 (29 Dec. 2014).
139. *Inmaris Perestroika Sailing Maritime Services GmbH and Others v. Ukraine*, Decision on Jurisdiction, ICSID Case No. ARB/08/8, para. 145 (8 Mar. 2010).

projected profitability based on violation of domestic law.[140] However, a foreign investor would not be entitled for protection in cases of egregious violations of domestic law.[141] False information and misrepresentation are instances of breach of good faith.[142] If it is established that the investment is not made in good faith and therefore not in accordance with domestic law, then the protection under BIT would not be available for the foreign investor.[143]

If the State allows the foreign investor to continue with an investment and cooperates with the investor in relation to that activity despite knowing about it then the defence of illegality is unavailable. The situation would be governed by the principle of estoppel. A corollary of the estoppel doctrine is that the illegality has to be committed by the investor and not by the State or an entity associated with the State. Illegalities committed with acquiescence of State or its instrumentalities do not deprive the foreign investor of protection under an investment treaty. The illegal act has to be on the part of the foreign investor. If a State enterprise violates the domestic law then foreign investor is not deprived of the protection of the invest entreaty.[144] Likewise, if the State enterprise acts outside its authority then the investor cannot be faulted.[145]

In *Inmaris v. Ukraine*, the Respondent State argued that the investment was illegal because as per the regulations on foreign exchange it was necessary that the investor obtained licence from the regulating authority. The investor had not obtained the licence. The Tribunal rejected the argument of Respondent State because the transaction took place through a government controlled company. It is the responsibility of the government owned company to obtain necessary licence. The government controlled company was aware of this regulation throughout, yet participated in the transaction. In such a case the foreign investor would not be responsible for the alleged illegality.[146] It is a fairly settled and convincing view that if a State entity participates in a transaction then it cannot thereafter allege that the transaction was illegal.

According to the Tribunal in *Fraport v. Philippines*, if a State 'knowingly overlooks' and 'endorses an investment' that violate its laws, then a State is estopped from raising a jurisdictional objection that the investments were illegal.[147] If a State knowingly engages with the foreign investor, then the State cannot retract.[148] However, it still remains to be seen if it was the State involved or officials acting outside the purview of their duty against public interest. In a country of India's size, it is difficult

---

140. *Fraport AG Frankfurt Airport Services Worldwide v. The Republic of Philippines*, supra n. 47, at para. 396.
141. *Ibid.*, at para. 397.
142. *Inceysa Vallisoletana S.L. v. Republic of El Salvador*, supra n. 29, at paras 235-6.
143. *Ibid.*, at para. 239.
144. *Southern Pacific Properties (Middle East) Limited v. Arab Republic of Egypt*, Award, 32 ILM 933 (1993), para. 81-5 (20 May 1992).
145. *Sergei Paushok, CJSC Golden East Company and CJSC Vostokneftegaz Company v. Government of Mongolia*, Award on Jurisdiction and Liability, UNCITRAL, paras 606-9 (28 Apr. 2011).
146. *Inmaris Perestroika Sailing Maritime Services GmbH and Others v. Ukraine*, supra n. 139, at paras 137-40.
147. *Fraport AG Frankfurt Airport Services Worldwide v. The Republic of Philippines*, supra n. 47, at para. 346.
148. *ADC Affiliate Limited and ADC & ADMC Management Limited v. Republic of Hungary*, Award, ICSID Case No. ARB/03/16, para. 475 (2 Oct. 2006).

to manage to keep a close eye on each investment. India is sub-divided into provinces, called states, and there are local bodies under the structure of provinces. They all have freedom to engage with foreign investors in different capacities, through public private partnership contracts, etc. It is possible that the government officers operating at different and complex levels may miss some non-compliances, which might come to light only at the stage of arbitration. If it is found that the investor deliberately committed illegality and the act did not come to the notice of the government, then should the Government of India be responsible? In these cases, India would not be faulted for mistakenly overlooking illegalities, unless the overlooking was knowingly done and the investment was endorsed. Furthermore, the application of estoppel by the Tribunal in *Fraport v. Philippines* was conscribed only to the jurisdictional stage. Thus, a host State could raise a defence that the investment is illegal when the claimant alleges breach of substantive standards at the merits stage. If the investment is obtained by deceitful conduct that violates the domestic law then it is contrary to the basic notion of international public policy.[149]

Estoppel applies for illegalities committed during the subsistence of the investments. This suggests that the legality requirement continues to operate. A host State is estopped from raising the illegality argument if it ignores the illegalities.[150] If the investment is concealed from the government then estoppel would not operate.[151] There is no specified period of limitation within which an objection would have to be raised. On one occasion a tribunal declined to entertain the objection of illegality on the ground of delay. The challenge was raised after five years. The tribunal found that under the domestic law of the host State this period would be beyond limitation, hence, the objection was time-barred.[152] In this case, the Respondent State was aware of the transaction and had participated. Therefore, it had knowledge. In cases where the State does not have knowledge, the period of limitation would start from the point of knowledge. There is no limitation period prescribed in international law. The tribunal decided to use the period under domestic law. It may not be a viable exercise since the period would differ from one host State to another. It may be convenient to use limitation period in the host State as a reference point. However, the period could not be rigidly applied through strict computation.

If the violations are by the host State or an entity controlled by the host State that is interacting with foreign investor, contrary to the domestic law, or the acts are beyond the purview of its authority, then the State cannot raise the argument of illegality. An investment tribunal would reject the argument of illegality if the host State was aware of the illegality and allowed the investor to continue – the idea is that 'a host State cannot avoid jurisdiction under the BIT by invoking its own failure to comply with its

---

149. *Plama Consortium Limited v. Republic of Bulgaria*, supra n. 84, at paras 143-4.
150. *Técnicas Medioambientales Tecmed S.A. v. United Mexican States*, Award, ICSID Case No. ARB (AF)/00/2, paras 149, 151, 174 (29 May 2003).
151. *Fraport AG Frankfurt Airport Services Worldwide v. The Republic of Philippines*, supra n. 47, at para. 347.
152. *ADC Affiliate Limited and ADC & ADMC Management Limited v. Republic of Hungary*, supra n. 148, at para. 456.

domestic law.'[153] In *Kardassopoulos v. Georgia*, the Respondent State argued that the investment is illegal and the foreign investor shall not be granted protection under the BIT because the State-owned enterprise had exceeded its authority in entering into a joint venture agreement and concession agreement with the foreign investor. This was a violation of the Georgian law and therefore the agreements were void *ab initio*. The Tribunal rejected this argument on the ground that the State cannot invoke violation of its laws when an entity controlled by itself is acting in excess of its authority.[154] A foreign investor cannot be faulted for violations of domestic law by the host State.

[E] Stage for Deciding Illegality

There is some academic debate about the appropriate stage for deciding illegality of investments.[155] The question of illegality, in the cases of wrongful entry or procurement of investments, is decided at the jurisdictional stage. Legality of the investment would be decided at the jurisdictional stage if 'in accordance with municipal law', it is tied to the definition of investment. If it is not, then the question would be decided at the time of deciding on the merits of the case.[156] In *Plama v. Bulgaria*, the Tribunal held that violations of local laws do not relate to the definition of investment and should be decided at merits stage, since allegations of misrepresentation are not directed towards the agreement to arbitrate but relate to the operation in relation to domestic law.[157] If the requirement of illegality is applicable to investments protected through a clause applying the treaty retrospectively, then a tribunal could decide the case at the stage of jurisdiction. The Tribunal did so in *Kardassopoulos v. Georgia*.[158] If the violation is manifest then the tribunal would deny jurisdiction and not proceed to the merits.[159] However, if it is manifest that the investment is performed in violation of the law, then judicial economy demands that legality is decided at the jurisdictional stage itself.[160]

In *Fraport v. Philippines*, the Tribunal held that failure to comply with host State law amounted to lack of jurisdiction *ratione materiae*.[161] Once it is established that the investment is illegal, then the tribunal would not exercise jurisdiction.[162] Whether decided at the jurisdictional or merits stage, the question of legality goes to the competence of a tribunal to try a dispute.[163] The presumption is that illegality is a substantive defence to alleged violations of an investment treaty. If a tribunal finds that

---

153. *Ioannis Kardassopoulos v. The Republic of Georgia, supra* n. 94, at para. 182.
154. *Ibid.*, at paras 183-4.
155. It has been argued that the appropriate stage is merits rather than jurisdiction. Cf. Stephan Schill, *Illegal Investment in Investment Treaty Arbitration*, 11 The Law and Practice of International Courts and Tribunals 281, 290-1 (2012).
156. *Khan Resources Inc., et al. v. Government of Mongolia*, Decision on Jurisdiction, UNCITRAL, para. 383-5 (25 Jul. 2012).
157. *Plama Consortium Limited v. Republic of Bulgaria, supra* n. 84, at paras 130-1, 229-30.
158. *Ioannis Kardassopoulos v. The Republic of Georgia, supra* n. 94, at para. 177.
159. *Phoenix Action, Ltd. v. The Czech Republic, supra* n. 58, at para. 102.
160. *Ibid.*, at para. 104.
161. *Fraport AG Frankfurt Airport Services Worldwide v. The Republic of Philippines, supra* n. 47, at para. 404; *Alasdair Ross Anderson et al v. Republic of Costa Rica, supra* n. 119, at para. 61.
162. *Ibid.*, at para. 60.
163. *Inceysa Vallisoletana S.L. v. Republic of El Salvador, supra* n. 29, at para. 155-6.

the investment is not protected then that determination relates to the jurisdiction of the tribunal, rather than a substantive defence.[164] The determination of illegality relates to the competence of the tribunal – depending on whether a State agreed to arbitrate disputes arising from illegal investments. Therefore, the question of legality is *ratione voluntatis*.[165]

If the illegality appeared at the merits stage, then tribunals have dealt with it at the merits stage.[166] At times a tribunal may find it best to decide the question of legality at the merits stage.[167] The extent of analysis of legal rights is such that the challenge of illegality cannot be decided at the jurisdictional stage. It will have to be decided on the merits.[168] In situations where illegality is not apparent from the outset, a tribunal may investigate legality while examining compliance with substantive standards.[169]

Based on the language of the treaty, illegality does not relate to the jurisdiction and has to be decided at the merits stage. In *Gustav Hamster v. Ghana*, the Tribunal held that jurisdiction of the tribunal would be affected only if the investor has obtained entry into State fraudulently. Frauds committed during the existence of the investment would have to be considered at the merits stage.[170] According to the Tribunal: 'Thus, on the wording of this BIT, the legality of the creation of the investment is a jurisdictional issue; the legality of the investor's conduct during the life of the investment is a merits issue.'[171]

The curial question is whether an investment would become illegal if during the life of investment, municipal law is changed and that results into the investment becoming illegal.

An investor cannot claim a vested right in an activity subsequently prohibited.[172] Thus legality continues to govern during the operation of the investment. In *Plama v. Bulgaria*, the investor alleged that due to retrospective imposition of environmental tax, the investment was destroyed. The challenge was to a regulation made during the course of the existence of the investment. The Tribunal found that there was no intention of the State to target the investor while adopting the environmental regulation.[173] The challenged regulation was made during the currency of the investment.

---

164. *Ibid.*, at para. 160.
165. *Ibid.*, at para. 161.
166. For example, *World Duty Free Company Limited v. Republic of Kenya*, *supra* n. 115, at para. 188. In this case, no jurisdictional objection was raised and the issue was decided at the merits stage.
167. *Plama Consortium Limited v. Republic of Bulgaria*, *supra* n. 84, at paras 126-30.
168. *Ibid.*, at paras 141, 151, 229-30.
169. Kriebaum, *supra* n. 127, at 307, 319.
170. *Gustav FW Hamester GmbH & Co KG v. Republic of Ghana*, *supra* n. 105, at para. 129.
171. *Ibid.*, at para. 127; *Teinver S.A., Transportes de Cercanías S.A. and Autobuses Urbanos del Sur S.A. v. Argentine Republic*, Decision on Jurisdiction, ICSID Case No. ARB/09/1, para. 257 (21 Dec. 2012); *Urbaser S.A. and Consorcio de Aguas Bilbao Biskaia, Bilbao Biskaia Ur Partzuergoa v. Argentine Republic*, Decision on Jurisdiction, ICSID Case No. ARB/07/26, para. 260 (19 Dec. 2012); *Quiborax S.A. and Non-Metallic Minerals S.A. v. Plurinational State of Bolivia*, Award, ICSID Case No. ARB/06/2, para. 219 (Award, 16 Sept. 2015).
172. *International Thunderbird Gaming Corporation v. The United Mexican States*, Award, UNCITRAL, para. 208 (26 Jan. 2006).
173. *Plama Consortium Limited v. Republic of Bulgaria*, *supra* n. 84, at para. 218.

Therefore, an investor would have to comply with regulatory changes that occur during the period of investment.

Legality relates to the consent to arbitrate by a State. In *Inceysa v. El Salvador*, the Respondent State argued that the consent to arbitrate is limited to investments made in compliance with host State's laws.[174] The Tribunal accepted this argument and held that consent to arbitrate is not blanket consent; it is subject to compliance with the host State laws.[175] States can always exclude certain types of disputes from the jurisdiction of ICSID, one of these types is the inclusion of 'in accordance with host State clause' in the BIT.[176]

Therefore, the foreign investor is under an obligation to not only enter the host State, i.e., India, as per the domestic law and continue to operate within the regulatory framework, but also follow the changes in law, as long as the changes are bona fide and not meant to defeat rights of investors.

---

174. *Inceysa Vallisoletana S.L. v. Republic of El Salvador, supra* n. 29, at para. 141.
175. *Ibid.*, at paras 164, 173.
176. *Ibid.*, at paras 184-5, 207.

CHAPTER 4
Applicable Laws and Jurisdiction

Applicable laws and jurisdiction are matters of procedural law in investment treaty arbitration (ITA). They impact the outcome of the judicial process and are discussed in this chapter. Applicable laws are the set of laws that an investment tribunal would apply to the substance as well as the procedure for conducting arbitration proceedings. Jurisdiction is the competence of an international tribunal to entertain and decide a dispute. An international tribunal is competent to decide its own jurisdiction, reflected in the principle *competence de la competence*.

§4.01 APPLICABLE LAWS

Most investment cases involve intricate and contested facts. The primary task faced by an investment tribunal is of determining the facts. After identifying the facts the tribunal applies legal principles to those facts. The set of legal principles applied to decide the dispute and to conduct the proceedings are the applicable laws. The laws regulating the conduct of proceedings are normally provided for in the bilateral investment treaty (BIT). Such as the UNCITRAL Rules on Arbitration, LCIA Rules of Arbitration, IBA Rules on Taking Evidence, etc. In investment arbitration, the laws regulating the conduct of the proceedings are similar to the rules applied in international commercial arbitration. But the substantive law applied in investment arbitration is very different from international commercial arbitration. The discussion here is focused on substantive applicable law.

In ITA the substantive law applied would be derived from domestic as well as international law. Most of the BITs entered into by India in the past contained a provision on applicable laws. Majority of those BITs used to contain a provision that the laws of the host State would govern the investments. They do not contain any express mention of international law. For example, Article 11 of the India-Germany BIT states that:

All investments shall, subject to this Agreement, be governed by the laws in force in the territory of the Contracting Party in which such investments are made.

Other BITs, on similar lines, contain only a reference to the domestic law and no reference to international law as such.[1] This does not mean that international law

---

1. Agreement between the Government of the Republic of India and the Government of the Kingdom of Denmark concerning the Promotion and Reciprocal Protection of Investments, Art. 12.1 (signed 6 Sept. 1995, entered into force 28 Aug. 1996, terminated 13 May 2017); Agreement between the Republic of India and the Kingdom of Netherlands for the Promotion and Protection of Investments, Art. 11 (signed 6 Nov. 1995, entered into force 1 Dec. 1996, terminated 1 Dec. 2016); Agreement between the Portuguese Republic and the Republic of India on the Mutual Promotion and Protection of Investments, Art. 12.1 (signed 28 Jun. 2000, entered into force 19 Jul. 2002); Agreement between the Swiss Confederation and the Republic of India for the Promotion and Protection of Investments, Art. 11.1 (signed 4 Apr. 1997, entered into force 16 Feb. 2000, terminated 6 Apr. 2017); Agreement between the Government of the Republic of India and the Government of the Republic of Armenia for the Promotion and Protection of Investments, Art. 12.1 (signed 23 May 2003, entered into force 30 May 2006); Agreement between the Government of the Republic of India and the Government of the Republic of Finland on the Promotion and Protection of Investments, Art. 12.1 (signed 7 Nov. 2002, entered into force 9 Apr. 2003); Agreement between the Government of the Republic of India and the Government of the Republic of Ghana for the Reciprocal Promotion and Protection of Investments, Art. 12(1) (signed 5 Aug. 2002); Agreement between the Czech Republic and Republic of India for the Promotion and Protection of Investments, Art. 11 (signed 11 Oct. 1996, entered into force 6 Feb. 1998); Agreement between the Government of the Republic of Croatia and the Government of the Republic of India on the Promotion and Reciprocal Protection of Investments, Art. 12.1 (signed 4 May 2001, entered into force 19 Jan. 2002, terminated 25 Apr. 2017); Agreement between the Government of the Republic of Austria and the Government of the Republic of India for the Promotion and Protection of Investments, Art. 12.1 (signed 8 Nov. 1999, entered into force 1 Mar. 2001, terminated 24 Mar. 2017); Agreement between the Government of the Republic of India and the Government of the Kingdom of Bahrain for the Promotion and Protection of Investments, Art. 12.1 (signed 13 Jan. 2004, entered into force 5 Dec. 2007); Agreement between the Government of the Republic of India and the Government of the People's Republic of Bangladesh for the Promotion and Protection of Investments, Art. 12.1 (signed 9 Feb. 2009, entered into force 7 Jul. 2011); Agreement between the Government of the Republic of India and the Government of the People's Republic of China for the Promotion and Protection of Investments, Art. 12 (signed 21 Nov. 2006, entered into force 1 Aug. 2007); Agreement between the State of Kuwait and the Republic of India for the Encouragement and Reciprocal Protection of Investment, Art. 14 (signed 27 Nov. 2001, entered into force 28 Jun. 2003); Agreement between the Government of the Republic of India and the Government of the Lao People's Democratic Republic for the Promotion and Protection of Investments, Art. 12.1 (signed 9 Nov. 2000, entered into force 5 Jan. 2003); Agreement between the Government of the Republic of Latvia and the Government of the Republic of India for the Promotion and Protection of Investments, Art. 12.1 (signed 18 Feb. 2010, entered into force 27 Nov. 2010); Agreement between the Government of Nepal and the Government of the Republic of India for the Promotion and Protection of Investments, Art. 12.1 (signed 21 Oct. 2011); Agreement between the Government of Australia and the Government of the Republic of India on the Promotion and Protection of Investments, Art. 14 (signed 26 Feb. 1999, entered into force 4 May 2000, terminated 23 Mar. 2017); Agreement between the Government of the Republic of Kazakhstan and the Government of the Republic of India for the Promotion and Reciprocal Protection of Investments, Art. 12.1 (signed 09 Dec. 1996, entered into force 26 Jul. 2001); Agreement between the Government of Republic of Korea and the Government of the Republic of India, Art. 10.1 (signed 26 Feb. 1996, entered into force 07 May 1996); Agreement between the Government of Israel and the Government of the Republic of India, Art. 12.1 (signed 29 Jan. 1996, entered into force 18 Feb. 1997); Agreement for the Promotion and Protection of Investments between the Republic of Colombia and the Republic of India, Art. 14 (signed 10 Nov. 2009, entered into force 2 Jul. 2012); Agreement between the Government of the Kingdom of Sweden and the Government of the Republic of India for the Promotion and Reciprocal Protection of Investments, Art. 12.1 (signed 4 Jul. 2000, entered into force 1 Apr.

Chapter 4: Applicable Laws and Jurisdiction §4.01

would not be applicable. A BIT is an international treaty and regulated by public international law.[2] According to Article 31(3)(c) of the Vienna Convention on the Law of Treaties, a treaty is to be interpreted 'any relevant rules of international law applicable in the relations between the parties.' In *AAPL v. Sri Lanka* the BIT did not even contain a provision on applicable law. The Tribunal concluded that BIT is not a closed system and has to be seen in a broader juridical context, which would include the BIT, customary international law and domestic law.[3] The Tribunal went further to conclude that:

> [T]he Bilateral Investment Treaty is not a self-contained closed legal system limited to provide for substantive material rules of direct applicability, but it has to be envisaged within a wider juridical context in which rules from other sources are integrated through implied incorporate on methods or by direct reference to certain supplementary rules, whether or international law character or of domestic law nature.[4]

Thus a BIT operates in the environment of international law. The 2015 Model BIT has elaborate provisions on applicable law. Article 23.3 states:

> The governing law for interpretation of this Treaty by a Tribunal constituted under this Article shall be: (a) this Treaty; (b) the general principles of public international law relating to the interpretation of treaties, including the presumption of consistency between international treaties to which the Parties are party; and (c) for matters relating to domestic law, the law of the Defending Party.

Clause (b) gives the impression that general international law would apply only to the extent of treaty interpretation. General principles of public international law is a broad phrase and should not be confused with 'general principles of law recognized by civilized nations' defined in Article 38(1) of the International Court of Justice (ICJ) Statute. 'General principles of international law' is a generic term used to represent the

---

2001); Agreement between the Government of the United Kingdom of Great Britain and Northern Ireland and the Government of the Republic of India for the Promotion and Reciprocal Protection of Investments, Art. 11.1 (signed 14 Mar. 1994, entered into force 6 Jan. 1995); Agreement on Reciprocal Protection and Promotion of Investments between the Government of the Republic of India and the Government of the Republic of Uzbekistan, Art. 13.1 (signed 18 May 1999, entered into force 28 Jul. 2000); Agreement between the Government of Malaysia and the Government of the Republic of India, Arts 10.1 (signed 03 Aug. 1995, entered into force 12 Apr. 1997, terminated on 23 May 2017); Agreement between the Government of the Mexico and the Government of the Republic of India, Art. 26 (signed 21 May 2007, entered into force 23 Feb. 2008).

2. *Wena Hotels Ltd. v. Arab Republic of Egypt*, Award, ICSID Case No. ARB/98/4, paras 78, 79 (8 Dec. 2000); *ADC Affiliate Limited and ADC & ADMC Management Limited v. The Republic of Hungary*, Award, ICSID Case No. ARB/03/16, paras 288-91 (2 Oct. 2006); *LG&E Energy Corp., LG&E Capital Corp., and LG&E International, Inc. v. Argentine Republic*, Decision on Liability, ICSID Case No. ARB/02/1, paras 85, 97-8 (3 Oct. 2006); *Saipem S.p.A. v. The People's Republic of Bangladesh*, Award, ICSID Case No. ARB/05/07, para. 99 (30 Jun. 2009); *Bayindir Insaat Turizm Ticaret Ve Sanayi A.S. v. Islamic Republic of Pakistan*, Award, ICSID Case No. ARB/03/29, paras 109, 110 (27 Aug. 2009).
3. *Asian Agricultural Products Ltd. v. Republic of Sri Lanka*, Final Award, ICSID Case No. ARB/87/3, paras 20-1 (27 Jun. 1990).
4. *Ibid.*, at paras 18-24.

entire body of international law originating in all the sources.[5] Clause (a) mentions the treaty, i.e., the BIT under which an investment claim is brought. This is a sufficient reference to apply the entire body of international law, even if, it is presumed that clause (b) allows application of some of the general principles of international law and not all.

Article 23.3 of the 2015 Model BIT grants a clear recognition to the application of domestic law as well as international law. Domestic law has an important place in investment disputes. A tribunal would have to pay due regard to national law because an award may be challenged before a domestic court or the investor would have to seek its enforcement.[6] Mandatory rules of administrative and regulatory nature are reserved for the host State and not subject to waiver.[7] Scholars have warned that respect and accommodation of domestic law is important to ensure that States continue to preserve arbitration as an instrument for settlement of disputes.[8]

There are practical reasons for relying on domestic law. The contents of international law are insufficient to address that issues that may arise particularly in investment arbitration. Domestic law plays an important role due to the effect of *renvoi* – it addresses issues for which international law does not have a response.[9] Commenting generally on paucity of rules in international law and the recourse to take in such situations, in the Barcelona Traction case, the ICJ held that: 'as to which rights international law has not established its own rules, it has to refer to the relevant rules of municipal law.'[10] Investments are normally held in the form of property. To establish jurisdiction of an investment tribunal, it has to be proved that the foreign investor possesses proprietary rights. In cases of expropriation, the first stage is deciding whether the foreign investor possessed proprietary rights.[11] International law does not contain any rules on determination of character of the asset and its features. The law of the State where the property is situated decides their nature as property.[12] Domestic

---

5. Refer to Analytical Report of the Study Group of the International Law Commission finalized by the Chairman M. Koskenniemi, *Fragmentation of International Law: Difficulties Arising from the Diversification and Expansion of International Law*, 251, 462, UN Doc A/CN.4/L.682, 13 Apr. 2006; *See* Anastasios Gourgourinis, *General/Particular International Law and Primary /Secondary Rules: Unitary Terminology of a Fragmented System*, 22(4) European Journal of International Law 1007-10 (2011).
6. Helen Elizabeth Kjos, *Applicable Law in Investor-State Arbitration*, 260-1 (1st ed., Oxford University Press 2013).
7. M. Sornarajah, *The Settlement of Foreign Investment Disputes*, 233 (Kluwer Law International 2000).
8. *See* B.M. Cremades and D.J.A. Cairnes, *The Brave New World of Global Arbitration*, 3 The Journal of World Investment 173, 207 (2002); J.F. Poudret and S. Besson, *Comparative Law of International Arbitration*, 610 (2nd ed., Thomson Sweet & Maxwell 2006); P. Mayer, *Mandatory Rules of Law in International Arbitration*, 2 Arbitration International 274, 285-6 (1986).
9. *En Cana Corporation v. Republic of Ecuador*, Award, LCIA Case No. UN3481, UNCITRAL, para. 184 (3 Feb. 2006); also *see* Monique Sasson, *Substantive Law in Investment Treaty Arbitration: The Unsettled Relationship between International Law and Municipal Law* (Kluwer Law International 2010).
10. *Case Concerning Barcelona Traction, Light and Power Company, Limited (Belgium v. Spain) Second Phase*, Judgement, ICJ Reports, para. 38 (5 Feb. 1970).
11. *Generation Ukraine, Inc v. Ukraine*, Award, ICSID Case No. ARB/00/9, para. 8.8 (16 Sept. 2003).
12. *See* Zachary Douglas, *The Hybrid Foundations of Investment Treaty Arbitration*, 74 British Yearbook of International Law 151, 197 (2003).

Chapter 4: Applicable Laws and Jurisdiction   §4.01

law is relevant for various purposes: it governs matters such as whether the investment is held in the territory of the host State,[13] the validity of those investments;[14] the question of whether the investment vests with the investor that is claiming protection under the BIT;[15] assurances given to the investment regarding protection under domestic law;[16] and the nature and scope of the governmental measure under challenge.[17] Violation of domestic law could be a defence against an investment claim. In *Fraport v. Philippines*, the Tribunals stated that:

> If, at the time of the initiation of the investment, there has been compliance with the law of the host state, allegations by the host state of violations of its law in the course of its investment, as a justification for state action with respect to the investment, might be a defense to claimed substantive violations of the BIT... .[18]

Investments are complex operations which involve numerous transactions of different kinds. Many of these transactions take place under domestic law and have a close connection with the laws of the host State.[19] There are a wide range of laws relevant, such as commercial law, company law, administrative law, labour law, tax law, foreign exchange regulations, real estate law.[20] In *Swembalt AC v. Latvia*, on the question of determination of a rate of interest on the amount of compensation, the tribunal stated that international law did not provide any guidance on the amount of compensation. The tribunal relied on Denmark law because that was the seat of arbitration and Swiss law – the law of the nationality of the investor – did not have sufficient link to the dispute. The parties had not provided any material about Latvian law on interest. The Denmark law was relied on based on general principles of law.[21]

---

13. *Philippe Gruslin v. Malaysia*, Award, ICSID Case No. ARB/99/3, paras 14.1 et seq. (27 Nov. 2000); *SGS Société Générale de Surveillance S.A. v. Islamic Republic of Pakistan*, Decision of the Tribunal on Objections to Jurisdiction, ICSID Case No. ARB/01/13, paras 136 et seq. (6 Aug. 2003); *SGS Société Générale de Surveillance S.A. v. Republic of the Philippines*, Decision of the Tribunal on Objections to Jurisdiction, ICSID Case No. ARB/02/6, paras 99 et seq. (29 Jan. 2004).
14. *Tokios Tokelés v. Ukraine*, Decision on Jurisdiction, ICSID Case No. ARB/02/18, paras 83-6 (29 Apr. 2004); *Fraport AG Frankfurt Airport Services Worldwide v. The Republic of the Philippines*, Award, ICSID Case No. ARB/03/25, paras 344 et seq. (16 Aug. 2007); *Ioannis Kardassopoulos v. The Republic of Georgia*, Decision on Jurisdiction, ICSID Case No. ARB/05/18, paras 142 et seq. (6 Jul. 2007).
15. *William Nagel v. The Czech Republic*, Final Award, SCC Case No. 049/2002, paras 158-62 (9 Sept. 2003); *CMS Gas Transmission Company v. The Republic of Argentina*, Award, ICSID Case No. ARB/01/8, paras 127-44 (12 May 2005).
16. *Alex Genin, Eastern Credit Limited, Inc. and A.S. Baltoil v. The Republic of Estonia*, Award, ICSID Case No. ARB/99/2, para. 348 (25 Jun. 2001); *Emilio Agustín Maffezini v. The Kingdom of Spain*, Award, ICSID Case No. ARB/97/7, paras 66-71 (13 Nov. 2000).
17. *Robert Azinian, Kenneth Davitian & Ellen Baca v. The United Mexican States*, Award, ICSID Case No. ARB (AF)/97/2, paras 105, 120 (1 Nov. 1999).
18. *Fraport AG Frankfurt Airport Services Worldwide v. The Republic of the Philippines*, supra n. 14, at para. 345.
19. Rudolf Dolzer and Christoph Schreuer, *Principles of International Investment Law*, 288 (2nd ed., Oxford University Press 2012).
20. Ibid.
21. *Swembalt AB, Sweden v. The Republic of Latvia*, Decision by the Court of Arbitration, 2 Stockholm Arbitration Reporter, para. 46 (23 Oct. 2000).

In *Eastern Sugar v. Czech Republic*, the tribunal applied Czech law wherever international law was silent – especially on the rate of interest.[22]

It is evident that domestic law and international law both are relevant. The challenge then is, what is the relationship between the two? Do they apply simultaneously? What is their respective role and what happens in case of a conflict?

International law and domestic law continue to apply alongside. In *CMS v. Argentina*, the tribunal held that the domestic law and international law are 'inseparable' and have to be applied in conjunction.[23] They entail different obligations and different consequences. Existence of obligation or breach under one does not imply the same for the other. Same set of actions may result into breach of either or both. In the *ELSI* case, the ICJ held that: 'what is a breach of a treaty may be lawful in the municipal law and what is unlawful in the municipal law may be wholly innocent of violation of a treaty provision.'[24] Therefore an action may be in breach of municipal law but not of international law and vice versa. In *Antoine Goetz v. Burundi*, the tribunal examined whether the host State was in breach of the host State domestic law and BIT and found that the host State was in breach of the BIT and not of the domestic law of the host State.[25] There is a close relationship between national and international law and '[a]ll of these rules are inseparable and will, to the extent justified, be applied by the Tribunal.'[26] In *Sempra v. Argentina*, the Tribunal observed the following regarding the relationship between national and international law:

> While writers and decisions have on occasion tended to consider domestic law and international law as mutually incompatible in their application, this is far from actually being the case. Both have a role to perform in the resolution of the dispute, as has been recognized.[27]

In *Goetz v. Burundi*, the tribunal's view represents an appropriate balance that has to be kept in mind while deciding which law would apply, whether domestic law or international law. According to the tribunal 'complementary relationship should be allowed to prevail'.[28] The Tribunal adopted a structured approach. It first saw whether the alleged actions of the host State violated the law of the host State. The Tribunal found that they were not breached.[29] Then the actions were tested based on

---

22. *Eastern Sugar B.V. (Netherlands) v. The Czech Republic*, Partial Award, SCC Case No. 088/2004, paras 196, 373 (27 Mar. 2007).
23. *CMS Gas Transmission Company v. The Republic of Argentina*, supra n. 15, at paras 127-44.
24. *Case Concerning Elettronica Sicula S.p.A. (ELSI) (United States of America v. Italy)*, Judgment, ICJ Reports, 15, 51, para. 73 (20 Jul. 1989).
25. *Antoine Goetz et consorts v. République du Burundi*, Award, ICSID Case No. ARB/95/3, paras 99, 119, 130-33 (10 Feb. 1999).
26. *CMS Gas Transmission Company v. The Republic of Argentina*, supra n. 15, at para. 117; *Occidental Petroleum Corporation and Occidental Exploration and Production Company v. The Republic of Ecuador*, Award, ICSID Case No. ARB/06/11, para. 93 (5 Oct. 2012).
27. *Sempra Energy International v. The Argentine Republic*, Award, ICSID Case No. ARB/02/16, para. 236 (28 Sept. 2007).
28. *Antoine Goetz et consorts v. République du Burundi*, supra n. 25, at para. 98.
29. *Ibid.*, at paras 100-19.

international law, and the Tribunal found that adequate and effective compensation was not yet paid. Therefore, there was breach of international law.[30]

Tribunals may apply a mix of domestic and international law to different situations. In *Maffezini v. Spain* to see if the alleged actions were attributable to the host State, the tribunal applied principles of State responsibility under international law,[31] whereas in order to understand the structure and operation of the administration it applied the domestic law of Spain.[32] This happens particularly in relation to the requirement of 'legality' of investments[33] or whether the investment satisfying the conditions of domestic law to be an asset. In *National Grid plc v. Argentina*, the Tribunal outlined the importance of applicable law in relation to determination of whether the foreign investor holds and asset and therefore satisfies the definition of investor to maintain an investment claim.[34] In *BG Group v. Argentina* observed that it is 'beyond dispute that the contours of the concept of "asset" included in the definition of "investment" in Article 1(a) of the Argentina-UK BIT, is governed by Argentine law'.[35] The domestic court of Mexico had held that the concession contract was invalid under domestic law. The tribunal in *Azinia v. Mexico* held that since there was no valid contract in existence, there was no expropriation.[36]

The conduct of the host State is to be checked on the basis of international law. International law decides if the host State would incur responsibility. The legal consequences of the wrongful actions of the State are determined on the basis of international law. The determination of existence of State responsibility and consequences thereof are primarily decided at the level of international law. Domestic law does not play any role at this stage.[37] International law is to fill the lacuna in the application of the domestic law thereby perform a gap-filling function.[38] In addition to a supplementary role, international law performs a supervening role, especially in case of a conflict.[39] Domestic law and international law would apply simultaneously but

---

30. *Ibid.*, at paras 120-33.
31. *Emilio Agustín Maffezini v. The Kingdom of Spain, supra* n. 16, at paras 50, 52, 57, 77, 83.
32. *Ibid.*, at paras 68-9.
33. Discussed in Chapter 4.
34. *National Grid plc v. The Argentine Republic*, Award, UNCITRAL, para. 81 (3 Nov. 2008).
35. *BG Group Plc v. The Republic of Argentina*, Final Award, UNCITRAL, para. 92 (24 Dec. 2007).
36. *Robert Azinian, Kenneth Davitian & Ellen Baca v. The United Mexican States, supra* n. 17, at para. 100; also see *William Nagel v. The Czech Republic, supra* n. 15, at pp. 161, 164.
37. Andrew Newcomb and Lluis Paradell, *Law and Practice of Investment Treaties: Standards of Treatment*, 99 (Wolters Kluwer: Law and Business 2009).
38. *Klöckner Industrie – Anlagen GmbH and others v. United Republic of Cameroon and Société Camerounaise des Engrais*, Decision on Annulment, ICSID Case No. ARB/81/2, para. 60 (3 May 1985); *Amco Asia Corporation and others v. Republic of Indonesia*, Ad hoc Committee Decision on the Application for Annulment, ICSID Case No. ARB/81/1, para. 20 (16 May 1986); *Amco Asia Corporation and others v. Republic of Indonesia*, Award in Resubmitted Proceeding, ICSID Case No. ARB/81/1, para. 40 (5 Jun. 1990); *Ioan Micula, Viorel Micula, S.C. European Food S.A, S.C. Starmill S.R.L. and S.C. Multipack S.R.L. v. Romania*, Decision on Jurisdiction and Admissibility, ICSID Case No. ARB/05/20, para. 151 (24 Sept. 2008); *Southern Pacific Properties (Middle East) Limited v. Arab Republic of Egypt*, Award, ICSID Case No. ARB/84/3, para. 80 (20 May 1992).
39. *Klöckner Industrie – Anlagen GmbH and others v. United Republic of Cameroon and Société Camerounaise des Engrais, supra* n. 38, at para. 69; *Liberian Eastern Timber Corporation v. Republic of Liberia*, Award, 2 ICSID Reports 343, 358-9; *Amco Asia Corporation and others v.*

there could be occasions where there is an overlap. In case of inconsistency, international law would prevail over domestic law.[40] In some situations, tribunals have found that the application of international law and national law lead to the same conclusion.[41] In these situations, there is no inconsistency or conflict. In situations of contradiction between the two, international law would apply.[42] If domestic law and international law contradict each other on a point then domestic law would have to give way. According to Article 27 of the VCLT and Article 3 of the ILC Draft Articles on State Responsibility, national law is not a defence for violation of international law obligations. In many situations the subject matter of challenge in investment arbitration is a domestic legislation. The tribunal would have to decide if the domestic law under challenge falls within the permissible framework of the BIT and international law.[43] This is an important aspect of investment arbitration. States are free to make laws as they chose. A host State may make laws that would infringe rights of foreign investors through law and then claim that the law is applicable and immune from review.

But mere identification of facts is insufficient because in order to decide the case, the tribunal has to thereafter apply legal rules to those facts. Moreover, awards of investment tribunals are challengeable and are to be enforced in municipal courts.[44] In investment cases where a State is a party to the ICSID Convention, the issue of challenge or enforcement does not arise. All other cases – which are mostly in majority – are covered by the New York Convention (NYC). The NYC provides that an award could be challenged on the ground that: '___contrary to laws applied to the award.' An investment tribunal, to ensure that the award that is delivered is finally enforced, has to first, identify the applicable law and second, apply that law carefully.

An important aspect is what happens if domestic laws are changed. Domestic laws are the creation of and within the control of the host State. They may be changed any time. They could be changed to prejudice and defeat the rights of the foreign investor under the investment treaty. If such legislations are passed or regulations are

---

Republic of Indonesia, Award in Resubmitted Proceeding, *supra* n. 38, at para. 38; *Southern Pacific Properties (Middle East) Limited v. Arab Republic of Egypt*, *supra* n. 38, at para. 84; *Autopista Concesionada de Venezuela, C.A. v. Bolivarian Republic of Venezuela*, Award, ICSID Case No. ARB/00/5, paras 101-5 (23 Sept. 2003).

40. *Sempra Energy International v. The Argentine Republic*, *supra* n. 27, at para. 239.
41. *Aguaytia Energy, LLC v. Republic of Peru*, Award, ICSID Case No. ARB/06/13, para. 72-3 (11 Dec. 2008); *Southern Pacific Properties (Middle East) Limited v. Arab Republic of Egypt*, *supra* n. 38, at para. 159; *Sempra Energy International v. The Argentine Republic*, *supra* n. 27, at para. 269; *M.C.I. Power Group L.C. and New Turbine, Inc. v. Republic of Ecuador*, Award, ICSID Case No. ARB/03/6, para. 305 (31 Jul. 2007).
42. *LG&E Energy Corp., LG&E Capital Corp., and LG&E International, Inc. v. Argentine Republic*, *supra* n. 2, at para. 94; *Compañia del Desarrollo de Santa Elena S.A. v. Republic of Costa Rica*, Award, ICSID Case No. ARB/96/1, paras 64, 65 (17 Feb. 2000); *Duke Energy International Peru Investments No. 1 Ltd. v. Republic of Peru*, Decision on Jurisdiction, ICSID Case No. ARB/03/28, para. 162 (1 Feb. 2006).
43. *MTD Equity Sdn. Bhd. and MTD Chile S.A. v. Republic of Chile*, Award, ICSID Case No. ARB/01/7, para. 204 (25 May 2004); *Consortium Groupement L.E.S.I. – DIPENTA v. République algérienne démocratique et populaire*, Award, ICSID Case No. ARB/03/08, para. 24 (10 Jan. 2005); *Técnicas Medioambientales Tecmed, S.A. v. The United Mexican States*, Award, ICSID Case No. ARB (AF)/00/2, para. 120 (29 May 2003).
44. *See* Chapter 6 below.

Chapter 4: Applicable Laws and Jurisdiction §4.01

adopted then those legislations and regulations could be challenged under the BIT. It is not that every regulation would amount to breach of treatment standards. Regulatory freedom of States is a customary international law right.[45] States could change laws as long as they are bona fide, non-discriminatory and in public interest. Customary international law operates alongside treaty law,[46] hence it would not amount to breach of treatment standards if these conditions are satisfied.

In relation to domestic law, the constitution, all legislations and judicial decisions (since India is a common law country) would apply. Article 141 of the Constitution of India declares that the judicial decisions are the law of the land in the following words:

> The law declared by the Supreme Court shall be binding on all courts within the territory of India.

The Constitution of the host State is an important source of domestic law. All laws draw their existence and force from the constitution. The constitution is the basic law. Other laws may change from time to time but the constitution is durable and influential. Investment tribunals have recognized the central position of the constitution. In *LETCO v. Liberia*, the Tribunal held that:

> The primary source of Liberian law and the basic document from which all other sources of law emanate is the Liberian Constitution; other sources include treaties, statutes and what may be called 'residual law'....In the absence of any relevant constitutional or statutory provision, residual law will be applied.[47]

In addition to the Constitution there are various other domestic laws applicable. The relevant domestic laws directly pertinent in relation to foreign investors were discussed in Chapter 3.

It is but natural that all sources of international law enshrined in Article 38(1) of the Statute of the ICJ would operate. This was recognized by the investment tribunal in *Merrill & Ring Forestry v. Canada*, where it was stated as follows:

> The meaning of international law can only understood today with reference to Article 38 (1) of the Stature of the International Court of Justice, where the sources of international law are identified as international conventions, international custom, general principles of law, and judicial decisions and the teachings of the

---

45. *Marvin Roy Feldman Karpa v. The United Mexican States*, Award, ICSID Case No. ARB (AF)/99/1, para. 100 (16 Dec. 2002); also see *Petrobart Limited v. The Kyrgyz Republic*, Award, SCC Case No. 126/2003, paras 103-6, 128-30 (29 Mar. 2005); *Saluka Investments BV (The Netherlands) v. The Czech Republic*, Partial Award, Permanent Court of Arbitration, paras 256-61 (17 Mar. 2006); *Link-Trading Joint Stock Company v. Department for Customs Control of the Republic of Moldova*, Final Award, UNCITRAL, paras 30, 33, 38, (18 Apr. 2002); *Methanex Corporation v. United States of America*, Final Award of the Tribunal on Jurisdiction and Merits, UNCITRAL, IV.D. paras 6-15 (3 Aug. 2005); *EnCana Corporation v. Republic of Ecuador, supra* n. 9, at paras 173-7, 193-5; *Chemtura Corporation v. Government of Canada (formerly Crompton Corporation v. Government of Canada)*, Award, UNCITRAL, paras 259-65 (2 Aug. 2010).
46. *Case Concerning Military and Paramilitary Activities in and Against Nicaragua (Nicaragua v. United States of America) Merits*, Judgment, ICJ Reports, 14, paras 173-7 (27 Jun. 1986).
47. *Liberian Eastern Timber Corporation v. Republic of Liberia*, ICSID Case No. ARB/83/2, Award, 26 ILM 647, 665 (1987) (31 Mar. 1986).

most highly qualified publicists as a subsidiary means for the determination of the rules of law.[48]

States are bound by treaties that they have agreed to. However it is necessary that both the disputing parties are members to that treaty. In the case of investment arbitration the link between the foreign investor and the host State that allows invocation of arbitration is the investment treaty. Therefore investment treaty is one of the applicable laws between the foreign investor and the host State. BIT is the treaty that the tribunal is fundamentally called upon to apply. This does not mean that investment tribunals can apply treaties other than the investment treaty, such as the World Trade Organization (WTO)[49] or human rights treaties.[50] The jurisdiction of an investment tribunal is limited to the subject matter of the treaty. Tribunals have resorted to customary law[51] and general principles.[52] There are various aspects of customary law that are relevant in investment disputes – such as denial of justice, State responsibility,[53] treaty interpretation, etc.

---

48. *Merrill & Ring Forestry L.P. v. Canada*, Award, ICSID Case. No. UNCT/07/1, para. 184 (31 Mar. 2010).
49. *Methanex Corporation v. United States of America*, supra n. 45, at II.B para. 5.
50. *Biloune and Marine Drive Complex Ltd. v. Ghana Investments Centre and the Government of Ghana*, Award on Jurisdiction and Liability, 1994 (95) International Law Reports 183, 203 (27 Oct. 1989); also *see Toto Construzioni Generali S.p.A. v. Republic of Lebanon*, Decision on Jurisdiction, ICSID Case No. ARB/07/12, paras 163, 165 (11 Sept. 2009). The Tribunal did venture to see if the International Convention on Civil and Political Rights was violated.
51. *Middle East Cement Shipping and Handling Co. S.A v. Arab Republic of Egypt*, Award, ICSID Case No. ARB/99/6, paras 85-7 (12 Apr. 2002); *Compañià de Aguas del Aconquija S.A. and Vivendi Universal S.A. v. Argentine Republic*, Award, ICSID Case No. ARB/97/3, para. 8.2.5 (20 Aug. 2007); *Philip Morris Brands Sàrl, Philip Morris Products S.A. and Abal Hermanos S.A. v. Oriental Republic of Uruguay*, Award, ICSID Case No. ARB/10/7, paras 291-5 (8 Jul. 2016); *CMS Gas Transmission Company v. The Republic of Argentina*, supra n. 15, at paras 304-31; *LG&E Energy Corp., LG&E Capital Corp., and LG&E International, Inc. v. Argentine Republic*, supra n. 2, at paras 89, 245-66; *Southern Pacific Properties (Middle East) Limited v. Arab Republic of Egypt*, supra n. 38, at para. 85; *Azurix Corp. v. The Argentine Republic*, Award, ICSID Case No. ARB/01/12, para. 50 (14 Jul. 2006); *Amco Asia Corporation and others v. Republic of Indonesia*, Award, ICSID Case No. ARB/81/1, para. 248(v) (20 Nov. 1984); *CMS Gas Transmission Company v. The Republic of Argentina*, Decision of the Ad Hoc Committee on the Application for Annulment, ICSID Case No. ARB/01/8, paras 101-50 (25 Sept. 2007); *Sempra Energy International v. The Argentine Republic*, supra n. 27, at paras 333-54, 392-97.
52. *Técnicas Medioambientales Tecmed, S.A. v. The United Mexican States*, supra n. 43, at para. 124; *Inceysa Vallisoletana S.L. v. Republic of El Salvador*, Award, ICSID Case No. ARB/03/26, paras 230 et seq. (2 Aug. 2006); *World Duty Free v. Republic of Kenya*, Award, ICSID Case No. ARB/00/7, paras 138-57 (4 Oct. 2006); *Mihaly International Corporation v. Democratic Socialist Republic of Sri Lanka*, Award, ICSID Case. No. ARB/00/2, para. 24 (15 Mar. 2002); *Generation Ukraine, Inc v. Ukraine*, supra n. 11, at paras 19.1, 19.4; *ADC Affiliate Limited and ADC & ADMC Management Limited v. The Republic of Hungary*, supra n. 2, at paras 474, 475; *Saipem S.p.A. v. The People's Republic of Bangladesh*, Decision on Jurisdiction, ICSID Case No. ARB/05/07, paras 154-58 (21 Mar. 2007); *Fraport AG Frankfurt Airport Services Worldwide v. The Republic of the Philippines*, supra n. 14, at paras 346, 347; *Autopista Concesionada de Venezuela, C.A. v. Bolivarian Republic of Venezuela*, supra n. 39, at para. 316.
53. Rudolf Dolzer and Christoph Schreuer, *supra* n. 19.

§4.02 JURISDICTION

In international adjudication, especially when States are involved consent to participate in judicial proceedings has to be clear. An international tribunal can entertain only those disputes that fall within the purview of that consent.[54] An investment tribunal can decide disputes only if it has jurisdiction to entertain a dispute as expressed in the jurisdictional requirements in a BIT. If the jurisdictional requirements are not satisfied then an investment tribunal cannot entertain the dispute even if substantive provisions of an investment treaty are violated. The jurisdictional requirements of investment treaties are: standing – the foreign investor should be a qualified investor (*ratione personae*); subject matter – the foreign investor should have made a qualified investment (*ratione materiae*); and the time of cause of action should be covered by the time of operation of the BIT (*ratione temporis*).

The definition of investor and investment has undergone immense transformation. The past BITs used to contain broad definitions of these terms. This would make it easy to establish jurisdiction for an investment tribunal. The 2015 Model BIT has narrowed both these definitions. This would have the inevitable consequence of limiting access to investment arbitration. The transformation from the old BITs to the new proposals under the 2015 Model BIT, which would form the basis of future negotiations is discussed hereunder:

[A] Investment

The definition of investment specifies which kinds of activities conducted in the home State by the foreign investor are protected and is normally placed in the early parts of the BIT. A standard example would be Indian-Armenia BIT, which is as follows:

> 'investment' means every kind of asset established or acquired including changes in the form of such investment, in accordance with the national laws of the Contracting Party in whose territory the investment is made and in particular, though not exclusively, includes:
>
> (i) movable and immovable property as well as other rights such as mortgages, liens or pledges;
> (ii) shares in and stock and debentures of a company and any other similar forms of participation in a company;
> (iii) rights to money or to any performance under contract having a financial value;
> (iv) intellectual property rights, in accordance with the relevant laws of the respective Contracting Party;

---

54. *See* Yuval Shany, *Questions of Jurisdiction and Admissibility before International Courts* (Cambridge University Press 2015).

(v) business concessions conferred by law or under contract, including concessions to search for and extract oil and other minerals.[55]

Virtually all other BITS used this language.[56]

---

55. Agreement between the Government of the Republic of Armenia and the Government of the Republic of India, *supra* n. 1, at Art. 1(2).
56. Agreement between the Government of the Republic of India and the Government of the Kingdom of Bahrain for the Promotion and Protection of Investments, *supra* n. 1, at Art. 1(b); Agreement between Bosnia and Herzegovina and The Republic of India for the Promotion and Protection of Investments, Art. 1(1) (signed 12 Sept. 2006, entered into force 13 Feb. 2008); Agreement between the Government of the Republic of India and The Government of His Majesty The Sultan and Yang Di-Pertuan of Brunei Darussalam on the Reciprocal Promotion and Protection of Investments, Art. 1(b) (signed 22 May 2008, entered into force 18 Jan. 2009); Agreement between the Government of the Republic of India and the Government of the Republic of Bulgaria for the Promotion and Protection of Investments, Art. 1(2) (signed 29 Oct. 1998, entered into force 23 Sept. 1999); Agreement between the Government of the Republic of India and the Government of the People's Republic of China for the Promotion and Protection of Investments, *supra* n. 1, at Art. 1(b); Agreement between the Government of the Republic of India and the Government of the Democratic Republic of Congo for the Mutual Promotion and Protection of Investments, Art. 1(b) (signed 13 Apr. 2010); Agreement between the Government of the Republic of Croatia and the Government of the Republic of India on the Promotion and Reciprocal Protection of Investments, *supra* n. 1, at Art. 1(1); Agreement between the Government of the Republic of Cyprus and the Government of the Republic of India for the Mutual Promotion and Protection of Investments, Art. 1(b) (signed 9 May 2002, entered into force 12 Jan. 2004); Agreement between the Government of the Republic of India and the Government of the Republic of Djibouti for the Promotion and Protection of Investments, Art. 1(b) (signed 19 May 2003); Agreement between the Government of the Arab Republic of Egypt and the Government of the Republic of India for the Promotion and Reciprocal Protection of Investments, Art. 1(b) (signed 9 Apr. 1997, entered into force 22 Nov. 2000, terminated on 29 Mar. 2016); Agreement between the Republic of India and the Federal Democratic Republic of Ethiopia for the Reciprocal Promotion and Protection of Investments, Art. 1(1) (signed 5 Jul. 2007); Agreement between the Government of the Republic of India and the Government of the Republic of Finland on the Promotion and Protection of Investments, *supra* n. 1, at Art. 1(1); Agreement between the Government of the Republic of India and the Government of the Republic of Ghana for the Reciprocal Promotion and Protection of Investments, *supra* n. 1, at Art. 1(2); Agreement between the Government of the Republic of India and the Government of the Republic of Iceland for the Promotion and Protection of Investments, Art. 1(b) (signed 29 Jun. 2007, entered into force 16 Dec. 2008); Agreement between the Government of the Republic of Indonesia and the Government of the Republic of India for the Promotion and Protection of Investments, Art. 1(1) (signed 10 Feb. 1999, entered into force 22 Jan. 2004, terminated on 4 Apr. 2016); Agreement between the Government of the Republic of India and the Government of the State of Israel for the Promotion and Protection of Investments, Art. 1(b) (signed 29 Jan. 1996, entered into force 18 Feb. 1997); Agreement between the Government of the Republic of Kazakhstan and the Government of the Republic of India for the Promotion and Reciprocal Protection of Investments, *supra* n. 1, at Art. 1(a); Agreement between the Government of the Republic of India and the Government of Kyrgyz Republic for the Promotion and Protection of Investments, Art. 1(b) (signed 16 May 1997, entered into force 12 May 2000); Agreement between the Government of the Republic of India and the Government of the Lao People's Democratic Republic for the Promotion and Protection of Investments, *supra* n. 1, at Art. 1(b); Agreement between the Government of the Republic of Latvia and the Government of the Republic of India for the Promotion and Protection of Investments, *supra* n. 1, Art. 1(a); Agreement between the Government of the Republic of India and the Great Socialist People's Libyan Arab Jamahiriya for the Promotion and Protection of Investments, Art. 1(b) (signed 26 May 2007, entered into force 23 Mar. 2009); Agreement between the Government of the Republic of India and the Government of the Republic of Lithuania for the Promotion and Protection of Investments, Art. 1(1) (signed 31 Mar. 2011, entered into force 1 Dec. 2011); Agreement

between the Government of the Republic of India and the Government of the Republic of Macedonia for the Promotion and Reciprocal Protection of Investments, Art. 1(1) (signed 17 Mar. 2008, entered into force 17 Nov. 2008); Agreement between the Government of the Republic of India and the Government of Mongolia for the Promotion and Protection of Investments, Art. 1(b) (signed 3 Jan. 2001, entered into force 29 Apr. 2002); Agreement between the Government of the Republic of Mozambique and the Government of the Republic of India for the Reciprocal Promotion and Protection of Investments, Art. 1(b) (signed 19 Feb. 2009, entered into force 23 Sept. 2009); Agreement between the Government of the Republic of India and the Government of the Union of Myanmar for the Reciprocal Promotion and Protection of Investments, Art. 1(b) (signed 24 Jun. 2008, entered into force 8 Feb. 2009); Agreement between the Government of Nepal and the Government of the Republic of India for the Promotion and Protection of Investments, *supra* n. 1, at Art. 1(b); Agreement between the Government of the Sultanate of Oman and the Government of the Republic of India for the Promotion and Protection of Investments, Art. 1(b) (signed 2 Apr. 1997, entered into force 13 Oct. 2000, terminated 22 Mar. 2017); Agreement between the Portuguese Republic and the Republic of India on the Mutual Promotion and Protection of Investments, *supra* n. 1, at Art. 1(1); Agreement between the Government of the Republic of India and the Government of the State of Qatar for the Reciprocal Promotion and Protection of Investments, Art. 1(2) (signed 7 Apr. 1999, entered into force 15 Dec. 1999); Agreement between the Government of the Republic of India and the Government of Romania for the Promotion and Reciprocal Protection of Investments, Art. 1(b) (signed 17 Nov. 1997, entered into force 9 Dec. 1999); Agreement between the Government of the Republic of India and the Government of the Republic of Senegal for the Promotion and Protection of Investments, Art. 1(a) (signed 3 Jul. 2008, entered into force 17 Oct. 2009); Agreement between the Government of the Republic of India and the Federal Government of The Federal Republic of Yugoslavia for the Reciprocal Promotion and Protection of Investments, Art. 1(a) (signed 31 Jan. 2003, entered into force 24 Feb. 2009); Agreement between the Government of the Republic of India and the Government of the Republic of Seychelles for the Promotion and Protection of Investments, Art. 1(b) (signed 2 Jun. 2010); Agreement between the Republic of India and the Slovak Republic for the Promotion and Reciprocal Protection of Investments, Art. 1(1) (signed 25 Sept. 2006, entered into force 27 Sept. 2007); Agreement between the Government of the Republic of India and the Government of the Republic of Slovenia for the Mutual Promotion and Protection of Investments, Art. 1(2) (signed 14 Jun. 2011); Agreement between the Government of the Democratic Socialist Republic of Sri Lanka and the Government of the Republic of India for the Promotion and Protection of Investments, Art. 1(b) (signed 22 Jan. 1997, entered into force 13 Feb. 1998); Agreement between the Government of the Republic of India and the Government of the Republic of Sudan for the Promotion and Protection of Investments, Art. 1(b) (signed 22 Oct. 2003, entered into force 18 Oct. 2010); Agreement between the Government of the Kingdom of Sweden and the Government of the Republic of India for the Promotion and Reciprocal Protection of Investments, *supra* n. 1, at Art. 1(a); Agreement between the Government of the Republic of India and the Government of the Syrian Arab Republic on the Mutual Promotion and Protection of Investments, Art. 1(1) (signed 18 Jun. 2008, entered into force 22 Jan. 2009); Agreement between the India Taipei Association in Taipei and the Taipei Economic and Cultural Center in New Delhi on the Promotion and Protection of Investments, Art. 1(1) (signed 17 Oct. 2002, entered into force 28 Nov. 2002); Agreement between the Government of the Republic of India and the Government of the Republic of Tajikistan for the Promotion and Protection of Investments, Art. 1(b) (signed 13 Dec. 1995, entered into force 14 Nov. 2003); Agreement between the Government of the Kingdom of Thailand and the Government of the Republic of India for the Promotion and Protection of Investments, Art. 1(b) (signed 10 Jul. 2000, entered into force 13 Jul. 2001); Agreement between the Government of the Republic of India and the Government of the Republic of Trinidad and Tobago for the Promotion and Protection of Investments, Art. 1(b) (signed 12 Mar. 2007, entered into force 7 Oct. 2007); Agreement between the Republic of Turkey and the Republic of India for the Reciprocal Promotion and Protection of Investments, Art. 1(2) (signed 17 Sept. 1998, entered into force 18 Oct. 2007); Agreement between the Government of the Republic of India and the Government of Turkmenistan for the Promotion and Protection of Investments, Art. 1(b) (signed 20 Sept. 1995, entered into force 27 Feb. 2006); Agreement between the Government of the Republic of India and the Government

Definition of investment comprises of two parts: *chapeau* and categories of investments covered. The *chapeau* normally states that the definition of investment is open-ended and non-exhaustive. This is represented in the words: investment 'means every kind of asset established or acquired, ... though not exclusively, includes: ...'. The *chapeau* also lays down the requirement that the asset should be acquired or any changes in the form of the asset should be 'in accordance with the national laws of the Contracting Party in whose territory the investment is made.' Some BITs do not include the words 'established and acquired' and only use 'changes in the form.'[57] India-Czech Republic BIT uses the same elements of investment as used in the general definition. It adds economic activity, it states: 'every kind of asset established or acquired in connection with economic activities by an investor.'[58] The Germany-India BIT simply states 'every kind of asset invested in accordance with the national laws'. It has no reference to 'established or acquired' or 'changes in the form of investment'.[59] The India-Morocco does not contain the *chapeau* thus there are no general requirements of 'investment' as contained in other BITs, the BIT contains only categories or kinds of investment and declares that change of the form of the kind of investment would also be covered.[60] The second part contains a non-exhaustive list of assets.

---

of Ukraine for the Promotion and Protection of Investments, Art. 1(b) (signed 1 Dec. 2001, entered into force 12 Aug. 2003); Agreement between the Government of the Republic of India and the Government of the United Arab Emirates on the Promotion and Protection of Investments, Art. 1(1) (signed 12 Dec. 2013, entered into force 21 Aug. 2014); Agreement between the Government of the United Kingdom of Great Britain and Northern Ireland and the Government of the Republic of India for the Promotion and Reciprocal Protection of Investments, *supra* n. 1, at Art. 1(b); Agreement on Reciprocal Protection and Promotion of Investments between the Government of the Republic of India and the Government of the Republic of Uzbekistan, *supra* n. 1, at Art. 1(2); Agreement between the Government of the Republic of India and the Government of the Socialist Republic of Vietnam for the Promotion and Protection of Investments, Art. 1(b) (signed 8 Mar. 1997, entered into force 1 Dec. 1999); Agreement between the Government of the Republic of India and the Government of the Republic of Yemen for the Promotion and Protection of Investments, Art. 1(b) (signed 1 Oct. 2002, entered into force 10 Feb. 2004);Agreement between the Government of the Republic of India and the Government of the Republic of Zimbabwe concerning the Promotion and Reciprocal Protection of Investments, Art. 1(a) (signed 10 Feb. 1999).

57. Agreement between the Government of the Republic of India and the Government of the Republic of Belarus for the Promotion and Protection of Investments, Art. 1 (signed 27 Nov. 2002, entered into force 23 Nov. 2003); Agreement between the Government of Malaysia and the Government of the Republic of India, *supra* n. 1, at Art. 1(2); Agreement between the Government of Nepal and the Government of the Republic of India for the Promotion and Protection of Investments, *supra* n. 1, at Art. 1(b).
58. Agreement between the Czech Republic and Republic of India for the Promotion and Protection of Investments, *supra* n. 1, at Art. 1(b); Agreement between the Republic of Hungary and Republic of India for the Promotion and Protection of Investments, Art. 1 (signed 3 Nov. 2003, entered into force 2 Jan. 2006, terminated 29 Mar. 2017).
59. Agreement between the Federal Republic of Germany and the Republic of India for the Promotion and Protection of Investments, Art. 1(b) (signed 10 Jul. 1995, entered into force 13 Jul. 1998, terminated 3 Jun. 2017).
60. Agreement between the Government of the Kingdom of Morocco and the Government of the Republic of India for the Promotion and Protection of Investments, Art. 1(1) (signed 13 Feb. 1999, entered into force 22 Feb. 2001); Agreement between the Swiss Confederation and the Republic of India for the Promotion and Protection of Investments, *supra* n. 1, at Art. 1(2).

Chapter 4: Applicable Laws and Jurisdiction §4.02[A]

The structure of the definition of 'investment' has led to a debate of whether investment is only one of the economic activities stipulated in the categories of investment or it involves something more i.e., whether there is a need of establishing 'objective' elements of the definition of investment in addition to the categories so mentioned. The debate about the need of an objective criteria for determining whether the activity amounts to investment has played out in detail in the context of Article 25 of the Convention on the Settlement of Investment Disputes Between States and Nationals of Other States (ICSID Convention). In the famous *Salini* case, the tribunal held that for a dispute to fall within the purview of ICSID Convention there is a need of satisfaction of objective criteria of investment, which are: contribution by the foreign investor to the host economy, certain duration of existence, undertaking risk of the transaction and contribution to economic development.[61] The presence of these objective elements ensures that the foreign investor has made an actual investment in good faith and is contributing into the host State economy. Although individual elements of investment are defined in a BIT, investment is a complex transition. In *CSOB v. Slovakia*, the Tribunal held that:

> An investment is frequently a rather complex operation, composed of various interrelated transactions, each element of which, standing alone, might not in all cases qualify as an investment. Hence, a dispute that is brought before the Centre must be deemed to arise directly out of an investment even when it is based on a transaction which, standing alone, would not qualify as an investment under the Convention, provided that the particular transaction forms an integral part of an overall operation that qualifies as an investment.[62]

In *Romak v. Uzbekistan*, a non-ICSID case, the Tribunal applied the 'objective' requirement test. According to the Tribunal, not doing so would convert every commercial activity into foreign investment capable of protection. BITs are not mean for protection of ordinary commercial transactions.[63] But in *White Industries v. Australia*, the tribunal declined to apply the *Salini* test outside ICSID cases.[64] Although it did conclude that the requirements of the *Salini* test were satisfied in that case.[65] Therefore, whether or not a tribunal would apply the objective test is unclear. The Model BIT removes such a possibility by incorporating the *Salini* test in the definition of investment. It requires that the assets of the enterprise should have:

---

61. *Salini Costruttori S.p.A and Italstrade S.p.A v. Kingdom of Morocco*, Decision on Jurisdiction, ICSID Case No. ARB/00/4, para. 53 (23 Jul. 2001).
62. *Ceskoslovenska Obchodni Banka, A.S. v. The Slovak Republic*, Decision on Jurisdiction, ICSID Case No. ARB/97/4, para. 54 (1 Dec. 2000); *Enron Corporation and Ponderosa Assets, L.P. v. Argentine Republic*, at para. 70; *Joy Mining Machinery Limited v. The Arabic Republic of Egypt*, Award on Jurisdiction, ICSID Case No. ARB/03/11, para. 54 (6 Aug. 2004); *Mr. Patrick Mitchell v. Democratic Republic of the Congo*, Decision on Annulment, ICSID Case No. ARB/99/7, para. 38 (1 Nov. 2006); *Duke Energy International Peru Investments No. 1 Ltd. v. Republic of Peru*, supra n. 42, at para. 92; *Saipem S.p.A. v. The People's Republic of Bangladesh*, supra n. 52, at paras 110, 114.
63. *Romak S.A. (Switzerland) v. The Republic of Uzbekistan*, Award, PCA Case No. AA280, paras 184-7 (26 Nov. 2009).
64. *White Industries Australia Limited v. The Republic of India*, Final Award, UNCITRAL, paras 7.4.8-7.4.9 (30 Nov. 2011).
65. *Ibid.*, at paras 7.4.10-7.4.19.

the characteristics of an investment such as the commitment of capital or other resources, certain duration, the expectation of gain or profit, the assumption of risk and a significance for the development of the Party in whose territory the investment is made.[66]

Investment tribunals have interpreted the categories of investment contained in the second part of the definition of investment broadly. Open-ended asset based definition broadens the jurisdiction of arbitral tribunals. For example, shareholders can independently bring a claim under a BIT.[67] This right is extended to minority shareholders also.[68]

---

66. *Model Text for the Indian Bilateral Investment Treaty*, Art. 1.4 (28 Dec. 2015) http://www.finmin.nic.in/reports/ModelTextIndia_BIT.pdf (accessed 18 Jul. 2017).
67. *See Antoine Goetz et consorts v. République du Burundi*, Decision on Liability, ICSID Case No. ARB/95/3 (2 Sept. 1998); *Emilio Agustín Maffezini v. The Kingdom of Spain*, Decision on Jurisdiction, ICSID Case No. ARB/97/7 (25 Jan. 2000); *Compañiá de Aguas del Aconquija S.A. and Vivendi Universal S.A. v. Argentine Republic*, Decision on Annulment, ICSID Case No. ARB/97/3 (3 Jul. 2002); *Azurix Corp. v. The Argentine Republic*, Decision on Jurisdiction, ICSID Case No. ARB/01/12 (8 Dec. 2003); *American Manufacturing & Trading, Inc. v. Republic of Zaire*, Award, ICSID Case No. ARB/93/1(21 Feb. 1997); *Alex Genin, Eastern Credit Limited, Inc. and A.S. Baltoil v. The Republic of Estonia*, supra n. 16; *CME Czech Republic B.V. v. The Czech Republic*, Partial Award, UNCITRAL (13 Sept. 2001); *Camuzzi International S.A. v. The Argentine Republic*, Decision on Jurisdiction, ICSID Case No. ARB/03/2, paras 12, 78-82, 140-2 (11 May 2005); *Gas Natural SDG, S.A. v. The Argentine Republic*, Decision on Jurisdiction, ICSID Case No. ARB/03/10, paras 32-5, 50-1 (17 Jun. 2005); *AES Corporation v. The Argentine Republic*, Decision on Jurisdiction, ICSID Case No. ARB/02/17, paras 85-9 (26 Apr. 2005); *Compañiá de Aguas del Aconquija S.A. and Vivendi Universal S.A. v. Argentine Republic*, Decision on Jurisdiction, ICSID Case No. ARB/97/3, paras 88-94 (14 Nov. 2005); *Continental Casualty Company v. The Argentine Republic*, Decision on Jurisdiction, ICSID Case No. ARB/03/9, paras 51-4, 76-89 (22 Feb. 2006); *Suez, Sociedad General de Aguas de Barcelona S.A., and InterAguas Servicios Integrales del Agua S.A. v. The Argentine Republic*, Decision on Jurisdiction, ICSID Case No. ARB/03/17, paras 46-51 (16 May 2006); *National Grid plc v. The Argentine Republic*, Decision on Jurisdiction, UNCITRAL, paras 147-58, 165 (20 Jun. 2006); *National Grid plc v. The Argentine Republic*, supra n. 34, at para. 126; *Pan American Energy LLC and BP Argentina Exploration Company v. The Argentine Republic*, Decision on Preliminary Objections, ICSID Case No. ARB/03/13, paras 209-22 (27 Jul. 2006); *Parkerings-Compagniet AS v. Republic of Lithuania*, Award, ICSID Case No. ARB/05/8, paras 250-4 (11 Sept. 2007); *Impregilo S.p.A. v. Argentine Republic*, Award, ICSID Case No. ARB/07/17, paras 110-40, 238-46, 271 (21 Jun. 2011).
68. *See Asian Agricultural Products Ltd. v. Republic of Sri Lanka*, supra n. 4; *Lanco International Inc. v. The Argentine Republic*, Decision on Jurisdiction, ICSID Case No. ARB/97/6 (8 Dec. 1998); *Compañiá de Aguas del Aconquija S.A. and Vivendi Universal S.A. v. Argentine Republic*, Decision on Annulment, supra n. 67; *CMS Gas Transmission Company v. The Republic of Argentina*, Decision on Jurisdiction, ICSID Case No. ARB/01/8 (17 Jul. 2003);*Champion Trading Company, Ameritrade International, Inc. v. Arab Republic of Egypt*, Decision on Jurisdiction, ICSID Case No. ARB/02/9 (21 Oct. 2003); *LG&E Energy Corp., LG&E Capital Corp., and LG&E International, Inc. v. Argentine Republic*, Decision on Jurisdiction, ICSID Case No. ARB/02/1, paras 50-63 (30 Apr. 2004); *LG&E Energy Corp., LG&E Capital Corp., and LG&E International, Inc. v. Argentine Republic*, Decision on Liability, supra n. 2, at paras 78-9; *Gami Investments, Inc. v. The Government of the United Mexican States*, Award, UNCITRAL (15 Nov. 2004); *Sempra Energy International v. The Argentine Republic*, Decision on Jurisdiction, ICSID Case No. ARB/02/16, paras 92-4 (11 May 2005); *El Paso Energy International Company v. The Argentine Republic*, Decision on Jurisdiction, ICSID Case No. ARB/03/15, para. 138 (27 Apr. 2006); *Phoenix Action, Ltd. v. The Czech Republic*, Award, ICSID Case No. ARB/06/5, paras 121-3 (15 Apr. 2009); *Hochtief AG v. The Argentine Republic*, Decision on Jurisdiction, ICSID Case No. ARB/07/31, paras 112-19 (24 Oct. 2011).

Chapter 4: Applicable Laws and Jurisdiction §4.02[A]

UNCTAD had advised States to adopt a closed list definition.[69] Therefore, States started including limitations on the definition of investment. One example of closed list of definition of investment is the India-Mexico BIT. It limits the categories of investments, only to those mentioned in the BIT. The Indian Model BIT adopts a closed list approach and goes a step further by introducing an enterprise-based definition.

The Indian Model BIT defines investment as an 'enterprise constituted, organized and operated in good faith by an investor in accordance with the law of the host state.'[70] An enterprise has been defined in turn as a legal entity that is 'constituted, organized and operated in compliance with the law' of the host State; and includes any company, corporation, limited liability partnership (LLP) or a joint venture and a branch of any such entity constituted in accordance with the laws of the host State.[71] The Model BIT aims to protect the assets of such an enterprise, which may be in the form of shares, stock, other equity instruments, debt instruments, licences, long-term contracts, copyrights, technical know-how, etc.[72] To fall within the definition of investment – unlike past – falling within one of the categories of investment is not adequate, the investment has to be made in an enterprise. The benefit of the enterprise-based definition is that the BIT would protect only those investment activities where the foreign investor has a real and effective presence in the host State. Therefore, only those investors actively present in the host State that are affected by a regulation would be covered by the BIT.

The 2015 Model BIT requires that the investment should be made in 'good faith' and constituted, organized and operated in accordance with the laws of the host State.[73] The specific reference to good faith would ensure that the foreign investor has created a physical presence for indulging into a serious activity in the host economy and not for simply seeking benefit of the BIT or the dispute resolution clause therein. An investor cannot claim protection by establishing an office in the host State without any actual and real intention to conduct investment related activity in the host State. Additionally, the investment has to be in accordance with the laws of host State at all times. This requirement is often referred to as the absence of illegality in investment law[74] and has been implied to exist, even if not specifically mentioned.[75]

---

69. United Nations Conference on Trade and Development, *Scope and Definition*, UNCTAD/DIAE/IA/2010/2, 10, 34-6 (UNCTAD Series on Issues in International Investment Agreements II, United Nations 2011) http://unctad.org/en/Docs/diaeia20102_en.pdf (accessed 18 Jul. 2017). For closed list approach, *see* Canada Model BIT, Art. 1 (2004) http://www.italaw.com/documents/Canadian2004-FIPA-model-en.pdf (accessed 18 Jul. 2017).
70. *Model Text for the Indian Bilateral Investment Treaty*, *supra* n. 66, at Art. 1.4.
71. *Ibid.*, at Art. 1.3.
72. *Ibid.*, at Art. 1.4(a)-(h).
73. *Ibid.*, at Art. 1.4. For a discussion on need of good faith in restructuring *see* Andrew D. Mitchell, M Sornarajah and Tania Voon (eds), *Good Faith and International Economic Law* 117-42 (Oxford University Press 2015).
74. *See* Stephan Schill, *Illegal Investments in Investment Treaty Arbitration*, 11 The Law and Practice of International Courts and Tribunals 281 (2012); Christian Klausegger and others (eds), *Austrian Yearbook on International Arbitration* 307-35 (CH Beck, Stämpfli and Manz 2010).
75. *Plama Consortium Limited v. Republic of Bulgaria*, Award, ICSID Case No. ARB/03/24, paras 138-9 (27 Aug. 2008) followed in *Phoenix Action, Ltd. v. The Czech Republic*, *supra* n. 68, at para. 101; *Fraport AG Frankfurt Airport Services Worldwide v. Republic of the Philippines[II]*, Award, ICSID Case No. ARB/11/12, para. 332 (10 Dec. 2014).

In addition to providing an enterprise-based definition with the need to satisfy objective requirements, the Model BIT excludes certain categories of investments. The exclusion list further narrows the scope of the definition of investment. Shares held in an enterprise amount to an investment but shares held simply on the share market as a portfolio is excluded.[76] There are good policy reasons for excluding portfolio investments from the definition of investment because they are merely speculative investments without any intention to hold on to them or contributing towards the presence and economic development of the host State.[77] Moreover, the investors regularly suffer losses due to movements in the market caused by regulations adopted or even announced by States. By excluding portfolio investments the chances of the host State being sued for regulations which result into losses in the share market are excluded.

Another category of investments that could result into challenges to regulatory actions of the host State relate to government bonds. Often in cases of government debt crises, governments are required to adopt various regulations that affect the entitlements of government bond and security holders.[78] The process of renegotiations between the government and the creditors is complex. Normally, the debts are renegotiated. If some of the creditors can access investment arbitration, then they could indulge into hold out litigation and hamper the prospects of renegotiations. In the case of Argentina, a tribunal has found that the bondholders could initiate arbitration based on the BIT.[79] Therefore allowing access to bondholders to investment arbitrations is problematic.[80] The Indian Model BIT excludes government bonds and other security interests from the definition of investment.[81]

The Model BIT excludes expenditures incurred prior to commencement of operations from the definition of investment.[82] Also, the protection of the treaty generally is not extended to pre-investment activity.[83] Pre-investment activity is defined as activities undertaken prior to establishment of the investment for 'compliance with sectoral limitations on foreign equity, and other limitations and conditions applicable under any law relating to the admission of investments' in the host country.[84] If protection is allowed to pre-operational activity then the regulatory

---

76. *Model Text for the Indian Bilateral Investment Treaty*, supra n. 66, at Art. 1.4(i).
77. Aniruddha Rajput, *Defining Investments: A Developmental Perspective*, 2(1) Indian Journal of Arbitration Law 12, 19-20 (2013). *See also* M. Sornarajah, *Portfolio Investments and Definition of Investment*, 24 ICSID Review – FILJ 516 (2009).
78. Argentina is a classic case where it had to undertake various regulatory measures after its economic crisis set in. For a discussion on the crises, *see* Peter Katel, *Argentina's Crisis Explained*, Time (20 Dec. 2001) http://content.time.com/time/world/article/0,8599,189393,00.html (accessed 18 Jul. 2017); Beniamino Moro and Victor A Beker (eds), *Modern Financial Crises: Argentina, United States and Europe*, 31 (Springer 2015).
79. *Abaclat and Others v. Argentine Republic* (formerly *Giovanna a Beccara and Others v. The Argentine Republic*), Decision on Jurisdiction and Admissibility, ICSID Case No. ARB/07/5, paras 352-6 (4 Aug. 2011).
80. *See* generally, Michael Waibel, *Opening Pandora's Box: Sovereign Bonds in International Arbitration*, 101 American Journal of International Law 711 (2007).
81. *Model Text for the Indian Bilateral Investment Treaty*, supra n. 66, at Art. 1.4(ii).
82. *Ibid.*, at Art. 1.4(iii).
83. *Ibid.*, at Art. 2.2.
84. *Ibid.*, at Art. 1.11.

freedom of the State would be constrained by an investment which has not even taken place yet. Tribunals have taken contradictory approach relating to pre-investment activity.[85]

Claims arising out of purely commercial transactions or extension of credit for those transactions are excluded from the definition of investment.[86] Commercial transactions as it is are excluded from the scope of investment arbitration because the objective of investment treaties is not to protect purely commercial transitions.[87] Yet in some cases, commercial transactions have been elevated to treaty claims.[88] The provision in the Model BIT clarifies the position so that an investment tribunal is constrained from include them within investment. If claims arising out of commercial transactions are allowed, then all commercial disputes would get transferred into investment claims. A wider set of regulations would then get covered.

The Model BIT excludes claims to money arising out of commercial transactions[89] and a judgment or order, which is an outcome of judicial, administrative or arbitral proceedings.[90] In *White Industries v. India*, claims to money were considered to be wide enough to include an unenforced commercial arbitration award.[91] In *Saipem v. Bangladesh*, the host State was found responsible for issuing injunction against arbitration proceedings.[92] If the foreign investor is involved in a commercial transaction with the government and has a commercial arbitration award in favour, then the investor could claim protection under the BIT. This naturally expands the access to investment arbitration. Therefore, claims to money as well as judicial decisions are excluded from the definition of investment. Even the US Model BIT adopts the same approach.[93]

In summary, to qualify as investment, the necessary attributes in the Model BIT have to be satisfied and then it has to be seen that the kind of investment is not excluded, only then can a foreign investor successfully complete the *ratione materiae* requirement of jurisdiction.

---

85. *Mihaly International Corporation v. Democratic Socialist Republic of Sri Lanka, supra* n. 52; *Fedax NV v. The Republic of Venezuela,* Decision of the Tribunal on Objections to Jurisdiction, ICSID Case No. ARB/96/3 (11 Jul. 1977).
86. *Model Text for the Indian Bilateral Investment Treaty, supra* n. 66, at Art. 1.7(iv)-(v).
87. *Romak S.A. (Switzerland) v. The Republic of Uzbekistan, supra* n. 63, at para. 189.
88. *Joy Mining Machinery Limited v. The Arabic Republic of Egypt, supra* n. 62, at para. 81; *SGS Société Générale de Surveillance S.A. v. Islamic Republic of Pakistan,* Decision on Jurisdiction, ICSID Case No. ARB/01/13, para. 166 (6 Aug. 2003).
89. *Model Text for the Indian Bilateral Investment Treaty, supra* n. 66, at Art. 1.4(iv)-(vi).
90. *Ibid.,* at Art. 1.4(vii).
91. *White Industries Australia Limited v. The Republic of India, supra* n. 64, at para. 7.3.8. *See also Saipem S.p.A. v. The People's Republic of Bangladesh, supra* n. 52, at para. 127; Loukas Mistellis, *Award as an Investment: The Value of an Arbitral Award or the Cost of Non-Enforcement,* 28 ICSID Review – FILJ 64 (2013).
92. *Saipem S.p.A. v. The People's Republic of Bangladesh, supra* n. 2, at para. 170.
93. US Model Bilateral Investment Treaty, Art. 1 (2012) http://www.state.gov/documents/organization/188371.pdf (accessed 19 Jul. 2017).

[B] Investor

Jurisdiction *ratione personae* requires that the person that is invoking arbitration proceedings under the BIT is qualified to do so. This is contained in the definition of 'investment' in the BIT.

In the old BITs, the definition of investor included 'natural' as well as 'legal' persons. 'Investor' was defined in the Indian BITs in three ways. The first was a very basic clause without any details. This clause would only state that natural and legal persons are investors. In the second, after setting out that both natural and legal persons are investors, detailed rules for natural and legal persons were specified. In the third case, different rules specified for each contracting party respectively, as to how whether the person is legal or natural would be decided. These structural differences were important because the interpretation of the definition of investor would change accordingly. The first and the simplest definition of investor is as under:

'investor' means any national or company of a Contracting Party.[94]

---

94. Agreement between the Government of the Republic of India and the Government of People's Republic of Bangladesh for the Promotion and Protection of Investments, *supra* n. 1, at Art. 1(c); Agreement between the Government of Bosnia & Herzegovina and the Government of the Republic of India, *supra* n. 56, at Art. 1(2); Agreement between the Government of the Republic of China and the Government of the Republic of India, *supra* n. 1, at Art. 1(a); Agreement between the Government of Cyprus and the Government of the Republic of India, *supra* n. 56, at Art. 1(c); Agreement between the Government of the Republic of India and the Government of the Kingdom of Denmark concerning the Promotion and Reciprocal Protection of Investments, *supra* n. 1, at Art. 1(4); Agreement between the Government of the Republic of Djibouti and the Government of the Republic of India, *supra* n. 56, at Art. 1(c); Agreement between the Government of the Egypt and the Government of the Republic of India, *supra* n. 56, at Art. 1(c); Agreement between the Government of Indonesia and the Government of the Republic of India, *supra* n. 56, at Art. 1(2); Agreement between the Government of Israel and the Government of the Republic of India, *supra* n. 1, at Art. 1(c); Agreement between the Government of the Hashemite Kingdom of Jordan and the Government of the Republic of India, Art. 1(b)(signed 30 Nov. 2006, entered into force 22 Jan. 2009); Agreement between the State of Kuwait and the Republic of India for the Encouragement and Reciprocal Protection of Investment, *supra* n. 1, at Art. 1(3); Agreement between the Government of Kyrgyz Republic and the Government of the Republic of India, *supra* n. 56, at Art. 1(c); Agreement between the Government of the Republic of India and the Government of the Lao People's Democratic Republic for the Promotion and Protection of Investments, *supra* n. 56, at Art. 1(c); Agreement between the Republic of India and the Great Socialist People's Libyan Arab Jamahiriya for the Promotion and Protection of Investments, *supra* n. 56, at Art. 1(c); Agreement between the Government of the Republic of India and the Government of Mongolia for the Promotion and Protection of Investments, *supra* n. 56, at Art. 1(c); Agreement between the Government of the Republic of Mozambique and the Government of the Republic of India for the Reciprocal Promotion and Protection of Investments, *supra* n. 56, at Art. 1(c); Agreement between the Republic of India and the Kingdom of the Netherlands for the Promotion and Protection of Investments, *supra* n. 1, at Art. 1(d);Agreement between the Government of the Sultanate of Oman and the Government of the Republic of India, *supra* n. 56, at Art. 1(c); Agreement between the Government of the Philippines and the Government of the Republic of India, Art. 1(4) (signed 28 Jan. 2000, entered into force 29 Jan. 2001); Agreement between the Government of Romania and the Government of the Republic of India, *supra* n. 56, at Art. 1(c); Agreement between the Government of the Republic of Sudan and the Government of the Republic of India, *supra* n. 56, at Art. 1(c); Agreement between the Government of the Kingdom of Sweden and the Government of the Republic of India for the Promotion and Reciprocal Protection of Investments, *supra* n. 1, at Art. 1(b); Agreement between the Government of the Republic of Tajikistan and the Government of

Some BITs improvised this provision and added the requirement that the investor has made an investment in the territory of the other State. The definition of investor in that case was as follows:

> 'investors' means any national or company of a Contracting Party, that has made investments in the territory of other Contracting Party.[95]

A slight variation of this drafting – however with little practical difference – could be seen in the India-Germany BIT:

> 'investors' means nationals or companies of a Contracting Party who have effected or are effecting investment in the territory of the other Contracting Party.[96]

This provision clearly required physical presence of the foreign investor in the host State.

Some definitions referred to the requirement of satisfaction of domestic legal conditions, whether as a national or a company in addition to the improvisation of

---

the Republic of India, *supra* n. 56, at Art. 1(c); Agreement between the Government of the Kingdom of Thailand and the Government of the Republic of India, *supra* n. 56, at Art. 1(c); Agreement between the Government of the Republic of Turkmenistan and the Government of the Republic of India, *supra* n. 56, at Art. 1(c); Agreement between the Government of the Republic of India and the Government of Ukraine for the Promotion and Protection of Investments, *supra* n. 56, at Art. 1(c); Agreement between the Government of the Republic of India and the Government of the United Arab Emirates on the Promotion and Protection of Investments, *supra* n. 56, at Art. 1(2); Agreement between the Government of the United Kingdom of Great Britain and Northern Ireland and the Government of the Republic of India for the Promotion and Reciprocal Protection of Investments, *supra* n. 56, at Art. 1(c); Agreement between the Government of the Republic of India and the Government of the Socialist Republic of Vietnam for the Promotion and Protection of Investments, *supra* n. 56, at Art. 1(c); Agreement between the Government of the Republic of India and the Government of the Republic of Yemen for the Promotion and Protection of Investments, *supra* n. 56, at Art. 1(c); Agreement between the Government of the Republic of India and the Government of the Republic of Zimbabwe for the Promotion and Reciprocal Protection of Investments, *supra* n. 56, at Art. 1(c).

95. Agreement between the Government of the Republic of India and the Government of His Majesty The Sultan And Yang Di-Pertuan of Brunei Darussalam on the Reciprocal Promotion and Protection of Investments, *supra* n. 56, at Art. 1(c); Agreement between the Government of the Republic of India and the Government of the Democratic Republic of Congo for the Mutual Promotion and Protection of Investments, *supra* n. 56, at Art. 1(c); Agreement between the Government of the Republic of Hungary and the Government of the Republic of India, *supra* n. 58, at Art. 1(2); Agreement between the Government of Iceland and the Government of the Republic of India, *supra* n. 56, at Art. 1(c); Agreement between the Government of the Republic of Kazakhstan and the Government of the Republic of India, *supra* n. 1, at Art. 1(b); Agreement between the Government of Republic of Korea and the Government of the Republic of India, *supra* n. 1, at Art. 1(3); Agreement between the Government of the Republic of Latvia and the Government of the Republic of India, *supra* n. 1, at Art. 1(b); Agreement between the Government of the former Yugoslav Republic of Macedonia and the Government of the Republic of India, *supra* n. 56, at Art. 1(2); Agreement between the Government of the Republic of the Union of Myanmar and the Government of the Republic of India, *supra* n. 56, at Art. 1(c); Agreement between the Government of Nepal and the Government of the Republic of India, *supra* n. 1, at Art. 1(c); Agreement between the Government of the Republic of India and the Government of the Republic of Seychelles for the Promotion and Protection of Investments, *supra* n. 56, at Art. 1(c); Agreement between the Government of the Republic of Trinidad and Tobago and the Government of the Republic of India, *supra* n. 56, at Art. 1(c).
96. Agreement between the Federal Republic of Germany and the Republic of India for the Promotion and Protection of Investments, *supra* n. 59, at Art. 1(c).

having presence in another State.[97] This clause would cover those in the process of investing.

Since there was a specific requirement of making of investment in the territory of another State, the need of actual physical presence was necessary. But the provision did not state the extent of presence that is necessary. In any case, the provision certainly excluded those investors who did not have a presence in the territory of another State.

The presence or absence of such a clause is immaterial, since BITs are meant to protect investors of one State inventing into another.

The drafting was seemingly simple but it had the potential to cause interpretative complications. Neither the word 'national' nor 'company' was defined. In absence of any guidance from the treaty, a tribunal would interpret both the terms broadly. India does not recognize dual nationality. International law gives deference to definition of nationality in municipal laws. Therefore, only a natural person who is a citizen of India can file a case against another contracting party. If the other contracting party recognizes dual nationality, then a person can bring a claim against India, if one of the nationalities belongs to the other contracting party. The word 'company' was also not defined. It could be argued that since the word company was used, the meaning under domestic law on companies has to be given. The Indian companies act defines a company as:

> company means a company incorporated under this Act or under any previous company law.[98]

A company would thus have to be incorporated under Indian law. This would be a restrictive definition since there could be various other forms of forming a legal entity to investment in a foreign country. Such an interpretation would exclude a large number of other legally incorporated entities such as private trusts and societies. Therefore, company has to be interpreted broadly.

The second category had separate and detailed rules for 'natural' and 'legal' persons. The natural as well as legal persons should have had invested in the territory of the other State in accordance with the law of that State.[99] A natural person had to be a citizen of either Contracting Party as per the laws of the home State.[100] Even if

---

97. Agreement between the Government of the Republic of Mauritius and the Government of the Republic of India for the Promotion and Protection of Investments, Art. 1(b) (signed 4 Sept. 1998, entered into force 20 Jun. 2000); Agreement between the Government of the Republic of Ghana and the Government of the Republic of India, *supra* n. 1, at Art. 1(c).
98. Section 2(20), The Indian Companies Act 2013.
99. Agreement between the Government of the Republic of India and the Government of the Republic of Armenia for the Promotion and Protection of Investments, *supra* n. 1, at Art. 1(3).
100. *Ibid.*, at Art. 1(3)(i); Agreement between the Government of Austria and the Government of the Republic of India, *supra* n. 1, at Art. 1(1)(a); Agreement between the Government of the Republic of India and the Government of Kingdom of Bahrain for the Promotion and Protection of Investments, *supra* n. 1, at Art. 1(a)(i); Agreement for the Promotion and Protection of Investments between the Republic of Colombia and the Republic of India, *supra* n. 1, at Art. 1.1(a); Agreement between the Government of Czech Republic and the Government of the Republic of India, *supra* n. 1, at Art. 1(a)(i); Agreement between the Republic of India and the Federal Democratic Republic of Ethiopia, *supra* n. 56, at Art. 1(2)(i);

conditions are mentioned separately for both countries; the conditions of compliance with local law of nationality for natural persons remains.[101] In some cases the requirement of investing in another State was mentioned along with the requirement of satisfying the national laws on nationality.[102] The legal person could be constituted in various forms. The definitions were broad to include various kinds of legal entities such as company, corporation, firm, association, etc. In some cases they were expressly required to be constituted as per the laws of a contracting party. This is the place of incorporation test. They used the words: incorporates, constituted or established.[103] In

---

Agreement between the Government of the Republic of Finland and the Government of the Republic of India, *supra* n. 1, at Art. 1(3)(a); Agreement between the Government of the Mexico and the Government of the Republic of India, *supra* n. 1, at Art. 1(8)(a); Agreement between the Government of the Kingdom of Morocco and the Government of the Republic of India for the Promotion and Protection of Investments, *supra* n. 60, at Art. 1(2)(a); Agreement between the Government of the Republic of India and the Government of the Republic of Poland for the Promotion and Protection of Investments, Art. 1(2)(a) (signed 7 Oct. 1996, entered into force 31 Dec. 1997); Agreement between the Government of Portugal and the Government of the Republic of India, *supra* n. 1, at Art. 1(3)(a); Agreement between the Government of the Russian Federation and the Government of the Republic of India, Art. 1(2)(a)(signed 23 Dec. 1994, entered into force 5 Aug. 1996); Agreement between the Government of the Republic of India and the Government of the Republic of Senegal for the Promotion and Protection of Investments, *supra* n. 56, at Art. 1(b)(i); Agreement between the Government of the Republic of India and the Federal Government of the Federal Republic of Yugoslavia for the Reciprocal Promotion and Protection of Investments, *supra* n. 56, at Art. 1(b)(i); Agreement between the Government of Republic of Slovakia and the Government of the Republic of India, *supra* n. 56, at Art. 1(3)(a); Agreement between the Government of the Republic of India and the Government of the Republic of Slovenia on the Mutual Promotion and Protection of Investments, *supra* n. 56, at Art. 1(1)(a); Agreement between the Swiss Confederation and the Republic of India for the Promotion and Protection of Investments, *supra* n. 1, at Art. 1(1)(a); Agreement between the Republic of Turkey and the Republic of India concerning the Reciprocal Promotion and Protection of Investments, *supra* n. 56, at Art. 1(1)(a).
101. Agreement between the Government of Qatar and the Government of the Republic of India, *supra* n. 56, at Arts 1(1)(i) (a) and (ii) (a); Agreement between the Government of the Republic of India and Government of the Kingdom of Saudi Arabia concerning the Encouragement and Reciprocal Protection of Investments, Arts 1(3) a) I and b) I (signed 25 Jan. 2006, entered into force 20 May 2008); Agreement between the Government of Syrian Arab Republic and the Government of the Republic of India, *supra* n. 56, at Art. 1(2)(a); Agreement on Reciprocal Protection and Promotion of Investments between the Government of the Republic of India and the Government of the Republic of Uzbekistan, *supra* n. 1, at Art. 1(1)(a); Agreement between the Government of Australia and the Government of the Republic of India on the Promotion and Protection of Investments, *supra* n. 1, at Art. 1(a)(ii); Agreement between the Government of the Republic of India and the Government of the Republic of Bulgaria for the Promotion and Protection of Investments, *supra* n. 56, at Arts 1(1)(a) and (b).
102. Agreement between the Government of the Republic of Croatia and the Government of the Republic of India on the Promotion and Reciprocal Protection of Investments, *supra* n. 1, at Art. 1(2)(a).
103. Agreement between the Government of the Republic of India and the Government of the Republic of Belarus for the Promotion and Protection of Investments, *supra* n. 57, at Art. 1(2)(b); Agreement between the Government of the Republic of India and the Government of the Republic of Bulgaria for the Promotion and Protection of Investments, *supra* n. 56, at Arts 1(1)(a) and (b); *ibid.*, at Art. 1(2)(b); Agreement between the Government of the Republic of India and the Government of the Republic of Poland for the Promotion and Protection of Investments, *supra* n. 100, at Art. 1(2)(b); Agreement between the Government of Qatar and the Government of the Republic of India, *supra* n. 56, at Art. 1(1)(i)(b); Agreement between the Government of the Russian Federation and the Government of the Republic of India, *supra*

some cases, further requirements were mentioned. Such as the need of having a registered office,[104] or 'head office'[105] or 'permanent seat'[106] or simply 'seat in the territory of that Contracting Party and making investment in the territory of the other Contracting Party',[107] 'economic activity.'[108] Some state the need of that the legal person shall be 'engaged in substantial business activities in the territory of' the home State.[109]

While mentioning legal persons, specific reference was also made to government agencies, corporations, etc. For example, the India-Qatar BIT had the following provision:

> (b) Government and Governmental agencies, corporations, companies, firms or business associations incorporated or constituted under the law in force in the State of Qatar and having their headquarters in the territory of the State of Qatar.[110]

Some simply stated to cover legal entity constituted as per the laws in force in either state: 'corporations, firms or business associations incorporated or constituted or established under the law in force in either of the Contracting Parties.'[111]

---

n. 100, at Art. 1(2)(b); Agreement between the Government of the Republic of India and the Government of the Republic of Senegal for the Promotion and Protection of Investments, *supra* n. 56, at Art. 1(b)(ii); Agreement between the Government of Syrian Arab Republic and the Government of the Republic of India, *supra* n. 56, at Art. 1(2)(b); Agreement between the Government of the Kingdom of Thailand and the Government of the Republic of India, *supra* n. 56, at Art. 1(a); Agreement on Reciprocal Protection and Promotion of Investments between the Government of the Republic of India and the Government of the Republic of Uzbekistan, *supra* n. 1, at Art. 1(1)b.

104. Agreement between the Government of the Republic of India and the Government of the Republic of Armenia for the Promotion and Protection of Investments, *supra* n. 1, at Art. 1(3)(ii); Agreement between the Government of the Republic of Finland and the Government of the Republic of India, *supra* n. 1, at Art. 1(3)(b).
105. Agreement between the Government of the Republic of India and Government of the Kingdom of Saudi Arabia concerning the Encouragement and Reciprocal Protection of Investments, *supra* n. 101, at Art. 1(3)(b)II.
106. Agreement between the Government of Czech Republic and the Government of the Republic of India, *supra* n. 1, at Art. 1(a)(ii).
107. Agreement between the Government of the former Yugoslav Republic of Macedonia and the Government of the Republic of India, *supra* n. 56, at Art. 1(b)(ii).
108. Agreement between the Republic of India and the Federal Democratic Republic of Ethiopia, *supra* n. 56, at Art. 1(2)(b).
109. Agreement for the Promotion and Protection of Investments between the Republic of Colombia and the Republic of India, *supra* n. 1, at Art. 1.1(b); Agreement between the Government of the Mexico and the Government of the Republic of India, *supra* n. 1, at Art. 8(b); Agreement between the Government of Portugal and the Government of the Republic of India, *supra* n. 1, at Art. 1(3)(b); Agreement between the Swiss Confederation and the Republic of India for the Promotion and Protection of Investments, *supra* n. 1, at Art. 1(1)(b); Agreement between the Republic of Turkey and the Republic of India concerning the Reciprocal Promotion and Protection of Investments, *supra* n. 56, at Art. 1(1)(b).
110. Agreement between the Government of Qatar and the Government of the Republic of India, *supra* n. 56, at Art. 1(1)(ii)(b); Agreement between the Government of the Republic of India and Government of the Kingdom of Saudi Arabia concerning the Encouragement and Reciprocal Protection of Investments, *supra* n. 101, at Art. 1(3)(b).III.
111. Agreement between the Government of the Republic of India and the Government of Kingdom of Bahrain for the Promotion and Protection of Investments, *supra* n. 1, at Art. 1(a)(ii).

Some BITs required control of the investment in the nationals of one of the States. For example, The India-Austria BIT stated that:

> (c) any juridical person, partnership or any other entity constituted or incorporated under the laws of a third State, which is controlled by investors referred to in (a) or (b), meaning that these investors have the ability to exercise decisive influence over the management and operation of the first mentioned entity, demonstrated specifically by way of:
> (i) ownership of at least 51% of shares or voting rights, or
> (ii) the ability to exercise decisive control over the composition of the Board of Directors making or having made an investment in the territory of the other Contracting Party.[112]

A similar requirement of control was stated in the India-Slovakia BIT:

> (i) in respect of the Republic of India: any entity that is incorporated, constituted, set up or otherwise duly organized under the laws and regulations of the Republic of India, whether or not for profit, whether privately or otherwise owned, with limited or unlimited liability, including any corporation, company, association, partnership, trust, joint venture, co-operatives or sole proprietorship. A legal person shall not include an entity, which is established and located in the territory of the Republic of India with negligible or nil business operations or with no real and continuous business activities carried out in its territory.
> (ii) in respect of the Slovak Republic: any entity which is incorporated or constituted in accordance with the laws and regulations of the Slovak Republic and which has its registered office, central administration or principal place of business in the Slovak Republic. However, should such a legal person have only its registered office in the territory of the Slovak Republic, its operations must possess a real and continuous link with the economy of that Contracting Party.[113]

The 2015 Model BIT is more in line with an elaborate definition. Although the changes are not substantial in comparison to the changes brought about in other BIT provisions. The definition of 'investor' is as follows:

> 'investor' means a natural or juridical person of a Party, other than a branch or representative office, that has made an investment in the territory of the other Party;
>
> For the purposes of this definition, a 'juridical person' means:
>
> (a) a legal entity that is constituted, organised and operated under the law of that Party and that has substantial business activities in the territory of that Party; or

---

112. Agreement between the Government of Austria and the Government of the Republic of India, *supra* n. 1, at Art. I(i)(c).
113. Agreement between the Government of Republic of Slovakia and the Government of the Republic of India, *supra* n. 56, at Art. 1(3)(a)(ii).

(b) a legal entity that is constituted, organised and operated under the laws of that Party and that is directly or indirectly owned or controlled by a natural person of that Party or by a legal entity mentioned under sub-clause (a) herein.[114]

Natural person is defined in the Model BIT, as follows:

'natural person' means a national or citizen of a Party in accordance with its law and regulations. A natural person who is a dual national or citizen shall be deemed to be exclusively a national or citizen of the country of her or his dominant and effective nationality/citizenship, where she/he ordinarily or permanently resides.[115]

Interpretation of definition of 'investor', particularly those of past BITs had created problems and resulted into inconsistent decision-making. In most cases, foreign investors are companies with presence in more than one country. These legal entities could be private as well as public corporations. Nationality of the investor serves as the link of the investor to the State based on which a relevant BIT is invoked. Nationality of the investors is important because, an investment tribunal would not have jurisdiction to entertain the dispute until the foreign investor question belongs to the State other than the State against which an investment claim is bought.[116]

For individuals, nationality is determined based on the law of country whose nationality is in issue.[117] A certificate issued by the State is a strong evidence of nationality.[118] Therefore if the investor acquires a new nationality and the old nationality lapses then the investor cannot bring a claim based on the old nationality.[119] If there is no effective nationality of the home State, access to investment arbitration would be declined.[120] Citizenship rather than residence is the decisive factor.[121]

It is complicated to determine the nationality of a corporation. A lot depends on the approach adopted in the BIT. In some cases, the test of incorporation or *siège social* is adopted.[122] The determination of the majority in the *Tokios Tokelés* has received attention in particular, and criticism due to a strong dissent by the President of the

---

114. *Model Text for the Indian Bilateral Investment Treaty*, supra n. 66, at Art. 1.5.
115. *Ibid.*, at Art. 1.9.
116. *Supra* n. 19, at 252-3.
117. *Victor Pey Casado and President Allende Foundation v. Republic of Chile*, Award, ICSID Case No. ARB/98/2, paras 254-60 (8 May 2008).
118. *Ioan Micula, Viorel Micula, S.C. European Food S.A, S.C. Starmill S.R.L. and S.C. Multipack S.R.L. v. Romania*, supra n. 38, at paras 70-106; *Señor Tza Yap Shum v. The Republic of Peru*, Decision on Jurisdiction, ICSID Case No. ARB/07/6, paras 42-77 (19 Jun. 2009).
119. *Hussein Nuaman Soufraki v. The United Arab Emirates*, Award, ICSID Case No. ARB/02/7, paras 42-6, 55 (7 Jul. 2004); *Waguih Elie George Siag and Clorinda Vecchi v. The Arab Republic of Egypt*, Decision on Jurisdiction, ICSID Case No. ARB/05/15, paras 195-201 (11 Apr. 2007).
120. *Champion Trading Company, Ameritrade International, Inc. v. Arab Republic of Egypt*, Decision on Jurisdiction, ICSID Case No. ARB/02/9, Section 3.4.1 (21 Oct. 2003).
121. *Marvin Roy Feldman Karpa v. United Mexican States*, Decision on Jurisdiction, ICSID Case No. ARB(AF)/99/1, paras 24-37 (6 Dec. 2000).
122. *Autopista Concesionada de Venezuela, C.A. v. Bolivarian Republic of Venezuela*, Decision on Jurisdiction, ICSID Case No. ARB/00/5, para. 107 (27 Sept. 2001); *Société Ouest Africaine des Bétons Industriels v. Senegal*, Decision on Jurisdiction, ICSID Case No. ARB/82/1, para. 29 (1 Aug. 1984).

Tribunal.[123] The investor was claiming breach of certain investment standards of the Ukraine-Lithuania BIT. Ukraine objected to the jurisdiction of the Tribunal on the ground that admittedly, 99% of the shares were owned, and two-thirds of the management composed of, Ukrainian nationals.[124] Allowing them to maintain a claim would be contrary to the International Convention for Settlement of Investment Disputes (ICSID) – setup to decide disputes between a Contracting Party and investors belonging to another Contracting Party – not nationals suing their own State.[125] The majority declined to pierce the corporate veil on the ground that the BIT was incorporated under the laws of that country only and not the nationality of the controlling shareholders or siege social.[126] The control test shall not be used to narrow the definition of investor under the BIT because the 'preamble expresses the Contracting Party's intent to "intensify economic cooperation to the mutual benefit of both States" and "create and maintain favourable conditions for investment by the investors of one State in the territory of the other State"'.[127] The Tribunal declared that there was no reason to pierce the corporate veil to find the true nationality of the corporation because the claimant corporation was not structured with the sole objective of gaining access of ICSID jurisdiction. The restructuring, as per the majority, was not for any improper purpose.[128] The President expressed a strong dissent. The interpretation of the majority was at odds with the object and purpose of the ICSID Convention and 'might jeopardize the future of the institution'.[129] In the words of the President of the Tribunal, the 'assumption that origin of capital is irrelevant flies in the face of object and purpose of the ICSID Convention, the Preamble and the Report of the Executive Directors.'[130] Further, the piercing of corporate veil need not happen only in cases of fraud, it may happen in situations which involve 'only and exclusively a question of giving effect to the object and purpose of the ICSID Convention....preserving its integrity'.[131] Although not the majority view, it does strongly emphasize the need of piercing corporate veil in certain situations. More so because ICSID has been time and again seen as a tool for promoting international public policy,[132] which will be defeated if misuse of its procedure is allowed.

---

123. *See* Andriy Alexeyev and Sergiy Vitocich, *Tokios Tokelés Vector: Jurisdictional Issues in ICSID Case Tokios Tokelés v. Ukraine*, 9 Journal of World Investment and Trade 519 (2008).
124. *Tokios Tokelés v. Ukraine*, *supra* n. 14, at para. 21.
125. *Ibid.*, at para. 22. Also *see* International Bank for Reconstruction and Development, *Report of the Executive Directors on the Convention on the Settlement of Disputes between States and Nationals of Other States*, paras 28-30 (2006) https://icsid.worldbank.org/en/Documents/resources/2006%20CRR_English-final.pdf (accessed 19 Jul. 2017).
126. *Ibid.*, at para. 30.
127. *Ibid.*, at para. 31.
128. *Ibid.*, at para. 56.
129. *Tokios Tokelés v. Ukraine*, Dissenting Opinion of Professor Prosper Weil, President, ICSID Case No. ARB/02/18, para. 1 (29 Apr. 2004).
130. *Ibid.*, at paras 6, 11.
131. *Ibid.*, at para. 25.
132. C.H. Schreuer, *The ICSID Convention: A Commentary*, 137 (2nd ed., Cambridge University Press 2009).

Prospective planning where there is a threat of nationalization, etc. would be permitted.[133] 'Prospective' means, before disputes have arisen.[134] If transfer is made after the dispute has arisen to seek benefit of the BIT then there is no requirement of protection.[135] Any transfer of ownership has to be bona fide.[136]

'Denial of benefits clauses' are used to exclude the benefits of a treaty to a company incorporated in a State but without any economic connection to that State.[137] The denial of benefits clause ensures that the foreign investor has a genuine link to the home State. The Model BIT of 2015 expressly includes this clause in the following words:

> Article 35. A Party may at any time, including after the institution of arbitration proceedings in accordance with Chapter IV of this Treaty, deny the benefits of this Treaty to:
> (i) an investment or investor owned or controlled, directly or indirectly, by persons of a non-Party or of the denying Party; or
> (ii) an investment or investor that has been established or restructured with the primary purpose of gaining access to the dispute resolution mechanisms provided in this Treaty.

The provisions in the Model BIT thus aim to reduce the possibility of abuse of the BIT particularly by shell or mailbox companies or investors of the home State trying to sue the home State through corporate entities incorporated in another State.

---

133. *Mobil Corporation, Venezuela Holdings, B.V., Mobil Cerro Negro Holding, Ltd., Mobil Venezolana de Petróleos Holdings, Inc., Mobil Cerro Negro, Ltd., and Mobil Venezolana de Petróleos, Inc. v. Bolivarian Republic of Venezuela*, Decision on Jurisdiction, ICSID Case No. ARB/07/27, paras 187-92, 200-5 (10 Jun. 2010); *Millicom International Operations B.V. and Sentel GSM SA v. The Republic of Senegal*, Decision on Jurisdiction, ICSID Case No. ARB/08/20, para. 84 (16 Jul. 2010).
134. *Société Générale In respect of DR Energy Holdings Limited and Empresa Distribuidora de Electricidad del Este, S.A. v. The Dominican Republic*, Decision on Jurisdiction, LCIA Case No. UN 7927, paras 109-10 (19 Sept. 2008).
135. *Banro American Resources, Inc. and Société Aurifère du Kivu et du Maniema S.A.R.L. v. Democratic Republic of the Congo*, Award, ICSID Case No. ARB/98/7 (1 Sept. 2000); *Phoenix Action, Ltd. v. The Czech Republic*, supra n. 68, at paras 142-4.
136. *Cementownia 'Nowa Huta' S.A. v. Republic of Turkey*, Award, ICSID Case No. ARB(AF)/06/2, paras 117, 156 (17 Sept. 2009).
137. *Supra* n. 19, at 55.

CHAPTER 5
Treatment Standards

Treatment standards are the legal standards according to which the host State must treat foreign investors. If the treatment of the foreign investors by the host State falls below these standards, then the host State is responsible for the breach of the BIT. They are the substantive provisions of an investment treaty, based on which the actions of the host State are checked. Treatment standards are the only substantive provisions that are enforceable. What is tested by the treatment standards are actions of the host State that are applied to foreign investors. These actions of the host State are generally referred to as 'measures'. The kinds of actions covered under a 'measure' are broad and include actions of all branches of government: executive, legislature and judiciary, and all levels of government: federal, provincial or local. The Indian Model BIT defines 'measure' as one which 'includes a law, regulation, rule, procedure, decision, administrative action, requirement or practice'.[1] The action which is alleged to be violating a treatment standard should fall within one of the categories mentioned in the definition of a 'measure'.

Indian BITs previously contained many standards of treatment. The most prominent amongst them were expropriation, fair and equitable treatment (FET), full protection and security (FPS), most favoured nation (MFN) and national treatment (NT). From these the 2015 Model BIT does not contain FET and MFN treatment. It continues expropriation and FPS, albeit with changes. NT has been continued as well and a new provision, an abridged form of international minimum standard is introduced. It is not clear from negotiations with other States whether the old treatment standards will continue or not. Therefore, for a holistic discussion, the contents of past BITs are discussed along with the contents of the 2015 Model BIT. In addition to discussing treaty provisions, this chapter will also elucidate the treatment standards

---

1. Ministry of Commerce and Industry, Government of India, *Model Text for the Indian Bilateral Investment Treaty*, Art. 1.8, http://indiainbusiness.nic.in/newdesign/upload/Model_BIT.pdf (accessed 1 Jul. 2017).

developed and applied in domestic law of India. This discussion is important since an investment tribunal has to apply international law as well as the law of the host State.[2]

§5.01 EXPROPRIATION

Expropriation is the oldest and prominent treatment standard. It exists in all BITs and has existed in the Friendship, Commerce and Navigation Treaties that preceded the modern-day BITs.[3]

Expropriation is the process whereby the government or any of its bodies takes over private property, which it may transfer to itself or to a third person. Expropriation is a wider concept and subsumes nationalization. Nationalization may be defined as 'a situation in which a State embarks on a wholesale taking of the property of foreigners to end their economic domination of the whole economy or of sectors of the economy' and expropriation as 'a specific term that could be used to describe the targeting of individual businesses for interference for specific economic or other reasons'.[4] Nationalization may involve either the taking away of the private property by the State or taking over of an activity such as banking, insurance, etc.[5]

As was discussed in Chapter 2 above, the period of 1960s and 1970s was the period when the newly independent States were trying to take back control of economic resources and industries that were mostly owned by the former colonial powers from foreign investors through nationalization. This was the time when the newly independent States announced the New International Economic Order (NIEO) and various General Assembly resolutions within that umbrella. Through these resolutions, the newly independent States announced that in international law they have the right to expropriate property. The BITs sought to undo the situation created by the NIEO. The elementary concern of the BITs was to insulate the effect of expropriation and in particular, the amount of compensation payable for expropriatory actions of the host State. Over the last few decades, instances of nationalization or expropriation have been few. States are keen on projecting themselves as pro-investment and pro-business. An expropriatory measure may create concern in the mind of foreign investors. This however may not be the case in future. With increase in economic nationalism, especially in the former capitalist and liberal economies, expropriation may not have lost its relevance entirely.

---

2. Applicable laws and the relationship between domestic law and international law was discussed in detail in Chapter 4.
3. For example, Treaty of Amity, Commerce and Navigation, United States-Congo, Art. 3 (24 Jan. 1891) 27 Stat. 926, T.S. No. 60; Treaty of Friendship, Commerce and Navigation, US-Nicaragua, Art. 9 (21 Jun. 1867), 15 Stat. 549, T S. 257.
4. M. Sornarajah, *The International Law on Foreign Investment*, 365-6 (3rd ed., Cambridge University Press 2010). A similar definition is proposed by Sacerdoti: 'By expropriation is meant the coercive appropriation by the State of private property, usually by means of individual administrative measures. Nationalizations do not differ in substance from expropriation except that they are directly statutorily based and have a wide coverage.' *See* G. Sacerdoti, *Bilateral Treaties and Multilateral Instruments on Investment Protection*, Recueil des Cours 261, 379 (1997); *See also* Ian Brownlie, *Principles of Public International Law*, 537 (7th ed., Oxford University Press 2008).
5. Konstantin Katzarov, *The Theory of Nationalisation*, 141-2 (Martinus Nijhoff 1964).

[A] Expropriation Provisions in Investment Treaties

The expropriation provision in the 2015 Model BIT is far more detailed than the earlier BITs. It would be appropriate to first analyse past BITs in order to properly appreciate the changes and the reasons for the changes brought about in the 2015 Model BIT.

Majority of investment treaties of the past contained a standard clause on expropriation and possessed five characteristics. First, they included direct and indirect expropriation or nationalization, and measures having effect equivalent to expropriation or nationalization. Second, they laid down conditions for legal expropriation. Third, they contained the standard of compensation payable in case of expropriation, along with interest. Fourth, they provided a right to the foreign investors to approach domestic courts or any other authority for challenging the measure undertaken by the host State that amounts to expropriation or nationalization; and an expectation that the domestic courts would decide the matter expeditiously. Fifth, they contained a provision that the shareholders of the contracting party would have a right to claim compensation to extent of losses they suffered due to expropriation of a company in which they held shares. There are variations within this framework, but this framework is consistent. A standard formulation would be:

> Investments of investors of either Contracting Party shall not be nationalized, expropriated or subjected to measures having effect equivalent to nationalization or expropriation (hereafter referred to as 'expropriation').[6]

Therefore, the scope of expropriatory measures covered are direct, indirect or having effect equivalent to expropriation. The Kuwait-India BIT also uses 'dispossession', in addition to nationalization and expropriation. It says: '…shall not be nationalized, expropriate, dispossessed or subjected to direct or indirect measures having

---

6. Agreement between the Government of the Republic of India and the Government of the Kingdom of Bahrain for the Promotion and Protection of Investments, Art. 5.1 (signed 13 Jan. 2004, entered into force 5 Dec. 2007); Agreement between the Government of the Republic of India and the Government of the People's Republic of Bangladesh for the Promotion and Protection of Investments, Art. 5.1 (signed 9 Feb. 2009, entered into force 7 Jul. 2011); Agreement between the Government of the Republic of India and the Government of the Republic of Bulgaria for the Promotion and Protection of Investments, Art. 5.1 (signed 29 Oct. 1998, entered into force 23 Sept. 1999); Agreement between the Government of the Republic of India and the Government of the Democratic Republic of Congo for the Mutual Promotion and Protection of Investments, Art. 5.1 (signed 13 Apr. 2010); Agreement between the Government of the Republic of India and the Government of Republic of Cyprus for the Mutual Promotion and Protection of Investments, Art. 5.1 (signed 9 Apr. 2002, entered into force 12 Jan. 2004); Agreement between the Czech Republic and the Republic of India for the Promotion and Protection of Investments, Art. 4.1 (signed 11 Oct. 1996, entered into force 6 Feb. 1998); Agreement between the Federal Republic of Germany and the Republic of India for the Promotion and Protection of Investments, Art. 5.1 (signed 10 Jul. 1995, entered into force 13 Jul. 1998); Agreement between the Republic of Hungary and the Republic of India for the Promotion and Protection of Investments, Art. 5.1 (signed 3 Nov. 2003, entered into force 2 Jan. 2006); Agreement between the Government of the Republic of India and the Government of the Republic of Korea on the Promotion and Protection of Investments, Art. 5.1 (signed 26 Feb. 1996, entered into force 7 May 1996).

effect equivalent to nationalization, expropriation or dispossession (hereinafter collectively referred as expropriation).'[7] Despite the use of dispossession, since all these terms are collectively referred to as 'expropriation', mere dispossession is insufficient. Dispossession has to have a characteristic of expropriation. Except for the India-Austria BIT, which is limited to direct expropriation,[8] rest of the BITs include indirect expropriation and measures having effect equivalent to expropriation.

Majority of the expropriation clauses use the phrase 'having effect equivalent to'. In the India-Columbia BIT, 'measure having effect equivalent to' has been replaced by 'other having similar effects' – which does not make much difference in terms of the effect.[9] The Mexico-India BIT uses 'tantamount to expropriation or nationalization' in the place of 'effect equivalent to'.[10] The India-Nepal BIT uses 'or any other measure having similar effects'.[11] The India-Qatar BIT says: '[t]he investments shall not be subject, either directly or indirectly, to any act of expropriation or nationalization or to any other procedure of similar effects'.[12] In the India-Armenia BIT, in addition to expropriation and nationalization, alienation is also used. However, it is clarified that "alienation" shall have the same meaning as "expropriation" or "nationalization"'.[13] In fact the expropriation clause is titled as 'alienation'. Therefore, although alienation is used, the treatment standard is limited to situations of traditional expropriation.

Most of the older BITs do not contain a definition or explanation of expropriation or indirect expropriation. The scope of indirect expropriation has been a matter of

---

7. Agreement between the State of Kuwait and the Republic of India for the Encouragement and Reciprocal Protection of Investment, Art. 7.1 (signed 27 Nov. 2001, entered into force 28 Jun. 2003).
8. Agreement between the Government of the Republic of Austria and the Government of the Republic of India for the Promotion and Protection of Investments, art 4.1 (signed 8 Nov. 1999, entered into force 1 Mar. 2001). It says: 'Investments of investor of either Contracting Party shall not be expropriated in the territory of the other Contracting Party'. The same language is used in Art. 6.1 of the India-Slovenia BIT: Agreement between the Government of the Republic of India and the Government of the Republic of Slovenia on the Mutual Promotion and Protection of Investments, Art. 6.1 (signed 14 Jun. 2011).
9. Agreement for the Promotion and Protection of Investments between the Republic of Columbia and the Republic of India, Art. 6.1 (signed 10 Nov. 2009, entered into force 2 Jul. 2012); Agreement between the Republic of Turkey and the Republic of India Concerning the Reciprocal Promotion and Protection of Investments, Art. 3.1 (signed 17 Sept. 1988, entered into force 18 Oct. 2007); Agreement between the Government of the Republic of India and the Government of the Republic of Yemen for the Promotion and Protection of Investments, Art. 5.1 (signed 1 Oct. 2002, entered into force 10 Feb. 2004).
10. Agreement between the Government of the United Mexican States and the Government of the Republic of India on the Promotion and Protection of Investments, Art. 7.1 (signed 21 May 2007, entered into force 23 Feb. 2008); Agreement between the Government of the Republic of India and Government of the Kingdom of Saudi Arabia Concerning the Encouragement and Reciprocal Protection of Investments, Art. 4.1 (signed 25 Jan. 2006, entered into force 20 May 2008).
11. Agreement between the Government of India and the Government of Nepal for the Promotion and Protection of Investments, Art. 5.1 (signed 21 Oct. 2011).
12. Agreement between the Government of the Republic of India and the Government of the State of Qatar for the Reciprocal Promotion and Protection of Investments, Art. 5.1 (signed 7 Apr. 1999, entered into force 15 Dec. 1999).
13. Agreement between the Government of the Republic of India and the Government of the Republic of Armenia for the Promotion and Protection of Investments, Explanation to Art. 5 (signed 23 May 2003, entered into force 30 May 2006).

debate in the field of international investment law.[14] The trend amongst investment tribunals has been to interpret indirect expropriation liberally and hold the host State responsible, based on the impact of the measure rather than looking at the basis for the measure or the nature of the measure.[15] All BITs entered into by India reflect clearly that the impact of the measure shall be the consequence of a measure undertaken for nationalization or expropriation. Only one BIT emphasizes solely on the impact of the measure, irrespective of what measure causes that effect, which is the India-France BIT. The clause on expropriation is as under:

> Neither Contracting Party shall take any measure of expropriation or nationalisation or any other measures having the effect of dispossession, direct or indirect, of investors of the other Contracting Party of their investments in its area, except in the public interest and provided that these measures are not discriminatory or contrary to a specific obligation entered into by Contracting Party not to take a measure of dispossession.[16]

To counter this problem some recent BITs provided an explanation of expropriation.[17] This practice of explaining contents of expropriation started with the US Model BIT of 2012. The 2015 Model BIT of India provides the following elements of expropriation:

> Article 5.3: The Parties confirm their shared understanding that:
>
> a) Expropriation may be direct or indirect:
>   (i) direct expropriation occurs when an investment is nationalised or otherwise directly expropriated through formal transfer of title or outright seizure; and
>   (ii) indirect expropriation occurs if a measure or series of measures of a Party has an effect equivalent to direct expropriation, in that it substantially or permanently deprives the investor of the fundamental attributes of property in its investment, including the right to use, enjoy and dispose of its investment, without formal transfer of title or outright seizure.
> b) The determination of whether a measure or a series of measures have an effect equivalent to expropriation requires a case-by-case, fact-based inquiry, that takes into consideration:
>   (i) the economic impact of the measure or series of measures, although the sole fact that a measure or series of measures of a Party has an adverse

---

14. *See* Sebastian López Escarcena, *Indirect Expropriation in International Law* (Edward Elgar Publishing Limited 2014).
15. The practice of looking at the impact of the measure is called the sole effects doctrine. Rudolf Dolzer and Christoph Schreuer, *Principles of International Investment Law*, 104-15, 125-6 (2nd ed., Oxford University Press 2012). The doctrine originated in the jurisprudence of the Iran-US Claims Tribunal in peculiar situations – very different than BITs. *See* Aniruddha Rajput, *Problems with the Jurisprudence of Iran-US Claims Tribunal on Indirect Expropriation*, 30 ICSID Review 589-615 (2015).
16. Agreement between the Government of the Republic of India and the Government of the Republic of France on the Reciprocal Promotion and Protection of Investments, Art. 6.1 (signed 2 Sept. 1997, entered into force 17 May 2000).
17. *See* Agreement between the Government of the Republic of India and the Government of the People's Republic of China for the Promotion and Protection of Investments (signed 21 Nov. 2006, entered into force 1 Sept. 2007); Agreement between the Government of India and the Government of Nepal for the Promotion and Protection of Investments, *supra* n. 11, at Art. 5.2.

effect on the economic value of an investment does not establish that an indirect expropriation has occurred;
(ii) the duration of the measure or series of measures of a Party;
(iii) the character of the measure or series of measures, notably their object, context and intent; and
(iv) whether a measure by a Party breaches the Party's prior binding written commitment to the investor whether by contract, licence or other legal document.

While the host State cannot undertake a measure that is expropriatory in one of the manners stated above, a State is entitled to expropriate property. But if a State expropriates a foreigner's property then in order for it to be a legal expropriation, some conditions have to be satisfied. Majority of the BITs contained provisions similar to the India-Bahrain BIT: 'public purpose, in accordance with law on a non-discriminatory basis and against fair and equitable compensation'.[18] Other conditions are: (a) public purpose, (b) non-discriminatory, (c) due process, and (d) compensation according to the laws of the host country. The India-Austria BIT refers to: 'public purpose on a non-discriminatory basis in accordance with law and against payment of compensation'.[19] The India-UAE BIT uses: '…public purpose related to the internal needs of that Contracting State and against expeditious, adequate and effective compensation and on a condition that such Measures are taken on a non-discriminatory basis and in accordance with the procedure established under law.'[20] The India-Lithuania BIT talks of: 'public purpose in accordance with law on a non-discriminatory basis and against

---

18. Agreement between the Government of the Republic of India and the Government of the Kingdom of Bahrain for the Promotion and Protection of Investments, *supra* n. 6, at Art. 7.1; Agreement between the Government of the Republic of India and the Government of the People's Republic of Bangladesh for the Promotion and Protection of Investments, *supra* n. 6, at Art. 5.1; Agreement between the Government of the Republic of India and the Government of the Republic of Belarus for the Promotion and Protection of Investments, Art. 5.1 (signed 27 Nov. 2002, entered into force 23 Nov. 2003; Agreement for the Promotion and Protection of Investments between the Republic of Columbia and the Republic of India, *supra* n. 9, at Art. 6.1; Agreement between the Government of the Republic of India and the Government of the Kingdom of Denmark Concerning the Promotion and Reciprocal Protection of Investments, Art. 5.1 (signed 6 Sept. 1995, entered into force 13 May 1996); Agreement between the Government of the Republic of India and the Government of the Republic of Djibouti for the Promotion and Protection of Investments, Art. 5.1 (signed 19 May 2003); Agreement between the Government of the Republic of Indonesia and the Government of the Republic of India for the Promotion and Protection of Investments, Art. 5.1 (signed 10 Feb. 1999, entered into force 22 Jan. 2004); Agreement between the Government of the Republic of India and the Government of the Republic of Ghana for the Reciprocal Promotion and Protection of Investments, Art. 5.1 signed (5 Aug. 2002); Agreement between the Government of the Republic of India and the Hashemite Kingdom of Jordan for the Promotion and Protection of Investments, Art. 5.1 (signed 30 Nov 2006, entered into force 22 Jan. 2009).
19. Agreement between the Government of the Republic of Austria and the Government of the Republic of India for the Promotion and Protection of Investments, *supra* n. 8, at Art. 4.1.
20. Agreement between the Government of the Republic of India and the Government of the United Arab Emirates on the Promotion and Protection of Investments, Art. 7.1(a) (signed 12 Dec. 2013, entered into force 21 Aug. 2014); Agreement between the State of Kuwait and the Republic of India for the Encouragement and Reciprocal Protection of Investment, *supra* n. 7, at Art. 7.1.

Chapter 5: Treatment Standards §5.01[A]

prompt, adequate and effective compensation'.[21] The India-France BIT uses: 'public interest...not discriminatory or contrary to specific obligations entered into by Contracting Party not to take a measure of dispossession'.[22]

These textual differences could not make a difference unless the difference has a substantive implication.

The extent of compensation payable and its computation differed between treaties. Different standards were adopted for determination of compensation and interest payable in situations of expropriation. The compensation 'shall amount to the genuine value of the investment',[23] 'compensation shall amount to market value of the investment',[24] 'compensation shall be determined in accordance with generally recognized principles of valuation and equitable principles taking into account the capital invested, depreciation, capital already repatriated, replacement value, and other relevant factors',[25] compensation to be determined 'in accordance with generally recognised principles of valuation';[26] 'adequate and reasonably prompt compensation, the amount of which shall be equal to the real value of the investments concerned and shall be set, indicating conditions of payment, in accordance with the normal economic situation prevailing prior to any threat of dispossession';[27] 'real market value';[28] 'such compensation shall amount to the fair market value of the investment

---

21. Agreement between the Government of the Republic of India and the Government of the Republic of Lithuania for the Promotion and Protection of Investments, Art. 5.1 (signed 31 Mar. 2011, entered into force 1 Dec. 2011); *See also* Agreement between the Government of the Republic of India and the Government of Malaysia for the Promotion and Protection of Investments, Art. 5.1 (signed 3 Aug. 1995, entered into force 12 Apr. 1997).
22. Agreement between the Government of the Republic of India and the Government of the Republic of France on the Reciprocal Promotion and Protection of Investments, *supra* n. 16, at Art. 6.1.
23. Agreement between the Government of the Republic of Austria and the Government of the Republic of India for the Promotion and Protection of Investments, *supra* n. 8, at Art. 5.1; Agreement between the Government of the Republic of India and the Government of the Kingdom of Bahrain for the Promotion and Protection of Investments, *supra* n. 6, at Art. 5.1; Agreement between the Government of the Republic of India and the Government of the Republic of Belarus for the Promotion and Protection of Investments, *supra* n. 18, at Art. 5.1; Agreement between the Government of the Republic of India and the Government of the People's Republic of China for the Promotion and Protection of Investments, *supra* n. 17, at Art. 5.1; Agreement between the Government of the Republic of India and the Government of the Arab Republic of Egypt for the Promotion and Reciprocal Protection of Investments, Art. 4.1 (signed 9 Apr. 1997, entered into force 22 Nov. 2000).
24. Agreement between the Government of the Republic of India and the Government of the People's Republic of Bangladesh for the Promotion and Protection of Investments, *supra* n. 6, at Art. 5.1.
25. Agreement between the Government of Australia and the Government of the Republic of India on the Promotion and Protection of Investments, Art. 7.2 (signed 26 Feb. 1999, entered into force 4 May 2000, Art. 7.2).
26. Agreement between the Government of the Republic of Austria and the Government of the Republic of India for the Promotion and Protection of Investments, *supra* n. 8, at Art. 4.2.
27. Agreement between the Government of the Republic of India and the Government of the Republic of France on the Reciprocal Promotion and Protection of Investments, *supra* n. 16, at Art. 6.2.
28. Agreement between the Government of the Republic of India and the Government of the State of Qatar for the Reciprocal Promotion and Protection of Investments, *supra* n. 12, at Art. 5.2.

expropriated...Where the market value cannot be ascertained properly, the compensation shall be determined in accordance with internationally recognised accounting principles';[29] compensation shall be 'equivalent to the fair market value of the investment expropriated';[30] 'fair value of the investments expropriated';[31] 'such compensation shall amount to the value of the investment expropriated'.[32] The Germany-India BIT only uses compensation, without any prefix.[33] The India-Finland BIT uses 'effective and adequate compensation'.[34] The Hungary-India BIT uses: 'fair compensation'.[35] The India-Portugal BIT states: 'by virtue of law, for a public purpose, on a non-discriminatory basis and against prompt compensation'.[36] The Kuwait-India BIT states that: 'compensation shall amount to the actual value of the expropriated investment and shall be determined and computed on the basis of the fair market value'.[37]

All the BITs imposed the obligation to make the payment expeditiously in a manner convertible and that could be withdrawn. The procedure of valuation differed between the BITs. It was payable as per the value of the property immediately before the expropriation or before the impending alienation became public, whichever is earlier. 'Valuation criteria shall include, without implying the exclusive validity of any single criteria, the going concern value, asset value, including declared tax value of tangible property, and other criteria, as appropriate, to determine the fair market value.'[38] The India-Brunei BIT states: 'Where the market value cannot be ascertained

---

29. Agreement between the Government of the Republic of India and the Government of His Majesty the Sultan and Yang Di-Pertuan of Brunei Darussalam on the Reciprocal Promotion and Protection of Investments, Art. 5.1 (signed 22 May 2009, entered into force 18 Jan. 2009).
30. Agreement for the Promotion and Protection of Investments between the Republic of Columbia and the Republic of India, *supra* n. 9, at Art. 6.3; Agreement between the Government of the Republic of India and the Government of the Republic of Finland on the Promotion and Protection of Investments, Art. 5.2 (signed 7 Nov. 2002, entered into force 9 Apr. 2003); Agreement between the Government of the Republic of India and the Government of the Republic of Latvia for the Promotion and Protection of Investments, Art. 5.1 (signed 18 Feb. 2010, entered into force 27 Nov. 2011).
31. Agreement between the Government of the Republic of India and the Government of Republic of Cyprus for the Mutual Promotion and Protection of Investments, *supra* n. 6, at Art. 5.1.
32. Agreement between the Czech Republic and the Republic of India for the Promotion and Protection of Investments, *supra* n. 6, at Art. 4.1; Agreement between the Federal Republic of Germany and the Republic of India for the Promotion and Protection of Investments, *supra* n. 6, at Art. 5.1.
33. Agreement between the Federal Republic of Germany and the Republic of India for the Promotion and Protection of Investments, *supra* n. 6, Art. 5.1; Agreement between the Republic of India and the Kingdom of the Netherlands for the Promotion and Protection of Investments, Art. 5.1 (signed 6 Nov. 1995, entered into force 1 Dec. 1996).
34. Agreement between the Government of the Republic of India and the Government of the Republic of Finland on the Promotion and Protection of Investments, *supra* n. 30, at Art. 5.1.
35. Agreement between the Republic of Hungary and the Republic of India for the Promotion and Protection of Investments, *supra* n. 6, at Art. 5.1.
36. Agreement between the Portuguese Republic and the Republic of India on the Mutual Promotion and Protection of Investments, Art. 5.1 (signed 28 Jun. 2000, entered into force 19 Jul. 2002).
37. Agreement between the State of Kuwait and the Republic of India for the Encouragement and Reciprocal Protection of Investment, *supra* n. 7, at Art. 7.1(b).
38. Agreement between the Government of the United Mexican States and the Government of the Republic of India on the Promotion and Protection of Investments, *supra* n. 10, at Art. 7.2(a).

properly the compensation shall be determined in accordance with internationally recognised accounting principles.'[39]

Interest was also payable on the amount of compensation but its rate differed from one BIT to another. The manner and amount of interest contemplated follows a different pattern in different BITs. Most BITs used the formula of 'fair and equitable rate of interest';[40] 'fair rate';[41] 'normal market rate';[42] 'appropriate market rate';[43]

---

39. Agreement between the Government of the Republic of India and the Government of His Majesty the Sultan and Yang Di-Pertuan of Brunei Darussalam on the Reciprocal Promotion and Protection of Investments, *supra* n. 29, at Art. 5.1.
40. Agreement between the Government of the Republic of India and the Government of the Republic of Armenia for the Promotion and Protection of Investments, *supra* n. 13, at Art. 5.1; Agreement between the Government of the Republic of India and the Government of the Kingdom of Bahrain for the Promotion and Protection of Investments, *supra* n. 6, at Art. 7.1; Agreement between the Government of the Republic of India and the Government of the People's Republic of China for the Promotion and Protection of Investments, *supra* n. 17, at Art. 5.1; Agreement between the Government of the Republic of India and the Government of the Democratic Republic of Congo for the Mutual Promotion and Protection of Investments, *supra* n. 6, at Art. 5.1; *See* Agreement between the Government of the Republic of Croatia and the Government of the Republic of India for the Promotion and Reciprocal Protection of Investments (signed 19 Jan. 2002, entered into force 25 Apr. 2017); Agreement between the Government of the Republic of India and the Government of the Republic of Djibouti for the Promotion and Protection of Investments, *supra* n. 18, at Art. 5.1; Agreement between the Republic of India and the Federal Democratic Republic of Ethiopia for the Reciprocal Promotion and Protection of Investments, Art. 5.1 (signed 5 Jul. 2007); Agreement between the Government of the Republic of India and the Government of the Republic of Iceland for the Promotion and Protection of Investments, Art. 5.1 (signed 29 Jun. 2007, entered into force 16 Dec. 2008); Agreement between the Government of the Republic of India and the Government of the State of Israel for the Promotion and Protection of Investments, Art. 5.1 (signed 29 Jan. 1996, entered into force 18 Feb. 1997); Agreement between the Government of the Republic of India and the Government of the Lao People's Democratic Republic for the Promotion and Protection of Investments, Art. 5.1 (signed 9 Nov. 2000, entered into force 5 Jan. 2003); Agreement between the Government of the Sultanate of Oman and the Government of the Republic of India for the Promotion and Protection of Investments, Art. 5.1 (signed 2 Apr. 1997, entered into force 13 Oct. 2000); Agreement between the Government of the Kingdom of Thailand and the Government of the Republic of India for the Promotion and Protection of Investments, Art. 6.1 (signed 10 Jul. 2000, entered into force 13 Jul. 2001); Agreement between the Government of the Republic of India and the Government of the Republic of Ghana for the Reciprocal Promotion and Protection of Investments, *supra* n. 18, at Art. 5.1.
41. Agreement between the Republic of Hungary and the Republic of India for the Promotion and Protection of Investments, *supra* n. 6, at Art. 5.1.
42. Agreement between the Government of Australia and the Government of the Republic of India on the Promotion and Protection of Investments, *supra* n. 25, at Art. 7.3; Agreement between the Government of the Republic of India and the Government of the People's Republic of Bangladesh for the Promotion and Protection of Investments, *supra* n. 6, at Art. 5.1; Agreement between the Government of the Republic of India and the Government of the Republic of Latvia for the Promotion and Protection of Investments, *supra* n. 30, at Art. 5.1; Agreement between the Portuguese Republic and the Republic of India on the Mutual Promotion and Protection of Investments, *supra* n. 36, at Art. 5.2.
43. Agreement between the Government of the Republic of India and the Government of the Republic of France on the Reciprocal Promotion and Protection of Investments, *supra* n. 16, at Art. 6.3.

'prevailing market rate';[44] 'prevailing rate';[45] 'interest at prevailing rate';[46] 'interest at a commercial rate established on a market basis';[47] 'commercially reasonable rate';[48] 'usual commercial interest';[49] 'interest calculated in the LIBOR basis';[50] 'interest at the prevailing commercial market rate, however, in no event less than the prevailing six months LIBOR';[51] 'rate applicable in the territory of that Contracting Party until the date of payment';[52] 'interest at prevailing commercial rate as agreed upon by both parties unless such rate is prescribed by law'.[53] The 2015 Model BIT requires that the compensation shall be adequate and 'at lease equivalent to the fair market value' on the day before expropriation takes place and 'shall not reflect any change in value occurring because the intended expropriation had become known earlier'.[54] The 2015 Model BIT gives the discretion to the host State to decide whether it wants to give compensation equivalent to the market value. At the same time, the fluctuation in

---

44. Agreement between the Government of the Republic of India and the Government of Republic of Cyprus for the Mutual Promotion and Protection of Investments, *supra* n. 6, at Art. 5.1.
45. Agreement between the Republic of Turkey and the Republic of India Concerning the Reciprocal Promotion and Protection of Investments, *supra* n. 9, at Art. 5.2.
46. Agreement between the Government of the Republic of Indonesia and the Government of the Republic of India for the Promotion and Protection of Investments, *supra* n. 18, at Art. 5.1.
47. Agreement between the Government of the Republic of Austria and the Government of the Republic of India for the Promotion and Protection of Investments, *supra* n. 8, at Art. 4.2; Agreement between the Government of the Republic of India and the Government of the Kingdom of Denmark Concerning the Promotion and Reciprocal Protection of Investments, *supra* n. 18, at Art. 5.2; Agreement between the Government of the Republic of India and the Government of the Republic of Finland on the Promotion and Protection of Investments, *supra* n. 30, at Art. 5.2; Agreement between the Federal Republic of Germany and the Republic of India for the Promotion and Protection of Investments, *supra* n. 6, at Art. 5.1; Agreement between the Government of the Russian Federation and the Government of the Republic of India for the Promotion and Mutual Protection of Investments, Art. 5.2 (signed 23 Dec. 1994, entered into force 5 Aug. 1996).
48. Agreement for the Promotion and Protection of Investments between the Republic of Columbia and the Republic of India, *supra* n. 9, at Art. 6.3; Agreement between the Government of India and the Government of Nepal for the Promotion and Protection of Investments, *supra* n. 11, at Art. 6.3.
49. Agreement between the Government of the Republic of India and the Government of the Republic of Zimbabwe Concerning the Promotion and Reciprocal Protection of Investments, Art. 4.2 (signed 10 Feb. 1999).
50. Agreement between the Government of the Republic of India and the Government of the Republic of Belarus for the Promotion and Protection of Investments, *supra* n. 18, at Art. 5.1; Agreement between the Government of the Republic of India and Government of the Republic of Macedonia for the Promotion and Reciprocal Protection of Investments, Art. 5.1 (signed 17 Mar. 2008, entered into force 17 Nov. 2008).
51. Agreement between the State of Kuwait and the Republic of India for the Encouragement and Reciprocal Protection of Investment, *supra* n. 7, at Art. 7.1(b); Agreement between the Government of the Republic of India and the Government of the State of Qatar for the Reciprocal Promotion and Protection of Investments, *supra* n. 12, at Art. 5.2; Agreement between the Government of the Republic of India and the Government of the United Arab Emirates on the Promotion and Protection of Investments, *supra* n. 20, at Art. 7.1(b).
52. Agreement between the Government of the Republic of India and the Government of the Republic of Bulgaria for the Promotion and Protection of Investments, *supra* n. 6, at Art. 5.1.
53. Agreement between the Government of the Republic of India and the Government of Malaysia for the Promotion and Protection of Investments, *supra* n. 21, at Art. 5.1(c).
54. Ministry of Commerce and Industry, Government of India, *Model Text for the Indian Bilateral Investment Treaty*, *supra* n. 1, at Art. 5.1.

Chapter 5: Treatment Standards §5.01[A]

value caused due to prior knowledge of expropriation does not affect the amount of compensation as per the 2015 Model BIT. Normally, the decision to expropriate in cases of direct expropriation is public and the value of the property gets affected. This does not apply in situations of indirect expropriation. The 2015 Model BIT provides a valuation criteria, which is:

> Valuation criteria shall include going concern value, asset value including declared tax value of tangible property, and other criteria, as appropriate, to determine fair market value.[55]

The 2015 Model BIT, that is now the basis of negotiations, has introduced the following provision on expropriation:

> 5.1 Neither Party may nationalize or expropriate an investment of an investor (hereinafter 'expropriate') of the other Party either directly or through measures having an effect equivalent to expropriation, except for reasons of public purpose, in accordance with the due process of law and on payment of adequate compensation. Such compensation shall be adequate and be at least equivalent to the fair market value of the expropriated investment immediately on the day before the expropriation takes place ('date of expropriation'), and shall not reflect any change in value occurring because the intended expropriation had become known earlier. Valuation criteria shall include going concern value, asset value including declared tax value of tangible property, and other criteria, as appropriate, to determine fair market value.
>
> 5.2 Payment of compensation shall be made in a freely convertible currency. Interest on payment of compensation, where applicable, shall be paid in simple interest at a commercially reasonable rate from the date of expropriation until the date of actual payment. On payment, compensation shall be freely transferable in accordance with Article 6. For the avoidance of doubt, where India is the expropriating Party, any measure of expropriation relating to land shall be for the purposes as set out in its Law relating to land acquisition and any questions as to 'public purpose' and compensation shall be determined in accordance with the procedure specified in such Law.

Problems are often faced in relation to expropriation and regulation. These are two different concepts. Expropriation relates to the exercise of 'eminent domain', whereas regulations are exercise of 'police powers'. The provisions on expropriation in the BIT are limited to eminent domain and do not cover police powers. It is incorrect to suggest that if the foreign investor suffers losses due to a legitimate regulatory exercise by the host State, it is an illegal expropriation. Regulatory freedom is a distinct rule of customary international law.[56]

---

55. *Ibid.*
56. *The Oscar Chinn Case (Belgium v. United Kingdom)* PCIJ Series A/B, No. 63, 65, 86, 88 (1934); *Emanuel Too v. Greater Modesto Insurance Associates*, Award No. 460-880-2, 29,23 Iran-USCTR 378, 378-9 (1989); *Sea-Land Service, Inc v. The Islamic Republic of Iran*, Award No. 135-33-1, 6 Iran-USCTR 149, 150-4 (1984); *Marvin Feldman v. Mexico*, Award, ICSID Case No. ARB (AF)/99/1, paras 98-100 (16 Dec. 2002); *Saluka Investments BV (The Netherlands) v. The Czech Republic*, Permanent Court of Arbitration, Partial Award, Mar. paras 256-61(17 Mar. 2006); *Link-Trading Joint Stock Company v. Department for Customs Control of Moldova*, Final Award,

The 2015 Model BIT excludes regulatory freedom as well as some other categories of State actions from the purview of expropriation. Non-discriminatory measures and judicial decisions 'that are designed and applied to protect legitimate public interest or public purpose objectives such as public health, safety and the environment shall not constitute expropriation'.[57] The 2015 Model BIT excludes impact of actions taken by the host State in commercial capacity.[58] This would ensure that the host State would not be responsible for losses caused to foreign investors due to participation of State-owned enterprises in economic activity by itself or through a public corporation.

[B] Expropriation under Domestic Law of India

The right to property has drastically transformed during the life of the Constitution of India. At the time of the commencement of the Constitution, the right to property was a 'fundamental right' recognized under Articles 19(1)(f) and 31 of the Constitution of India. Successive governments reduced its rigour through constitutional amendments until its character was changed from a 'fundamental right' to a 'legal right' through the amendment in 1978. The fundamental right status was removed by the Constitution (Forty-Fourth Amendment) Act, 1978. The Amendment declared that:

> Property, while ceasing to be a fundamental right, would, however, be given express recognition as a legal right, provision being made that no person shall be deprived of his property save in accordance with law.[59]

It is necessary to understand the reasons why the governments reduced the scope and subsequently the character of the right to property in the Indian constitutional structure. Due to the colonial past, there was concentration of property in the hands of few large land-owners (zamindars) and former rulers of princely states who had aligned themselves with the British government and exploited the masses. To achieve an equitable distribution of property and equitable growth of society, various measures were adopted by governments and necessary legislations were passed. The Government undertook steps to reconstruct the agrarian economy, whereby ownership rights were transferred from those who owned large tracts of lands to the tillers of those lands. Limitations on the extent of agricultural land an individual could possess were set out, and the surplus land was distributed amongst the landless. Second, to provide urban housing to all, clear the slums and achieve planned town development, limitations on the extent of land individuals could own in the urban areas was imposed. Third, for financial inclusion, some private banks were nationalized. Most of these

---

UNCITRAL, paras 64-71 (18 Apr. 2002); *Methanex Corporation v. United States of America*, Final Award of the Tribunal on Jurisdiction and Merits, UNCITRAL, Aug. Part IV-Chapter D (3 Aug. 2005).
57. Ministry of Commerce and Industry, Government of India, *Model Text for the Indian Bilateral Investment Treaty, supra* n. 1, at Art. 5.5.
58. *Ibid.*, at Art. 5.4.
59. Constitution (Forty-Fourth) Constitutional Amendment Act (India), Statement of Object and Reasons, para. 5 (1978).

steps were taken to give effect to the Directive Principles of State Policy[60] contained in Part IV of the Constitution.[61] Even fundamental rights are not absolute and are amenable to reasonable restrictions in the interest of general public, and, accordingly the zamindari system was abolished in India.[62]

The difference between a constitutional and a fundamental right is that fundamental rights cannot be abridged by the Government. The Parliament may amend fundamental rights but it cannot amend those fundamental rights that constitute the basic feature of the Constitution.[63] The Constitution of India possesses some basic features which cannot be amended.[64] Right to property is not a basic feature of the Constitution of India and therefore it was open for amendment/alteration.[65] By placing fundamental rights in the group of mere legal rights, the prospects of its non-abridgability by the Government are reduced. This should not give the impression that the right has become redundant. It still carries value and is a way of checking arbitrary taking of property by the Government. It is therefore still very much an important right. As decided by the Supreme Court, 'the right to property is a human right as also a constitutional right. But it is not a fundamental right. Each and every claim to property would not be property right'.[66]

Capturing the consequences of the changes in the law, the Supreme Court has stated that:

> It would thus be clear that acquisition of the property by law laid in furtherance of the directive principles of State policy was to distribute the material resources of the community including acquisition and taking possession of private property for public purpose. It does not require payment of compensation or indemnification to the owner of the property expropriated. It is the very negation of the effectuating the public purpose. Payment of market value in lieu of acquired property is not *sine qua* non-for acquisition. Acquisition and payment of amount are part of the scheme and they cannot be dissected. However, fixation of the amount or specification of the principles and manner in which the amount is to be determined must be relevant to the fixation of amount. The amount determined need not bear reasonable relationship. In other words, it is not illusory. The adequacy of the resultant amount cannot be questioned in a Court of law. However, the validity of irrelevant principles are amenable to judicial scrutiny.[67]

Presently, the extent of protection of private property under domestic law of India is regulated by Article 300-A of the Constitution of India. It provides: 'No person shall be deprived of his property save by authority of law.'

Explaining the purport of Article 300-A, the Supreme Court has observed that:

---

60. Directive Principles on State Policy were the goals that the makers of the Indian Constitution had added to the Constitution, which the future governments were to achieve.
61. M.P. Jain, *Indian Constitutional Law*, Vol. 2 1802 (6th ed., revised by Samaraditya Pal and Ruma Pal, Lexis Nexis Butterworths Wadhwa 2010).
62. *K. T. Plantation (P) Ltd. v. State of Kerala* 9 SCC 1, para. 146 (2011).
63. *Keshavananda Bharati v. State of Kerala* 4 SCC 225 (1973).
64. Ibid.
65. *Jilubhai Nanbhai Khachar v. State of Gujarat* Supp. (1) SCC 596 (1995).
66. *Indian Handicrafts Emporium v. Union of India* 7 SCC 589, para. 111 (2003).
67. *Jilubhai Nanbhai Khachar v. State of Gujarat*, *supra* n. 65.

Article 300-A enables the State to put restrictions on the right to property by *law*. That law has to be reasonable. It must comply with other provisions of the Constitution. The limitation or restriction should not be arbitrary or excessive or what is beyond what is required in public interest. The limitation or restriction must not be disproportionate to the situation or excessive.[68]

There is no reference of need of compensation in Article 300-A. Whether compensation is to be provided and the amount thereof would depend on the laws in question. Article 300-A intends to control only the power of the Executive. Property cannot be deprived through an executive fiat.[69] The effect of Article 300-A is that the hands of Executive to expropriate property are tied. Property can be taken only by law and not by the Executive without any basis in the law.[70] There is an inherent right of the State to take away property without the consent of the owner.[71] But that cannot take place in an arbitrary manner and if compensation is not provided for, then there should be necessary and sufficient reasons provided for, in the statute that does not allow compensation.

The Courts have expressed the need that the measures of taking property will have to be reasonable, otherwise the Courts could strike down the order of taking of property, and direct payment of further compensation. The Constitution does not expect payment of compensation anymore. This does not mean that courts would not allow payment of compensation. These elements would be pubic purpose and compensation.[72] It would be too much to expect that the courts would grant compensation in each case. Such an interpretation would defeat the purpose of the constitutional amendment.[73] Also, the courts would not impose a certain standard of compensation.[74] As held by the Supreme Court:

> At this stage we may clarify that there is a difference between 'no' compensation and 'nil' compensation. A law seeking to acquire private property for public purposes cannot say that 'no compensation shall be paid'. However, there could be a law awarding 'nil' compensation in cases where the State undertakes to discharge the liabilities charged on the property under acquisition and onus is on the Government to establish validity of such law. In the latter case, the Court in exercise of judicial review will test such a law keeping in mind the above parameters.[75]

The court has continued to hold that the property cannot be deprived without compensation.[76] The first task after independence was abolition of zamindari – which involved taking away of private property. It was not possible to compensate the owners as per the market value, hence, the word compensation was not preceded by 'just' or

---

68. *K. T. Plantation (P) Ltd. v. State of Kerala*, supra n. 62, at para. 190.
69. *Bishamber Dayal Chandra Mohan v. State of Uttar Pradesh* 1 SCC 39 (1982).
70. *State of Mysore v. K. C. Adiga* (2) SCC 495 (1976); *Bishamber Dayal Chandra Mohan v. State of Uttar Pradesh*, supra n. 69.
71. *Chairman, Indore Vikas Pradhikaran v. Pure Industrial Coke & Chemicals Ltd.* 8 SCC 705 (2007).
72. Jain, supra n. 61, at 1868-9.
73. Ibid., at 1869-70.
74. Ibid., at 1870.
75. *K. T. Plantation (P) Ltd. v. State of Kerala*, supra n. 62, at para. 192.
76. *M. Naga Venkata Lakshmi v. Visakhapatnam Municipal Corporation* 8 SCC 748, 750 (2007).

'fair'. Those words came to be introduced by the Courts. In response, the Parliament amended the Constitution further to exclude activities of taking properties for welfare purposes from the purview of judicial review.[77] The Court will be careful not to step into the shoes of the Executive and interfere with policy decisions. The Court would focus on investigating the correctness of the decision-making process, because:

> Plea of unreasonableness, arbitrariness, proportionality, etc. always raises an element of subjectivity on which a court cannot strike down a statute or a statutory provision, especially when the right to property is no more a fundamental right. Otherwise the court will be substituting its wisdom to that of the legislature, which is impermissible in our constitutional democracy.[78]

Any deprivation of private property while exercising eminent domain must be for a public purpose.[79] Although presence of public purpose is necessary the need for payment of compensation and the amount to be paid would depend on the purpose for which the property is taken and the public good that the government seeks to achieve while depriving someone of private property.[80]

Expropriations would mostly take place under the Right to Fair Compensation and Transparency in Land Acquisition, Rehabilitation and Resettlement Act, 2013. It provides for a compensation based on market value.[81] It is possible that the Parliament could enact more legislations for expropriating property and adopt appropriate standards depending on the nature of the legislation.

Property has been interpreted broadly in the domestic law. It includes shares but not rights accruing to the shareholder.[82] Right to property is a bundle of rights which includes the right to transfer property.[83] Right to a sum of money was treated as property.[84] Property would include every form of property: tangible, intangible, including debts.[85] Mills, machinery, stock and contractual rights constitute property.[86] However, the right to property was subject to reasonable restrictions. The Courts have upheld reasonable restrictions on exercise of property.[87] Control of property, short of deprivation, does not entitle payment of compensation.[88]

Provisions on expropriation in the Indian Constitution relate to exercise of State power in the capacity of eminent domain. But actions undertaken as a part of police

---

77. Jain, *supra* n. 61, at 1840-2.
78. *K. T. Plantation (P) Ltd. v. State of Kerala, supra* n. 62, at para. 205.
79. *Ibid.*, at para. 180.
80. *Ibid.*, at para. 189.
81. Sections 26-8, Right to Fair Compensation and Transparency in Land Acquisition, Rehabilitation and Resettlement Act, 2013.
82. *Chiranjit Lal v. Union of India*, SCR 869 (1950).
83. *DLF Qutab Enclave Complex Educational Charitable Trust v. State of Haryana*, 5 SCC 622 (2003).
84. *Bombay Dyeing & Manufacturing Co. v. State of Bombay* 1958 SCR 1122; *State of Madhya Pradesh v. Ranojirao Shinde* SCR 489 (1968).
85. *M. M. Pathak v. Union of India*, (2) SCC 50 (1978).
86. *Dwarka v. Sholapur Mills*, SCR 674 (1954); Commissioner, *Hindu Religious Endowment v. Lakshmindra*, SCR 1005 (1954).
87. *V. J. Ferreira v. Bombay Municipality*, 1 SCC 70 (1972). For a detailed discussion on various laws restricting use of property that have been upheld, *see* Jain, *supra* n. 61, at 1808.
88. *Indian Handicrafts Emporium v. Union of India*, 7 SCC 589 (2003).

powers are excluded from the purview of provisions relating to property deprivation.[89] The Supreme Court of India is conscious about the distinction between the police powers doctrine and eminent domain.[90]

There is no doubt that the extent of property protection envisaged under the Constitution and the interpretation of the Supreme Court would extend to foreign investors. The Supreme Court has stated this in very clear words:

> 220. Deprivation of property may also cause serious concern in the area of foreign investment, especially in the context of international law and international investment agreements. Whenever a foreign investor operates within the territory of a host country the investor and its properties are subject to the legislative control of the host country, along with the international treaties or agreements. Even if the foreign investor has no fundamental right, let them know, that the rule of law prevails in this country.[91]

§5.02 FET AND FPS

Foreign investors have frequently and successfully invoked the FET standard to hold States responsible. It is comparatively easier to find breach of the FET standard than other standards.[92] Therefore the 2015 Model BIT does not contain the FET standard. It only contains FPS. One does not know if other States would be comfortable during negotiations. It would be worthwhile to analyse the way these provisions were drafted in past BITs.

[A] Treaty Practice

The FET and FPS are discussed together because they mostly appear together. For example, the India-Senegal BIT states:

> The investments of investors of each Contracting Party shall always be treated fairly and equitably and shall enjoy full protection and security in the territory of the other Contracting Party, in accordance with its laws and regulations. No Contracting Party shall impede, in any way, the management, preservation, use, increase or disposal of such investments through discriminatory measures.[93]

But in many treaties, there is no provision on FPS, only FET.[94] The FET and FPS provisions in Indian BITs were complex and differently drafted. No generalizations can be made.

---

89. Jain, *supra* n. 61, at 1835-8.
90. *K. T. Plantation (P) Ltd. v. State of Kerala*, *supra* n. 62, at para. 141.
91. *K. T. Plantation (P) Ltd. v. State of Kerala*, *supra* n. 62.
92. Dolzer and Schreuer, *supra* n. 15, at 130.
93. Agreement between the Government of the Republic of India and the Government of the Republic of Senegal for the Promotion and Protection of Investments, Art. 3.2 (signed 3 Jul. 2008, entered into force 17 Oct. 2009).
94. Agreement between the Government of the Republic of India and the Government of the Republic of Armenia for the Promotion and Protection of Investments, *supra* n. 13, at Art. 3;

Chapter 5: Treatment Standards §5.02[A]

The simplest formulation was that of the Russia-India BIT, which stated:

> Investments of the Investors of each Contracting Party shall at all times be accorded fair and equitable treatment and shall enjoy full protection and security in the territory of the State of the other Contracting Party.[95]

It would be an unnecessarily extensive task to reproduce all the differences. But some of the prominent ones are discussed. In some BITs, FET was in a separate clause than FPS but still under the same article.[96]

Agreement between the Government of the Republic of India and the Government of the Kingdom of Bahrain for the Promotion and Protection of Investments, *supra* n. 6, at Art. 3.2; India-Bangladesh BIT, *supra* n. 6, Art. 3.2; Agreement between the Government of the Republic of India and the Government of the Republic of Belarus for the Promotion and Protection of Investments, *supra* n. 18, at Art. 3; Agreement between the Government of the Republic of India and the Government of the Republic of Bulgaria for the Promotion and Protection of Investments, *supra* n. 6, at Art. 3; Agreement between the Government of the Republic of India and the Government of the People's Republic of China for the Promotion and Protection of Investments, *supra* n. 17, at Art. 3.2; Agreement between the Government of the Republic of India and the Government of the Democratic Republic of Congo for the Mutual Promotion and Protection of Investments, *supra* n. 6, at Art. 3.2; Agreement between the Government of the Republic of India and the Government of Republic of Cyprus for the Mutual Promotion and Protection of Investments, *supra* n. 6, at Art. 3.2; Agreement between the Czech Republic and the Republic of India for the Promotion and Protection of Investments, *supra* n. 6, at Art. 2(2); Agreement between the Government of the Republic of India and the Government of the Arab Republic of Egypt for the Promotion and Reciprocal Protection of Investments, *supra* n. 23, at Art. 2.2; Agreement between the Government of the Republic of Indonesia and the Government of the Republic of India for the Promotion and Protection of Investments, *supra* n. 18, at Art. 3; Agreement between the Government of the Republic of India and the Government of the State of Israel for the Promotion and Protection of Investments, *supra* n. 40, at Art. 3.2; Agreement between the Government of the Republic of India and the Hashemite Kingdom of Jordan for the Promotion and Protection of Investments, *supra* n. 18, at Art. 3.2; Agreement between the Government of India and the Government of Nepal for the Promotion and Protection of Investments, *supra* n. 11, at Art. 3.2; Agreement between the Government of the Republic of India and the Government of the Republic of Poland for the Promotion and Protection of Investments, art 3.2 (signed 7 Oct. 1996, entered into force 31 Dec. 1997).

95. Agreement between the Government of the Russian Federation and the Government of the Republic of India for the Promotion and Mutual Protection of Investments, *supra* n. 56, at Art. 3.2; Agreement between the Federal Republic of Germany and the Republic of India for the Promotion and Protection of Investments, *supra* n. 6, at Art. 3.2; Agreement between the Government of Australia and the Government of the Republic of India on the Promotion and Protection of Investments, *supra* n. 25, at Art. 3.2; Agreement between the Government of the Republic of India and the Government of the Republic of Ghana for the Reciprocal Promotion and Protection of Investments, *supra* n. 18, at Art. 3.2; Agreement between the Republic of Hungary and the Republic of India for the Promotion and Protection of Investments, *supra* n. 6, at Art. 3.2; Agreement between the Government of the Republic of India and the Government of the Republic of Iceland for the Promotion and Protection of Investments, *supra* n. 40, at Art. 3.2; Agreement between the Republic of India and the Kingdom of the Netherlands for the Promotion and Protection of Investments, *supra* n. 33, at Art. 4.

96. Agreement between the Government of the Republic of Mauritius and the Government of the Republic of India for the Promotion and Protection of Investments, Art. 4.1 (signed 4 Sept. 1998, entered into force 20 Jun. 2000); Agreement between the Government of the Republic of India and the Government of the Republic of Trinidad and Tobago for the Promotion and Protection of Investments, Art. 3.2 (signed 12 Mar. 2007, entered into force 7 Oct. 2007). Agreement between the Government of the Republic of Austria and the Government of the Republic of India for the Promotion and Protection of Investments, *supra* n. 8, at Art. 2.3; Agreement between the

The provision in the Australia-India BIT was unique. It contained a different provision on FET and FPS. The standard of FPS was limited to domestic law. It stated:

> A Contracting Party shall, subject to its laws, accord within its territory protection and security to investments and shall not impair management, maintenance, use, enjoyment or disposal of investment.[97]

The FPS in this case shall be granted to the extent that it is provided for in domestic law. Also, FPS would not extent to stability of the legal framework.

In some cases FET appears along with the most favoured and NT and FPS appears with arbitrary or discriminatory measure. The Kuwait-India BIT has the following provisions:

> Each Contracting State shall at all time ensure investments and associated activities, made in its territory by investors of the other Contracting State, fair and equitable treatment. Such treatment shall not be less favourable than that which its accords in like situations to investments of its own investors or investors of any third State, whichever is the most favourable.[98]...investments by investors of either Contracting State shall enjoy full protection and security in the territory of the other Contracting State in a manner consistent with the provisions of this Agreement and applicable rules of international law Neither Contracting State shall in any way impair by arbitrary or discriminatory measures. The management, maintenance. use. enjoyment, or disposal of investments.[99]

In some cases, FET, FPS and non-discrimination, all appeared in the same provision.[100]

The FET standard has been removed from the 2015 Model BIT, and it appears that the Government may not be keen on having it in future BITs. This is due to the interpretation of FET. FET has been interpreted to encompass many things, such as

---

Portuguese Republic and the Republic of India on the Mutual Promotion and Protection of Investments, *supra* n. 36, at Art. 3.1.

97. Agreement between the Government of Australia and the Government of the Republic of India on the Promotion and Protection of Investments, *supra* n. 25, at Art. 3.3; exactly the same as Agreement between the Government of the Republic of India and the Government of the Republic of Latvia for the Promotion and Protection of Investments *supra* n. 30, at Art. 3.3; Compare Agreement between the Government of the Republic of India and Government of the Republic of Macedonia for the Promotion and Reciprocal Protection of Investments, *supra* n. 50, at Art. 3.2.
98. Agreement between the State of Kuwait and the Republic of India for the Encouragement and Reciprocal Protection of Investment, *supra* n. 7, at Art. 5.1; Agreement between the Government of the Republic of India and the Government of the United Arab Emirates on the Promotion and Protection of Investments, *supra* n. 20, at Art. 5.
99. Agreement between the State of Kuwait and the Republic of India for the Encouragement and Reciprocal Protection of Investment, *supra* n. 7, at Art. 4.1.
100. Agreement between the Government of the Italian Republic and the Government of the Republic of India on the Promotion and Protection of Investments, Art. 3.2 (signed 23 Nov. 1995, entered into force 26 Mar. 1998); Agreement between the Government of the Republic of India and the Government of the Republic of Lithuania for the Promotion and Protection of Investments, *supra* n. 21, at Art. 3.2; Agreement between the Government of the Republic of India and Government of the Kingdom of Saudi Arabia Concerning the Encouragement and Reciprocal Protection of Investments, *supra* n. 10, at Art. 3.2.

denial of justice,[101] representations made to the investor,[102] due process in administrative decision-making,[103] discrimination,[104] transparency,[105] good faith,[106] and freedom from harassment by State authorities.[107] The determination of the contents of FET cannot be reached in abstract. A lot would depend on facts[108] with which the uncertainty of the standards that would be applied by an investment tribunal.

The problem with the FET is that it lacks precise contents. Tribunals have used it as a flexible standard for holding host States responsible for principles relating to due process or a principle embodying general rule of law.[109] There has been disagreement as to whether FET is a standard equivalent to the customary international minimum standard or higher than that.[110] It is argued that the FET goes far beyond procedural obligations on host States and encompasses even substantive obligations.[111] If it were to be interpreted to have more requirements than the customary international law standard of the international minimum standard, then the responsibility on the host State would be higher. The FET is interpreted to impose an obligation on States to actively promote and stimulate foreign investments and create conducive environment for those purposes.[112] The FET is said to create an expectation in the minds of the investor that the host State would not alter the regulatory framework which existed when the foreign investor entered the host State.[113] Such an interpretation has the effect of freezing the regulatory framework and restraining the host State from making any changes to its laws. An important constituent of the FET is legitimate expectations of the foreign investor. The legitimate expectations would depend on the regulatory

---

101. Discussed in detail in Chapter 7.
102. Campbell McLachlan, Laurence Shore and Matthew Weiniger, *International Investment Law: Substantive Principles*, 237-8 (Oxford University Press 2008).
103. McLachlan, Shore and Matthew Weiniger, *supra* n. 102, at 239; Dolzer and Schreuer, *supra* n. 15, at 154-6.
104. McLachlan, Shore and Matthew Weiniger, *supra* n. 102, at 239-40.
105. McLachlan, Shore and Matthew Weiniger, *supra* n. 102, at 240-2; Dolzer and Schreuer, *supra* n. 15, at 149-52.
106. McLachlan, Shore and Matthew Weiniger, *supra* n. 102, at 242; Dolzer and Schreuer, *supra* n. 15, at 156-8.
107. McLachlan, Shore and Matthew Weiniger, *supra* n. 102, at 242-3; Dolzer and Schreuer, *supra* n. 15, at 159-60.
108. *Mondev International Ltd. v. United States of America*, Award, ICSID Case No. ARB(AF)/99/2, para. 118 (11 Oct. 2002); *Waste Management, Inc. v. United Mexican States*, Award, ICSID Case No. ARB(AF)/00/3, para. 99 (30 Apr. 2004); *Ronald S. Lauder v. The Czech Republic*, Final Award, UNCITRAL, para. 292 (3 Sept. 2001); *CMS Gas Transmission Company v. The Republic of Argentina*, Award, ICSID Case No. ARB(AF)/01/8, para. 273 (12 May 2005); *Noble Ventures, Inc. v. Romania*, Award, ICSID Case No. ARB(AF)/01/11, para. 181 (12 Oct. 2005).
109. Stephen Vasciannie, *The Fair and Equitable Treatment Standard in International Investment Law and Practice*, 70 The British Year Book of International Law 99, 100, 104, 145 (1990); Prosper Weil, *The State, the Foreign Investor, and International Law: The No Longer Stormy Relationship of a Ménage À Trois*, 15 ICSID Review 401, 415 (2000); Stephan Schill, *Fair and Equitable Treatment, the Rule of Law and Comparative Public Law*, in International Investment Law and Comparative Public Law 151 (Stephan Schill (ed.), Oxford University Press, 2010).
110. Dolzer and Schreuer, *supra* n. 15, at 134-41.
111. Stephen Schewebel, *Justice in International Law*, 163 (Cambridge University Press 1994).
112. *MTD Equity Sdn. Bhd. and MTD Chile S.A. v. Republic of Chile*, Award, ICSID Case No. ARB/01/7, para. 13 (25 May 2004).
113. *Técnicas Medioambientales Tecmed, S.A. v. The United Mexican States*, Award, ICSID Case No. ARB (AF)/00/2, para. 89 (29 May 2003).

framework existing in the host State at the time of entry. Tribunals have held that once such expectations are formed on the basis of the regulatory framework existing at the time of entry, then the host State cannot change it to prejudice the interest of foreign investor.[114] A stable and predictable environment has to be maintained.[115] In some situations, tribunals have found violation of contractual terms to amount to breach of the FET standard.[116] Investment tribunals may not shy away from additional elements to FET as they go along deciding disputes. According to Sornarajah, the contents of the FET laid down by the tribunals do not have support in the text of the investment treaties and the contents identified by the tribunals are vague as well. In effect, they open the possibility of excessive jurisdiction being exercised by arbitrators beyond that which is allowed by the investment treaty.[117]

One of the associated debates on FET is whether the FET standard is equivalent to or higher than international minimum standard. The fair and equitable standard has had a complex relationship with the customary international law minimum standard.[118] In some treaties customary international law or international minimum standard has been specified along with the fair and equitable standard.[119] Some scholars take the view that FET constitutes an independent standard that is higher than customary international law.[120] Tribunals have also taken this view.[121] Tribunals have considered that the FET is broad and is by itself capable of evolving.[122] After the tribunals started taking expansive view, States have clarified that FET does not expect treatment any higher than the international minimum standard. Article 1105(1) of NAFTA states that:

---

114. Dolzer and Schreuer, *supra* n. 15, at 146. The host State was held responsible for changes in the domestic taxation law. *Occidental Exploration and Production Company (OEPC) v. The Republic of Ecuador*, Final Award, LCIA Case No. UN3467, paras 184-91 (1 Jul. 2004).
115. *CMS Gas Transmission Company v. The Republic of Argentina*, *supra* n. 108, at paras 274-6.
116. *SGS Société Générale de Surveillance S.A. v. Republic of Philippines*, Decision of Tribunal on Objections to Jurisdictions, ICSID Case No. ARB/02/6, para. 162 (29 Jan. 2004); *Noble Ventures, Inc. v. Romania*, *supra* n. 108, at para. 182; *SGS Société Générale de Surveillance S.A. v. The Republic of Paraguay*, Decision on Jurisdiction, ICSID Case No. ARB/07/29, paras 144-51 (10 Feb. 2012); *Mondev International Ltd. v. United States of America*, *supra* n. 108, at para. 134.
117. M. Sornarajah, *Resistance and Change in the International Law on Foreign Investment*, 254-7 (Cambridge University Press 2015).
118. *See* Hussein Haeri, *A Tale of Two Standards: 'Fair and Equitable Treatment' and the Minimum Standard in International Law*, 27(1) Arbitration International (2011).
119. United States-Singapore Free Trade Agreement, Art. 15.5 (signed 6 May 2003, entered into force 1 Jan. 2004); Trans Pacific Partnership Agreement (Auckland, 4 Feb. 2016) https://ustr.gov/trade-agreements/free-trade-agreements/trans-pacific-partnership/tpp-full-text (accessed 10 Sept. 2016).
120. Vasciannie, *supra* n. 109, at 104-5; Iona Tudor, *The Fair and Equitable Treatment Standard in International Law of Foreign Investment*, 54-68 (Oxford University Press 2008).
121. *Compañiá de Aguas del Aconquija S.A. and Vivendi Universal S.A. v. Argentine Republic*, Award, ICSID Case No. ARB/97/3, para. 745 (20 Aug. 2007).
122. *ADF Group Inc. v. United States of America*, Award, ICSID Case No. ARB (AF)/00/1, para. 179 (9 Jan. 2003); *Merrill & Ring Forestry L.P. v. The Government of Canada*, Award, UNCITRAL, ICSID Administered Case, para. 213 (31 Mar. 2010).

Each Party shall accord to investments of investors of another Party treatment in accordance with international law, including fair and equitable treatment and full protection and security.

The Free Trade Commission (FTC) of NAFTA issued a clarification in 2001 stating that the FET expects treatment no higher than the international minimum standard.[123] The clarifications issued by the FTC are issued jointly by the State Parties to NAFTA, which are binding. The view is expressed that the FET standard is different from the international minimum standard and if States wish to impose international minimum standard they could have specified the same.[124] Even in situations where the treatment standard is tied to the international minimum standard, arguably, the standard is prone to evolution.[125] Some tribunals have gone to the extent of stating that FET standard has become a part of customary international law.[126] It is a doubtful proposition since the provision is used very differently in each treaty and now some States are not even keeping it in their treaties. The constitute elements of custom: State practice and opinio juris are absent. Therefore, claims that FET has become a custom are unfounded.

Indian BITs do not have a reference to international minimum standard, except the India-Columbia and Mexico-India BIT, where the treaty clauses first set out the standard and thereafter, clarify that the standard expects a treatment no higher than the international minimum standard.[127]

Traditionally, FPS has been understood to mean physical protection.[128] FPS has been liberally interpreted by investment tribunals to claim that it imposes an obligation on the host State not only to the extent of physical protection. It goes beyond and involves ensuring stability of the legal framework.[129] In *CME v. Czech Republic*, the Tribunal interpreted FPS to mean that the host State 'is obliged to ensure that neither by amendment of its laws not by actions of its administrative bodies is the agreed and

---

123. Organization of American States: NAFTA Free Trade Commission, NAFTA: Notes on Interpretation of Certain Chapter 11 Provisions (31 Jul. 2001) http://www.sice.oas.org/tpd/nafta/Commission/CH11understanding_e.asp (accessed 1 Jul. 2017).
124. *Biwater Gauff (Tanzania) Ltd. v. United Republic of Tanzania*, Award, ICSID Case No. ARB/05/22, para. 591 (24 Jul. 2008); Rudolf Dolzer and Margarete Stevens, *Bilateral Investment Treaties*, 60 (Martinus Nijhoff Publishers 1995); UNCTAD, *Fair and Equitable Treatment: UNCTAD Series on Issues in International Investment Agreements II*, 13, 17, 37-40, 53, 61 (United Nations Publications 2012); Vasciannie, *supra* n. 109, at 104-5, 139-44; Tudor, *supra* n. 120, at 54-68.
125. *Chemtura Corp. v. Government of Canada*, Award, UNCITRAL paras 121, 236 (2 Aug. 2010).
126. *Merrill & Ring Forsty v. Canada*, *supra* n. 122, at para. 210.
127. Agreement for the Promotion and Protection of Investments between the Republic of Columbia and the Republic of India, *supra* n. 9, at Art. 3; Agreement between the Government of the United Mexican States and the Government of the Republic of India on the Promotion and Protection of Investments, *supra* n. 10, at Art. 5.3(a).
128. *Asian Agricultural Products Ltd. v. Republic of Sri Lanka*, Final Award, ICSID Case No. ARB/87/3, para. 45 (27 Jun. 1990); *Wena Hotels Ltd. v. Arab Republic of Egypt*, Award, ICSID Case No. ARB/98/4, para. 84 (8 Dec. 2000); *American Manufacturing & Trading, Inc. v. Republic of Zaire*, Award, ICSID Case No. ARB/93/1, para. 6.02 (21 Feb. 1997).
129. *Azurix Corp. v. The Argentine Republic*, Award, ICSID Case No. ARB/01/12, paras 406-8 (14 Jul. 2006); *Siemens A.G. v. The Argentine Republic*, Award, ICSID Case No. ARB/02/8, para. 303 (17 Jan. 2007); *Compañiá de Aguas del Aconquija S.A. and Vivendi Universal S.A. v. Argentine Republic*, *supra* n. 121, at para. 7.4.15; *Frontier Petroleum Services Ltd. v. The Czech Republic*, Final Award, UNCITRAL para. 263 (12 Nov. 2010).

approved security and protection of foreign investor's investment withdrawn or devalued.'[130] Therefore, unless the prefix 'legal' is added there is no reason to interpret FPS clause to include anything more than physical protection. This is only rarely the case in Indian treaty practice. The India-Argentina BIT contains such a provision:

> Investments and returns of investors of each Contracting Party shall at all times be accorded fair and equitable treatment and shall enjoy full *legal* protection and security in the territory of the other Contracting Party.[131] (emphasis added)

Otherwise, the protection should be more than physical protection. To ensure that an investment tribunal does not adopt a liberal approach, few BITs had clarified this position.[132] The 2015 Model BIT puts it beyond doubt that FPS should not be extended to beyond physical protection and security in the following words:

> Each Party shall accord in its territory to investments of the other Party and to investors with respect to their investments full protection and security. For greater certainty, 'full protection and security' only refers to a Party's obligations relating to physical security of investors and to investments made by the investors of the other Party and not to any other obligation whatsoever.[133]

As already stated, the 2015 Model BIT does not contain FET. India is not the first State to exclude FET, some other States have also done so.[134] It does contain a novel standard, which could be called an abridged form of international minimum standard, and it reads as under:

> No Party shall subject investments made by investors of the other Party to measures which constitute a violation of customary international law through:

---

130. *CME Czech Republic B.V. v. Czech Republic*, Partial Award, UNCITRAL, para. 613(13 Sept 2001).
131. Agreement between the Government of the Republic of India and the Government of the Argentine Republic on the Promotion and Reciprocal Protection of Investments, Art. 3(2) (signed 20 Aug. 1999, entered into force 12 Aug. 2002).
132. Agreement for the Promotion and Protection of Investments between the Republic of Columbia and the Republic of India, *supra* n. 9, at Art. 4(b).
133. Ministry of Commerce and Industry, Government of India, *Model Text for the Indian Bilateral Investment Treaty*, *supra* n. 1, at Art. 3.2.
134. Framework Agreement on the ASEAN Investment Area (Makati) (signed 7 Oct. 1998, entered into force 25 May 1999) http://www.asean.org/7994.pdf (accessed 1 Jul. 2017); Comprehensive Economic Cooperation Agreement between the Republic of India and the Republic of Singapore (New Delhi) (signed 29 Jun. 2005 entered into force 1 Aug. 2005); The Agreement between New Zealand and Singapore on a Closer Economic Partnership (signed 14 Nov. 2000, entered into force 1 Jan. 2001), https://web.archive.org/web/20150922202457/http://www.mfat.govt.nz/Trade-and-Economic-Relations/2-Trade-Relationships-and-Agreements/Singapore/Closer-Economic-Partnership-Agreement-text/index.php (accessed 1 Jul. 2017); Agreement between New Zealand and Thailand on a Closer Economic Partnership Agreement (signed 30 Nov. 2004, entered into force 1 Jul. 2005), https://www.mfat.govt.nz/assets/_securedfiles/FTAs-agreements-in-force/Thailand-FTA/thainzcep-agreement.pdf (accessed 1 Jul. 2017); Agreement between the Government of the Republic of Albania and the Government, of the Republic of Croatia for the Encouragement and Reciprocal Protection of Investments (signed 10 May 1993, entered into force 16 Apr. 1994); Agreement between the Government of the Republic of Croatia and the Government of Ukraine for the Promotion and Reciprocal Protection of Investments (signed 15 Dec. 1997, entered into force 5 Jun. 2001).

(i) Denial of justice in any judicial or administrative proceedings; or
(ii) fundamental breach of due process; or
(iii) targeted discrimination on manifestly unjustified grounds, such as gender, race or religious belief; or
(iv) manifestly abusive treatment, such as coercion, duress and harassment.[135]

[B] Analysis of Domestic Law

The understanding of these principles in domestic law is equally important. The Indian courts have emphasized on the need of fairness and lack of unreasonableness in governmental action. The present-day Government is a welfare State, and it has wide powers for regulating and dispensing special services such as leases, licences, contracts, etc. While performing these functions, the Government is expected not to act like private individuals, but abide by certain standards and norms. When the Court says that the Government cannot behave like private individuals, it has public interest in mind. In distinguishing the objectives of private individuals, against those expected of the Government, it is commented that the private individuals are 'guided by economic considerations of self-gain' and the law allows them to enter into transitions that operate contrary to their self-interest or act on terms favourable to the interests of some of the other parties, if not all. Whereas on the other hand, the Government is not free to act the way it wants because it is tied by the constraints of a democratic society. It is conferred with a constitutional power that cannot be exercised in an arbitrary, capricious or unprincipled manner. The Government has to exercise its powers with public good in mind. All activities of the Government involve a public element and thus must be 'informed with reason and guided by public interest.'[136] Whatever the actions, they 'should not be arbitrary, irrational or irrelevant', rather 'justifiable on the basis of some policy or valid principles which by themselves are reasonable and not discriminatory.'[137]

The other side of the coin when it comes to protection of public interest is that although the Government has to be fair in its dealing with private entities, it is the custodian of public interest. The State and its instrumentalities may affect private interest to protect public interest. Especially, on matters of economic policy, the Government has to resort to experimentation – 'trial and error'. It is thus not possible to judge the actions of the Government, guided by policy, through a pre-determined rigid formula.[138] The Government must have freedom to operate and discretion to decide what is in public interest, on its own genuine judgment. Thus, the Court cannot strike down a policy decision solely because it feels another policy decision would have been 'fairer or wise or more scientific or logical.'[139]

---

135. Ministry of Commerce and Industry, Government of India, *Model Text for the Indian Bilateral Investment Treaty, supra* n. 1, at Art. 3.1.
136. *Kasturi Lal Lakshmi Reddy v. State of Jammu and Kashmir* 4 SCC 1, para. 11 (1980).
137. *Union of India v. Hindustan Development Corporation* 3 SCC 499, para. 7 (1993).
138. *R. K. Garg v. Union of India* 4 SCC 675, para. 8 (1981).
139. *State of Madhya Pradesh v. Nandlal Jaiswal* 4 SCC 566, para. 34 (1986).

Prominently in matters of economic policy, the regulations have to ensure that the public interest does not suffer adversely at the behest of unreasonable individual economic interests. The Government may validly adopt regulations for equitable distribution of commodities at a fair price in the best interest of general public. Furthermore, it is obvious that measures undertaken for the achievement of greater public interest also promote efficiency in the industry.[140]

[C] Legitimate Expectations

In arbitral jurisprudence, 'legitimate expectations' has emerged as one of the important ingredients for testing presence of FET. In *Tecmed v. Mexico*, the phrase, 'legitimate expectations' was explained as follows:

> in light of the good faith principle established by international law, requires the Contracting Parties to provide to international investments treatment that does not affect the basic expectations that were taken into account by the foreign investor to make the investment. The foreign investor expects the host State to act in a consistent manner, free from ambiguity and totally transparently in its relations with the foreign investor, so that it may know before-hand any and all rules and regulations that will govern its investments, as well as the goals of the relevant policies and administrative practices or directives, to be able to plan its investment and comply with such regulations. Any and all State actions confirming to such criteria should relate not only to the guidelines, directives are requirements issued, or the resolutions approved thereunder, but also the goals underlying such regulations.[141]

This analysis of the Tribunal about legitimate expectations as one of the factors in determining breach of FET is not informed in its understanding as in general public international law. Understandably so, because there is no such interpretation adopted in international law. The emergence and content of legitimate expectations arises from British administrative law.[142] Administrative law developed in domestic jurisdictions can be seen to have a better-informed understanding of the meaning of FET. The doctrine of legitimate expectations in substantive sense has been admitted in Indian jurisprudence as well, unless there is overriding public interest.[143]

The Supreme Court of India has defined the doctrine of legitimate expectations in the following words:

> [T]he doctrine of 'legitimate expectation' imposes in essence a duty on public authority to act fairly by taking into consideration all relevant factors relating to

---

140. *Sitaram Sugar Co. Ltd. v. Union of India* 3 SCC 223, para. 13 (1990).
141. *Tecmed v. Mexico*, *supra* n. 113, at para. 154; *see also Occidental v. Ecuador*, *supra* n. 114, at para. 183; *CMS v. Argentina*, *supra* n. 108, at para. 89; *CME Czech Republic B.V. v. The Czech Republic*, *supra* n. 130, at para. 356; *International Thunderbird Gaming Corporation v. The United States of Mexico*, Arbitral Award, UNCITRAL, para. 147 (26 Jan. 2006).
142. Chester Brown and Kate Miles, *Evolution in Investment Treaty Law and Arbitration*, 650 (Cambridge University Press 2011); *see* Francisco Orrego-Vicuna, *Foreign investment Law: How Customary Is Custom?*, ASIL Proceedings 98 (2005); McLachlan, Shore and Matthew Weiniger, *supra* n. 102, at p. 238.
143. *Punjab Communications Ltd. v. Union of India*, 4 SCC 727, para. 37 (1999).

such 'legitimate expectation'. Within the conspectus of fair dealing in case of 'legitimate expectation', the reasonable opportunities to make representation by the parties likely to be affected by any change of consistent past policy come in.[144]

Legitimate Expectations doctrine has developed in the context of reasonableness and natural justice.[145] Within the sphere of public law, legitimate expectations could arise in cases of contracts with the Government, distribution of largess, discretionary grant of licence permits, their renewal or reissue. But if the actions are taken by the Government in public interest or pursuant to change in the policy or by way of legislation, there cannot be legitimate expectation.[146] In certain situations it may extend to substantive protection, but it is predominantly procedural in nature.[147]

These are two facets of the legitimate expectations doctrine. First, it is legitimate to expect that the Government would adopt fair procedures. Second, expectations may be generated by persons who may be affected by the decision of the Government, as long as the expectations are reasonable or legitimate. The Government must consider the second aspect and give due weight to it in the decision-making process.[148] Although legitimate expectations operate at these two levels and control the manner of behaviour of the Government, they cannot stifle public interest. According to the Supreme Court of India:

> Every legitimate expectation is a relevant factor requiring due consideration in a fair decision making process. Whether the expectations of claimant are reasonable or legitimate in the context is a question of fact in each case. Whenever the question arises, it is to be determined not according to the claimant's perception but in larger public interest wherein other more important considerations may outweigh what would otherwise have been the legitimate expectations of the claimant. A bona fide decision of the public authority reached in this manner would satisfy the requirement of non-arbitrariness and withstand judicial scrutiny. The doctrine of legitimate expectation gets assimilated in the rule of law and operates in our legal system in this manner and to this extent.[149]

The Supreme Court of India, in the case of *Union of India v. Hindustan Development Corporation*, addressed the specific details of nature of the expectation, who possesses it, when does it become legitimate, what are its foundations, and the duties that it imposes upon administrative authorities, while taking decisions in cases involving legitimate expectation. The Court has distinguished 'legitimate expectations' from 'anticipation' in following terms:

> For legal purposes, the expectation cannot be the same as anticipation. It is different from a wish, a desire or a hope nor can it amount to a claim or demand on the ground of a right. However earnest and sincere a wish, a desire or a hope may be and however confidently one may look to them to be fulfilled, they by

---

144. *Navjyoti Co-operative Group Housing Society v. Union of India*, 4 SCC 477, para. 16 (1992).
145. *National Buildings Construction Corporation v. S. Raghunathan*, 7 SCC 66, para. 19 (1998).
146. *Union of India v. Hindustan Development Corporation*, supra n. 137, at para. 35.
147. *MP Oil Extraction v. State of MP*, 7 SCC 592, para. 44 (1997).
148. *Food Corporation of India v. Kamdhenu Cattle Feed Industries*, 1 SCC 71, para. 7 (1993).
149. *Ibid.*, at para. 8.

themselves cannot amount to an assertable expectation and a mere disappointment does not attract legal consequences. A pious hope even leading to a moral obligation cannot amount to a legitimate expectation.[150]

The expectation should be 'justifiable legitimate and protectable', it need not 'by itself fructify into a right and therefore it does not amount to a right in the conventional sense.'[151]

It then explained the parameters for determining legitimacy of the expectations: 'legitimacy of an exception can be inferred only if it is founded on the sanction of law or custom or an established procedure followed in regular and natural sequence.'[152]

Legitimate expectations would arise if there is a consistent practice which creates legitimate expectations. Legitimate expectations normally arise in situations where, in the past, a particular treatment has been awarded and this treatment is changed. This results in the frustration of the expectation. This frustration is legitimate as long as the change in situation that caused frustration is based on some rational grounds, which are communicated.[153] If such expectations are created then the person whose expectations would be frustrated by the action of the Government should be heard.[154] Legitimate expectations have certain consequences. One such consequence is that the Government should not act in a manner that defeats the legitimate expectations, unless there is overriding public policy. In such situations, the aggrieved person may be given an opportunity of representation.[155] The person holding the expectation does not hold a legal right, but the expectation is an outcome of the circumstances, dependent on his placement – as a group or individual adversely affected by the actions of the Government. The existence of this doctrine is dehors any legal right, hence any unbridled and expansive interpretation could hugely impair legitimate regulations by Governments. The doctrine is thus to be applied with circumspection, and it loses its force in situations of supervening public interest. A legitimate expectation arising from the practice of the Government certainly limits the right of the Executive, but it cannot impair that right in entirety while acting in a bona fide manner in public interest.[156]

The protection of legitimate expectations does not imply disregard of regulatory flexibility of the host State. The Tribunal, in *Saluka v. Czech Republic*, observed that:

> No investor may reasonably expect that the circumstances prevailing at the time the investment is made remain totally unchanged. In order to determine whether frustration of the foreign investor's expectations was justified and reasonable, the host State's legitimate right subsequently to regulate domestic matters in the public interest must be taken into consideration as well.[157]

---

150. *Union of India v. Hindustan Development Corporation*, supra n. 137, at para. 28.
151. *Ibid.*
152. *Ibid.*
153. *Council of Civil Service Unions v. Minister for the Civil Service*, 3 All ER 935, 408-9 (1984).
154. *Navjyoti Co-operative Group Housing Society v. Union of India*, supra n. 144, at para. 15.
155. *Ibid.*
156. See *Council of Civil Service Unions v. Minister for the Civil Service*, 3 All ER 935 (1984), cited with approval in *Navjyoti Co-operative Group Housing Society v. Union of India*, supra n. 144, and *Union of India v. Hindustan Development Corporation*, supra n. 137.
157. *Saluka Investments BV (The Netherlands) v. The Czech Republic*, supra n. 56, para. 305. See also, *Azurix Corp. v. The Argentine Republic*, Award, ICSID Case No. ARB/01/12, paras 406-8

Also, in Indian law, the acknowledged exception to legitimate expectations doctrine is of public interest. Municipal courts applying this principle have given overriding status to public interest, and Indian courts have also adhered to this practice. After surveying the state of the law, as decided in cases by various common law jurisdictions, the Indian courts have adopted the position that the doctrine of legitimate expectations is confined to the right of a fair hearing before a decision removing a promise or withdrawing an undertaking is taken. It is not available as a remedy to challenge the decision of administrative authorities on substance because in cases of legitimate expectations, crystallized rights are not formed.[158] Legitimate expectations cannot be fulfilled in situations where overriding public interest demands otherwise. In other words, according to the Supreme Court of India, 'where a person's legitimate expectation is not fulfilled by taking a particular decision then decision maker should justify the denial of such expectation by showing some overriding public interest.'[159] Thus, even if the protection under legitimate expectations would extend to substantive protection in certain cases, it does not contemplate granting an absolute right to a particular person. A case for legitimate expectations could arise if the body generating expectation through representation or past practice already possessed that power to fulfil the expectations. The person claiming legitimate expectations has to satisfy that there is 'foundation and thus has locus standi to make such a claim.' Such a situation would arise only if the following conditions are satisfied:

(a) the decision taken by the authority shall be arbitrary, unreasonable and not taken in public interest;
(b) if it is a matter of policy, including change of policy, the courts cannot interfere with the decision;
(c) whether a legitimate expectation was created is essentially a question of fact;
(d) if all these tests are satisfied then the question to be asked is whether there was failure to give a hearing which has resulted into failure of justice.[160]

The Court adopted a narrow interpretation of the phrase because of its nature in comparison to a legal right – 'legitimate expectation ought to be protected though not guaranteed.'[161]

The question of public interest is not to be decided based on the perception of the claimant.[162] It is necessary that there is a representation and the claimant has relied on the statement to his detriment and suffered losses.[163] This requirement by itself is not

---

(14 Jul. 2006); *Siemens A.G. v. The Argentine Republic*, Award, ICSID Case No. ARB/02/8, para. 303 (17 Jan. 2007); *Compañiá de Aguas del Aconquija S.A. and Vivendi Universal S.A. v. Argentine Republic*, *supra* n. 121, at para. 7.4.15; *Frontier Petroleum Services Ltd. v. The Czech Republic*, Final Award, UNCITRAL para. 263 (12 Nov. 2010); Dolzer and Schreuer, *supra* n. 15, at 148; *See EDF (Services) v. Romania*, Award, ICSID Case No. ARB/05/13 (8 Oct. 2009).
158. *Union of India v. Hindustan Development Corporation*, *supra* n. 137, at para. 33.
159. *Ibid.*
160. *Ibid.*
161. *Ibid.*, at para. 34.
162. *National Buildings Construction Corporation v. S. Raghunathan*, *supra* n. 166, at para. 30.
163. *Ibid.*, at para. 18.

sufficient to create legitimate expectations, because then no difference will remain between estoppel and legitimate expectations. The only decision where the Supreme Court expressly recognizes substantive the legitimate expectations right is *Punjab Communications Ltd. v. Union of India*. The Court held that:

> The result is that a change in policy can defeat a substantive legitimate expectation if it can be justified on *Wednesbury* reasonableness. We have noticed that in *Hindustan Development Corporation Case* also, it was laid down that the decision maker has to choose in the balancing of the pros and cons relevant to the change in policy. It is, therefore, clear that the choice of the policy is for the decision-maker and not for the court. The legitimate substantive expectation merely permits the court to find out if the change in policy which is the cause for defeating the legitimate expectation is irrational or perverse or one which no reasonable person could have made.[164]

In my view, bona fide regulations would satisfy these requirements. The Supreme Court is clear about the principle: 'the judgment whether public interest overrides the substantive legitimate expectation of individuals will be for the decision-maker who has made the change in the policy and the courts will intervene in that decision only if they are satisfied that the decision is irrational or perverse'.[165]

The change of policy however can be investigated on the basis of proportionality – whether it is substantively fair and appropriately balanced.[166] While using general principles of law as a guiding principle, the principle imported into international law need not be a perfect replica of the municipal law. It is rarely the case. Same legal principles would be interpreted and applied differently in similar legal systems. This is obvious since the process of law-making and decision-making by the judges is influenced by the status and thinking of its society. Generalizations are not only impossible but dangerous. In view of this problem, a reduced status for general principle as a source of international law is understandable. Only those ingredients of a legal principle that have achieved substantial agreement in municipal law spheres may be considered.

The circumstances of invocation of legitimate expectation are limited and if there is no violation of natural justice, then the Court cannot interfere, because it cannot usurp the discretion of public authority.[167] It is also not necessary that all situations would require a hearing. This can be the case if the discretion rests entirely with the authority and the authority has acted objectively and fairly. For example, if the authority has freedom to renew a licence then a new application cannot claim that he had a legitimate expectation and the licence could not have been renewed.[168] Reflecting on the limitations inherent in the legitimate expectations doctrine, the Supreme Court stated that:

---

164. *Punjab Communications Ltd. v. Union of India, supra* n. 164, at para. 40.
165. *Ibid.*, at para. 42.
166. *Ibid.*, at para. 38.
167. *Union of India v. Hindustan Development Corporation, supra* n. 137, at para. 35.
168. *Ibid.*, at para. 35.

It would thus appear that there are stronger reasons as to why the legitimate expectation should not be substantively protected than the reasons as to why it should be protected. In other words, such a legal obligation exists whenever the case supporting the same in terms of legal principles of different sorts, is stronger than the case against it....It depends very much on the facts and general principles of administrative law applicable to such facts and the concept of legitimate expectation which is the latest recruit to a long list of concepts fashioned by the courts for the review of administrative actions, must be restricted to the general limitations applicable and binding the manner of future exercise of administrative power in a particular case. It follows that the concept of legitimate expectation is 'not the key which unlocks the treasure of natural justice and it ought not to unlock the gates which shuts the court out of review on the merits', particularly when the element of speculation and uncertainty is inherent in that very concept.[169]

§5.03 MFN TREATMENT AND NT

The MFN and NT are aimed at creating a level playing field between all foreign investors and national investors. MFN ensures that a foreign investor is not treated less favourably in comparison to any other similarly placed foreign investor, whereas NT ensures that a foreign investor is not treated less favourably in comparison to any other similarly placed domestic investor.

The standard pattern of all Indian BITs is that they limit the application of MFN and NT to the investments and or matters relating to control, management and returns from investments. MFN and NT clauses do not apply to all provisions of the treaty. This is the situation with BITs between some other States. For example the Spain-Argentina BIT states that: 'In all matters subject to this Agreement, this treatment shall not be less favourable than that extended by each Party to the investments made in its territory by investors of a third country.'[170] In these cases, the applicability of MFN and NT is not limited to 'treatment' but applies to 'all matters subject to this agreement'.[171] This has been used as a basis by tribunals to extend the benefit of the MFN and NT to the entire BIT, including dispute resolution clauses. The two consequences have been that on the

---

169. *Ibid.*
170. Agreement between the Kingdom of Spain and the Argentine Republic for the Promotion and Reciprocal Protection of Investments, Art. 4.2 (signed 3 Oct. 1991, entered into force 28 Sept. 1992, Art. 4.2); Agreement between the Government of Australia and the Government of the Republic of India on the Promotion and Protection of Investments, *supra* n. 25, at Art. 4.2; Agreement between the Government of Australia and the Government of the Republic of Indonesia concerning the Promotion and Protection of Investments, Art. 4.1 (signed 17 Nov. 1992, entered into force 29 Jul. 1993); Agreement between the Government of the Kingdom of Sweden and the Government of the Republic of Argentina on the Promotion and Reciprocal Protection of Investments, Art. 3.1 (signed 22 Nov. 1991, entered into force 28 Sept. 1992); Agreement on the Mutual Promotion and Protection of Investments between the Republic of Korea and the Kingdom of Spain, Art. 3.1 (signed 17 Jan. 1994, entered into force 19 Jul. 1994); Agreement on the Promotion and Reciprocal Protection of Investments between the Government of the Republic of Albania and the Government of Ukraine, Art. 4(1) (signed 25 Oct. 2002); Agreement between the Government of the United Kingdom of Great Britain and Northern Ireland and the Government of the Republic of Argentina for the Promotion and Protection of Investments, Art. 3.1 (signed 11 Dec. 1990, entered into force 19 Feb. 1993).
171. Dolzer and Schreuer, *supra* n. 15, at 208.

basis of MFN, beneficial treatment clauses contained in other BITs entered into by the home State are said to apply to the concerned foreign investor as well. At the same time, tribunals have imported beneficial dispute resolution clauses – with lesser waiting period or other procedural restrictions – from BITs entered into by host State with other States to be applicable to the concerned investor. This however could happen because the language of the MFN clause was not limited to 'treatment' as is the case with Indian BITs. Therefore, the interpretation proposed by *Maffezini v. Spain* and followed by some other tribunals is inapplicable in the case of Indian BITs. This however did not stop the tribunal in *White Industries v. India* to use MFN to import favourable treatments standards form other BITs although the MFN applied only to treatment and not to the entire BIT.

There are certain common features that all MFN/NT clauses of Indian BITs contain. There are differences in language employed but they are mostly same. Except in some cases, fair and equitable is introduced but limited in scope to MFN or NT. First, MFN and NT all appear next to each other. Second, they apply to 'investments of investor' and 'operation, management, maintenance, use, enjoyment or disposal' of the investment. Third, they always contain two exceptions: exclusion of benefits granted under regional agreements, unions or preferential arrangements entered with other States and international agreements or matters relating wholly or mainly to taxation.

There are certain fundamental norms in relation to MFN that need to be kept in mind: it is a treaty-based standard and must be contained in a specific treaty; it requires comparison of two similarly placed foreign investors – therefore, 'a relative standard and must be applied to similar objective situations'; and governed by the *ejusdem generis* rule, whereby 'it may only apply to issues belonging to the same subject matter or the same category of subjects to which the clause relates'.[172]

MFN has existed in international economic treaties for centuries. MFN is the cornerstone of the international trading system envisaged under the WTO and enshrined in Article I of General Agreement on Tariffs and Trade (GATT).[173] They are not a part of customary law and are imposed only through a treaty. Their goal is 'to ensure that the relevant parties treat each other in a manner at least as favourable as they treat third parties.'[174] The term 'most favoured' is misleading. It does not mean granting most favoured treatment, rather the treatment shall not be less favourable than that granted to another entity under the treaty in question. MFN is a relative standard and would not come into operation if the host State does not grant any special benefit to any particular investor as opposed to the foreign investor in question. Once such a benefit is granted, it has to be equally applied to all.[175]

Three elements are involved in determination of violation of NT standard: (a) whether the foreign investor and the domestic investor are in a comparable situation –

---

172. UNCTAD, *Most-Favoured-Nation Treatment: UNCTAD Series on Issues in International Investment Agreements II* 22-7 (United Nations Publications 2010).
173. John Jackson, *The World Trading System*, 157-8 (2nd ed., The MIT Press 1997).
174. Dolzer and Schreuer, *supra* n. 15, at 206.
175. *Ibid.*

i.e., like circumstances; (b) whether the treatment accorded to the foreign investor is less favourable that that accorded to the domestic investor; and (c) if differentiation exists then whether there are grounds to justify the differentiation.[176] Treaties do not provide any guidance about how to apply these elements and what are its components.

The issues of 'like circumstances'[177] and justification for differential treatment under NT continue to apply in relation to MFN.[178] There are two aspects involved while deciding the alleged breach of an MFN/NT treatment clause. The first stage is of determination of whether the requirements of MFN and NT, which are inherent in the definition of the terms applied and thereafter, it is seen whether any of the exceptions cover them.

The first stage of analysis requires the identification of a comparable domestic investor. MFN and NT are not free standing standards they are dependent on other standards to determine their content. They are comparable standards. The challenge really is to determine with whom they are to be compared with and could be compared with. Many BITs do not contain the requirement of 'like circumstances', yet it continues to operate, since it is implicit in the concept of MFN.[179] None of the BITs use the 'like circumstances' test except the Mexico-India, India-Columbia and India-Slovakia BITs. The challenge is whether the domestic investor shall be in the same sector or the same business. This is a controversial area.

The further complication is in terms of which situation ought to be compared.[180] In *Feldman v. Mexico*, the tribunal found that 'in like circumstances' means same business, which was exporting cigarettes in that case.[181] In *Occidental v. Ecuador*, the tribunal declined to compare exclusively based on the sector in which the particular activity was undertaken.[182]

The interpretation of 'like circumstances' has to take place keeping in mind the broader framework and objective of the BIT and then it is to be decided whether 'like circumstances' should be interpreted broadly or narrowly.[183] Investment tribunals have applied inconsistent standards for comparison. For some, there should be the same sector with high degree of competition.[184] Some tribunals have interpreted sector widely: The concept of 'like circumstances' invites an examination of whether a

---

176. *Ibid.*, at 199; Also check *United Parcel Services v. Government of Canada*, Award on Merits, ICSID Case No. UNCT/02/1, para. 83 (24 May 2007).
177. *Bayindir Insaat Turizm Ticaret Ve Sanayi A.S. v. Islamic Republic of Pakistan*, Award, ICSID Case No. ARB/03/29, para. 388 (27 Aug. 2009); *Parkerings-Compagniet A.S. v. Republic of Lithuania*, Award, ICSID Case No. ARB/05/8, paras 377-430 (11 Sept. 2007); *Archer Daniels Midland Company v. The United Mexican States*, Award, ICSID Case No. ARB (AF)/04/5, paras 197-204 (21 Nov. 2007); *Corn Products International Inc. v. The United Mexican States*, Decision on Responsibility, ICSID Case No. ARB (AF)/04/1, paras 120 et seq. (15 Jan. 2008); UNCTAD, *supra* n. 172, at 29 et seq.
178. *Parkerings-Compagniet A.S. v. Republic of Lithuania*, *supra* n. 177, at paras 368 et seq.
179. UNCTAD, *supra* n. 172, at 54.
180. *Consortium RFCC v. Royaume du Maroc*, Arbitral Award, ICSID Case No. ARB (AF)/00/6, para. 53 (22 Dec. 2003).
181. *Feldman v. Mexico*, *supra* n. 56, at para. 171.
182. *Occidental v. Ecuador*, *supra* n. 114, at para. 173.
183. *S. D. Myers v. Government of Canada*, Partial Award, UNCITRAL, para. 250 (12 Nov. 2000).
184. *Ibid.*; *Pope & Talbot Inc. v. The Government of Canada*, Award on the Merits of Phase 2, UNCITRAL (10 Apr. 2001) para. 73. Both are in the same business of reselling/exporting

non-national investor complaining of less favourable treatment is in the same 'sector' as the national investor. Economic sector may be the same,[185] to the extent of the concepts of 'economic sector' and 'business sector'.[186]

Different treatment by itself does not amount to less favourable treatment. There has to be an element of discriminatory treatment.[187] The second requirement is of discrimination. Discrimination may take the form of de jure or de facto. A discrimination is de jure where the intention to discriminate is manifest and evident, and it is de facto when on the face of it, there is no discrimination but in fact, it does exist.[188] This position was summarized by the Tribunal in *Corn Products* in the following words:

> existence of discrimination is not a requirement for a breach ..., where such an intention is shown, that is sufficient to satisfy the third requirement [treatment less favourable, see para 117]. But the Tribunal would add that, even if an intention to discriminate has not been shown, the fact that the adverse effects of the tax were felt exclusively..., all of them foreign-owned, to the benefit of the sugar products, the majority of which were Mexican-owned, would be sufficient to establish that the third requirement of 'less favourable treatment' was satisfied.[189]

In *Thunderbird*, the tribunal expressed the view that there is no need to establish intention to discriminate, the presence of less favourable treatment is adequate.[190] If the differentiation caused is purely accidental due to a misguided policy decision then that is inadequate to establish that there was differential treatment.[191]

The third element of NT is whether there are adequate grounds to defend the discriminatory measures. Even if this justification is not present in treaties, it is widely accepted that such a defence exists.[192] For example, in *GAMI v. Mexico*, the tribunal found the objective of protecting solvency of an important local industry (sugar in that case) was a legitimate regulation, not aiming at discriminating against foreign investors.[193] In *ADF v. USA*, the Tribunal did not find violation of NT standard, even when

---

cigarettes. *Feldman v. Mexico, supra* n. 56, at paras 171-2; only like to be compared: *Nykomb Synergetics Technology Holding AB v. The Republic of Latvia*, Arbitral Award, SCC, para. 34 (16 Dec. 2003).
185. See *S. D. Myers v. Government of Canada, supra* n. 183, at para. 250; *Methanex Corp. v. USA, supra* n. 56, at Part IV-Chapter B; *Occidental v. Ecuador, supra* n. 114, at paras 173-4; *United Parcel Service of America Inc. v. Canada*, Separate Statement of Dean Ronald A. Cass: Award on Merits, para. 16 (24 May 2007).
186. *S. D. Myers v. Government of Canada, supra* n. 185.
187. UNCTAD, *supra* n. 172, at 28-9.
188. World Trade Organisation, European Communities – Measures Prohibiting the Importation and Marketing of Seal Products, *European Union's Responses to the Questions from the Panel following Second Meeting*, DS400, DS401, paras 157, 158 (Geneva, 23 May 2013); Jonathan Bonnitcha and Ors, *The Political Economy of the Investment Treaty Regime*, 96 (1st ed., Oxford University Press 2017).
189. *Corn Products International Inc. v. The United Mexican States, supra* n. 177, at para. 138.
190. *Thunderbird v. Mexico, supra* n. 183, at para. 177.
191. *Gami Investments Inc. v. The Government of the United Mexican States*, Award, UNCITRAL (15 Nov. 2004) at para. 114.
192. Dolzer &Schreuer, *supra* n. 15, at 202.
193. *Gami Investments Inc. v. The Government of the United Mexican States, supra* n. 191, at paras 114-5.

the US required locally produced steel to be used for government projects – because it applied equally to national and foreign contractors.[194]

In *Thunderbird v. Mexico*, the tribunal expressed the opinion that a claim of NT could not be made if the conduct of the foreign investor was illegal according to the national law, even if the national law was not uniformly enforced – in that case, it was gambling.[195] Tribunals have held that presence of intention is not necessary in determination of presence of discrimination. The Tribunal, in *Siemens v. Argentina*, stated that: 'The Tribunal concurs that intention is not decisive or essential for a finding of discrimination, and that the impact of the measure on the investment would be the determining factor to ascertain whether it had resulted in non-discriminatory treatment.'[196] Some tribunals have held that discriminatory intent is necessary.[197]

An element of the determination would be whether a differentiation has taken place and whether it had some justification. The existence of 'like circumstances' has been determined by tribunals in light of the question of whether the entities were subjected to 'like legal requirement' in their regulatory treatment.[198] Insisting on the important of regulatory freedom as an exception from NT, the tribunal, in *SD Myers v. Canada*, stated that: 'The assessment of "like circumstances" must also take into account circumstances that would justify governmental regulations that treat them differently in order protect the public interest.'[199] Exceptions have been interpreted differently by tribunals. The Tribunal, in *National Grid v. Argentina*, held that MFN would apply to jurisdiction as well, and was not limited to the exceptions (customs union, free trade area, economic community, taxes, etc.).[200] In *Palma v. Bulgaria*, the Tribunal did not adopt this interpretation. It interpreted 'privilege' in the exception to mean that MFN applied only to substantive protection and did not extend to jurisdiction.[201]

All investment treaties contain exceptions to MFN and NT:

'3. The provisions of paragraphs 1 and 2 above shall not be construed to require Contracting Party to extend to the investors of the other Party the benefit of any treatment, preference or privilege resulting from:

---

194. *ADF Group Inc. v. United States of America*, Award, ICSID Case No. ARB (AF)/00/1, paras 156-8 (9 Jan. 2003).
195. *Thunderbird v. Mexico*, supra n. 183, at para. 183.
196. *Siemens v. Argentina*, supra n. 129, at para. 321; *Feldman v. Mexico*, supra n. 56, at para. 181; *Bayindir v. Pakistan*, supra n. 177, at para. 309; *Corn Products International Inc. v. The United Mexican States*, supra n. 177, at 201; *S. D. Myers v. Government of Canada*, supra n. 183, at paras 254-5.
197. *Alex Genin v. The Republic of Estonia*, Award, ICSID Case No. ARB/99/2, para. 369 (25 Jun. 2001); *Methanex Corp. v. USA*, supra n. 56, Part, at para. 12.
198. *Grand River Enterprises Six Nations Ltd. v. United States of America*, Award, UNCITRAL, para. 166 (12 Jan. 2011).
199. *S. D. Myers v. Government of Canada*, supra n. 183, at para. 250.
200. *National Grid plc v. The Argentine Republic*, Decision on Jurisdiction, UNCITRAL, para. 82 (20 Jun. 2006).
201. *Plama Cosortium Ltd. v. Republic of Bulgaria*, Decision on Jurisdiction, ICSID Case No. ARB/03/24, para. 191(8 Feb. 2005).

(a) Any existing or future agreement of free trade zone, customs union, market or a similar regional agreement in which Contracting Party is or may be a party, or
  (b) Any international agreement or arrangement relating, wholly or mainly to taxes, or any domestic legislation relating wholly or mainly to taxes, or
  (c) Any bilateral agreement providing for special financing concluded by Contracting Party with a third country.'[202]
(3) The provisions of paragraphs (1) and (2) above shall not be construed so as to oblige one Contracting Party to extend to the investors of the other the benefit of any treatment, preference or privilege resulting from:
  (a) any existing or future free trade area, customs unions, monetary union or similar international agreement or other forms of regional cooperation to which one of the Contracting Parties is or may become a party, or
  (b) any matter pertaining wholly or mainly to taxation.[203]
(4) This Article shall not require a Contracting Party to extend to investments any treatment, preference or privilege resulting from:
  (a) any customs union, economic union, free trade area or regional economic integration agreement to which the Contracting Party belongs; or
  (b) the provisions of a double taxation agreement with a third country; or
  (c) any legislation relating wholly or mainly to taxation.[204]
3. The provisions of paragraph (1) shall not be constructed as to oblige one Contracting Party to extend to the investors of the other Contracting Party and their investments the present or future benefit of any treatment, preference or privilege resulting from
  (a) any present or future customs union, common market, free trade area or membership in an economic community or a similar international agreement.
  (b) any matter, including international agreements, pertaining wholly or mainly to taxation.[205]
(3) The provisions of paragraphs (1) and (2) above shall not be construed so as to oblige one Contracting Party to extend to the investors of the other the benefit of any treatment, preference or privilege resulting from:
  (a) any existing or future customs union, free trade area or regional cooperation organisation or similar international agreement to which either of the Contracting Parties is or may become a party, or
  (b) any international agreement or arrangement, or any domestic legislation, relating wholly or mainly to taxation.[206]
(3) The provisions of paragraphs (1) and (2) above shall not be construed so as to oblige one Contracting Party to extend to the investors of the other Contracting Party the benefit of any treatment, preference or privilege resulting from:
  (a) any existing or future customs unions or similar international agreement to which it is or may become a party; or

---

202. Agreement between the Government of the Republic of India and the Government of the Argentine Republic on the Promotion and Reciprocal Protection of Investments, *supra* n. 131, at Art. 4.3.
203. Agreement between the Government of the Republic of India and the Government of the Republic of Armenia for the Promotion and Protection of Investments, *supra* n. 13, at Art. 4.3.
204. Agreement between the Government of Australia and the Government of the Republic of India on the Promotion and Protection of Investments, *supra* n. 25, at Art. 4.4.
205. Agreement between the Government of the Republic of Austria and the Government of the Republic of India for the Promotion and Protection of Investments, *supra* n. 8, at Art. 3.3.
206. Agreement between the Government of the Republic of India and the Government of the Kingdom of Bahrain for the Promotion and Protection of Investments, *supra* n. 6, at Art. 4.3.

Chapter 5: Treatment Standards §5.03

(b) any matter pertaining wholly or mainly to taxation.[207]

The China-India BIT also contains a similar language. There is an additional sentence after clause (b) that clarifies that all taxation matters would be dealt with under the avoidance of double taxation treaty between India and China.[208] The India-Iceland BIT has a similar clause and adds the following to sub-clause (b): 'Nothing in this Agreement shall affect the rights and obligations of either Contracting Party derived from any tax convention. In the event of any inconsistency between the provisions of this Agreement and any tax convention, the provisions of the latter shall prevail.'[209]

---

207. Agreement between the Government of the Republic of India and the Government of the People's Republic of Bangladesh for the Promotion and Protection of Investments, *supra* n. 6, at Art. 4.3; Agreement between the Government of the Republic of India and the Government of the Republic of Belarus for the Promotion and Protection of Investments, *supra* n. 18, at Art. 4.3; Agreement between the Government of the Republic of India and the Belgo-Luxembourg Economic Union for the Promotion and Protection of Investments, Art. 4.3 (signed 31 Oct. 1997, entered into force 8 Jan. 2001); Agreement between the Government of the Republic of India and the Government of His Majesty the Sultan and Yang Di-Pertuan of Brunei Darussalam on the Reciprocal Promotion and Protection of Investments, *supra* n. 29, at Art. 4.3; Agreement between the Government of the Republic of India and the Government of the Republic of Bulgaria for the Promotion and Protection of Investments, *supra* n. 6, at Art. 4.3(b); Agreement between the Government of the Republic of India and the Government of the Democratic Republic of Congo for the Mutual Promotion and Protection of Investments, *supra* n. 6, at Art. 4.3; Agreement between the Government of the Republic of Croatia and the Government of the Republic of India for the Promotion and Reciprocal Protection of Investments, *supra* n. 40, at Art. 4.3; Agreement between the Czech Republic and the Republic of India for the Promotion and Protection of Investments, *supra* n. 6, at Art. 3.3; Agreement between the Government of the Republic of India and the Government of the Republic of Djibouti for the Promotion and Protection of Investments, *supra* n. 18, Art. 4.3; Agreement between the Government of the Republic of India and the Government of the Arab Republic of Egypt for the Promotion and Reciprocal Protection of Investments, *supra* n. 23, at Art. 3.3; Agreement between the Government of the Republic of India and the Government of the Republic of France on the Reciprocal Promotion and Protection of Investments, *supra* n. 16, at Art. 5.4; Agreement between the Government of the Republic of India and the Government of the Republic of Ghana for the Reciprocal Promotion and Protection of Investments, *supra* n. 18, at Art. 4.3; Agreement between the Government of the Republic of India and the Government of the Hellenic Republic on the Promotion and Protection of Investments, Art. 4.3(b) (signed 26 Apr. 2007 entered into force 12 Apr. 2008); Agreement between the Government of the Republic of India and the Government of the State of Israel for the Promotion and Protection of Investments, *supra* n. 40, at Art. 4.3; Agreement between the Government of the Republic of Kazakhstan and the Government of the Republic of India for the Promotion and Reciprocal Protection of Investments, Art. 4(3)(b) (signed 9 Dec. 1996, entered into force 26 Jul. 2001); Agreement between the Government of the Republic of India and the Government of the Republic of Korea on the Promotion and Protection of Investments, *supra* n. 6, at Art. 3.4; Agreement between the Government of the Republic of India and the Government of the Lao People's Democratic Republic for the Promotion and Protection of Investments, *supra* n. 40, at Art. 4.3.
208. For a similar language, *see* The Government of the Kingdom of Morocco and the Government of the Republic of India for the Promotion and Protection of Investments, Art. 3.3(b) (signed 13 Feb. 1999, entered into force 22 Feb. 2001); Agreement between the Government of the Republic of India and the Government of the Union of Myanmar for the Reciprocal Promotion and Protection of Investments, Art. 4.3 (signed 24 Jun. 2008, entered into force 8 Feb. 2009).
209. Agreement between the Government of the Republic of India and the Government of the Republic of Iceland for the Promotion and Protection of Investments, *supra* n. 40, at Art. 4.4.

Article 4. The provisions of this Agreement relative to the granting of treatment not less favourable than that accorded to the investors of each Contracting Patty or of any third State shall not be construed so as to oblige one Contracting Party to extend to the investors of the other Contracting Party the benefit of any treatment, preference or privilege resulting from:

(a) membership of any existing or future Regional Economic Integration Organisation or customs union of which one of the Contracting Parties is or may become a party, or
(b) any matter pertaining wholly or mainly to taxation.[210]

3. The provisions of paragraphs 1 and 2 above shall not be construed so as to oblige one Contracting Party to extend to the investors of the other Contracting Party the benefit of any treatment, preference or privilege accorded to investors of any third State resulting from:
   a) any existing or future customs union, free trade area, economic union or similar international agreement to which it is or may become a party, or
   b) agreements on avoidance of double taxation or any other international arrangements pertaining wholly or mainly to taxation.[211]

On exclusion of regional and free trade unions, the provision of the Germany-India BIT is very similar. However, it paraphrases the taxation exemption that is granted through legislation or arrangements. The exception to MFN and NT is framed in Article 4 as follows:

(2) The Provisions of paragraph 1 shall not relate to privileges which either Contracting Party accords to investors of third States on account of its membership of, or association with, a customs or economic union, a common market or a free trade area.
(3) The Provisions of paragraph 1 shall also not relate to advantages which either Contracting Party accords to its own investors or to investors of third Stats by virtue of an agreement, legislation or arrangements consequent to such legislation regarding matters of taxation, including an agreement on the avoidance of double taxation.[212]

A similar reference to domestic legislation based on taxation arrangements is contained in the India-Latvia BIT.[213]

MFN has emerged as a controversial treatment standard due to the interpretation given to it by some investment tribunals. In *Maffezini v. Spain*, the Tribunal disregarded the eighteen month-waiting period under the Spain-Argentina BIT, because

---

210. Agreement between the Government of the Republic of India and the Government of the Kingdom of Denmark Concerning the Promotion and Reciprocal Protection of Investments, *supra* n. 18, at Art. 4.
211. Agreement between Bosnia and Herzegovina and the Republic of India for the Promotion and Protection of Investments, Art. 4.3(b) (signed 12 Sept. 2006, entered into force 13 Feb. 2008).
212. Agreement between the Federal Republic of Germany and the Republic of India for the Promotion and Protection of Investments, *supra* n. 6, at Art. 4(2) & (3).
213. Agreement between the Government of the Republic of India and the Government of the Republic of Latvia for the Promotion and Protection of Investments, *supra* n. 30, at Art. 4.3.

under the Spain-Chile BIT, there was no such restriction and the Spain-Argentina BIT contained an MFN clause.[214] The Tribunal went further to clarify that:

> As a matter of principle, the beneficiary of the clause should not be able to override public policy considerations that the contracting parties might have envisaged as fundamental conditions for their acceptance of the agreement in question, particularly if the beneficiary is a private investor, as will often be the case. The scope of the clause might thus be narrower than it appears at first sight. It is clear, in any event, that a distinction has to be made between the legitimate extension of rights and benefits by means of the operation of the clause, on the one hand, and disruptive treaty-shopping that would play havoc with the policy objectives of underlying specific treaty provisions, on the other hand.[215]

The unusual interpretation given by the Tribunal has sparked a debate and divided arbitral tribunals and the possibility of conciliation of views is absent.[216] The decision has focused the debate in investment arbitration from the meaning and interpretation of MFN to the question of its applicability to dispute resolution clauses and importing beneficial treatment standards from other treaties.[217] Many tribunals thereafter took the view that such an extension is possible.[218] All matters include dispute resolution and since the exclusion clause in MFN does not contain dispute resolution, MFN can be applied.[219] On the other hand many tribunals have rejected the *Maffezini* approach.[220] In *Wintershall v. Argentina* this was rejected because jurisdiction is based on consent of States and the jurisdictional clauses in a treaty cannot be interpreted flexibly to import beneficial provisions.[221]

---

214. *Emilio Agustín Maffezini v. The Kingdom of Spain*, Decision of the Tribunal on the Objections of Jurisdiction, ICSID Case No. ARB/97/7, para. 56 (25 Jan. 2000).
215. *Ibid.*, at paras 62-3.
216. UNCTAD, *supra* n. 172, at 2-4.
217. *Ibid.*, at 5-6.
218. *Siemens A.G. v. The Argentine Republic*, Decision on Jurisdiction, ICSID Case No. ARB/02/8, para. 102 (3 Aug. 2004); *Gas Natural SDG, S.A. v. The Republic of Argentina*, Decision of the Tribunal on Preliminary Questions on Jurisdiction, ICSID Case No. ARB/03/10, para. 49 (17 Jun. 2005); *Suez, Sociedad General de Aguas de Barcelona S.A., and InterAguas Servicios Integrales del Agua, S.A. v. The Republic of Argentina*, Decision on Jurisdiction, ICSID Case No. ARB/03/17, para. 57 (16 May 2006).
219. *Camuzzi International S.A. v. The Republic of Argentina*, Decision of the Tribunal on Objections to Jurisdiction, ICSID Case No. ARB/03/7, para. 120 (10 Jun. 2005); *National Grid plc v. Republic of Argentina*, supra n. 200, at para. 82-3; *AWG Group Ltd v. The Republic of Argentina*, Decision on Jurisdiction, UNCITRAL, para. 68 (3 Aug. 2006); *RosInvestCo UK Ltd. v. The Russian Federation*, Award, SCC, Case No. 079/2005, paras 131-2 (October 2007).
220. *Salini Costruttori S.p.A. and Italstrade S.p.A. v. The Hashemite Kingdom of Jordan*, Decision on Jurisdiction, ICSID Case No. ARB/02/13, para. 115 (29 Nov. 2004); *Plama Cosortium Ltd. v. Republic of Bulgaria*, supra n. 201, at paras 209, 212-3; *Telenor Mobile Communications A.S. v. The Republic of Hungary*, Award, ICSID Case No. ARB/04/15, paras 92-5 (13 Sept. 2006); *Vladimir Berschader and Moise Berschader v. The Russian Federation*, Award, SCC, Case No. 080/2005, paras 178, 181 (21 Apr. 2006); *Tza Yap Shum v. The Republic of Peru*, Decision on Jurisdiction and Competence, ICSID Case No. ARB/07/6, paras 196, 198, 216. (19 Jun. 2009).
221. *Wintershall Aktiengesellschaft v. The Argentine Republic*, Award, ICSID Case No. ARB/04/14, paras 106 (3), 167, 185-6 (8 Dec. 2008).

MFN applies to procedural as well as substantive principles.[222] The presence of FET in MFN clauses is interpreted to mean that other substantive obligations in other BITs of the host State could be applied in relation to any investor. The Tribunal in *MTD v. Chile* held that:

> The Tribunal has concluded that, under the BIT, the fair and equitable treatment standard of treatment has to be interpreted in the manner most favourable to investments. The Tribunal considers that to include as part of the protection of the BIT those included in Article 3(1) of the Denmark BIT and Article 3 (3) and (4) of the Croatia BIT is in consonance with this purpose. The Tribunal is further convinced of this conclusion by the fact that the exclusions in the MFN clause relate to tax treatment and regional cooperation, matters alien to the BIT but that, because of the general nature of the MFN clause, the Contracting Parties considered it prudent to exclude. *A contratio sensu*, other matters that can be construed to be part of the fair and equitable treatment of investors would be covered by the same clause.[223]

The state of the law on MFN is in confusion, and it is difficult to say in which direction the jurisprudence will proceed.[224] There is clearly a divide in approaches of tribunals which is irreconcilable.

In any case, some tribunals have viewed the possibility of invocation of FET contained in another BIT on the basis of MFN.[225]

MFN is seen by these tribunals as a treatment standard that applies to the conditions expected in the host State, rather than a treaty provision applicable to actions of the government. If treatment is interpreted to mean conditions in the host State then the scope of MFN gets widened and transgresses the scope of State consent. Whereas in realty MFN applies to treatment, rather than conditions in the host State. BITs do not state that conditions have to be in conformity with MFN, they only expect the treatment granted to the foreign investor complies with MFN.

The India-Columbia BIT employs the same language and excludes the operation of MFN from double taxation treaty by using the following words: '(b) Any matter pertaining wholly or mainly to taxation including an agreement for the avoidance of double taxation.'

The India-Columbia BIT also counters the trend amongst investment tribunals in interpreting MFN to import favourable treatment standards from other treaties or extending MFN to dispute resolution clauses in the following words:

> 3. The most favourable treatment to be granted in like circumstances referred to in this Agreement does not encompass mechanisms for the settlement of investment disputes, such as those contained in Articles 9 (Settlement of Disputes between One Contracting Party and an Investor of the Other Contracting Party) and 10

---

222. *Hochtief AG v. The Argentine Republic*, Decision on Jurisdiction, ICSID Case No. ARB/07/31, para. 67 (24 Oct. 2011).
223. *MTD Equity Sdn. Bhd. and MTD Chile S.A. v. Republic of Chile*, supra n. 112, at paras 103-4.
224. Dolzer and Schreuer, *supra* n. 15, at 211.
225. *Bayindir v. Pakistan*, Decision on Jurisdiction ICSID Case No. ARB/03/29, paras 231-2 (14 Nov. 2005), *supra* n. 177, at paras 163-7.

(Settlement of Disputes between the Contracting Parties) of this Agreement, which are provided for in treaties or international investment agreements.

This clause is also called the *Maffezini* clause because it is meant to counter the effect of decision in the *Maffezini* case.[226] In order to tackle all these problems, the 2015 Model BIT does not contain an MFN clause.

The 2015 Model BIT does not contain MFN but contains only NT, albeit with clarifications. It clarifies the meaning of like circumstances – an important element of any comparative standard yet undefined in BITs in the past. Article 4 of the 2015 defines MFN as follows:

> 4.1 Each Party shall not apply to investor or to investments made by investors of the other Party, measures that accord less favourable treatment than that it accords, in like circumstances, to its own investors or to investments by such investors with respect to the management, conduct, operation, sale or other disposition of investments in its territory.
>
> 4.2 The treatment accorded by a Party under Article 4.1 means, with respect to a Sub-national government, treatment no less favourable than the treatment accorded, in like circumstances, by that Sub-national government to investors, and to investments of investors, of the Party of which it forms a part.

For greater certainty, whether treatment is accorded in 'like circumstances' depends on the totality of the circumstances, including whether the relevant treatment distinguishes between investors or investments on the basis of legitimate regulatory objectives. These circumstances include, but are not limited to: (a) the goods or services consumed or produced by the investment; (b) the actual and potential impact of the investment on third persons, the local community, or the environment; (c) whether the investment is public, private, or State-owned or controlled; and (d) the practical challenges of regulating the investment.

---

226. *See* UNCTAD, *supra* n. 172, at 84-7.

CHAPTER 6
Dispute Resolution and Enforcement of Investment Awards

The dispute resolution process under investment arbitration takes place based on the clauses on dispute resolution in the investment treaty. The procedure for appointment of an arbitral tribunal is mentioned therein. Indian BITs have always contained provisions on mandatory dispute resolution through investor-State arbitration. The 2015 Model BIT does contain a provision for investor-State arbitration but with certain procedural requirements. There are elaborate provisions on other areas relating to dispute resolution. All these aspects are discussed in this chapter. This chapter would also discuss the procedure and consequences post an investment award, particularly in relation to the enforcement of an investment award.

§6.01 DISPUTE RESOLUTION PROVISIONS

Consent of the host State to arbitration is represented in three modes: consent expressly mentioned in the domestic legislation,[1] unilateral offer to arbitrate contained in a BIT[2] or direct agreement between the parties to submit the dispute to investment arbitration.[3] India does not have a domestic legislation that gives consent to arbitration. Most cases are covered in the BITs. International adjudication is consensual, meaning thereby that the consent to arbitration by the State has to be expressly mentioned. The dispute resolution provisions contained in BITs are in the nature of an offer to arbitrate.[4] They do not represent an agreement with each investor and specific to the disputes that have arisen. Tribunals have held that the dispute resolution provisions

---

1. C.H. Schreuer, *The ICSID Convention: A Commentary*, paras 392-409 (2nd ed., Cambridge University Press 2009).
2. *Ibid.*, at paras 427-8.
3. *Ibid.*, at paras 382-91.
4. *See* generally, Jan Paulsson, *Arbitration Without Privity*, 10(2) Foreign Investment Law Journal (ICSID Review 1995).

mentioned in the BIT are sufficient and there is no need of any additional consent to dispute settlement by an investment tribunal.[5]

There are two categories of disputes covered under the dispute resolution provisions in BITs: State-to-State disputes and investor-State disputes. Disputes regarding the interpretation and application of the BIT between the States could be decided through the provision on State-to-State disputes. The Indian BITs in the past also contained this provision. For example, the India-United Kingdom BIT has the following provision:

> (1) Disputes between the Contracting Parties concerning the interpretation or application of this Agreement should, if possible, be settled through negotiation.
> (2) If a dispute between the Contracting Parties cannot thus be settled within six months from the time the dispute arose, it shall upon the request of either Contracting Party be submitted to an arbitral tribunal.
> (3) Such an arbitral tribunal shall be constituted for each individual case in the following way. Within two months of the receipt of the request for arbitration, each Contracting Party shall appoint one member of the tribunal. Those two members shall then select a national of a third State who on approval by the two Contracting Parties shall be appointed Chairman of the tribunal. The Chairman shall be appointed within two months from the date of appointment of the other two members.
> (4) If within the periods specified in paragraph (3) of this Article the necessary appointments have not been made, either Contracting Party may, in the absence of any other agreement, invite the President of the International Court of Justice to make any necessary appointments. If the President is a national of either Contracting Party or if he is otherwise prevented from discharging the said function, the Vice-President shall be invited to make the necessary appointments. If the Vice-President is a national of either Contracting Party or if he too is prevented from discharging the said function, the Member of the International Court of Justice next in seniority who is not a national of either Contracting Party shall be invited to make the necessary appointments.
> (5) The arbitral tribunal shalt reach its decision by a majority of votes. Such decision shall be binding on both Contracting Parties. Each Contracting Party shall bear the cost of its own member of the tribunal and of its representation in the arbitral proceedings; the cost of the Chairman and the remaining costs shall be borne in equal parts by the Contracting Parties. The tribunal may, however, in its decision direct that a higher proportion of costs shall be borne

---

5. *Ibid.*, at 232-57; *American Manufacturing & Trading, Inc. v. Republic of Zaire*, Award, ICSID Case No. ARB/93/1, para. 5.19 (21 Feb. 1997); *Salini Costruttori S.p.A. and Italstrade S.p.A. v. Kingdom of Morocco*, Decision on Jurisdiction, ICSID Case No. ARB/00/4, para. 27 (23 Jul. 2001); *Salini Costruttori S.p.A. and Italstrade S.p.A. v. The Hashemite Kingdom of Jordan*, Decision on Jurisdiction, ICSID Case No. ARB/02/13, para. 66 (29 Nov. 2004); *Impregilo S.p.A. v. Islamic Republic of Pakistan*, Decision on Jurisdiction, ICSID Case No. ARB/03/3, para. 109 (22 Apr. 2005); *LG&E Energy Corp., LG&E Capital Corp., and LG&E International, Inc v. Argentine Republic*, Decision on Jurisdiction, ICSID Case No. ARB/02/1, para. 73 (30 Apr. 2004); *El Paso Energy International Company v. The Argentine Republic, Decision on Jurisdiction*, ICSID Case No. ARB/03/15, para. 36 (27 Apr. 2006); *Tokios Tokelés v. Ukraine, Decision on Jurisdiction*, ICSID Case No. ARB/02/18, para. 94 (29 Apr. 2004).

by one of the two Contracting Parties, and this award shall be binding on both Contracting Parties. The tribunal shall determine its own procedure.[6]

A similar provision is seen in other Indian BITs as well.[7] The 2015 Model BIT also contains a similar provision under Article 31, which is as under:

Disputes between Parties
31.1 Disputes between the Parties concerning:
    (i) the interpretation or application of this Treaty, or
    (ii) whether there has been compliance with obligations to consult in good faith under Articles 30 or 36, should, as far as possible, be settled through consultation or negotiation, which may include the use of non-binding third-party mediation or other mechanisms.
31.2 If a dispute between the Parties cannot be settled within six months from the time the dispute arose, it shall upon the request of either Party be submitted to a Tribunal.
31.3 Such a Tribunal shall be constituted for each individual case in the following way: Within two months of the receipt of the request for arbitration, each Party shall appoint one member of the Tribunal. Those two members shall then select a national of a third State who, on approval by the two Parties, shall be appointed Chairman of the Tribunal. The Chairman shall be appointed within two months from the date of appointment of the other two members.
31.4 If within the periods specified in Article 31.3 the necessary appointment(s) have not been made, either Party may, in the absence of any other agreement, invite the President of the International Court of Justice to make any necessary appointment(s). If the President is a national of either Party or if he or she is otherwise prevented from discharging the said function, the Vice President shall be invited to make the necessary appointment(s). If the Vice President is a national of either Party or if he or she too is prevented from discharging the said function, the member of the International Court of Justice next in seniority who is not a national of either Party shall be invited to make the necessary appointment(s).

---

6. Agreement between the Government of the United Kingdom of Great Britain and Northern Ireland and the Government of the Republic of India for the Promotion and Reciprocal Protection of Investments, Art. 10 (signed 14 Mar. 1994, entered into force 6 Jan. 1995).
7. Agreement between the Government of the Republic of India and the Government of Republic of Iceland for the Promotion and Protection of Investments, Art. 10 (signed 29 Jun. 2007, entered into force 16 Dec. 2008); Agreement between the Government of the Republic of India and the Federal Government of the Federal Republic of Yugoslavia for the Reciprocal Promotion and Protection of Investments, Art. 10 (signed 31 Jan. 2003, entered into force 24 Feb. 2009); Agreement between the Government of the Republic of India and the Government of the Republic of Poland for the Promotion and Protection of Investments, Art. 10 (signed 7 Oct. 1996, entered into force 31 Dec. 1997); Agreement between the Republic of India and the Great Socialist People's Libyan Arab Jamahiriya for the Promotion and Protection of Investments, Art. 10 (signed 26 May 2007, entered into force 23 Mar. 2009); Agreement between the Government of the Republic of India and the Government of the Republic of Armenia for the Promotion and Protection of Investments, Art. 10 (signed 23 May 2003, entered into force 30 May 2006); Agreement between the Government of the Republic of India and the Government of Kingdom of Bahrain for the Promotion and Protection of Investments, Art. 10 (signed 13 Jan. 2004, entered into force 5 Dec. 2007); Agreement between the Government of the Republic of India and the Government of People's Republic of Bangladesh for the Promotion and Protection of Investments, Art. 10 (signed 9 Feb. 2009, entered into force 7 Jul. 2011); Also refer to Indian Model Agreement for the Promotion and Protection of Investments, Arts 9, 10 (2003).

31.5 The arbitral tribunal shall reach its decision by a majority of votes. Such decision shall be binding on both Parties.
31.6 The Parties to the arbitration shall share the costs of the arbitration, including the arbitrator fees, expenses, allowances and other administrative costs. Each Party shall bear the cost of its representation in the arbitral proceedings. The Tribunal may, however, in its discretion direct that the entire costs or a higher proportion of costs shall be borne by one of the two disputing Parties and this determination shall be binding on both disputing Parties.
31.7 The Tribunal shall decide all questions relating to its competence and, subject to any agreement between the disputing Parties, determine its own procedure, taking into account the PCA Optional Rules.[8]

These provisions have never been invoked by India or against India by any other State. However, there have been many instances where States have resorted to these provisions.[9]

Prior to invocation of arbitration, the dispute resolution provisions provide certain procedures. They specify that the parties to dispute should engage in negotiations for a period of six months. If the disputes are not resolved in that period then arbitration could be commenced.[10] This period is also known as the 'cooling-off' period. The objective behind this is that the parties may succeed in arriving at a

---

8. *Model Text for the Indian Bilateral Investment Treaty*, Art. 31 (28 Dec. 2015) http://www.finmin.nic.in/reports/ModelTextIndia_BIT.pdf (accessed 12 Jul. 2017).
9. For example, refer to *Republic of Ecuador v. United States of America*, Request of the Republic of Ecuador, PCA Case No. 2012-5, paras 7, 8 (28 Jun. 2011); *Italian Republic v. Republic of Cuba*, Interim Award (sentence preliminaire) Ad hoc State-State arbitration, para. 6 (15 Mar. 2005); *see Peru v. Chile* (2003), where Art. 9(1) and (2) of the dispute settlement clause in the BIT stated 'Controversias entre las Partes Contratantes' [Disputes between Contracting States] of the Chile-Peru BIT (2000) reads: '1. Las controversias entre las Partes Contratantes relativas a la interpretación o aplicación del Convenio serán resueltas mediante canales diplomáticos. 2. En caso de que ambas Partes Contratantes no pudieren llegar a un acuerdo dentro de seis meses, la controversia será, a petición de cualquiera de las Partes Contratantes, remitida a un tribunal arbitral compuesto por tres miembros. Cada Parte Contratante deberá designar a un árbitro, y esos dos árbitros deberán designar a un Presidente, que deberá ser nacional de un tercer Estado'; For *Peru v. Chile* (2003) also refer to L.E. Peterson, *ICSID Tribunal Declines to Halt Investor Arbitration in Deference to State-to-State Arbitration*, IISD INVEST-SD: Investment Law and Policy Weekly News Bulletin (19 Dec. 2003) http:// www.iisd.org/pdf/2003/investment_investsd_dec19_2003.pdf (accessed 12 Jul. 2017); *Mexico v. United States (in the Matter of Cross-Border Trucking Services)*, Final Report of the Panel, NAFTA Chapter 20 State-to-State arbitration, paras 15-24 (6 Feb. 2001); Also generally refer to Nathalie Bernasconi-Osterwalder, *State-State Dispute Settlement in Investment Treaties Best Practices Series*, 8-16 (The International Institute for Sustainable Development October 2014).
10. Agreement between the Government of the Republic of Armenia and the Government of the Republic of India, *supra* n. 7, at Art. 9(1) and 9(2); Agreement between the Government of Bangladesh and the Government of the Republic of India, *supra* n. 7, at Art. 9(1) and 9(2); Agreement between the Government of Czech Republic and the Government of the Republic of India, Art. 8(1) and 8(2) (signed 11 Oct. 1996, entered into force 6 Feb. 1998); Agreement between the Government of Israel and the Government of the Republic of India, Art. 9(1) and 9(2) (signed 29 Jan. 1996, entered into force 18 Feb. 1997); Agreement between the Government of Malaysia and the Government of the Republic of India, Art. 7(1) and 7(2) (signed 3 Aug. 1995, entered into force 12 Apr. 1997, terminated on 23 May 2017); Agreement between the Government of Portugal and the Government of the Republic of India, Art. 10(1) and 10(2) (signed 28 Jun. 2000, entered into force 19 Jul. 2002); Agreement between the Government of Qatar and the Government of the Republic of India, Art. 8(1) and 8(2) (signed 7 Apr. 1999, entered into force 15 Dec. 1999).

Chapter 6: Dispute Resolution and Enforcement §6.01

peaceful settlement obviating the need to go for arbitration. Peaceful negotiations cannot be an empty formality. Parties have to make a 'good faith' effort.[11] It is not mandatory that they arrive at some settlement.

Some tribunals took the position that there is no need to wait for the six-month 'cooling-off' period and arbitration could be initiated immediately after disputes arose. This happened in the *Maffezini* case where the tribunal held that since the underlying BIT contained a most favoured nation (MFN) clause, the investment tribunal could import beneficial provisions from other BITs.[12] One of the beneficial provisions is the absence of the need to wait for six months. Some tribunals have followed this approach,[13] whereas others have not.[14] There are various policy reasons for not taking such a stand.[15] It is not clear how a tribunal would interpret such a provision. Indian Model BIT has ended this debate by excluding the application of MFN to dispute resolution clauses by removing MFN altogether from the Model BIT. Also, the dispute resolution provisions contain an express provision that arbitration proceedings could be initiated only against violation of treaty standards provided in the present BIT.[16] This obviates the possibility of provisions from another BIT being imported.

The old BITs provided that the parties to dispute have to appoint arbitrators within two months.[17] If parties fail to appoint arbitrator within a period of two months

---

11. *Case concerning Pulp Mills on the River Uruguay (Argentina v. Uruguay)*, Judgment, ICJ Reports, paras 143-50 (20 Apr. 2010); *Murphy Exploration and Production Company International v. Republic of Ecuador*, Award on Jurisdiction, ICSID Case No. ARB/08/4, para. 154 (15 Dec. 2010); *Enron Corporation and Ponderosa Assets, L.P. v. Argentine Republic*, Award on Jurisdiction, ICSID Case No. ARB/01/3, para. 88 (14 Jan. 2004); *See* generally Matthias Goldmann, *Putting your Faith in Good Faith: A Principled Strategy for Smoother Sovereign Debt Workouts*, 41(2) Yale Journal of International Law (2016); Joseph F. O'Connor, *Good Faith in International Law*, 45-79 (1991); Andreas R. Ziegler and Jorun Baumgartner, *Good Faith as a General Principle of (International) Law*, 9 (Andrew D. Mitchell, et al. (eds), 2015); Friedrich Kessler and Edith Fine, *Culpa in Contrahendo, Bargaining in Good Faith, and Freedom of Contract: A Comparative Study*, 77, 401, 404 Harvard Law Review (1964); Robert Kolb, *Principles as Sources of International Law (with Special Reference to Good Faith)*, 53 Netherlands International Law Review 1, 17-8 (2006); Anthony D'Amato, *Good Faith in Encyclopaedia of Public International Law* 2, 599 (Rudolf Bernhardt ed. 1995); *See* generally Anne Peters, *International Dispute Settlement: A Network of Co-operational Duties*, Vol. 14 No. 1, 1-34 (EJIL 2003).
12. *Maffezini v. Kingdom of Spain*, Decision on Jurisdiction, ICSID Case No. ARB/97/7, 56-64 (25 Jan. 2000).
13. *Siemens A.G. v. Argentine Republic*, Decision on Jurisdiction, ICSID Case No. ARB/02/8, 32-110 (3 Aug. 2004); *National Grid PCL v. Argentina*, Decision on Jurisdiction, UNCITRAL (20 Jun. 2006); *Gas Natural SDG, S.A. v. The Argentine Republic*, Decision on Jurisdiction, ICSID Case No. ARB/03/10, 24-31, 41-9 (17 Jun. 2005).
14. *Wintershall Aktiengesellschaft v. Argentine Republic*, Award, ICSID Case No. ARB/04/14, 163-74 (8 Nov. 2008); *Salini Costruttori S.p.A. and Italstrade S.p.A. v. The Hashemite Kingdom of Jordan*, *supra* n. 5, at 119; *Plama Consortium Limited v. Republic of Bulgaria*, Decision on Jurisdiction, ICSID Case No. ARB/03/24, 183,184,227 (8 Feb. 2005); *Telenor Mobile Communications A.S. v. The Republic of Hungary*, Award, ICSID Case No. ARB/04/15, 90-100 (13 Sept. 2006).
15. United Nations Conference on Trade and Development, *Most Favoured Nation Treatment*, UNCTAD/DIAE/IA/2010/1, 97-102 (UNCTAD Series on Issues in International Investment Agreements II, United Nations 2010) http://unctad.org/en/Docs/diaeia20101_en.pdf (accessed 27 Jun. 2017).
16. *Supra* n. 8, at Art. 13.2.
17. Agreement between the Government of the Republic of Armenia and the Government of the Republic of India, *supra* n. 7, at Art. 9(3)(c)(ii); Agreement between the Government of the

then an appointing authority could appoint arbitrators. The appointing authority is normally the President, Vice-President or next senior judge of the ICJ who is not a national of either Contracting Party.[18] The third arbitrator shall not be a national of either Party.[19]

The Model BIT also provides for a 'cooling-off' period of six months in which the parties shall use their 'best efforts' to resolve the dispute through 'meaningful' consultation and other mechanisms.[20] If the dispute cannot be resolved amicably, the investor can submit the claim to arbitration, subject to these conditions: (a) not more than six years have elapsed from the date on which the disputing investor first acquired knowledge of the measure at issue or loss or damage to investment; (b) not more than twelve months have elapsed from the conclusion of domestic proceedings; (c) the investor has waived its right to pursue other domestic remedies under the law of any

---

Republic of Cyprus and the Government of the Republic of India, Art. 9(3)(c)(ii) (signed 9 May 2002, entered into force 12 Jan. 2004); Agreement between the Government of the Republic of Djibouti and the Government of the Republic of India, Art. 9(3)(c)(ii) (signed 19 May 2003); Agreement between the Government of the Republic of Finland and the Government of the Republic of India, Art. 9(3)(c)(ii) (signed 7 Nov. 2002, entered into force 9 Apr. 2003); Agreement between the Government of the Republic of Hungary and the Government of the Republic of India, Art. 9(2)(ii) (signed 3 Nov. 2003, entered into force 2 Jan. 2006, terminated on 29 Mar. 2017); Agreement between the Government of Iceland and the Government of the Republic of India, *supra* n. 7, at Art. 9(3)(c)(ii).

18. Agreement between the Government of the Republic of Armenia and the Government of the Republic of India, *supra* n. 7, at Art. 9(3)(c)(i); Agreement between the Government of Iceland and the Government of the Republic of India, *supra* n. 7, at Art. 9(3)(c)(i); Agreement between the Government of the Hashemite Kingdom of Jordan and the Government of the Republic of India, Art. 9(3)(b)(i) (signed 30 Nov. 2006, entered into force 22 Jan. 2009); Agreement between the Government of the Republic of Kazakhstan and the Government of the Republic of India, Art. 9(3)(c)(i) (signed 9 Dec. 1996, entered into force 26 Jul. 2001); Agreement between the Government of Kyrgyz Republic and the Government of the Republic of India, Art. 9(3)(c)(i) (signed 16 May 1997, entered into force 12 May 2000); Agreement between the Government of the Republic of Latvia and the Government of the Republic of India, Art. 9(2)(d)(i) (signed 18 Feb. 2010, entered into force 27 Nov. 2010); Agreement between the Government of the Republic of Lithuania and the Government of the Republic of India, Art. 9(2)(c)(iii)(a) (signed 31 Mar. 2011, entered into force 1 Dec. 2011); Agreement between the Government of the Republic of the Union of Myanmar and the Government of the Republic of India, Art. 9(2)(c)(i) (signed 24 Jun. 2008, entered into force 8 Feb. 2009).
19. Agreement between the Government of the Republic of Armenia and the Government of the Republic of India, *supra* n. 18; Agreement between the Government of the Sultanate of Oman and the Government of the Republic of India, Art. 9(3)(c)(i) (signed 2 Apr. 1997, entered into force 13 Oct. 2000, terminated on 22 Mar. 2017); Agreement between the Government of the Republic of Poland and the Government of the Republic of India, *supra* n. 7, at Art. 9(3)(c)(i); Agreement between the Government of the Republic of Sudan and the Government of the Republic of India, Art. 9(3)(c)(i) (signed 22 Oct. 2003, entered into force 18 Oct. 2010); Agreement between the Government of the Republic of Tajikistan and the Government of the Republic of India, Art. 9(3)(c)(i) (signed 13 Dec. 1995, entered into force 14 Nov. 2003); Agreement between the Government of the Kingdom of Thailand and the Government of the Republic of India, Art. 9(3)(c)(i) (signed 10 Jul. 2000, entered into force 13 Jul. 2001); Agreement between the Government of the Republic of Trinidad and Tobago and the Government of the Republic of India, Art. 9(3)(c)(i) (signed 12 Mar. 2007, entered into force 7 Oct. 2007); Agreement between the Government of the Republic of Turkmenistan and the Government of the Republic of India, Art. 9(3)(c)(i) (signed 20 Sept. 1995, entered into force 27 Feb. 2006).
20. *Supra* n. 8, at Art. 15.4.

Contracting Party, or other dispute settlement procedures; (d) a notice of intention to submit to claim to arbitration has been submitted to the defending party at least ninety days before submitting any claim to arbitration.[21]

The Model BIT also provides for an elaborate procedure for appointment of arbitrators, especially for challenging their appointment and strict conditions for conflict of interest and disclosures for arbitrators. A list of guidelines to determine whether there exist 'justifiable doubts as to an arbitrator's independence or impartiality or freedom from conflicts of interest' has also been incorporated by way of Article 19.10 in the Model BIT. An arbitrator's inability to access conflict and disclosure related information independently nor unavailability of such information in the public sphere will relieve him/her of the duty to make disclosures.[22] The Model BIT also seeks to reserve the power to further adopt a separate code of conduct for arbitrators for addressing issues such as disclosures, confidentiality, impartiality, etc.[23]

The BIT further provides that the arbitration shall be held in a territory signatory to the NYC and such choice shall be made after taking into account factors such as convenience of the parties and arbitrators, the location of the subject matter, proximity of the evidence, and special consideration to the capital city of the Defending Party.[24] The Model BIT also states that a tribunal shall not have the power to compel production of documents which the State asserts to be protected from disclosure under the confidentiality and privilege related rules under its domestic law.[25]

The Model BIT also addresses the issue of 'frivolous claims' and empowers the tribunal to address other preliminary objections of the claim being: (a) outside the scope of the Tribunal's jurisdiction; (b) manifestly without legal merit;[26] (c) unfounded as a matter of law.[27] In case such a preliminary objection is made, the Tribunal shall suspend the proceedings on merits, consider such objections first and issue an award within 150 days. In case the defending party requests a hearing, the tribunal may take additional 30 days to issue the award. The tribunal may also award reasonable legal costs incurred in submitting or opposing the objection.

A novel feature of the Model BIT is the incorporation of transparency related rules. It provides that the notice of dispute and arbitration; pleadings and other written submissions, hearings' transcripts, decisions, orders and awards issued by the Tribunal shall be available to public, subject to the applicable law regarding confidential information.[28] The confidential information may be redacted if the defending party determines it to be in the public interest. A duty has also been cast on the tribunal to facilitate public access to hearings, subject to the need to protect confidential information.

---

21. *Ibid.*, at Art. 15.5.
22. *Ibid.*, at Art. 19.2.
23. *Ibid.*, at Art. 19.11.
24. *Ibid.*, at Art. 20.
25. *Ibid.*, at Art. 20.3.
26. *See* generally ICSID Rules of Procedure for Arbitration Proceedings (Arbitration Rules), ICSID/15, Rule 41(5), 99 (April 2006), https://icsid.worldbank.org/en/Documents/resources/2006%20CRR_English-final.pdf (accessed 13 Jul. 2017).
27. *Supra* n. 20.
28. *Ibid.*, at Art. 22.

Some old BITs provided that even if parties fail to agree to a peaceful resolution, they could mutually agree to refer the dispute to competent, judicial, arbitral or administrative body as per the laws of the host State or conduct conciliation.[29] Some other BITs used to contain 'Fork-In-The-Road' clauses which attach finality to the investor's choice of dispute resolution mechanism, i.e., either the domestic courts or investment arbitration.[30] The effect of such clauses is that an investor must choose between the approaching domestic courts or initiate investment arbitration. The Model BIT of 2015 has introduced rigorous provisions that require the foreign investor to first approach domestic courts and initiate investment arbitration only if that procedure fails or does not result into an outcome within five years from the date on which investor acquired knowledge of the measure at issue or loss or damage to the investment.[31] The investor must submit its claim within one year from the date on which it acquired knowledge of the measure at issue or loss or damage to the investment. However, this requirement shall not be applicable if the investor can demonstrate that the local remedies are not capable of reasonably providing any relief. Presently terminated Indian BITs contained two avenues for arbitration: ICSID[32] or ad hoc.[33] Under the Model BIT, an investor can submit its claim either under the ICSID

---

29. Agreement between the Government of the Republic of Armenia and the Government of the Republic of India, *supra* n. 7, at Art. 19(2); Agreement between the Government of the Republic of China and the Government of the Republic of India, Art. 9(2) (signed 21 Nov. 2006, entered into force 1 Aug. 2007); Agreement between the Government of Czech Republic and the Government of the Republic of India, *supra* n. 10, at Art. 8(2); Agreement between the Government of the Republic of Ghana and the Government of the Republic of India, Art. 9(2) (signed 5 Aug. 2002); Agreement between the Government of Israel and the Government of the Republic of India, *supra* n. 10, at Arts 9(1) and 9(2); Agreement between the Government of the Republic of Kazakhstan and the Government of the Republic of India, *supra* n. 18, at Art. 9(2); Agreement between the Government of Malaysia and the Government of the Republic of India, *supra* n. 10, at Art. 7(2); Agreement between the Government of Nepal and the Government of the Republic of India, Art. 9(2) (signed 21 Oct. 2011).
30. Agreement between the Government of Indonesia and the Government of the Republic of India, Art. 9(2) (signed 10 Feb. 1999, entered into force 22 Jan. 2004, terminated on 4 Apr. 2016); Agreement between the Government of the Republic of Lithuania and the Government of the Republic of India, *supra* n. 18, at Art. 9(3); Agreement between the Government of Romania and the Government of the Republic of India, Art. 9(2)(b) (signed 17 Nov. 1997, entered into force 9 Dec. 1999); Agreement between the Government of Czech Republic and the Government of the Republic of India, *supra* n. 10, at Art. 9(4).
31. *Supra* n. 8, at Art. 15.
32. Agreement between the Government of the Republic of Armenia and the Government of the Republic of India, *supra* n. 7, at Art. 9(3)(a); Agreement between the Government of Bosnia & Herzegovina and the Government of the Republic of India, Art. 9(3)(1) (signed 12 Sept. 2006, entered into force 13 Feb. 2008); Agreement between the Government of Republic of Korea and the Government of the Republic of India, Art. 8(3)(a) (signed 26 Feb. 1996, entered into force 7 May 1996); Agreement between the Government of the Republic of Latvia and the Government of the Republic of India, *supra* n. 18, at Art. 9(2)(b); Agreement between the Government of Republic of Slovakia and the Government of the Republic of India, Art. 8(2)(a) (signed 25 Sept. 2006, entered into force 27 Sept. 2007); Agreement between the Government of Syrian Arab Republic and the Government of the Republic of India, Art. 9(3) (signed 18 Jun. 2008, entered into force 22 Jan. 2009); Agreement between the Government of Austria and the Government of the Republic of India, Art. 9(3)(a) (signed 8 Nov. 1999, entered into force 1 Mar. 2001).
33. Agreement between the Government of the Republic of Armenia and the Government of the Republic of India, *supra* n. 7, at Art. 9(3)(b); Agreement between the Government of Israel and the Government of the Republic of India, *supra* n. 10, at Art. 9(3)(b); Agreement between the

Convention, Additional Facility Rules or the UNCITRAL Arbitration Rules.[34] This cannot be interpreted as an agreement to take to dispute to ICSID Arbitration. ICSID Convention is an international treaty, and any State cannot be bound by it unless that State has joined the Convention. Since India has not joined the ICSID, the reference to ICSID in Indian BITs is of no consequence. A reason for having those provisions may be to contemplate a situation in future, where India may want to join ICSID. They may have been included at the insistence of the other Contracting Party.

§6.02 ENFORCEMENT OF INVESTMENT AWARDS

Indian BITs do not contain any provision in relation to enforcement of awards. The past BITs would normally state that an award should contain reasons and give the basis of its conclusions.[35] An award is final and binding on the parties.[36] The 2015 Model BIT has detailed provisions in relation to the award. The award has to be public except for redaction of certain sensitive information.[37] The 2015 Model BIT states that the provision of the BIT that has been breached shall be clearly stated and the decision has

---

Government of the Republic of Latvia and the Government of the Republic of India, *supra* n. 18, at Art. 9(2)(d); Agreement between the Government of the Russian Federation and the Government of the Republic of India, Art. 9(2) (signed 23 Dec. 1994, entered into force 5 Aug. 1996); Agreement between the Government of the Brunei Darussalam and the Government of the Republic of India, Art. 9(3)(c) (signed 22 May 2008, entered into force 18 Jan. 2009); Agreement between the Government of Cyprus and the Government of the Republic of India, *supra* n. 17, at Art. 9(3)(c); Agreement between the Government of Czech Republic and the Government of the Republic of India, *supra* n. 10, at Art. 8(2)(c).

34. *Supra* n. 8, at Art. 16.
35. Agreement between the Government of the Republic of Armenia and the Government of the Republic of India, *supra* n. 7, at Art. 9(3)(c)(iv); Agreement between the Government of Bangladesh and the Government of the Republic of India, *supra* n. 7, at Art. 9(3)(c)(iv); Agreement between the Government of Belarus and the Government of the Republic of India, Art. 9(3)(c)(iv) (signed 27 Nov. 2002, entered into force 23 Nov. 2003; Agreement between the Government of the Brunei Darussalam and the Government of the Republic of India, *supra* n. 33, at Art. 9(3)(c)(iv); Agreement between the Government of Czech Republic and the Government of the Republic of India, *supra* n. 10, at Art. 8(2)(c)(iii); Agreement between the Government of the Egypt and the Government of the Republic of India, Art. 8(3)(c)(iv) (signed 9 Apr. 1997, entered into force 22 Nov. 2000, terminated on 29 Mar. 2016); Agreement between the Government of Finland and the Government of the Republic of India, *supra* n. 17, at Art. 9(3)(c)(iii).
36. Agreement between the Government of the Republic of Armenia and the Government of the Republic of India, *supra* n. 7, at Art. 9(3)(c)(v); Agreement between the Government of Israel and the Government of the Republic of India, *supra* n. 10, at Arts 9(3)(b)(v); Agreement between the Government of the United Kingdom and the Government of the Republic of India, *supra* n. 6, at Art. 10(9); Agreement between the Government of the Republic of Latvia and the Government of the Republic of India, *supra* n. 18, at Art. 9(4); Agreement between the Government of the Republic of Lithuania and the Government of the Republic of India, *supra* n. 18, at Art. 9(4); Agreement between the Government of the former Yugoslav Republic of Macedonia and the Government of the Republic of India, Art. 9(5) (signed 17 Mar. 2008, entered into force 17 Nov. 2008); Agreement between the Government of the Mexico and the Government of the Republic of India, Art. 19(3) (signed 21 May 2007, entered into force 23 Feb. 2008); Agreement between the Government of the Philippines and the Government of the Republic of India, Art. 9(3)(c)(iii) (signed 28 Jan. 2000, entered into force 29 Jan. 2001).
37. *Supra* n. 8, at Art. 22.3.

to be arrived at by majority.[38] A tribunal can award only monetary damages, which 'shall not be greater than the loss suffered by the investor or, as applicable, the locally established enterprise, reduced by any prior damages or compensation already provided by a Party'.[39] The tribunal may reduce compensation based on mitigating factors.[40]

Although, award may have been declared as final and binding in a BIT, it has to be recognized and enforced by domestic courts. An investment award is intentional in nature but has to be enforced in national courts of some State or other, and the domestic courts of that State play a role in the process of enforcement. The ICSID Convention declares that an investment arbitration award passed by an ICSID tribunal shall be treated as a decision of the highest court of the State against which the award is passed.[41] It would not be possible to challenge the validity of an award passed by an ICSID tribunal by the State against whom the award is passed. Yet, to realize the amounts and directions granted in the award a judicial authority of a national court has to be approached. If the assets of the losing State are in different jurisdictions which are not a party to the ICSID Convention, then proceedings under the New York Convention (NYC) will have to be initiated. In substance the NYC remains an important instrument for enforcement of an investment arbitration award, whether or not the host State is party to the ICSID Convention. Additionally, in case of India, since it is not a party to the ICSID Convention, NYC is the only method of enforcement of investment arbitration awards.

In relation to every award, including an investment arbitration award, there are three processes under the NYC: recognition, enforcement and setting aside. Recognition and enforcement is the process whereby the winning party tries to get the award endorsed as valid and get it enforced. There is a difference between recognition and enforcement as well. An award maybe recognized without enforcing.[42] However, if the award is enforced by a court, then it means that it has been recognized as well[43] – thus the process of enforcement includes recognition, whereas recognition does not involve enforcement. Recognition is quintessentially used as a defence. Whenever any other party to the dispute initiates proceedings in relation to some aspects of the award, the winning party would use the process of recognition. The existence of an award is used to resist the proceedings on the ground of res judicata. The judicial authority will then decide whether all the issues were decided in the arbitration proceedings. If they have

---

38. *Ibid.*, at Art. 26.1.
39. *Ibid.*, at Art. 26.3.
40. *Ibid.* Mitigating factors are defined in foot note 4 as: 'Mitigating factors can include, current and past use of the investment, the history of its acquisition and purpose, compensation received by the investor from other sources, any unremedied harm or damage that the investor has caused to the environment or local community or other relevant considerations regarding the need to balance public interest and the interests of the investor.'
41. See Chapter 8 for further discussion.
42. *Dallal v. Bank Mellat*, X1 Yearbook of Commercial Arbitration, 547 at 553 (1986). In this case, the English Judge held that the decision of the Iran-US Claims Tribunal was not enforceable under the New York Convention; however, he recognized the award as a valid judgment of a competent tribunal.
43. Nigel Blackaby and Ors, *Redfern and Hunter on International Arbitration*, 627 (5th ed., Oxford University Press 2009).

been so decided then the judicial authority would not proceed. Whereas, if there are certain issues that have not been decided in the arbitration proceedings then the judicial authority could decide other issues.[44] Enforcement goes a step further than recognition. In enforcement proceedings, the court is requested to enforce the award – that is to apply legal sanctions to compel carrying out of the award against the losing party. The enforcement proceedings can be initiated in any State where the losing party has assets. Explaining the challenge at the stage of recognition and enforcement, the explanatory note in UNCITRAL Model Law states that: 'recourse means actively attacking the award; a party is, of course, not precluded from seeking court control by way of defence in enforcement proceedings'.[45] Which means that an unsuccessful party can resist enforcement of an award in any country, irrespective of the seat of the arbitration, that is the country where the award is delivered.[46] The court of the seat of arbitration, where the award is challenged is primarily concerned about ensuring that the decision of the private tribunal is in accordance with the fundamental notions of justice of that jurisdiction where the award is rendered. The enforcing court has to balance between finality and justice.[47]

Setting aside of an award is the process whereby the competent court can review the award under Article V of the NYC and decline the enforcement of the award. These grounds are incorporated into domestic laws of all States that are parties to the NYC. The municipal courts enjoy a certain degree of interpretation and application of those provisions. If the application for setting aside is accepted by the municipal courts then that is refusal of enforcement. Refusal of enforcement of an award has an effect limited to the country where the decision is made. Whereas the setting aside of an award has an *erga omnes* effect. Once the enforcement of an award is declined in a jurisdiction, then it cannot be enforced in any other jurisdiction.[48] This situation exists because the jurisdiction within which the arbitration took place has the primary jurisdiction and all other States have secondary jurisdiction.[49] One of the drafters of the NYC, Professor Sanders wrote in private capacity after the drafting of the NYC if an award was set aside in the country of origin, the 'Courts will…refuse the enforcement as there no longer exists an arbitral award and enforcing a non-existing arbitral award would be an impossibility or even go against the public policy of the country of enforcement.'[50]

---

44. *Ibid.*, at pp. 627-8.
45. Explanatory Note by the UNCITRAL Secretariat on the Model Law on International Commercial Arbitration, para. 41, https://www.mcgill.ca/arbitration/files/arbitration/ExplanatoryNote-UNCITRALSecretariat.pdf (accessed 13 Jul. 2017); *See* generally Explanatory Note by the UNCITRAL Secretariat on the 1985 Model Law on International Commercial Arbitration as amended in 2006, http://www.uncitral.org/pdf/english/texts/arbitration/ml-arb/MLARB-explanatoryNote20-9-07.pdf (accessed 13 Jul. 2017).
46. K.S. Harisankar, *Annulment versus Enforcement of International Arbitral Awards: Does the New York Convention permit Issue Estoppel?*, International Arbitration Law Review 47, 48 (2015).
47. *Ibid.*
48. Albert Jan van den Berg, *The New York Arbitration Convention of 1958: Towards a Uniform Judicial Interpretation*, 355-7 (Walters Kluwer 1981).
49. *Karaha Bodas Co. LLC v. Perusahaan Pertambangan Minyak Dan Gas Bumi Negara et al.*, 29 Yearbook of Commercial Arbitration 1262 (US Court of Appeals, 5th Circuit, 23 Mar. 2004).
50. P. Sanders, *New York Convention on the Recognition and Enforcement of Foreign Arbitral Awards*, Netherlands International Law Review 43, 55 (1959); *IPOC International Growth Fund*

In addition to domestic law, the enforcement proceedings in domestic courts are constrained by the law of sovereign immunity.[51] In international law, 'the jurisdictional immunities of States and their property are generally accepted as a principle of customary international law'.[52] State immunity cannot be invoked in relation to commercial matters[53] or in case of commercial arbitration proceedings in which a State is participating.[54] Immunity may not apply based on the nature of the judicial proceedings, but it continues to apply based on the nature of property against which enforcement proceedings are initiated. Immunity applies to 'warships, or naval auxiliaries, nor does it applies to other vessels owned or operated by a State and used, for the time being, only on government non-commercial service.'[55] Article 21(1) of the UN Convention on Jurisdictional Immunities of States and Their Property excludes certain categories of properties from execution in the following words:

> Specific categories of property
> 1. The following categories, in particular, of property of a State shall not be considered as property specifically in use or intended for use by the State for other than government non-commercial purposes under article 19, subparagraph (c):
>   (a) property, including any bank account, which is used or intended for use in the performance of the functions of the diplomatic mission of the State or its consular posts, special missions, missions to international organizations or delegations to organs of international organizations or to international conferences;
>   (b) property of a military character or used or intended for use in the performance of military functions;
>   (c) property of the central bank or other monetary authority of the State;
>   (d) property forming part of the cultural heritage of the State or part of its archives and not placed or intended to be placed on sale;
>   (e) property forming part of an exhibition of objects of scientific, cultural or historical interest and not placed or intended to be placed on sale.[56]

Immunity of certain assets from execution is an important challenge to enforcement. All properties owned by the State for performance of its functions are protected by immunity. For example, after winning the investment award when the foreign investor tried to attach securities and cash held by third parties in London on behalf of

---

Ltd v. L V Finance Group Ltd., 22 Yearbook of Commercial Arbitration 406 (Court of Appeal British Virgin Islands, 18 Jun. 2008): 'The decision of the Swiss Supreme Court confirms the Second Convention Award. Had that court set aside the award, the appeal would have fallen away altogether because there would be no Award that could be the subject of enforcement proceedings.'

51. Matthew Saunders and Claudia Salomon, *Enforcement of Arbitral Awards Against States and State Entities*, 23(3) Arbitration International 467, 476 (2007).
52. Preamble, United Nations Convention on Jurisdictional Immunities of States and Their Property, A/RES/59/38 (2 Dec. 2004), http://www.refworld.org/docid/4280737b4.html (accessed on 14 Jul. 2017).
53. *Ibid.*, at Art. 10.
54. *Ibid.*, at Art. 17.
55. *Ibid.*, at Art. 16(2).
56. For a detailed discussion on case law *see* Hazel Fox and Philippa Webb, *The Law of State Immunity*, 518-35 (3rd ed., (revised and updated) Oxford University Press 2003).

the National Bank of Kazakhstan, the English Court declined to execute its award. The property was immune from enforcement since it was not intended for commercial purposes.[57] An American Court declined to execute an investment award against taxes payable to the host State.[58] In a subsequent application, the court refused to execute orders against the bank accounts of the Embassy of Libya.[59]

In *Sedelmayer v. Russia*,[60] the investor attempted to execute an investment award against the Government of Russia in German courts, by seeking an attachment order of the payments payable by Lufthansa airlines to the Russian Government for over flight. The Federal Court of Justice (the highest court in Germany) declined the relief over flight rights, including transit and entry fee assets on the ground that they were of public nature and not private contract type transactions and therefore the assets were made public in nature as per German Law. Therefore, sovereign immunity applied and the award cannot be enforced.[61]

§6.03 PROCEEDINGS UNDER INDIAN ARBITRATION ACT

All proceedings in relation to the NYC take place under the Indian Arbitration and Conciliation Act, 1996 (Arbitration Act). It is the domestic statute implementing the NYC. In order to initiate proceedings under the Arbitration Act, certain preconditions have to be satisfied.

India has a commercial reservation to the NYC, hence only commercial arbitration awards could be enforce in India.[62] If proceedings relating to investment arbitration award, for enforcement (referred collectively to represent 'enforcement' and 'recognition' for convenience in this section) or setting-aside are to be initiated the test of 'commercial' under the Arbitration Act has to be satisfied. A study of genesis of the word 'commercial' shows that in civil law countries only commercial matters were arbitrable, whereas non-commercial matters could not be arbitrated. To qualify as commercial, the dispute should involve economic matters. For example, a commercial contract between two traders could be arbitrated, but a contract for allocation of

---

57. *AIG Capital Partners Inc and others v. Republic of Kazakhstan and others* (2006) 1 All ER 284 [2006] EWHC Civ 1529.
58. Refer *Liberian Eastern Timber Corporation (LETCO) v. Government of the Republic of Liberia*, 659 F Supp. 73.
59. *Ibid.*, at 606.
60. *Sedelmayer v. Russian Federation (Germany/Soviet Union BIT)*, Decision on Jurisdiction and Final Award, 2 Stockholm Int'l Arb. Rev. 1 (7 Jul. 1998); Alan Alexandrosff and Ian Laird, *Compliance and Enforcement*, 1182 (September 2008) http://alanalexandroff.com/wp-content/uploads/2010/11/asa_laird_ch29.pdf (accessed 17 Jul. 2017).
61. *See Beschluss des VII Zicilsenats* Vol. 4.10.2005-VII ZB 9/05, 2 (5) TDM (Bundesgerichtsh of (German Federal Supreme Court 2005)).
62. The declaration and reservation of India is as follows: '*In accordance with Article I of the Convention, the Government of India declare that they will apply the Convention to the recognition and enforcement of awards made only in the territory of a State, party to this Convention. They further declare that they will apply the Convention only to differences arising out of legal relationships, whether contractual or not, which are considered as commercial under the law of India.*', available at: http://www.newyorkconvention.org/countries.

property on the marriage of their children could not be.[63] Therefore, the distinction between commercial and non-commercial was based on the permissibility of arbitration of the domestic law within the domestic legal regime.

The distinction between 'commercial matters' and 'any other matters' was stipulated in the Geneva Protocol – which allowed States to exclude those matters they did not consider to fall within the purview of commercial as per their domestic law.[64] The word commercial was neither defined in the Geneva Protocol nor in the NYC. There was some discussion during the drafting of the UNCITRAL Model Arbitration Law. There was lack of agreement, and it was decided, not to define 'commercial' in a text, but footnote was added. The contents of the footnote describe 'commercial' which is very broad, and the contents of the footnote are as under:

> The term 'commercial' should be given a wide interpretation so as to cover matters arising from all relationships of a commercial nature, whether contractual or not. Relationships of a commercial nature include, but are not limited to, the following transactions: any trade transaction for the supply or exchange of goods or services; distribution agreement; commercial representation or agency; factoring; leasing; construction of works; consulting; engineering; licensing; investment; financing; banking; insurance; exploitation agreement or concession; joint venture and other forms of industrial or business cooperation; carriage of goods or passengers by air, sea, rail or road.

The footnote includes the 'investment'. It also includes various other activities such as licensing, services and other relationships of a commercial nature in which the foreign investor would be involved in the host State. The footnote should be used to interpret commercial in the context of the NYC.[65] Therefore the word commercial in relation to investment arbitration needs to be interpreted differently than under commercial arbitration for the purposes of the NYC. Therefore, the NYC would continue to apply to investment arbitration awards. In almost all jurisdictions where investment arbitration awards have been challenged or enforced, they have been treated as 'commercial arbitration award' for the purpose of Article 1(3) of the NYC.[66] The Supreme Court of India has interpreted the word 'commercial' liberally.[67]

Indian courts would and could have a role in enforcement of investment arbitration award proceedings in more than one way. The most obvious case is of enforcement proceedings brought by a foreign investor to enforce an award against India or India seeking to set aside such an award in India. If the arbitration proceedings

---

63. *Supra* n. 43, at p. 13.
64. Protocol on Arbitration Clauses, League of Nations, Geneva, Art. 1 (24 Sept. 1923).
65. In *R.M. Investment & Trading Co. Pvt. Ltd. v. Boeing Co. and Anr.* 1 SCR 837, para. 14 (1994).
66. See *United Mexican States v. Metaclad*, 5 ICSID Report 236, 246-7 (Supreme Court of British Columbia, Canada 2 May 2001); *Czech Republic v. CME Czech Republic*, 9 ICSID Report 439, Case No. T 8735-01 (*Svea Court of Appeal*, Sweden 15 May 2003); *BG Group plc v. Republic of Argentina*, 1 572 US 9, 15 (US Supreme Court 2014).
67. *R.M. Investment & Trading Co. Pvt. Ltd. v. Boeing Co. and Anr.* 1 SCR 837, para. 12 (1994); See *Renusagar Power Co. Ltd. v. General Electric Co. and Anr*, 4 SCC 679, at pp. 723-4 (1984); See *Koch Navigation Inc v. Hindustan Petroleum*, 4 SCC 259, p. 75 at para. 8 (1989).

have taken place in India then Part I of the Arbitration Act applies.[68] If the proceedings took place outside India then Part II would apply.

The difference resulting from the application of Part I and II is the extent of intervention possible on the part of domestic courts. Part I contains provisions relating to interim measures, appointment of arbitrators, etc. These rules facilitate conduct of arbitration and therefore act as *lex fori* or *lex loci arbitrai*: rules of the seat of arbitration are applicable. Part I also contains provisions on recognition, enforcement and setting aside of an arbitration award. If the arbitration proceedings are conducted in India then Part I would apply.[69] The requirement of seat is that the 'legal seat' has to be in India. The proceedings may actually be conducted outside India but the seat as agreed by the agreement of the parties has to be India.[70] This fiction operates because when a legal seat for arbitration is chosen, parties agree to apply the *lex fori arbitri* to their proceedings.[71] Second, if the arbitration proceedings have taken place outside India then the proceedings in relation to the award could take place in India. This may happen when India is a party to an investment claim or the assets of the losing party are located in India. If India has won a claim against a foreign investor in investment arbitration and the foreigner has assets in India, Indian courts would have jurisdiction to entertain the petition. A foreign investor could initiate proceedings in Indian courts against a foreign country that has assets in India. In this case, since the seat of arbitration is outside India, Part II of the Arbitration Act would apply.[72]

Article 48 of the Arbitration Act, 1996 specifies conditions for refusal of enforcement of an award. Its contents are as under:

> 48. Conditions for enforcement of foreign awards. –
> (1) Enforcement of a foreign award may be refused, at the request of the party against whom it is invoked, only if that party furnishes to the court proof that-
> (a) The parties to the agreement referred to in section 44 were, under the law applicable to them, under some incapacity, or the said agreement is not valid under the law to which the parties have subjected it or, failing any indication thereon, under the law of the country where the award was made; or

---

68. Section 2(2), The Arbitration and Conciliation Act 1996.
69. *Bharat Aluminum Co. v. Kaiser Aluminum Technical Service, Inc.*, 9 SCC 552, para. 122 (2012).
70. *Ibid.*, at para. 100.
71. *Ibid.*, at para. 95: 'Learned counsel for the appellants have submitted that Section 2(1)(e), Section 20 and Section 28 read with Section 45 and Section 48(1)(e) make it clear that Part I is not limited only to arbitrations which take place in India. These provisions indicate that Arbitration Act, 1996 is subject matter centric and not exclusively seat centric. Therefore, "seat" is not the "centre of gravity" so far as the Arbitration Act, 1996 is concerned. We are of the considered opinion that the aforesaid provisions have to be interpreted by keeping the principle of territoriality at the forefront. We have earlier observed that Section 2(2) does not make Part I applicable to arbitrations seated or held outside India. In view of the expression used in Section 2(2), the maxim expressum facit cessare tacitum, would not permit by interpretation to hold that Part I would also apply to arbitrations held outside the territory of India. The expression "this Part shall apply where the place of arbitration is in India" necessarily excludes application of Part I to arbitration seated or held outside India. It appears to us that neither of the provisions relied upon by the learned counsel for the appellants would make any section of Part I applicable to arbitration seated outside India. It will be apposite now to consider each of the aforesaid provisions in turn.'
72. *Supra* n. 69, at para. 76.

(b) The party against whom the award is invoked was not given proper notice of the appointment of the arbitrator or of the arbitral proceedings or was otherwise unable to present his case; or

(c) The award deals with a difference not contemplated by or not falling within the terms of the submission to arbitration, or it contains decisions on matters beyond the scope of the submission to arbitration:
Provided that, if the decisions on matters submitted to arbitration can be separated from those not so submitted, that part of the award which contains decisions on matters submitted to arbitration may be enforced; or

(d) The composition of the arbitral authority or the arbitral procedure was not in accordance with the agreement of the parties, or, failing such agreement, was not in accordance with the law of the country where the arbitration took place; or

(e) The award has not yet become binding on the parties, or has been set aside or suspended by a competent authority of the country in which, or under the law of which, that award was made.

(2) Enforcement of an arbitral award may also be refused if the court finds that-

(a) The subject-matter of the difference is not capable of settlement by arbitration under the law of India; or

(b) The enforcement of the award would be contrary to the public policy of India. Explanation. -Without prejudice to the generality of clause (b) of this section, it is hereby declared, for the avoidance of any doubt, that an award is in conflict with the public policy of India if the making of the award was induced or affected by fraud or corruption.

(3) If an application for the setting aside or suspension of the award has been made to a competent authority referred to in clause (e) of sub-section (1) the court may, if it considers it proper, adjourn the decision on the enforcement of the award and may also, on the application of the party claiming enforcement of the award, order the other party to give suitable security.

The contents of Section 48 replicate Article V of the NYC. The jurisprudence of the Court therein would become relevant in the case of enforcement proceedings of investment arbitration.[73] The focus here is limited to the most controversial topic: public policy.

Public policy of India would be a ground for enforcement of an award. Absence of challenge of an award does not make the award automatically valid. The award needs to be tested on the ground of public policy at the place of enforcement. The setting aside of an award at the seat has a universal effect, but the recognition and enforcement or dismissal of setting aside application does not have a universal effect. The refusal for enforcement has no effect in other jurisdictions.[74] It is possible to challenge the award at the time of enforcement even if proceedings for setting it aside

---

73. *See* Justice R.S. Bachawat, *Law of Arbitration and Conciliation*, Vol. 1 (Wadhwa, A, Krishnan, A (eds), Lexis Nexis 2010); P.C. Markanda, Naresh Markanda and Rajesh Markanda, *Law Relating to Arbitration and Conciliation* (9th ed., Lexis Nexis 2016); O.P. Malhotra and Indu Malhotra, *Law and Practice of Arbitration and Conciliation* (3rd ed., Lexis Nexis 2006).
74. Albert van den Berg, *Enforcement of Arbitral Awards Annulled in Russia*, 27(2) Journal of International Arbitration 179-82 (2010).

were never initiated at the seat of arbitration.[75] The rationale is that 'an international decision of justice and its validity must be examined according to the applicable rules of the country where its recognition and enforcement are sought.'[76] The NYC provides for the ground of 'public policy' to refuse enforcement of an award. But, no definition is provided for. It is left for the domestic courts to interpret public policy based on their concerns and priorities. Indian Courts have understood public policy to 'connote some matter which concerns the public good and the public interest.'[77] It is not a static concept, and it would vary from time to time because public good or public interest changes from time to time.[78] In private international law, public policy has been often invoked to deny enforcement of foreign judgments or awards in a country because they contradict public interest and public good in a country where enforcement is sought.[79] The judges enjoy wide range of discretion in these issues. As stated by the Supreme Court:

> The difficulty of discovering what public policy is at any given moment certainly does not absolve the judges from the duty of doing so. In conducting an enquiry, as already stated, judges are not hide-bound by precedent. The judges must look beyond the narrow field of past precedents, though this still leaves open the question, in which direction. They must cast their gaze. The judges are to base their decision on the opinions of men of the world, as distinguished from opinions based on legal learning. In other words, the judges will have to look beyond the jurisprudence and that in so doing, they must consult not their own personal standards or predilections but those of the dominant opinion at a given moment, or what has been termed customary morality. The judge must consider the social consequences of the rules propounded, especially in the light of the factual evidence available as to its probable results. Of course, it is not to be expected that men of the world are to be subpoenaed as expert witnesses in the trial of every action raising a question of public policy. It is not open to the judges to make a sort of referendum or hear evidence or conduct an inquiry as to the prevailing moral concept. Such an extended extra, judicial enquiry is wholly outside the tradition of courts where the tendency is to 'trust the judge to be a typical representative of his day and generation'. Our law relies, on the implied insight of the judge on such matters. It is the judges themselves, assisted by the bar, who here represent the highest common factor of public sentiment and intelligence see Percy H. Winfield, 'Public Policy in English Common Law' 42 Harvard Law Rev. 76 and also, Dennis

---

75. *French Seller v. German Buyer* (Oberlandesgericht Munich 23 Nov. 2009) and *French Seller v. German Buyer*, Bundesgerichtshof (16 Dec. 2010), 36 YB Com Arb 273 (2011); *Actival International SA v. Conservas El Pilar SA*, 27 YB Com Arb 528-32 (Tribunal Supremo (Supreme Court) Madrid 2002); *Minmetals Germany GmbH v. Ferco Steel Ltd*, 1 All ER (Comm) 315, 331 (England 1999); *PT First Media TBK (formerly known as PT Broadband Multimedia TBK) v. Astro Nusantara International BV and others*, SGCA 57, 90 (Singapore 2013); also *see* Albert van den Berg, *Should the Setting Aside of the Arbitral Award be Abolished?*, 29 ICSID Review 1, 8 (2014); James Allsop, *The.-Authority of the Arbitrator*, Clayton Utz Sydney of University International Arbitration Lecture (2013) https://www.claytonutz.com/ialecture/content/previous/2013/speech_2013 (accessed on 14 Jul. 2017).
76. *See P T Putrabali Adyamulia v. SA Rena Holding*, Cour de cassation (France 2007) http://newyorkconvention1958.org/index.php?lvl=notice_display&id=176 (accessed on 14 Jul. 2017).
77. *Central Inland Water Transport Corpn Ltd. v. Brojo Nath Ganguly* 3 SCC 156, 217 (1986).
78. *Ibid.*
79. *Renusagar Power Co Ltd. v. General Electric Co*, supra n. 67, at 50.

Lloyd, 'Public Policy' (1953), pp. 124-125. No doubt, there is no assurance that judges will interpret the mores of their day more wisely and truly than other men. But this is beside the point. The point is rather that this power must be lodged somewhere and under our Constitution and laws, it has been lodged in the judges and if they have to fulfill their function as judge's, it could hardly be lodged elsewhere.[80]

Therefore, if the award relates to a contract for gambling and gambling is illegal and contrary to public interest in that State, then the enforcement of the contract could be denied on the ground of public policy. There are two kinds of public policy: one governed under domestic law and the other under conflict of laws. The Supreme Court of India has interpreted 'public policy' in relation to enforcement of an international commercial arbitration award under the NYC to mean 'international public policy'. In the *Renusagar Case*, the Court elaborated on it in the following words:

> In view of the absence of a workable definition of 'international public policy' we find it difficult to construe the expression 'public policy' in Article V(2)(b) of the New York Convention to mean international public policy. In our opinion the said expression must be construed to mean the doctrine of public policy as applied by the courts in which the foreign award is sought to be enforced. Consequently, the expression 'public policy' in Section 7(1)(b)(ii) of the Foreign Awards Act means the doctrine of public policy as applied by the courts in India. This raises the question whether the narrower concept of public policy as applicable in the field of public international law should be applied or the wider concept of public policy as applicable in the field of municipal law.[81]

The application of public policy in the field of conflict of laws, according to the Supreme Court of India is 'more limited than that in the domestic law and the courts are slower to invoke public policy in cases involving a foreign element than when a purely municipal legal issue is involved.'[82] Elaborating on the relative scope of operation of these two principles, the Supreme Court has observed that:

> It is thus clear that the principles governing public policy must be and are capable, on proper occasion, of expansion or modification. Practices which were considered perfectly normal at one time have today become obnoxious and oppressive to public conscience. If there is no head of public policy which D covers a case, then the court must in consonance with public conscience and in keeping with public good and public interest declare such practice to be opposed to public policy. Above all, in deciding any case which may not be covered by authority our courts have before them the beacon light of the Preamble to the Constitution. Lacking precedent, the court can always be guided by that light and the principles underlying the Fundamental Rights and the Directive Principles enshrined in our Constitution.[83]

A lot would depend on the seat of arbitration. If the arbitration proceedings took place in India then the domestic law standard of public policy would be applied

---

80. *Murlidhar Aggarwal v. State of UP*, 2 SCC 472, para. 32 (1974).
81. *Supra* n. 79, at para. 63.
82. *Ibid.*, at para. 51.
83. *Supra* n. 77, at para. 110.

Chapter 6: Dispute Resolution and Enforcement §6.03

because the proceedings would be covered under Part I of the Arbitration Act. If the seat of arbitration was outside India then Part II would apply and the standard of public policy would be narrower as compared to that applied in case of Part I. In Part I, setting aside of an award is governed by Section 34 of the Arbitration Act. This provision has been interpreted broadly by the Supreme Court to even include violations of domestic law. The Court held that the award could be set aside, if it is contrary to:

(a) fundamental public policy of India; or
(b) the interest of India; or
(c) justice or morality; or
(d) in addition, if it is patently illegal.

Illegality must go to the root of the matter and if the illegality is of trivial nature it cannot be held that award is against the public policy. Award could also be set aside if it is so unfair and unreasonable that it shocks the conscience of the court. Such award is opposed to public policy.[84]

All these terms are vague and open to interpretation. Realizing these problems, the Arbitration Act was amended in 2015 to restrict the possibilities of its broad interpretation, which may go to the extent of conducting a substantive review of the arbitral award. Following two explanations have been added to Sections 34 and 48:

Explanation 1.-For the avoidance of any doubt, it is clarified that an award is in conflict with the public policy of India, only if,-

(i) the making of the award was induced or affected by fraud or corruption or was in violation of section 75 or section 81; or
(ii) it is in contravention with the fundamental policy of Indian law; or
(iii) it is in conflict with the most basic notions of morality or justice.

Explanation 2.-For the avoidance of doubt, the test as to whether there is a contravention with the fundamental policy of Indian law shall not entail a review on the merits of the dispute.

It is thus clear that the Courts cannot expand the scope of these provisions to conduct a substantive review of the award. Until now no investment award has been challenged or enforced in India. However, this situation may arise in future.

---

84. *ONGC Ltd v. Saw Pipes Ltd*, 5 SCC 705, para. 28 (2003).

CHAPTER 7
Indian Judiciary and Investment Treaty Arbitration

Indian judiciary is a prominent and influential institution in India that commands a lot of respect with the general public. There are many potential reasons why foreign investor interests and the activities of the judiciary may be at cross-roads. The relationship, therefore, is paradoxical. The relationship is paradoxical because the judiciary actively protects private rights without discrimination: whether Indian or foreign. At the same time, judicial decisions can form the basis of an investment claim. There is every prospect that the activism of Indian judiciary could result into potential investment claims. This chapter elucidates this relationship. It is first, necessary to understand the structure and working of the Indian judiciary so that the paradoxical relationship could be fully understood.

§7.01 THE STRUCTURE AND NATURE OF THE INDIAN JUDICIARY

The Indian judiciary comprises of three levels: the Supreme Court, the High Courts and the subordinate judiciary. The Supreme Court is the highest court of the land. It is the last appellate court[1] for civil,[2] criminal matters[3] and against decisions of any other body or authority in India.[4] It also works as a constitutional court.[5] Since India is a common law jurisdiction, it follows the rule of precedent. The decisions delivered by the Supreme Court become the law of the land and all other courts have to follow those decisions.[6] The Supreme Court also has the power to do complete justice between

---
1. Article 132, Constitution of India 1950.
2. *Ibid.*, at Art. 133.
3. *Ibid.*, at Art. 134.
4. *Ibid.*, at Art. 136.
5. *Ibid.*, at Art. 32.
6. *Ibid.*, at Art. 141; *Sahara India Real Estate Corporation Ltd and Ors. v. Securities and Exchange Board of India and Anr*, 10 SCC 603, para. 52 (2012); *Ramachandra Rao v. State of Karnataka*, 4

parties based on equity, which is a discretion that only the Supreme Court enjoys.[7] These powers are exercised only in exceptional circumstances, where there is no legal provision to grant a remedy or if the legal provision itself comes in way of granting such a remedy.[8] These powers are exercised rarely and with circumspection.[9] This is an obvious area where the actions of the Supreme Court may come into conflict with the interests of foreign investors – especially if the Supreme Court interferes with the rights of foreign investors while doing complete justice. There are many such instances of judicial decisions affecting foreign investors, which are discussed in detail below.

The High Court is the highest Court of Appeal at the provincial level but is subject to the final decision and authority of the Supreme Court. The High Courts operate as Court of Appeal for civil and criminal matters and as an original court for constitutional matters. In constitutional matters, the jurisdiction is exercisable under Article 226 of the constitution, which contains the writ jurisdiction of the court. The High Court exercises wide jurisdiction and discretion under this provision. The provision could be used by foreign investors for seeking protection and at the same time, could become a basis for an investment claim (discussed in detail below).

The subordinate judiciary comprises of two streams: civil and criminal cases. The subordinate judiciary works under the supervision and control of a High Court.[10]

All the three levels of Indian judiciary are independent of the executive and legislature. The Constitution of India ensures functional independence. The integrity and independence of judiciary have been ensured by the Constitution through the procedure of appointment as well as the conditions of service. Appointments of judges of the Supreme Court and the High Court are made by the executive, but the judiciary has a very important role in deciding these appointments.[11] The Chief Justice of India is to be consulted while making these appointments and 'consultation' is interpreted as binding advice.[12] The terms of service of the judges of the Supreme Court, including their salary cannot be altered after their appointment.[13] The judges of the High Court are protected likewise.[14] The Supreme Court has the power to appoint other administrative and supportive staff,[15] and the administrative expenses, including salaries, etc.,

---

SCC 578, paras 28, 33 (2002); *South Central Railway Employees Cooperative Credit Society Employees Union v. B. Yashodabai and Others*, 2 SCC 727, para. 15 (2015); *Director of Settlements, A.P. and Others v. M.R. Apparao & Anr*, 4 SCC 638, para. 7 (2002).

7. *Supra* n. 1, at Art. 142; *Rupa Ashok Hurra v. Ashok Hurra and Anr.*, 4 SCC 388, at pp. 46-7 (2002); *Re Vinay Chandra Mishra*, 2 SCC 585, para. 47 (1995); *Supreme Court Bar Assn v. Union of India*, 4 SCC 409, para. 47 (1998).
8. *Supreme Court Bar Association v. Union of India & Anr.*, 4 SCC 409, para. 48 (1998).
9. *Ashok Sadarangani & Anr v. Union of India*, 11 SCC 321, para. 25 (2012); *Delhi Development Authority v. Skipper Construction Co. (P) Ltd.*, 4 SCC 62, para. 16 (1996); *Chandrakant Patil v. State*, 3 SCC 38, para. 13 (1998); Durga Das Basu, *Commentary on the Constitution of India*, Vol. V, §§5991-2 (8th ed., LexisNexis Butterworths Wadhwa Nagpur 2009).
10. *Supra* n. 1, at Chapter VI, Arts 233-7.
11. For a general discussion on the process refer to *Supreme Court Advocates on Record Association & Anr v. Union of India*, 5 SCC 808 (2016).
12. *Supreme Court Advocates on Record Association v. Union of India*, 4 SCC 441, para. 485 (1993).
13. *Supra* n. 1, at Art. 125(2).
14. *Ibid.*, at Art. 221(2).
15. *Ibid.*, at Art. 146(1).

are paid from the Consolidated Fund.[16] Likewise, the Chief Justices of the High Courts can appoint supporting staff, and the expenses of the High Court, including salaries and other expenses which are paid from the Consolidated Fund of the State.[17] This ensures that other branches do not strangulate the administration of justice by interference with the flow of resources necessary for the running of judicial structure of the country.

The executive head of the provincial government can transfer a judge of the High Court only after 'consultation' with the Chief Justice of India.[18] The High Courts of each province have the power to make rules regarding issues that relate to 'administration of justice',[19] which ensures that all matters relating to functioning of the judiciary is under the control of the judiciary and are not encroached upon by the other branches. The judges of the subordinate judiciary are appointed by the executive head of the provinces in consultation with the High Court of that province.[20] The control of the lower judiciary, especially regarding posting, promotion, conditions of service, etc. are all under the control of the High Court.[21] The High Courts – being one limb of the higher judiciary – are responsible for superintendence over all courts and tribunals within its province. They possess extensive powers, such as calling for records, issuing the rules and forms regulating practice, etc.[22] and transfer of cases from the subordinate courts to itself in cases involving substantial question of law as to interpretation of the Constitution.[23]

The separation of powers, between the legislature, executive and judiciary branches is strongly entrenched in India due to the jurisprudence and practice of the courts in India. There are no allegations of racial discrimination or other prejudice against the system. The concerns of foreign investors have arisen mostly out of delays in court proceeds or on an interpretative approach towards certain legal provisions. The writ jurisdiction continues to attract most of the disputes of corporations, including those of foreign investors. The manner in which the judiciary could protect rights of foreign investors through adjudication in domestic courts is discussed in the next part.

§7.02 INDIAN JUDICIARY AND PROTECTION OF FOREIGN INVESTMENT

The writ jurisdiction is exercised under the Indian Constitution. There is no legislation dealing specifically with the writ remedy, but there is abundant judicial precedent in this field. The jurisprudence has emerged as a part of interpretation of the Constitution.

The public law remedy of writ is exercised by the Supreme Court under Article 32 of the Constitution and by the High Courts under Article 226. The jurisdiction of the Supreme Court under Article 32 is limited since it extends only to violations of

---

16. *Ibid.*, at Art. 146(3).
17. *Ibid.*, at Art. 230.
18. *Ibid.*, at Art. 222(1).
19. *Ibid.*, at Art. 225.
20. *Ibid.*, at Art. 233(1).
21. *Ibid.*, at Art. 235.
22. *Ibid.*, at Art. 227.
23. *Ibid.*, at Art. 228.

fundamental rights. In practice, the Supreme Court exercises this jurisdiction only in serious cases. Whereas the jurisdiction of the High Courts is broad since it goes beyond violations of fundamental rights and extends to 'any other purpose'. High Courts regularly exercise this jurisdiction. The phrase 'any other purpose' is used to protect a wide range of legal rights.[24] In theory, purely contractual or commercial disputes may not be included within the scope of the public law remedies. But if two conditions are satisfied then the nature of the claim is immaterial: first, the government has to act fairly and second, whenever there is an element of public interest involved, the Courts would not decline jurisdiction. It does not matter that it is operating in a contractual sphere.[25] According to the Supreme Court, the nature of the underlying transaction is irrelevant:

> Every action of the State executive authority must be subject to rule of law and must be informed by reason. So, whatever be the activity of the public authority, in such monopoly or semi-monopoly dealings, it should meet the test of Article 14 of the Constitution.[26]

A breach of contract associated with the performance of public functions of the State would result in violation of legal right within Article 226.[27] The underlying principle is that the State cannot behave like a private individual. Its actions cannot be dictated by personal preferences and choices. It ought to be objective and impartial all the time, even if it is operating in a contractual or commercial sphere. Explaining this doctrine, the Supreme Court observed:

> **22.** There is an obvious difference in the contracts between private parties and contracts to which the State is a party. Private parties are concerned only with their personal interest whereas the State while exercising its powers and discharging its functions, acts indubitably, as is expected of it, for public good and in public interest. The impact of every State action is also on public interest. This factor alone is sufficient to import at least the minimal requirements of public law obligations and impress with this character the contracts made by the State or its instrumentality.[28]

Furthermore, Article 298 of the Constitution allows the Government into commercial and contractual activity conducted by the Government.[29] A 'decision of the State/public authority under Article 298 of the Constitution, is an administrative

---

24. Durga Das Basu, *Shorter Constitution of India*, Vol. II, §§1201-4 (14th ed., LexisNexis Butterworths Wadhwa Nagpur Reprint 2010).
25. *Shrilekha Vidyarthi (Kumari) v. State of Uttar Pradesh*, 1 SCC 212, para. 28 (1991).
26. *Mahabir Auto Stores v. Indian Oil Corporation* 3 SCC 752, para. 12 (1990).
27. *Supra* n. 24, at pp. 1218-20.
28. *Supra* n. 25, at para. 22.
29. Refer to *supra* n. 1, at Art. 298, which reads as under: The executive power of the Union and of each State shall extend to the carrying on of any trade or business and to the acquisition, holding and disposal of property and the making of contracts for any purpose:

    Provided that–

    (a) the said executive power of the Union shall, in so far as such trade or business or such purpose is not one with respect to which Parliament may make laws, be subject in each State to legislation by the State; and

decision and can be impeached on the ground that the decision is arbitrary or violative of Article 14 of the Constitution of India on any of the grounds available in public law field'.[30]

Often foreign investors are engaged with the government through a public procurement contract. Situations such as failure of the Government to grant licences, approvals, etc. can be challenged under the writ remedy. It is possible that failure of a public body to pay amounts due to a private party could form the basis of a writ remedy.[31]

Thus, even in contractual cases if the State fails to behave reasonably, the writ jurisdiction of the higher judiciary is available. This is a liberal approach towards contractual disputes as compared to investment tribunals. Tribunals have maintained a conscious distinction between breaches arising out of contract and breaches arising out of an investment treaty. The possibility of converting contractual disputes into treaty claims is possible only in cases of umbrella clauses. The Tribunals are not consistent on the point that in each case the breach of contract would be converted into treaty breach, independent of treaty breaches.[32] The prevailing view does not favour a liberal interpretation of umbrella clauses. It retains the distinction between contractual breaches and treaty breaches and rejects the conversion of contractual breaches into treaty breaches, unless there are independent treaty breaches.[33] In treaties without an umbrella clause, breach of purely contractual terms would not result into violation of treaty terms.[34] To this extent, the writ remedy is extensive and effective to subsume contractual breaches.

The writ remedies are available against the Government at the national level or regional level. It is available against different entities associated with the Government.[35] Courts have liberally interpreted the other entities to include private entities performing public functions. These would include several corporations and companies constituted by the Government exclusively for trading purposes. Public functions are functions undertaken for the collective benefit of public or a section of public. Bodies may intervene in social and economic affairs in public interest and in such a case they

---

      (b) the said executive power of each State shall, in so far as such trade or business or such purpose is not one with respect to which the State Legislature may make laws, be subject to legislation by Parliament.

30. *Supra* n. 26, at para. 19.
31. *Supra* n. 25, at paras 17-22, 24; *Life Insurance Corporation of India v. Escorts Ltd.*, 1 SCC 264, paras 22-8 (1986); *Joshi Technologies International Inc. v. Union of India*, 7 SCC 728, paras 68, 69 (2015).
32. *SGS Société Générale de Surveillance S.A. v. Islamic Republic of Pakistan*, Jurisdiction, ICSID Case No. ARB/01/13, para. 162 (6 Aug. 2003). *See* contra *SGS Société Générale de Surveillance S.A. v. Republic of the Philippines*, Jurisdiction, ICSID Case No. ARB/02/6, paras 119-28 (29 Jan. 2004).
33. *El Paso Energy International Company v. The Argentina Republic*, ICSID Case No. ARB/03/15, Jurisdiction, paras 85-8 (27 Apr. 2006); *El Paso Energy International Company v. The Argentina Republic*, Award, ICSID Case No. ARB/03/15, paras 532-8 (31 Oct. 2011).
34. *Waste Management Inc v. United Mexican States*, ICSID Case No. ARB(AF)/00/3, Award, paras 171-6 (30 Apr. 2004).
35. *Supra* n. 1, at Art. 12.

are accountable to public law principles.[36] The kind of authorities included within the writ jurisdiction is much wider in comparison to investment arbitration. For claiming responsibility of a State for the actions of its organs in investment arbitration, reference to the ILC Draft Articles on Responsibility of States for Internationally Wrongful Acts becomes necessary. Investment treaties do not stipulate rules of attribution. The actions of different organs of State can be attributed to a State.[37] The actions of persons or entities that are not an organ of the State are also attributable to the State, 'empowered by the law of that State to exercise elements of the governmental authority'; further, 'the person or entity is acting in that capacity in the particular instance'.[38] The number of authorities covered within these provisions is limited in comparison to those covered under the writ jurisdiction of the courts.

The standard based on which the actions of a public body are tested are based on a cumulative reading of Articles 14, 19 and 21 of the Constitution of India. Article 14 is most well suited for protecting foreign investors. It says: '14. Equality before law: The State shall not deny to any person equality before the law or the equal protection of laws within the territory of India.' This provision ensures national treatment (NT) for investors once they have validly entered and established their investments. They would also have to additionally satisfy the standing requirement elaborated below.

Additionally, Article 19 grants 'fundamental freedoms' to citizens, such as: freedom of expression (which includes commercial speech such as advertisement[39]); association; move freely throughout the country; carry out any occupation, trade or business. Article 21 protects right to life and personal liberty. Article 21 may appear irrelevant but the constitutional jurisprudence has developed in such a fashion that it sees all the three provisions comprehensively. They constitute different aspects of fundamental rights.[40] Fairness in action is a deeply embedded principle in the Constitution – '[a]rbitratiness is the very negation of the rule of law.'[41] All arms of the State are to ensure that their behaviour is devoid of arbitrariness, capriciousness, colourable, etc. These remedies are meant to prevent abuse of power and neglect of duties by public authorities. The Supreme Court has emphasized that denial of free trial amounts to violation of Article 14. It approved the standard of free trial of the European Convention for the Protection of Human Rights and Fundamental Freedoms, 1950.[42]

The requirement of standing is subsumed within the language of the substantive protection principles under the Constitution. A foreign investor can seek relief under writ jurisdiction through Articles 14 and 21. The problem with Article 19 is that it applies only to citizens, and an incorporated body cannot be treated as a citizen.[43] This does not mean that protection under Article 19 would not be available at all. In the

---

36. *Binny Ltd. v. V Sadasivan*, 6 SCC 657, paras 11, 29 (2005).
37. Draft Articles on Responsibility of States for Internationally Wrongful Acts, Supplement No. 10 (A/56/10), chp.IV.E.1, Art. 4 (November 2001), 2 Y.B. International Law Commission.
38. *Ibid.*, Art. 5.
39. *Tata Press Ltd. v. Mahanagar Telephone Nigam Ltd.*, 5 SCC 139, paras 17-23 (1995).
40. *Maneka Gandhi v. Union of India*, 1 SCC 248, paras 4-7 (1978).
41. *Supra* n. 25, at para. 35.
42. *Dwarka Prasad Agarwal v. B D Agarwal*, 6 SCC 230, para. 38 (2003).
43. *Tata Engineering and Locomotive Co. Ltd. v. State of Bihar*, 6 SCR 885, pp. 901-2 (1964).

Chapter 7: Indian Judiciary and Investment Treaty Arbitration §7.02

matter of protection of fundamental freedoms, the law does not distinguish between the rights of shareholders and the rights of a company. They are considered to be co-extensive and a shareholder can bring proceedings on behalf of the company.[44]

In the Bank Nationalisation case, the Supreme Court held as follows:

> A measure executive or legislative may impair the rights of the company alone, and not of its shareholders; it may impair the rights of the shareholders not of the Company; it may impair the rights of the shareholders as well as of the company. Jurisdiction of the Court to grant relief cannot be denied, when by State action the rights of the individual shareholder are impaired, if- that action, impairs the rights of the Company as well. The test in determining whether the shareholder's right is impaired is not formal; it is essentially qualitative; if the State action impairs the right of the shareholders- as well as of the Company, the Court will not, concentrating merely upon the technical operation of the action, deny itself jurisdiction to grant relief.[45]

The rulings in Sakal Papers case and Express Newspapers case also support the competence of the petitioners to maintain the proceedings.[46]

Under Article 226, since the only requirement is the existence of a legal right, Indian nationality is not required to file these proceedings. Courts have entertained petitions filed by companies that had foreign shareholders.[47]

The Courts can grant appropriate orders as necessary, depending on the circumstances of the case,[48] including monetary relief.[49] Normally investment tribunals cannot strike down tax legislations, unless they are confiscatory and result into violation of one of the treatment standards in the investment treaty.[50] The taxing powers are protected as police powers in international law.[51] The high judiciary is responsible for safeguarding the constitution. Thus, it possesses greater power to check whether the authority imposing tax possesses necessary authority and has strictly followed the procedure. A tax regulation would be cancelled irrespective of the extent of its effect.[52] In the constitutional law jurisprudence, once a right is established the subject matter of inquiry is the validity of the measure on the touchstone of constitutional principles. The economic impact is not a supervening factor. The constitutional courts enjoy a liberal jurisdiction. The language of the treaties limits the jurisdiction of

---

44. *Delhi Cloth and General Mills v. Union of India*, 4 SCC 166, para. 12 (1983).
45. *R.C. Cooper v. Union of India*, 3 SCR 530, para. 15 (1970).
46. *Sakal Papers (P) Ltd. and Others v. Union of India*, 3 SCR 842, paras 27, 28, 31, 34, 38, 41, 49 (1962); *Express Newspapers (P) Ltd. v. Union of India*, 3 SCR Supl. 382, paras 135-8 (1985).
47. *Zaheer Mauritius v. Director of Income Tax* (International Taxation)-II, 7 HCC (Del) 271, paras 3, 35 (2014); *Niko Resources Limited v. Union of India*, 374 ITR 369 (Guj), paras 1, 64 (2015); *Timken India Limited and Others v. Deputy Commissioner of Income Tax and Others*, 4 TMI 592, para. 25 (2016).
48. *Dwarka Nath v. ITO*, AIR SC 81, p. 85 (1966).
49. *ABL International Ltd. v. Export Credit Guarantee Corporation of India*, 3 SCC 553, paras 26-7 (2004).
50. *Marvin Roy Feldman Karpa v. United Mexican States*, Award, ICSID Case No. ARB(AF)/99/1, para. 103 (16 Dec. 2002).
51. *Link-Trading Joint Stock Company v. Department for Customs Control of Moldova*, Final Award, UNCITRAL, paras 69, 72 (18 Apr. 2002).
52. *Mafatlal Industries Ltd. v. Union of India*, 5 SCC 536, para. 108 (1997).

investment tribunals. The challenge to a measure becomes irrelevant unless it fits the frame of standards of treatment.

The protection under municipal law, in most situations is higher than that provided by investment tribunals. Furthermore, the extent of discretion enjoyed by the municipal courts in granting and molding a relief to suit the circumstances of a case is peculiar. The attractive feature is their enforceability. Any non-compliance with the orders passed under writ jurisdiction would amount to contempt of Court.[53] Government and its officials are extremely careful to ensure that they do not cross this line. The time taken to decide writ cases is much lesser. The proceedings are mostly documents based. They involve only one level of appeal and in some cases two. This also reduces the time spent at different levels of appeals. The standard of protection available under public law is much higher than investment tribunals. Some issues cannot be effectively addressed under the writ jurisdiction. The writ court cannot decide complicated and heavily disputed questions of fact. It would avoid situations where extensive oral testimonies are to be heard. The experience of White Industries shows that in situations where the order of the Court itself – including delays – is the basis of cause of action in an investment claim, the protection under municipal law is futile. Denial of justice is bound to be a ground to challenge judicial decisions.

The writ jurisdiction of the High Courts continues to attract cases filed by foreign investors against Government at different levels (central, provincial and local). For example in the *Vodafone case*, the dispute was involving a foreign investor in India, which had acquired a company overseas and the Indian tax authorities had raised demand notices for taxing the said transaction.[54] The Supreme Court held that the offshore transaction that took place was 'a bona fide structured FDI investment into India which fell outside India's territorial tax jurisdiction, hence not taxable.'[55] The Court further observed that: 'FDI flows towards locations with a strong governance infrastructure which includes enactment of laws and how well the legal system works. Certainty is integral to the rule of law. Certainty and stability form the basic foundation of any fiscal system. Tax policy certainly is crucial for taxpayers (including foreign investors) to make rational economic choices in the most efficient manner....Investors should know where they stand. It also helps the tax administration in enforcing the provisions of the taxing laws.'[56]

The Government had decided to change the law to overcome the decision of the Supreme Court, against which the foreign investor filed an investment claim.[57] In May 2017, Vodafone filed a second investment arbitration claim against India, even as the first arbitration continues.

In addition to writ remedy, a suit can be filed against any governmental authority in the subordinate courts under Sections 79-82 (Suits by or against the Government or

---

53. *Supra* n. 1, at Arts 129, 215; Section 2, Contempt of Courts Act, 1961.
54. The restructuring carried out was very complex. For a detailed discussion *see* Vodafone *International Holdings BV v. Union of India*, 6 SCC 613, paras 4-59 (2012).
55. *Ibid.*, at para. 179.
56. *Ibid.*, at para. 180.
57. *See* Vodafone *International Holdings BV v. India*, Notice of Arbitration (not public), UNCITRAL, (17 Apr. 2014).

public officers in their official capacity) and Order 27 of the Code of Civil Procedure, 1908 (CPC).

According to Section 79 of the CPC, in a suit by or against the Government, the authority to be named as plaintiff or defendant, as the case may be, shall be (a) in the case of a suit by or against the Central Government, the Union of India, and (b) in the case of a suit by or against a State Government, the State. Thus allowing that the Government of India may sue or be sued by the name of the Union of India and the Government of a State may sue or be sued by the name of the State.[58] Section 80 requires that advance notice shall be given to the Government.

This provision is rarely used since writ remedy is available and easily accessible. If one approaches the lower judiciary then the time taken for the appeals and the matter to be disposed of finally would take a very long time.

The higher judiciary provides fast justice at relatively low costs through the writ jurisdiction. This could be one of the reasons why India was not sued, since India entered into a bilateral investment treaty (BIT) in 1994 until the White Industries case in 2009, where the investment claim was based on a cause of action rising out of the actions of the judiciary. The ethos of fairness and insistence on the rule of law in the thinking of the Indian judiciary is represented in the following passage from the judgment of the Supreme Court in the KT Plantation case:

218. The rule of law as a principle, it may be mentioned, is not an absolute means of achieving equality, human rights, justice, freedom and even democracy and it all depends upon the nature of the legislation and the seriousness of the violation. The rule of law as an overarching principle can be applied by the constitutional courts, in the rarest of rare cases, in situations, we have referred to earlier and can undo laws which are tyrannical, violate the basic structure of our Constitution, and our cherished comes of law and justice.
219. One of the fundamental principles of a democratic society inherent in all the provisions of the Constitution is that any interference with the peaceful enjoyment of possession should be lawful. Let the message, therefore, be loud and clear, that the rule of law exists in this country even when we interpret a statue, which has the blessings of Article 300-A.[59]

§7.03 THE RESPONSIBILITY OF INDIA FOR THE ACTS OF JUDICIARY

The experience is that the judiciary has steadfastly protected its independence and ensured that there is no interference of other branches of the State in its operation. Despite this position, the Indian State would be responsible for the actions of the judiciary.[60] Interestingly, international law on State responsibility for actions of judiciary has evolved over time. The earlier position was that in States where the judiciary is independent from other branches, the State was not necessarily responsible

---

58. *The State of Kerala v. General Manager, Southern Railways*, AIR SC 2538, para. 5 (1976); *State of Punjab v. O. G. B. Syndicate*), 5 SCR 387, para. 21 (1964).
59. *KT Plantation (P) Ltd. v. State of Kerala*, 9 SCC 1 (2011).
60. *See* Prabhash Ranjan and Deepak Raju, *Bilateral Investment Treaties and the Indian Judiciary*, 46 Georg Washington International Law Review 809 (2013-2014).

for actions of judiciary.[61] However this principle came to be rejected by overwhelming opinion to the contrary of scholars.[62] A State is responsible for the actions of the judiciary because, in international law, a State is considered to be and treated as a single entity – the principle of unity.[63] International law does not recognize that certain organs of the State are capable of generating international responsibility while certain cannot.[64] The nature of structure and distribution of authority internally in the State is irrelevant. In the words of the International Law Commission (ILC), a 'State is treated as a unity, consistent with its recognition as a single legal person in international law'.[65] For the purposes of State responsibility the distinction between executive, judicial and legislative is irrelevant.[66] Judiciary has been specifically included as an organ and States have been found responsible for the actions of their judiciary.[67] This rule is a customary international law rule.[68] Hence it cannot be suggested that judiciary is excluded from consideration for holding India responsible in international law. The internal division within the State is irrelevant and inconsequential. Therefore the fact that the Indian judiciary is independent is no reason to think that India would not be responsible for the actions of the courts. Article 4(1) of the ILC Draft Articles on Responsibility of States for Internationally Wrongful Acts declares that:

> 1. The conduct of any State organ shall be considered an act of that State under international law, whether the organ exercises legislative, executive, judicial or

---

61. T. Baty, *The Canons of International Law*, 127-8 (John Murray 1930); In the *Yuille Shortridge & Co case*, the Senate of Hamburg, while adjudicating the British case for private loss suffered due to the decision of a Portuguese court, declared that Portugal cannot be held responsible because as per the Portuguese Constitution the judiciary is completely independent of the other branches and thus other branches were unable to exert influence on the judiciary. Hence the State would not attract responsibility for the actions of its judiciary: A. de Lapradelle and N. Politis, *Rescuil des arbitrages internationaux*, Vol. I, 78, 103, para. 30 (21 Oct. 1861); Gustavo Gurrero, Annexure to Questionnaire No. 4, Committee of Experts for the Progressive Codification of International Law, Report of the Sub-Committee, League of Nations Document C.196.M70.1927.V.
62. Charles Dupuis, *Liberté des voices de communication et le Relations internationales*, Recueil des Cours, Vol. I 129, 354 (1924); Gerald Fitzmaurice, *The Meaning of the Term 'Denial of Justice'* 13 British Yearbook of International Law 93, 108 (1932); Alwyn Freeman, *The International Responsibility of Sates for Denial of Justice*, 31 (Longman 1938); Jiménez de Aréchaga, *International Law in the Past Third of a Century*, 159 Recueil des Cours, I, 278 (1978).
63. *See* Eduardo Jiménez de Aréchaga, *International Law in the Past Third of a Century*, 159 Recueil de Cours 1, 278 (1978).
64. Draft Articles on Responsibility of States for Internationally Wrongful Acts with commentaries, 2 Y.B. International Law Commission, Official Records of the General Assembly, Fifty-Sixth session, Supplement No. 10 (A/56/10), chp.IV.E.2, Part two, 40 (2001).
65. *Ibid.*, at p. 35.
66. *Salvador Commercial Company*, UNRIAA, Vol. XV (Sale No. 66, V.3), 455 at para. 477 (1902); *Chattin Case (US v. Mexico)* IV (Sale No. 1951, V.1) RIAA 282, at paras 285-6 (23 Jul. 1927); *Disputes Concerning the Interpretation of Article 79 of the Treaty of Peace*, RIAA, Vol. XIII (Sales No. 64.V.3), 389 at para. 438 (1955).
67. *Certain German Interests in Polish Upper Silesia*, Merits, Judgment No. 7, PCIJ Series A No. 7, 19 (1926); *S.S. Lotus (Fr. V. Turk)*, Judgment No. 9, PCIJ Series A No. 10, 24 (1927); *Jurisdiction of the Courts of Danzig*, Advisory Opinion, PCIJ Series B, No. 15, 26-7 (1928); *Ambatielos*, Merits, Judgment, ICJ Reports, 10 at paras 21-2 (1953); *Application of the Convention of 1902 Governing the Guardianship of Infants*, Judgment, ICJ Reports, 55 at para. 65 (1958).
68. *Differences Relating to Immunity from Legal Process of a Special Rapporteur of the Commission on Human Rights*, Advisory Opinion, ICJ Reports, 62 at para. 62 (1999).

any other functions, whatever position it holds in the organization of the State, and whatever its character as an organ of the central Government or of a territorial unit of the State.

BITs also provide the foundation for responsibility of the State for actions of judiciary. A State is responsible for the 'measures' that it adopts that affect foreign investors. The definition of 'measure' is defined in international investment agreements (IIAs).[69] 'Measure' includes all actions including judicial. Law includes judge made law as well and all three branches are covered.[70] There is no reason to exclude judicial decisions from the purview of measures.[71] The basis of responsibility is that the courts of the host State may take a decision in accordance with its domestic law. But if that decision violates international law, then the host State is responsible for that decision.[72] The decision of whether an action is wrongful has to be based on international law. As per Article 3 of the ILC Draft Articles on State Responsibility, its characterization under domestic law is irrelevant.[73] Therefore, the decision of the judiciary in relation to foreign investor may be defended under the domestic law but if it violates international law, then the State is still responsible. Article 32 is a corollary to Article 3. The responsible State cannot rely on its domestic law to defend its actions.[74] The actions of the Indian judiciary may be defended under domestic law of India or the Constitution of India, but this cannot constitute a defence from international responsibility once an international law rule is breached.

In the ordinary course, in case of failure of State or an entity related to the State, to respect legal and contractual rights of foreign investor, the foreign investor has to approach the domestic courts for remedy.[75] If the domestic courts fail to provide appropriate remedy then the home State of the investor could espouse the claim of its nationals on the grounds of denial of justice.[76] In the absence of an investment treaty a foreign investor would be required to go to domestic courts for redressal of its grievances.

According to the Permanent Court of International Justice (PCIJ) in *Treatment of Polish Nationals Case*: 'a state cannot adduce as against another State its own Constitution with a view to evading obligations incumbent upon it under international

---

69. ASEAN Comprehensive Investment Agreement (adopted 26 Feb. 2009, entered into force 29 Feb. 2012); Treaty between the Government of the United States of America and the Government of Rwanda Concerning the Encouragement and Reciprocal Protection of Investment (Rwanda – United States of America) (adopted 19 Feb. 2008, entered into force 1 Jan. 2012); Investment Agreement for the COMESA Common Investment Area (23 May 2007).
70. *Loewen Group, Inc. and Raymond L. Loewen v. United States of America*, Award, ICSID Case No. ARB(AF)/98/3, para. 40 (26 Jun. 2003).
71. *Ibid.*, at paras 54, 60.
72. *Supra* n. 50, at para. 140; Also see *Himpurna California Energy Ltd. v. Indonesia*, Interim Award, (2000) XXV Y.B.Comm'l Arb. 11, para. 181 (26 Sept. 1999); *Martini Case (Italy v. Venezuela)*, X RIAA 644 (8 Jul. 1904).
73. *Supra* n. 37, at Art. 3.
74. *Ibid.*, at Art. 32.
75. Robert Jennings and Arthur Watts (ed.), *Oppenheim's International Law*, Vol. I: Peace, 927-31, (9th ed., Oxford University Press 2008).
76. *Ibid.*, at pp. 934-5.

law or under general international law.'[77] A similar provision is also contained in Article 27 of the Vienna Convention on the Law of Treaties, 1969. This rule applies to all legal provisions passed by whichever authority.[78] This provision covers all aspects of internal law: 'whether written or unwritten and whether they take the form of constitutional or legislative rules, administrative decrees of judicial decisions.'[79] At the same time, the final decision-maker on whether a State has committed an international delict is an international tribunal; it would be inappropriate to expect that the same authority will be judging whether its own actions are correct. It would also make the possibility of an international adjudication inconsequential and fruitless. Since a State is one entity – from the standpoint of international law – it would be treated that one arm is judging another within the same structure.[80] Thus the independence of judiciary under domestic legal system is disregarded in international law.

An investment claim could arise out of and maintained on one of the following grounds.

[A] Judicial Activism and Other Problems

Judicial activism means 'judicial philosophy which motivates judges to depart from strict adherence to judicial precedent in favour of progressive and new social policies which is not always consistent with the restraint expected of appellate judges.'[81] It is the making of new public policies through the decisions by the judges.[82] Some scholars have also called the practice of courts in stepping beyond their domain and commenting on political and other issues juristocracy.[83] There are cases of instances and voluminous literature where the Courts have exercised judicial activism. They are not discussed here since it is beyond the scope of the present work.

The Supreme Court has explained the rationale for judicial activism in the following words:

---

77. *Treatment of Polish Nationals and Other Persons of Polish Origin or Speech in the Danzing Territory*, Advisory Opinion, PCIJ Series A/B, No. 44, 4, 24 (1932). Also *see SS Wimbledon (Britain v. Germany)*, Judgment of 17 Aug. 1923, PCIJ Series A, No. 1, 29-30 (1923); *Free Zones of Upper Savoy and the District of Gex*, Order of 6 December 1930, PCIJ Series A/B No. 46, 96, 167 (1930); *Greco-Bulgarian 'Communities'*, Advisory Opinion, PCIJ Series B, No. 17, 32 (1930); *Elettronica Sicula S.p.A (ELSI)*, Judgment, ICJ Reports 15, 73, 94 (1989); I.L.C. Draft Declaration on Rights and Duties of States, General Assembly Resolution 375 (IV), Annex, Art. 13 (6 Dec. 1949).
78. *LaGrand (Germany v. United States)*, Provisional Measures, Order of 3 Mar. 1999, ICJ Reports, 9 at para. 28 (1999).
79. *Supra* n. 64, at p. 38.
80. Chittaranjan Amerasinghe, *State Responsibility for Injuries to Aliens*, 215 (Oxford University Press: Clarendon Press 1967).
81. Bryan A. Garner, (ed.), *Black's Law Dictionary* (9th ed., West Group 2009).
82. *See* generally Jay M. Shafritz, *The Harper Collins Dictionary of American Government and Politics* (Harper Perennial 1993).
83. V.R. Krishna Iyer, *Quality of Justice Is Not Strained*, Indian Express (27 Nov. 2003); *See* Ran Hirschl, *The Origins and Consequences of New Constitutionalism*, 294 (Harvard University 2004).

it is the duty of the executive to fill the vacuum by executive orders because its field is coterminous with that of the legislature, and where there is inaction even by the executive, for whatever reason, the judiciary must step in, in exercise of its constitutional obligations under the aforesaid provisions to provide a solution till such time as the legislature acts to perform its role by enacting proper legislation to cover the field.[84]

The Supreme Court and the High Courts exercise jurisdiction under public interest litigation.[85] The courts have expanded the scope of standing – i.e., the ability to bring proceedings before the Court for violation of fundamental rights.[86] Any 'public spirited' person can bring issues to the notice of the Court and there is no need to follow formal procedures, as are normally followed in the Court of law.[87] In these proceedings various issues can be and are brought. For example, Article 21 that encompasses 'right to life' has been interpreted extensively by the courts to include right to good, air,[88] environment,[89] water, and compulsory licensing of life saving drugs as an exception to protection of intellectual property rights.[90] The word 'public interest' has been widely and liberally interpreted by Indian courts. They may also have a direct impact on the interest of foreign investors. These proceedings are normally in between the 'public spirited' claimant and the State. The affected foreign investor may not even be a party to such proceedings and a decision may be rendered in his absence.

According to a commentary, the Supreme Court of India is all powerful, and the judges decide virtually on all aspects of life: from election of Prime Minister and conduct of legislature to petty administrative issues about roads and fair means in examination.[91] It is natural that a Court would comment or adjudicate on issues that affect foreign investors. Foreign investors often work on large contracts which have an element of public interest involved – may it be construction of an airport, road or other infrastructure, management of watersupply for a municipal corporation or some such services.[92] It is natural and but obvious that some elements of the dispute would come before the Court, and the Court will deliver a judgment that would adversely affect a foreign investor. For example a lot of environmental regulation happened through the Supreme Court.[93] Now a lot of this activity is undertaken by the National Green Tribunal that was constituted subsequently. In public interest the court interferes with many public service deliveries, such as water, road, transport, etc. If a foreign investor

---

84. *Vincent Narain v. Union of India*, 1 SCC 226, para. 52 (1999).
85. *Mumbai Kamgar Sabha, Bombay v. M/S Abdulbhai Faizullabhai & Ors*, AIR SC 1455, p. 1458 (1976).
86. *Sunil Batra v. Delhi Administration* 4 SCC 494 (1978); *Bandhua Mukti Morcha v. Union of India (UOI) and Ors* 3 SCC 161 (1984).
87. *Ibid.*
88. *Subhash Kumar v. State of Bihar and Ors*, 1 SCR 5 (1991).
89. *Vellore Citizens Welfare Forum v. Union Of India & Ors*, AIR SC 2715 (1986).
90. *Novartis AG and others v. Union Of India & Others*, AIR SC 1311 (2013).
91. Sudhansu Ranjan, *Justice: Judocracy and Democracy in India*, 2-3 (Taylor & Francis Group 2012).
92. *See* for example *Centre for Public Interest Litigation v. Union of India* (2G Spectrum case) 1 CGBCLJ 209 (2012); *Manohar Lal Sharma v. Principal Secretary* (Coal Block Allocation Case) 9 SCC 516 (2014); *Flemingo Duty Free Shop Ltd. v. Union of India* (110) BomLR 1730 (2008).
93. Shyam Divan and Armin Rosencranz, *Environmental Law and Policy in India*, 41-2, 50-4, 105-10, 147-9 (2nd ed., Oxford University Press 18 Apr. 2002).

has invested in such an enterprise or has undertaken it under a contract, its contractual rights could be affected by due judicial decisions. Judicial activism can act as a potential for conflict between the interest of foreign investor or adjudication by courts.

Delays are the most notorious feature of the Indian judicial system. Excessive caseload is causing delay. A lack of case management results into uncertainty about the date when the case would be heard. This often causes financial losses and wasteful expenditure in preparation for the case. Lack of designated day and time are a major problem that brings in uncertainty.[94] This issue was raised in the *White and Industries case*, discussed below.

At times there are concerns that due to the power of the Supreme Court to overrule its decisions, there is a tendency to introduce inconsistency in the jurisprudence.[95] Uncertainty is one of the worrying factors for a foreign investor. A foreign investor wants to be certain about the legal framework that the investor is entering. Inconsistent decision-making affects profits and the value of investments, especially in taxation matters and other cases that have an economic impact. The fair and equitable treatment (FET) has been interpreted in a manner to State that legitimate expectations is one of the vital components of the FET standard. As a part of legitimate expectations the foreign investor expects that the legal framework which existed while the investor entered would not be suddenly altered to cause prejudice and loss of foreign investment.

[B] Denial of Justice

Denial of justice is a standard under customary international law and is one of the well-developed branches of international law.[96] Paulsson defines denial of justice as a situation where: 'a state incurs responsibility if it administers justice to aliens in a fundamentally unfair manner.'[97] The applicability of concerned laws under international law is distinct from that under domestic law. There is no legislature or any other centralized law making body in international law. The sources of international law are specified in Article 38(1) of the Statute of the International Court of Justice (ICJ). Two important sources that are relevant for our discussion are treaty and customary international law. In the case of investment disputes, an investment tribunal is required to decide disputes based on all the sources specified in Article 38(1) of the Statute of the ICJ – primarily treaty and custom. The treaty that would be applied in an investment dispute is the investment treaty under which a foreign investor would file an investment claim. At the same time, customary international law rules continue to apply. The rule that relates to activities of the judiciary is the rule of denial of justice. Therefore, there have been instances where the ground of denial of justice has been invoked, even if it was not contained in the IIA.[98] In *Saipem v. Bangladesh*, the tribunal declined to

---

94. Fali Nariman, *India's Legal System: Can it be Saved?*, 140-7 (Penguin Books 2006).
95. *Ibid.*, at p. 137.
96. Jan Paulsson, *Denial of Justice in International Law*, 2 (Cambridge University Press 2005).
97. *Ibid.*, at p. 4.
98. *Supra* n. 70, at paras 127-9, 137.

invoke denial of justice on the ground that it was not present in the BIT.[99] The tribunal committed an error by ignoring that denial of justice would continue to apply as a part of customary international law.

Vattel has identified three instances of denial of justice: (a) not allowing foreigners to establish their rights before ordinary courts, (b) delays which are ruinous or equivalent to refusal, (c) judgments that are 'manifestly unjust or one sided'.[100] These three elements encapsulate the philosophy behind the rule of denial of justice.

It is the duty of each State under customary international law to maintain a working and fair judicial system of a minimum international standard, capable of administering justice, at least in relation to foreigners.[101] The ground of denial of justice is available only to foreigners. Nationals of a State cannot seek redress against their own courts before an international tribunal by invoking the denial of justice. The violation that may be invoked is of international law and not domestic law. An international tribunal is not concerned with violations of domestic law. On the contrary, even if domestic laws were violated an international tribunal would not be concerned with it.[102] The foreign investor will have to go to domestic courts for redress of those rights. In some cases 'exceptionally outrageous or monstrously grave' breaches of municipal law could be treated as denial of justice.[103]

Although investment treaties allow a foreign investor to make a claim directly to in investment tribunal, for the rule of denial of justice to trigger, exhaustion of local remedies is necessary. As per this rule, all remedies available in domestic courts are to be exhausted. This rule ensures that the courts in the State have had an opportunity of correcting errors in the judgment. Paulsson has described this situation aptly:

> If aliens are allowed to bypass those mechanisms and bring international claims for denial of justice on the basis of alleged wrongdoing by the justice of the peace of any neighborhood, international law would find itself intruding intolerably into internal affairs. For a foreigner's international grievance to proceed as a claim of denial of justice, the national system must have been tested. Its perceived failings cannot constitute an international wrong unless it has been given a chance to correct itself.[104]

However, the rule of exhaustion of local remedies has to be understood in a 'rational manner', it does not make the rights of foreigners delusive.[105] The rule of exhaustion of local remedies would not be available where there are no remedies

---

99. *Saipem S.p.A. v. The People's Republic of Bangladesh*, Award, ICSID Case No. ARB/05/07, 121, 181 (30 Jun. 2009).
100. Emer de Vattel (translated by Charles Fenwick), *The Law of Nations or the Principles of Natural Law (Le droit de gens, ou principles de la loi naturelle)*, Vol. II, 350 (William S. Hein & Co. 1995).
101. *Supra* n. 96, at pp. 1-2.
102. *Supra* n. 64, at p. 36.
103. *See* Pleadings of Spain in the *Barcelona Traction Case*, Jiménez de Aréchaga, *International Law in the Past Third of a Century*, 159 Recueil des Cours, Vol. I, 185 (1978); *Martini Case (Italy v. Venezuela)*, X RIAA 644 (8 Jul. 1904).
104. *Supra* n. 96, at p. 108.
105. *Montano Case (Peru v. USA)*, 2 Moore International Arbitrations 1630, 1637 (1863).

available.¹⁰⁶ A victim of denial of justice is not expected to follow improbable remedies or undertake efforts beyond the normal course for seeking justice.¹⁰⁷ The rule of exhaustion of local remedies cannot be absolute, otherwise it would result into improbable outcomes. An appropriate exception is the absence of a reasonable possibility of an effective remedy.¹⁰⁸ The responsibility is on the person alleging that these conditions constrained the exhaustion of local remedies.¹⁰⁹ India cannot insist that the foreign investor waits for unreasonably long period that all the courts in India decide the case decisively. Delays of Indian courts could be termed as unreasonable – the decision, however, would depend on a case-by-case basis because there cannot be an arithmetical formula to determine what is unreasonable. One has to be careful since a delay could be seen as defect in the judicial system, which would be treated to amount to denial of justice.¹¹⁰ In *White Industries v. India*, the Tribunal rejected the argument of the claimant that the Indian courts were responsible for denial of justice because there were delays in adjudication. It had been eight years since the arbitration award was pending enforcement in Indian courts and at the time when arbitration proceedings were initiated, it was pending before the Supreme Court undecided.¹¹¹ The Tribunal held that there were multiple proceedings initiated by the claimant. Although it took time before the Supreme Court, at other levels the adjudication was fairly quick. Considering the caseload of the Supreme Court, it could not be said that the delay has raised concerns about the 'judicial propriety of the outcome'.¹¹² The Tribunal acknowledged that India has a huge population with a seriously overstretched judiciary. The Tribunal said that:

> The Tribunal considers it also to be relevant, when examining the behavior of the courts, to bear in mind that India is a developing country with a population of over 1.2 billion people with a seriously overstretched judiciary.¹¹³

The Tribunal conducted independent analysis of the time spent at each level of proceedings to conclude that the delay was not unreasonable.¹¹⁴

Although the Indian Courts were not held responsible for denial of justice, the Tribunal circuitously arrived at the same conclusion by relying on the MFN clause in

---

106. *Elettronica Sicula S.p.A (ELSI)*, supra n. 77, at paras 15, 94.
107. *Supra* n. 96, at p. 113.
108. *Ibid.*, at p. 118.
109. Third Report on Diplomatic Protection, International Law Commission, UN Doc. A/CN. 4/523, para. 19 (2002).
110. *El Oro Mining Railway Company (Great Britain) v. Mexico*, V RIAA 191, 198; *Great Britain v. Mexico Claims Commission*, Decision No. 55, 198 at para. 10 (18 Jun. 1931): The Tribunal found a nine-year delay to amount to denial of justice. The tribunal held that: 'the amount of work incumbent on the Court and the multitude of law suits which they are confronted, may explain, but not excuse, the delay. If this number is so enormous as to occasion an arrear of nine years, the conclusion cannot be other than the judicial machinery is defective'.
111. For a description of facts refer to *White Industries Australia Ltd. v. Republic of India*, Final Award, UNCITRAL, 3.2.33-3.2.65 (30 Nov. 2011).
112. *Ibid.*, at para. 10.4.12.
113. *Ibid.*, at para. 10.4.18.
114. *Ibid.*, at paras 10.4.21, 10.4.22.

India-Australia BIT to import 'effective means' standard from the Kuwait BIT. In a highly unusual manner the Tribunal abruptly concluded that:

> In these circumstances, and even though we have decided that the nine years of proceedings in the set aside application do not amount to a denial of justice, the Tribunal has no difficulty in concluding the Indian judicial system's inability to deal with White's jurisdictional claim in over nine years, and the Supreme Court's inability to hear White's jurisdictional appeal for over five years amounts to undue delay and constitutes a breach of India's voluntarily assumed obligation of providing White with 'effective means' of asserting claims and enforcing rights.[115]

Therefore, India was responsible for the actions of the judiciary, which were found to contract the India-Kuwait BIT.

While deciding question of delay, various factors would be important: contribution of the foreign investor in the delay through the number of proceedings and adjournments and caseload of Indian courts would be important considerations before declaring if in a case in question the delay may be termed as unreasonable. Judicial delays constitute denial of justice and an unreasonable situation, which would act as an exemption from the rule of exhaustion of local remedies.[116]

If a foreign investor is kept in jail in relation to a criminal matter during the pendency of the trial, then it may be treated as denial of justice.[117] Indian courts are known for long detention of under trials. This has been one of the important concerns.[118] Denial of justice is present if the inadequate measures are taken against perpetrators of crimes against foreign investors.[119] The criminal justice system suffers from some serious drawbacks and delays. There are chances that criminal cases filed against those committing criminal actions affecting foreign investors may take a long time. At the same time the sentencing policy in India is uncertain.[120] It is plausible that the punishment awarded may be treated as inadequate.

---

115. *Ibid.*, at para. 11.4.19.
116. *Antoine Fabiani (no 1) (France v. Venezuela)*, 5 Moore International Arbitrations 4878, 4909 (31 Jul. 1905).
117. *Chattin Case, supra* n. 66: The foreigner was kept in detention for five months while unsuccessful appeals were being filed in courts.
118. Jayanth K. Krishnan, Kumar C. Raj, *Delay in Process, Denial of Justice: The Jurisprudence and Empirics of Speedy Trials in Comparative Perspective*, Paper 155 (Articles by Maurer Faculty: 2011); *Bhim Singh v. Union of India* 4 RCR (Criminal) 234 (2014); *In Re: Inhuman Conditions in 1382 Prisons* 3 SCC 700 (2016); Seventy-Eighth report on Congestion of Under-Trial prisoners in Jails, Law Commission of India, D.O. No. F.2 (19)/78-L.C., (February 1979); Report No. 239, Expeditious Investigation and Trial of Criminal Cases Against Influential Public Personalities (Submitted to the Supreme Court of India in W P (C) NO. 341/2004, *Virender Kumar Ohri v. Union of India & Others*), Law Commission of India, (March 2012); Vrinda Bhandari, *On Trial the Criminal Justice System*, The Indian Express (25 Sept. 2014), http://indianexpress.com/article/opinion/columns/on-trial-the-criminal-justice-system/ (accessed 10 Jul. 2017).
119. *Supra* n. 96, at pp. 170-3.
120. *Baldev Singh v. State of Punjab*, AIR SC 1231 (2011); Anup Surendranath, *Death Is Entirely Discriminatory*, The Hindu (17 Sept. 2012), http://www.thehindu.com/todays-paper/tp-opinion/death-is-entirely-discriminatory/article3905516.ece; (accessed 10 Jul. 2017); Live Law News Network, *The Unending Uncertainty in the Death Sentencing Policy of Indian Courts*, Livelaw.in (13 May 2015), http://www.livelaw.in/the-unending-uncertainty-in-the-death-sentencing-policy-of-indian-courts/ (accessed 10 Jul. 2017); *Purushottam Dashrath Borate & Anr v. State of Maharashtra* 6 SCC 652 (2015); *See Santosh Kumar Satish Bhusan Bariyar v.*

States are under an obligation to provide a fair and efficient system of justice and not to undertake that there would be no judicial misconduct at all.[121] There are limitations in respect of the extent to which an international tribunal can investigate the decision of the national courts while taking decision on the existence of denial of justice. It must be kept in mind that claims of denial of justice do not include a complete review by an international tribunal. In *Azinia v. Mexico*, the Tribunal stated that:

> The possibility of holding a State internationally liable for judicial decisions does not, however, entitle a claimant to seek international review of the national court decisions as though the international jurisdiction seized has plenary appellate jurisdiction. This is not true generally, and it is not true for NAFTA.[122]

In situations of denial of justice, the action of judiciary constitutes the cause of action for an international claim. Denial of justice is different from appellate jurisdiction exercised in municipal law. Under municipal law, the appellate court exercises wide ranging powers, including the power to review the decision on its merits. In denial of justice, an international tribunal exercises a limited jurisdiction, spanning only to the extent of checking fairness in procedure.[123] While performing appellate functions the higher court is concerned with correcting the errors of the lower court, whereas, in situations of denial of justice, the international tribunal would hold the host State responsible for the judicial actions. The actions of the domestic court constitute the cause of action for an international claim.

It is impossible to exhaustively enumerate instances of denial of justice.[124] Denial of justice is always procedural unless the substantive mistakes are so egregious wrong that no honest or competent court could have rendered such a decision.[125] Freeman considered denial of justice as a broad concept to include all actions of the judiciary that are contrary to international law.[126] Procedural unfairness would include judgments tainted by fraud, bias, dishonesty or malice.[127] Denial of justice included procedural and substantive denial of justice as per Freeman, but later scholars do not agree with this position. A State is not responsible for violations of substantive international law.[128] Paulsson argues that if the courts render decisions contrary to international law then those actions are not covered under denial of justice.[129] A State

---

State of Maharashtra 6 SCC 498 (2009), where the Supreme Court had declared that imposition of death penalty was per incurium in at least three cases. Furthermore, Indian Penal Statutes do not have gradation in Sentencing, and the same has been discussed in the Verma Committee Report.
121. *Supra* n. 96, at p. 100.
122. *Robert Azinian v. United Mexican States*, Final Award, ICSID, ARB(AF)/97/2, Paulsson.Civiletti.Wobeser-Hoepfner, 83,99 (1 Nov. 1999).
123. *Supra* n. 96, at pp. 4-5.
124. *Ibid.*, at pp. 93-8.
125. *Ibid.*, at p. 98.
126. Alwyn Freeman, *supra* n. 62, at 178, 309.
127. *Supra* n. 96, at pp. 88-9.
128. *Ibid.*, at pp. 81-2.
129. *Ibid.*, at pp. 69-73.

is not responsible for bona fide errors of the judiciary on the substance of international law.[130] According to Paulsson:

> But international law does not impose a duty on states to treat foreigners fairly at every step of the legal process. The duty is to create and maintain a *system of justice* which ensures that unfairness to foreigners either does not happen, *or is corrected...* .[131]

In Ambatielos Claim, it was observed that: 'it is the whole system of legal protection, as provided by municipal law, which must have been put to the test.'[132]

This is understandable since there is no concept of perfect justice. Additionally, the domestic judges may not be well versed in international law. Even while applying international law, they are considering international law in the context of municipal law. Extreme cases would be 'dealt with on the footing that they are so unjustifiable that they could have been only the product of bias or some other violations of the right to *due process*.'[133] Situations of bad faith would be where:

> An unjust judgment may and often does afford strong evidence that the court was dishonest, or rather it raises a strong presumption of dishonesty. It may even afford conclusive evidence, it the injustice be sufficiently flagrant, so that the judgment is of a kind which no honest and competent court could possibly have given.[134]

In *Azinia v. Mexico*, the Tribunal rejected the argument of the claimant that the domestic courts had committed an error of law on the ground that there was insufficient evidence. The Tribunal did open the possibility of merits review, but was very clear that it should raise to the level of being arbitrary or malicious. In the words of the Tribunal:

> If the Claimant cannot convince the Arbitral Tribunal that the evidence for this finding was so insubstantial or so bereft of a basis in law, that the judgments were in effect arbitrary or malicious, they simply cannot prevail.[135]

Failure of the judge to hear a foreign investor would be a situation of gross procedural unfairness. The decision could arise after the foreign investor was heard and could be based on reasoning justified in national law, but not under international law. Denial of justice cannot be lightly inferred – as held by the Great Britain-Mexico Claims Commission:

---

130. Gerald Fitzmaurice, *supra* n. 62, at 112-3.
131. *Supra* n. 96, at p. 7.
132. *Ambatielos Claim (Greece v. UK)*, XII RIAA 83, 120 (6 Mar. 1956).
133. *Supra* n. 96, at p. 82.
134. *Supra* n. 130, at p. 113.
135. *Supra* n. 122, at para. 105.

It is obvious that such a grave reproach can only be directed against a judicial authority upon evidence of the most convincing nature.[136]

Denial of justice may be found in various instances such as refusal to judge,[137] illegitimate assertion of jurisdiction,[138] discrimination of prejudice,[139] arbitrariness,[140] gross incompetence[141] and pretense of form.[142] The judicial structure and the constitutional mechanism of the judicial operations are such that these problems would not arise in India and even if they do at some stage of judicial proceedings, the systems are adept to contain and correct such errors. As discussed, denial of justice does not contemplate State responsibility for stray actions of a judge, but rather looks at the entire judicial institution – whether the State has maintained a minimal workable judicial structure to redress concerns of foreigners in an unbiased manner. From this standard, the judicial performance and integrity of the Indian judiciary are certainly of a high standard manned with competent persons.

Denial of justice would exist if there are fundamental breaches of due process.[143] This situation would not arise in India because administrative law principle of *audi alterem partem* is followed strictly,[144] whereby no person is to be condemned unheard. Also, this has to be effective and not a mere formality.[145] If the lower judiciary fails to comply, the appellate courts would always interfere and correct such decision. According to Paulsson:

> But international law does not impose a duty on states to treat foreigners fairly at every step of the legal process. The duty is to create and maintain a *system of justice* which ensures that unfairness to foreigners either does not happen, *or is corrected....*[146] In Ambatielos Claim, it was observed that: 'it is the whole system of legal protection, as provided by municipal law, which must have been put to the test.'[147]

India may be required to pay compensation for the losses caused to the foreign investor due to the judicial actions or restitution may also be directed by an investment tribunal.[148]

---

136. *Supra* n. 110, at p. 198, para. 9. There is a possibility that a tribunal may decline to follow that decision and claim that the law has evolved bringing down the standard. In any case, a tribunal would enjoy extensive latitude in deciding whether that standard has been met, even if the bar has been set very high.
137. *Supra* n. 96, at pp. 176-7.
138. *Ibid.*, at pp. 178-9.
139. *Ibid.*, at pp. 192-5.
140. *Ibid.*, at pp. 196-8.
141. *Ibid.*, at pp. 200-2.
142. *Ibid.*, at pp. 202-4.
143. *Supra* n. 96, at pp. 180-92.
144. *Canara Bank v. Debashish Das* AIR SC 2041, paras 15, 21 (2003); *National Central Cooperative Bank v. Ajay Kumar* AIR. SC 39, para. 5 (1994).
145. *Dhakeswari Cotton Mills v. CIT* 26 ITR 775, para. 9 (1954).
146. *Supra* n. 96, at p. 7.
147. *Supra* n. 132.
148. *Supra* n. 96, at pp. 207-27.

[C] FET

There is a close relationship between denial of justice and FET. Often the arguments of denial of justice would be made as a part of the FET argument. These arguments relate to assessment of unfairness or discriminatory by a judicial body.[149]

In the ELSI case, the ICJ held that an arbitrary conduct would be a 'willful disregard of due process of law, which shocks, or at least surprises, a sense of judicial propriety.'[150]

In *Mondev v. USA*, the Tribunal held that it is fine for courts to change view, because 'even if it had done so its decision would have fallen within the limits of common law adjudication. There is nothing here to shock or surprise even a delicate judicial sensibility.'[151] But there cannot be constant reversal of decisions. The constant reversal could create a sense of instability.

Legitimate expectations are an important component of the FET.[152] These legitimate expectations are based on the legal framework that exists when the investor enters the host State. The legal framework that an investor is entitled to is based on legislation, treaties and assurances contained in decrees, licences, executive statements, contractual undertakings made explicitly or implicitly.[153] Reversal of assurances would result into violation of FET.[154] There can be no assurance that the judicial decisions would be decided in a particular way. An investor could allege that the FET is violated if a particular regulatory framework promised and instituted by the executive or legislature was reversed by the judiciary. Procedural propriety and due process are a part of FET.[155]

In *White Industries v. Australia*, the foreign investor alleged that the timely enforcement of a commercial arbitration award is a legitimate expectation and by failing to enforce the commercial arbitration award in a timely manner, it amounts to breach of the FET. The Tribunal rejected the argument of the claimant on the following grounds:

> Quite apart from the point that an investor must generally take a host State (including its court system) as it finds it, on these facts, and absent an express assurance from India that any award would be enforced in a particular manner or timeframe, it is simply not possible for White, legitimately, to have had the expectation as to the timely enforcement of the Award that it now asserts.[156]

---

149. *Ibid.*, at p. 6.
150. *Supra* n. 106, at para. 128 (1989).
151. *Mondev v. USA*, Award, ICSID Case No. ARB(AF)/99/2, 133 (11 Oct. 2002).
152. Discussed above in FET Chapter.
153. Rudolf Dolzer and Christoph Schreuer, *Principles of International Investment Law*, § 145 (2nd ed., Oxford University Press 2012).
154. *See* generally W. Michael Reisman and Mahnoush Arsanjani, *The Question of Unilateral Governmental Statements as Applicable Law in Investment Disputes*, 19 (2) ICSID Review – FILJ 328, 2004.
155. *Supra* n. 153, at pp. 154-6.
156. *Supra* n. 111, at para. 10.3.15.

The investor also alleged that there was lack of transparency in proceedings before the Indian courts. The Tribunal rejected this argument as well due to lack of evidence to that effect.[157] Therefore, lack of transparency could be raised as an argument, but the investor would have to present convincing evidence. In the absence of such evidence, lack of transparency and consequential breach of FET would not be found.

If a claimant foreign investor alleges that the judiciary is acting at the behest of the executive or has failed to follow due process, then the foreign investor has to establish this. If there is no enough evidence then it cannot be said that the judiciary has breached the fair and equitable standard.[158] If the foreign investor has availed of the appellate procedure and the appellate courts have given a fair hearing and revised some of the decisions of the lower court then it would not be established that the judiciary has not acted in conformity with the FET.[159]

[D] Expropriation

The treatment standard of expropriation comprises of direct, expropriation, indirect expropriation and measures tantamount to or equivalent to expropriation.[160] Direct expropriation involves an action of direct taking of property, which would take place through a legislative or executive action. Judiciary would never take property directly. It may only contribute to the extent that the order of taking given by the executive or legislature may be upheld by the judiciary. In *Rumeli Telekom v. Kazakhstan*, the Tribunal expressed the view that since judicial decisions are rendered for administration of justice and execution of law of the host State, they satisfy the requirement of 'public purpose' for direct expropriation.[161] This oversimplification ignores that in direct expropriation there is a clear objective of taking the property. The consequence of a judicial decision may be loss of property but to suggest that by delivering a decision the courts are taking private property is stretching the concept of expropriation too far and beyond the original purpose of expropriation clauses.

Indirect expropriation claim against actions of judiciary is complex. There are two principal streams of interpretation of indirect expropriation: the nature of the measure and the sole effects doctrine.[162] If the sole effects doctrine is adopted then the impact of the measure would be the sole criteria for holding the host State responsible and the impact on the property shall amount to neutralization of the assets. If a judicial decision has to result into invocation of the sole effects doctrine then the effect of the judicial decision would be such that the foreign investment completely loses its value due to the judicial decision. In all judicial decisions the losing party is always impacted

---

157. *Ibid.*, at para. 10.3.20.
158. *Rumeli Telekom A.S. and Telsim Mobil Telekomunikasyon Hizmetleri A.S. v. Republic of Kazakhstan*, Award, ICSID Case No. ARB/05/16, 619 (29 Jul. 2008).
159. *Ibid.*
160. The contents of expropriation clauses and their interpretation has already been discussed above in Chapter 5.
161. *Supra* n. 158, at paras 705-8.
162. Both the concepts have been discussed above in Chapter 5.

– thus each judicial decision where an investor loses would be indirect expropriation for the losing party – without any further need of establishing malafides on the part of judiciary. Although judicial expropriation is an impractical concept, it has found favour with some tribunals.[163] And there is a possibility that the actions of Indian judiciary could be scrutinized under judicial expropriation. In *Saipem v. Bangladesh*, the tribunal found that the failure of Bangladesh to enforce a commercial arbitration award amounted to indirect expropriation: a measure having similar effects as expropriation.[164] If the basis for deciding indirect expropriation is the nature of the measure then the nature of the judicial decision would have to be analysed. This analysis will inevitably involve the elements of denial of justice such as failure to follow due process and manifest injustice.

One of the kinds of expropriation is creeping expropriation, where a State undertakes a range of measures, which individually may not amount to creeping expropriation but would do so if seen together. The action of the judiciary may be one of the actions in this chain of events and may not be individually expropriatory, but it would be so if it is a part of that chain.[165]

§7.04 CONCLUSIONS

Although the host State is responsible for the actions of the judiciary, it is not that all actions of the judiciary causing loss to the foreign investor amount to breach of an IIA. It must be established that the actions of the judiciary have resulted into breach of treaty provisions or denial of justice.

There are deeper philosophical and sensitive issues that coalesce the practice of an international tribunal reviewing actions of domestic courts, including the highest Court of Appeal or a constitutional court of the State. The domestic courts are conscious of the political, social and economic realities and almost inevitable factor in those considerations while taking decisions – especially those that relate to or affect public policy and public interest. An international tribunal is aloof and unaware of these realities. The members of the tribunal often are not exposed to the sensitivities or practicalities of the State where the decisions are taken by court and how the courts try to strike a balance and achieve justice. Despite these theoretical arguments and their merits, States have agreed to subject the judicial decisions of their courts to be reviewed by an international tribunal. They cannot complain now. This is a necessary evil, and States have to face it. An international tribunal has to be careful and sensitive about this fact. This does not mean that it should be deferential towards the decision of national court. But, be careful in ensuring that they operate within the limitations of the rules of denial of justice and look only at whether there were procedural problems – not touch the merits or not try to indirectly touch merits by usurping appellate functions.

---

163. *Supra* n. 99, at paras 128,129; *Sistem Muhendislik Sanayi Ve Ticaret A.S. v. Kyrgyz Republic*, Award, ICSID Case No. ARB(AF)/06/1, 118-9, 121 (30 Sept. 2009).
164. *Supra* n. 99, at para. 129.
165. *Supra* n. 158, at para. 708.

It is argued that an international tribunal should be review actions of domestic courts to uphold the rule of law. It is fine as long as an international tribunal is operating within the sphere of its authorization. Once it expands its jurisdiction and tries to get into other issues, it becomes problematic.

The sensitive thing for the Indian judiciary is that it would not be the last word on the rights of foreign investors. On all other issues, the Supreme Court of India has the final word as per the Constitution of India under Article 141. A conflict is created between obligations of India under international law and the constitutional provisions. This issue has not arisen in Indian courts yet, but it has arisen in other countries such as Ecuador[166] and Bolivia.[167] In these conflicting situations, international obligation will supersede the constitutional obligations. Through the Model BIT of 2015, India has managed to reduce the scope of denial of justice in customary international law. A State will continue to remain responsible for the actions of its judiciary unless otherwise provided in the treaty.[168]

---

166. Refer to Art. 422, Ecuadorean Constitution 2008, which reads as follows: 'Treaties or international instruments where the Ecuadorian State yields its sovereign jurisdiction to international arbitration entities in disputes involving contracts or trade between the State and natural persons or legal entities cannot be entered into'; R. Jijón-Letort & J.M. Marchán- Pérez Bustamante & Ponce, *National and International Arbitration in Ecuador*, 43 (The Arbitration Review of the Americas, Global Arbitration Review 2012); UNCTAD, *Denunciation of the ICSID Convention and BITs: Impact on Investor-State Claims*, IIA Issues Note No. 2, 1 (December 2010); *World Investment Report 2010: Investing in a Low-Carbon Economy*, 85-6 (UN 2010).
167. Articles 320, 366, Bolivia Constitution 2009; Catharine Titi, *Investment Arbitration in Latin America The Uncertain Veracity of Preconceived Idea*, 30(2) Arbitration International: The Journal of the London Court of International Arbitration 368 (2014).
168. *See, Model Text for the Indian Bilateral Investment Treaty*, Art. 14.2(ii)(b) (2015) https://www.mygov.in/sites/default/files/master_image/Model%20Text%20for%20the%20Indian%20Bilateral%20Investment%20Treaty.pdf (accessed 10 Jul. 2017): 'In addition to other limits on its jurisdiction, a tribunal constituted under this article shall not have the jurisdiction to review the merits of a decision made by a judicial authority of the Host State.' This provision reduces ISDS claims against India in respect of judicial actions, thereby excluding the judiciary from the purview of international responsibility under the BIT.

CHAPTER 8
India and ICSID

International Center for Settlement of Investment Disputes (ICSID) is an important institution in the field of international investment law. It is the first and only dispute resolution facility dedicated exclusively for resolution of investment disputes.[1] It was created by a multilateral treaty, the International Convention on Settlement of Investment Disputes between States and Nationals of Other States (ICSID Convention),[2] and it administers the process of settlement of disputes between foreign investors and host States. About 161 States have signed the ICSID Convention and 153 States have deposited their instruments of ratification till date.[3]

India has an important share in the flow of foreign investment and has recently faced many investment claims. Yet, India is not a party to the ICSID Convention. It would be important to explore the relationship between ICSID and India. Therefore, this chapter would discuss the background and reasons for the creation of ICSID, the structure and working of ICSID, reasons for India not joining ICSID and finally the pros and cons of joining ICSID.

§8.01 REASONS, BACKGROUND AND NEGOTIATING HISTORY OF ICSID

The Executive Directors of the International Bank for Reconstruction and Development (IBRD) formulated the ICSID Convention, famously known as the 'World Bank'. The Executive Directors submitted the ICSID Convention with accompanying Report to the

---

1. ICSID Annual Report, Report No. 81806, p. 5 (2013), http://documents.worldbank.org/curated/en/608571468336018162/pdf/818060WBAR0ENG00Box379835B00PUBLIC0.pdf (accessed 19 Jul. 2017).
2. ICSID Convention Regulations and Rules, 7, Art. 1(1) (2006), International Centre for Settlement of Investment Disputes, https://icsid.worldbank.org/en/Documents/resources/2006%20CRR_English-final.pdf (accessed 19 Jul. 2017).
3. ICSID, List of Contracting States and Other Signatories of the Convention as of 12 Apr. 2016 https://icsid.worldbank.org/apps/ICSIDWEB/icsiddocs/Documents/List%20of%20Contracting%20States%20and%20Other%20Signatories%20of%20the%20Convention%20-%20Latest.pdf (accessed 1 Jul. 2017).

Member States of the World Bank for signature and ratification on 18 March 1965. The Convention entered into force on 14 October 1966, when it was ratified by twenty countries.[4] ICSID is a member of the World Bank Group with close links to it, yet it is an autonomous international organization.[5] The Executive Directors were strongly of the view that there should be a close link between the Bank and the Center, and this thinking was reflected in drafts that were negotiated and finally accepted.[6]

[A] Reasons and Background

The reason for involvement of the World Bank with issues relating to foreign investment is its background in the field of growth and development. As the name of the Bank suggests, the Bank was originally created with the objective of 'reconstruction' and 'development' after the devastation caused by the Second World War. The initial objective was to give credit to help rebuild European countries devastated by the War. Once the post-war reconstruction and development priorities were taken care of, the Bank diversified its activities. It extended credit to countries from other regions such as Latin America, Africa and Asia. In the 1950s and 1960s, the focus was on funding for large infrastructure projects, such as dams, electrical grids, irrigation systems, and roads. Soon the Bank aimed at social development by providing credit for education, communications, cultural heritage, and good governance.[7]

The need for a convention for protection of foreign investment was evident from the fact that a large number of countries had become independent and joined the World Bank. From 1957 to 1962, thirty newly independent States joined the UN and by early 1960s they joined the IBRD, thereby taking the number of developing countries in IBRD to almost 50%.[8] It was realized that development is an important component for ensuring international peace and security.[9] Developed countries of the West undertook different aids and programmes and different institutions came into being. The European Development Bank established a facility for the developing countries in 1958, called the European Investment Fund.[10] Inter-American Development Bank was created in the next year. In 1956, the World Bank established a private financing facility through the IFC.[11] The rising participation of developing countries meant that greater capital would have to be provided for development in these newly independent countries. By joining institutions such as the World Bank, the expectation was that the developing States would get access to capital from it.

---

4. ICSID Convention Regulations and Rules, *supra* n. 2, at p. 5.
5. World Bank, *A Guide to the World Bank* 27-9 (3rd ed., The World Bank, Washington DC 2011).
6. Antonio Parra, *The History of ICSID*, 41 (Oxford University Press 2012).
7. The World Bank, *History* http://www.worldbank.org/en/about/archives/history (accessed 1 Jul. 2017).
8. Parra, *supra* n. 6, at 12.
9. Preamble of UN Charter, declaration of Sixth Committee, other articles on the right to development.
10. D. Kapoor and others, *The World Bank: Its First Half Century*, 152 (Brookings Institution Press 1997).
11. Parra, *supra* n. 8.

Chapter 8: India and ICSID §8.01[A]

Capital plays an important role in spurring growth. Availability of capital has been a challenge in the developing world. Capital could be facilitated for States in the form of credit, investment or aids. The contribution of aid to Governments in spurring economic growth has been doubted.[12] The World Bank provides institutional credit i.e., a loan for certain activities on definite terms. In addition to the terms and conditions of lending, the lending by the World Bank has its own limitations. It is project specific and targeted. Investments made by the Bank were limited to lending for capital infrastructure projects.[13] There was a need for movement of capital into various sectors especially private sector to generate jobs and growth. The Bank could invest in limited areas. The investments that go in infrastructure are capable of generating employment only in the public sector. No direct contribution is made to the private sector, which is a crucial contributor towards employment generation and growth in the economy.

The flow of private capital plays an important role in the overall growth and development of national economies. Additionally, there are limitations to the amount of investment that can flow into an economy through institutional debts. The limitation of the public sector funds was their availability. The private sector could provide funds and also technical skills, management, know-how and necessary marketing.[14] Private capital is available in larger quantity and can freely move into different sectors of the economy. With proper channelization, the flow of private funds could be attuned to the developmental objectives of the State receiving capital. The ICSID Convention is conscious of the role of private capital. Therefore, the ICSID Convention has highlighted the importance of private capital in its preamble in the following words:

> Considering the need for international cooperation for economic development, and the role of private international investment therein.

The primary aim of the ICSID Convention is to promote economic development, and the movement of private capital is seen as an important contributor in that direction.[15] The Report of the Executive Directors acknowledges this.[16] In addition to the text of the Convention, the Report of the Executive Directors is an influential document for interpretation of the Convention. It is a part of the Convention and has been relied upon by the investment tribunals.[17]

---

12. Raghuram Rajan and Arvind Subramanian, *Aid and Growth: What Does the Cross-Country Evidence Really Show?*, NBER Working Paper No. 11513 (August 2005, rev. February 2007) http://www.nber.org/papers/w11513.pdf (accessed 1 Jul. 2017).
13. Parra, *supra* n. 6, at 28.
14. Andreas Lowenfeld, *The ICSID Convention: Origins and Transformation*, 38 Georgia Journal of International and Comparative Law 47, 49 (2009).
15. Christoph Schreuer, et al., *ICSID Convention: A Commentary*, 4 (2nd ed., Cambridge University Press 2009).
16. ICSID, *Report of the Executive Directors on the ICSID Convention*, paras 9, 12 https://icsid.worldbank.org/en/Pages/icsiddocs/REPORT-OF-THE-EXECUTIVE-DIRECTORS-ON-THE-ICSID-CONVENTION.aspx (accessed 19 Jul. 2017).
17. *Tokios Tokelés v. Ukraine*, Decision on Jurisdiction (Dissenting Opinion by Mr Prosper Weil), ICSID Case No. ARB/02/18 (29 Apr. 2004).

Private capital would not be ready to undertake the risk of investing in foreign countries unless they were awarded adequate protection. ICSID was meant to serve this crucial purpose of providing comfort to the foreign investors that their investments would not be affected prejudicially. Various strategies were conceived to persuade private investors to invest in developing countries. Many developed countries such as the US and Germany offered insurance schemes for their investors investing abroad. However, the national insurance support was not very popular, hence a multilateral scheme for insurance was proposed.[18] Also, a code of conduct for the host State was proposed and, after failed efforts at creating a multilateral treaty with wide coverage, ICSID was proposed.[19]

The fear of political risks was one of the vital deterrents for foreign capital to flow in the developing countries. For encouraging flow of private capital, it is necessary that the country intending to receive capital has a stable and attractive environment. The stability has to be legal and political and the attraction has to be economic. Most of the developing countries have an economic dividend because raw material and labour is cheaply available thereby the manufacturing cost is low as compared to advanced economies. Normally, the developing States preferred investments that would generate employment and contribute towards the development of the economy. A foreign investor would establish presence in the host State by incorporating a company, establishing a manufacturing plant, etc. In this process, there is a transfer of technical know-how and imparting of skills to the local populace. If a foreign investor is expected to undertake such a heavy financial cost for establishing presence in an unknown jurisdiction, political and legal stability is necessary. Legal stability to a great extent is associated with the political stability. The political establishment has the freedom to alter and amend the laws. There is a need for some assurance to the foreign investor that their investments would not be expropriated or nationalized or treated prejudicially. Only then will private investment will be comfortable to flow into relatively unknown jurisdictions. Therefore, one of the priorities of the World Bank was to promote flow of private capital into different parts of the world that were in early stages of development. A foreign investor, after making such massive investments, is prone to various political risks. There is a possibility of change of regime, change in laws and other measures which may be used to destroy the investment directly or indirectly. These fears dissuade investors from investing in unknown jurisdictions. The perception of political or non-commercial risks and threat of nationalization and expropriation made private investors reluctant to invest in these developing countries.[20] These risks limit the flow of capital. It was felt that a multilateral framework ought to be in place where by foreign investors are assured that their investments would not be destroyed through use of sovereign power. The investors would be assured of protection in States joining such a multilateral convention. The ICSID Convention did not aim at countering all political risks. It had a specific objective of ensuring that disputes that arise out of such events should be resolved expeditiously.

---

18. Parra, *supra* n. 6, at 13-4.
19. *Ibid.*, at pp. 16-7.
20. *Ibid.*, at p. 13.

The Work Bank perceived that it would help to improve the investment climate by reducing unresolved conflicts, and it would also diffuse standoffs between the host country and the national state of the investor. Therefore, the Bank aimed at creating a forum for voluntary dispute resolution.[21] The existence of unresolved disputes is an obstacle for smooth transfer of resources from developed to less developed countries. The ICSID Convention plays an important role in this regard. The prospect of getting a dispute resolved gives confidence to multinational corporations (MNCs) to invest in developing countries. It also acts as a deterrent for host countries and foreign investors engaging in wrangling or arbitrary behaviour.

The ICSID Convention does not impose any substantive obligations on State Parties. It simply provides a forum to facilitate dispute resolution. Some large investors had managed to negotiate agreements containing arbitration clauses, which would contain detailed rules regarding the appointment of arbitrators, conduct of arbitrations and the rules to be applied to the dispute. However, the host States could deny the validity of such agreements. The solution was seen to lie in creating a treaty which will ensure that arbitration agreements voluntarily entered into would be implemented. Such an international treaty would create an institutional mechanism to settle investment disputes.[22]

This was also the time when various steps were taken by the international community to promote peaceful settlement of disputes, particularly through arbitration and provision for enforcement mechanisms to facilitate and foster international trade. The International Law Commission (ILC) adopted Model Rules on Arbitral Procedure in 1958.[23] The New York Convention on the Recognition and Enforcement of Foreign Awards (NYC) was also adopted by State parties. Although NYC came into being and commercial arbitration was administered through International Chamber of Commerce (ICC), it was felt that there was a need to have a body that would arbitrate commercial disputes but would not be associated with such disputes. Such a body would be readily acceptable to States since this body will have a public nature to dispute resolution.[24] The disputes that the future Center was expected to decide were between individuals and States and to be decided on the basis of principles of public international law.

At around the same time, many institutions were suggesting that such services may be offered where the disputes would be between a State and a foreign investor.[25] The Report of the Secretary-General strongly recommended the creation of an independent body where private investment related disputes could be decided.

The World Bank ventured into the project of dispute resolution because the Articles of Agreement of the Bank gave it the power to promote private foreign capital

---

21. Chittaranjan Amerasinghe, *The International Centre for Settlement of Investment Disputes and Development through the Multinational Corporations*, 9 Vanderbilt Journal of Transnational Law 793, 795 (1976).
22. *Ibid.*
23. International Law Commission, II Yearbook of International Law Commission 82 (1958).
24. United Nations Economic and Social Council, *The Promotion of the International Low of Private Capital: Progress Report by Secretary General*, E/3325, 8, 80-1 (26 Feb. 1960).
25. Permanent Court of Arbitration started offering such services. International Law Association and International Bar Association also offered similar proposals. Parra, *supra* n. 6, at 18-9.

in member countries.²⁶ The Bank also relied on markets for raising capital and was aware that if investment disputes do not get resolved quickly then the credibility of the Bank would come in question. There would be problems in ensuring credit flow in countries and problems for the Bank in raising capital for itself. Therefore, a robust mechanism for resolution of investment disputes was felt necessary.²⁷ The Bank was interested in resolving disputes quickly and was seen as a well-qualified expert to resolve such disputes. The Bank had offered its services in past for resolution of disputes through good offices, mediation or conciliation.²⁸

While providing arbitration services, the Bank did not intend to be an active party in dispute resolution. None of the persons associated with the Bank took up the responsibility of sitting as arbitrator in disputes in the past and only provided good offices, mediation or conciliation services.²⁹ Even today, it provides services but does not resolve the disputes. It never took up the role of an adjudicator and giving binding awards. Presently, the Bank provides arbitration as well as conciliation services. Its expertise in the latter field is longstanding.³⁰

At the time when the ICSID Convention came into force, the developed States had entered into Friendship Commerce and Navigation (FCN) Treaties, and there were long-term contracts between foreign investors and host States for exploration of oil and other natural resources. Bilateral investment treaties (BITs) were not in vogue at that time. Germany had entered into the first BIT. The discussions for the preparation of the ICSID Convention reflect that the objective of the Convention was to include disputes arising from BITs as well.³¹ The Convention does not stipulate any substantive provisions for investor protection. It merely provides an institutional framework for dispute resolution. The few substantive requirements that get imposed on parties to the dispute are an outcome of jurisdictional and procedural requirements of the ICSID Convention.

Expeditious disposal of disputes with the state of destination of investment was to provide a sense of confidence for investors. Also, the fact of joining an international framework operated as a limitation on the States from mistreating foreign investors. Yet the highly distinguishable factor of the ICSID Convention was an effort to remove foreign investment disputes from the shackles of diplomatic protection. One of the principal aims of the Convention was to enable a private party to bring a claim against a foreign State before an international arbitral tribunal, rather than seeking diplomatic protection or the home State bringing an international claim. Under customary international law, the primary responsibility of protection of foreign investors abroad is of the home State. The home State would grant diplomatic protection to its investors investing abroad.³² However, home States are under no obligation to extend that

---

26. *Ibid.*, at p. 22.
27. *Ibid.*, at pp. 22-3.
28. *Ibid.*, at pp. 23.
29. *Ibid.*, at p. 25.
30. *Ibid.*, at p. 26.
31. *Ibid.*, at pp. 42-3.
32. *The Ambatielos Claim (Greece, United Kingdom of Great Britain and Northern Ireland)*, Vol. XII, Reports of International Arbitral Awards, 83-153 (6 Mar. 1956).

protection to foreign investors.³³ There have been instances where this protection has been denied. There could be various reasons for not granting protection. For example, the relations between the host State and the home State may be friendly or there may not be any diplomatic relations between the States. In such a situation, the protection of private foreign investor is at the mercy of the discretion of the host State. A Convention would ensure that the foreign investor is not dependent on the home State to espouse the claim. The aim of ICSID was to create an institution where the disputes between the foreign investor and the host State could be submitted without the need of intervention by the home State.³⁴

The home State may have strong diplomatic ties with the Host State or may not be in a politically strong position to take the step of estranging the relations.³⁵ It was felt necessary to depoliticize the process. One of the objectives of ICSID was to get over the political process of diplomatic protection by removing it and introducing a prospective State consent.³⁶ ICSID Convention states that:

> No Contracting State shall give diplomatic protection, or bring an international claim, in respect of a dispute which one of its nationals and another Contracting State shall have consented to submit or shall have submitted to arbitration under this Convention, unless such other Contracting State shall have failed to abide by and comply with the award rendered in such dispute.³⁷

The ICSID Convention has not only removed the requirement of diplomatic protection but also made a negative stipulation that it cannot be granted. This would ensure that once arbitration is initiated under ICSID, the home State cannot defeat the arbitration by invoking diplomatic protection and insist that the dispute shall be taken to another forum. Therefore, the right to diplomatic protection of the home State was waived. However, the right to diplomatic protection of the home State could revive in case the host State violated the obligations under the Convention.³⁸

[B] Negotiating History

The negotiating process for the drafting and adoption of the ICSID Convention was unique. The circumstances and the environment in which the ICSID Convention was negotiated dictated its peculiarity.

The Directors of the Bank that were representing Latin American countries opposed the idea of creation of a Convention. They were insisting that the Center may be established administratively or through a simple resolution of the Board of Governors or of the Executive Directors of the Bank. Aron Broches, the General Counsel of the Bank and the brain behind the Convention, insisted that there should be a binding

---

33. Hersch Lauterpacht, *Oppenheim's International Law*, 686 (Longmans, Green & Company 1955).
34. Parra, *supra* n. 6, at 17-8.
35. Lauterpacht, *supra* n. 33, at 686-7.
36. Jan Paulsson, *Arbitration Without Privity*, 10 ICSID Review 232 (1995).
37. ICSID Convention Regulations and Rules, *supra* n. 2, at Art. 27(1).
38. Parra, *supra* n. 6, at 36.

treaty rather than a simple administrative order. It would provide certain rules and not allow the arbitral process to be frustrated.[39]

In February 1963, Broches made a proposal to a Committee of 'the Whole' comprising of all the Executive Directors organized as an ad hoc committee without reference to their respective voting power. There were three elements of that proposal. First, the Draft OECD Convention on the Protection of Property, which was never adopted. Second, was a proposal for insurance, which was the basis of the Multilateral Investment Guarantee Agreement (MIGA) – but only in the 1980s. Third, was the role of the Bank for setting out the rules for conduct of arbitration or conciliation.[40] The essence of the third element was that if the parties agreed to avail the services of the Center for arbitration, then the government would not be permitted to refer the dispute with the private party to the government's national courts, and the private party would not be permitted to seek the protection of its own government. The Convention would provide that the awards so passed by the Center would be enforceable in all the countries that are ready to become parties.[41]

The States were not involved in the drafting process. The staff members of the Bank prepared working papers and drafts for consideration of the Executive Directors. The Executive Directors authorized the President to convene regional meetings of experts in 1963. They were meant for consultation only, and the reactions received were to become guide for the Executive Directors to decide the further course. Thereafter, member countries were invited to send representatives for a meeting with the Legal Committee to assist the Executive Directors further. After deliberations, the text was finalized which was sent to member countries for consideration with a view of signature and ratification, acceptance or approval.[42]

The consultations did not take place with all the States together. Rather they were undertaken in regional groups. The report was thereafter submitted to the Executive Directors.[43] After receiving comments from the regional committees, the draft was presented to the Directors who decided to constitute a group of experts to be nominated by the Governments. This group was expected to present frank exchange of views between capital-exporting and capital-importing States.[44] These experts were acting

---

39. *Ibid.*, at 39.
40. Lowenfeld, *supra* n. 14, at 47, 48.
41. International Center for Settlement of Investment Disputes, *Convention on the Settlement of Investment Disputes Between States and Nationals of Other States: Documents Concerning the Origin and the Formulation of the Convention*, 2, 80 (1968).
42. *See* Executive Directors Resolution No. 65-14 (18 Mar. 1965), Parra, *supra* n. 6, at 94; ICSID, *Report of the Executive Directors on the ICSID Convention*, *supra* n. 16.
43. 'Regional Consultative Meetings of Legal Experts on Settlement of Investment Dispute, Chairman's Report on Issues raised and Suggestions made with respect to the Preliminary Draft of a Convention on the Settlement of Investment Disputes Between States and Nationals of Other States' found at ICSID, *History of the ICSID Convention: Documents concerning the Origin and the Formulation of the Convention*, Vol. II-1, 557 (2009) https://icsid.worldbank.org/en/Documents/resources/History%20of%20ICSID%20Convention%20-%20VOLUME%20II-1.pdf (accessed 19 Jul. 2017); Parra, *supra* n. 6, at 65.
44. Settlement of Investment Disputes Consultative Meeting of Legal Experts, Summary record of Proceedings, 458-89 (20 Jul. 1964) https://icsid.worldbank.org/en/Documents/resources/History%20of%20ICSID%20Convention%20-%20VOLUME%20II-1.pdf (accessed 19 Jul. 2017).

under instructions of the member countries unlike the experts in the regional groups.[45] The procedure was convenient and fast. It reduced the possibility of developing countries getting together and putting up a coordinated objection.

The central responsibility of drafting was with the Executive Directors, which is a small group of persons, therefore not completely representative in nature of the membership. This shortcoming was sought to be cured through discussions in regional groups and the proceedings of the Legal Committee which were to provide technical expertise and advice.[46] Additionally, the Work Bank followed weighted voting system. The voting rights of Directors were disparate and concentrated within the industrialized countries. To cure this problem, the weightage voting formula was replaced with consensus. The voting system was used only for dealing with Bank operations or Bank policy and not for semi-extracurricular activities such as an international agreement.[47]

The ICSID Convention deliberately omitted any reference to substantive obligations between the host State and the foreign investor. The Convention was meant to be an arbitration convention rather than a convention concerning with international law on foreign investment.[48] According to Lowenfeld, a diplomatic conference was not convened in order to avoid the controversy around drafting substantive provisions in a convention. Instead four regional meeting were convened – 'Consultative Meetings of Legal Experts' – and involved technical experts deliberating on a draft prepared in advance.[49] The Convention did not lay down standards for treatment of property of aliens by States or with the merits of investment disputes.[50]

The Executive Directors took final action on the Convention on 18 March 1965, and the Convention entered into force on 14 October 1966 after receiving necessary ratifications.[51]

§8.02 THE STRUCTURE AND WORKING OF ICSID

On the administrative side, the Center consists of Administrative Council and the Secretariat. The Administrative Council consists of one representative of each Contracting State.[52] It possesses the power to adopt administrative and financial regulations, rules of procedure for institution, conduct of arbitration and conciliation proceedings, and other administrative functions in relation to terms of service and budget.[53] It does not perform any direct role in the dispute resolution process. The Secretariat is the custodian of the arbitration process. The Secretariat consists of

---

45. Parra, *supra* n. 6, at 67.
46. Amerasinghe, *supra* n. 21, at 797.
47. *Ibid.*
48. Lowenfeld, *supra* n. 14, at 47, 51.
49. *Ibid.*, at 47, 52.
50. *Ibid.*, at 47, 53.
51. Amerasinghe, *supra* n. 21, at 798.
52. ICSID Convention Regulations and Rules, *supra* n. 2, at Art. 4.1.
53. *Ibid.*, at Art. 6.

Secretary-General, one or more Deputy Secretaries-General and staff.[54] The Secretary-General 'shall perform the function of registrar and shall have the power to authenticate arbitral awards rendered pursuant to…(the) Convention, and to certify copies thereof.'[55] ICSID provides an independent facility of arbitration and conciliation. For this purpose, the Secretariat is responsible for maintaining a Panel of Arbitrators and a Panel of Conciliators.[56] The Panel of Arbitrators and the Panel of Conciliators consist of 'qualified persons'[57] with 'high moral character and recognized competence in the fields of law, commerce, industry or finance, who may be relied upon to exercise independent judgment. Competence in the field of law shall be of particular importance in the case of persons on the Panel of Arbitrators.'[58] The parties are not restricted to the Panels for appointing a conciliator or arbitrator.[59] This enables them to appoint persons of their choice who enjoy their special confidence.[60] Conversely, an arbitrator need not belong to the Panel in order to be appointed for a dispute conducted by ICSID. However, the Chairman, in making such appointments, is restricted to the Panels.[61] The same restriction applies when a party appointed conciliator or arbitrator resigns without consent of the tribunal and the Chairman appoints a replacement[62] and when making appointments to an ad hoc committee for annulment proceedings.[63] The ICSID would appoint arbitrators if one of the parties fails to appoint an arbitrator within stipulated time. Also, all members of the ad hoc Annulment Committee are appointed by the ICSID.

The Center performs the function of administering the ICSID Convention. It possesses full international legal personality. The phrase '"international" legal personality' connotes the distinction between the Center's capacity to act on the international level and capacity to act on the municipal level.[64] Some of the other recently constituted international organizations have also been *expressis ver bis* acknowledged to have an 'international' legal personality. For example, African Development Bank,[65] International Fund for Agriculture Development (IFAD),[66] International Seabed Authority (ISA)[67] and International Criminal Court (ICC).[68]

---

54. *Ibid.*, at Art. 9.
55. *Ibid.*, at Art. 11.
56. *Ibid.*, at Art. 3.
57. *Ibid.*, at Art. 12.
58. *Ibid.*, at Art. 14(1).
59. *Ibid.*, at Arts 31(1) and 40(1).
60. Schreuer, *supra* n. 15, at 509.
61. ICSID Convention Regulations and Rules, *supra* n. 59.
62. *Ibid.*, at p. 99, at Art. 56(3).
63. *Ibid.*, at Art. 52(3).
64. ICSID, *History of the ICSID Convention: Documents concerning the Origin and the Formulation of the Convention*, *supra* n. 43, at 737.
65. Agreement establishing the African Development Bank, Art. 50 (4 Aug. 1963) T.S, Vol. 510, p. 3, and Vol. 569, p. 353 (corrigendum to Vol. 510).
66. Agreement establishing the International Fund for Agricultural Development, Art. 10 (13 Jun. 1976) https://treaties.un.org/pages/ViewDetails.aspx?src=TREATY&mtdsg_no=X-8&chapter=10&clang=_en (accessed 19 Jun. 2017).
67. UN General Assembly, Convention on the Law of the Sea, Art. 176 (10 Dec. 1982) http://www.refworld.org/docid/3dd8fd1b4.html (accessed 19 Jul. 2017).

It has the capacity to contract, acquire movable and immovable property, and institute legal proceedings.[69] The property and assets of the Center enjoy immunity from all legal processes except where the Center has waived the immunity.[70] In May 2013, Jack Grynberg of RSM Production Corporation sued the Center in a district court in Columbia, USA over alleged lack of accountability but later withdrew the complaint.[71] The Center enjoys immunities and privileges in the territory of the Contracting States for performing its functions under the Convention.[72] The archives of the Center are inviolable. With regard to the official communications, the Contracting States shall accord no less treatment to the Center than is what is accorded to other international organizations.[73] The arbitrators, conciliators and some of the administrative staff enjoy immunity with respect to acts performed by them in the exercise of their functions, except when the Center waives the immunity.[74] This protection is important so that the arbitrators can adjudicate without the worry of facing legal proceedings in any State for their judicial actions. It is but natural that this protection would be extended to parties, agents, counsel, advocates, witnesses or experts appearing in the proceedings conducted by the Center.[75]

The cases are administered under the ICSID Convention, ICSID Additional Facility, arbitration rules of the United Nations Commission on International Trade Law (UNCITRAL Arbitration Rules) and rules of other institutions such as ICC, LCIA, etc. as per the request of the parties.[76]

§8.03 WHY DID INDIA NOT JOIN ICSID?

Direct evidence giving explicit reasons for India not joining the ICSID is not available. But the historic context and the process of creation of ICSID allows some conclusions to be drawn regarding non-participation of India in the ICSID.

As was discussed in Chapter 2, India was a prominent leader of the movement for reclaiming control of vital sectors of economy and natural resources from the former colonial powers in the UN. At the UN, resistance characterized India's attitude towards protection of foreign property. That attitude represents one of the natural reasons for India to not join the ICSID. The decade of the 1950s and 1960 was characterized by the declarations on Permanent Sovereignty over Natural Resources and the New International Economic Order (NIEO) in the UN. This was the time when negotiations for the ICSID Convention were ongoing. This was also the time when OECD Draft Convention

---

68. UN General Assembly, Rome Statute of the International Criminal Court (last amended 2010) Art. 4(1) (17 Jul. 1998) ISBN No. 92-9227-227-6 http://www.refworld.org/docid/3ae6b3a84.html (accessed 19 Jul. 2017).
69. ICSID Convention Regulations and Rules, *supra* n. 2, at Art. 18.
70. *Ibid.*, at Art. 20.
71. Tom Moore, *Grynberg Drops World Bank Lawsuit* (5 Nov. 2013) https://www.cdr-news.com/categories/usa/4557-grynberg-drops-case-against-world-bank (accessed 1 Jul. 2017).
72. ICSID Convention Regulations and Rules, *supra* n. 2, at Art. 19.
73. *Ibid.*, at Art. 23.
74. *Ibid.*, at Art. 21.
75. *Ibid.*, at Art. 22.
76. ICSID Annual Report, *supra* n. 1, at 18.

on Protection of Foreign Property 1967 was issued. Capital-exporting States resisted it since it contained substantive provisions unacceptable to States. It was a challenge to float a multilateral project in this environment.[77] The ICSID Convention succeeded because it was limited only for providing a mechanism for dispute resolution rather than stipulating substantive provisions. When ICSID Convention was being negotiated the substantive provisions were expected to be covered in contracts between foreign investors and host States since at that time BITs were not in vogue.[78]

India adopted socialist pattern of economy. The word 'socialist' was specifically added to the Indian Constitution to reaffirm and strengthen India's commitment to creating an economically egalitarian society through social justice and equality.[79] Although these developments took place after the coming into force of the ICSID Convention the influence of this thinking cannot be discarded.

In the period when the NIEO resolutions were passed, the Asian, African and Latin American States were opposed to any international standards for protection of foreign property. They insisted that the protection has to be granted as per the domestic law of the state of investment and the foreign investors have to approach the domestic courts. By sharing this position with other newly independent and Latin American States India expressed support for primacy of national laws over international law to regulate and protect foreign investment in India.[80] It was obvious for India to not to participate in an institution creating an international forum for investment disputes because India has resisted the idea of invocation of international law for protection of foreign investment. India resisted the idea of State responsibility for injury to aliens and their property at all fora.[81]

Other participants in the resolution on Declaration on Sovereignty over Natural Resources and the NIEO sought to assert national control over natural resources and foreign property but joined ICSID. India did not. These may be collective reasons for India to not join ICSID, but they by themselves are insufficient to represent India's resistance. There possibly could have been some specific objections in relation to ICSID.[82]

After independence, India adopted a mixed economy, where government as well as private sector would equally participate in the economic activity. However, the private sector was heavily controlled. The Constitution of India was amended in 1976

---

77. Stephan Schill, *The Multilateralization of International Investment Law*, 35-7 (Cambridge University Press 2009).
78. The first BIT between Germany and Pakistan was entered into in 1959, yet the BITs had not picked up until then.
79. Section 2(a), Constitution (Forty-Second) Constitution Amendment Act, 1976; M.P. Jain, *Indian Constitutional Law*, 14 (LexisNexis Butterworths Wadhwa 2011).
80. Prabhash Ranjan, *India and Bilateral Investment Treaties – A Changing Landscape*, ICSID Review 1, 50 (2014).
81. Even at the International Law Commission, where State responsibility was being codified, India resisted the idea of State responsibility for injury to aliens. *See* 9th Session of the International Law Commission, Yearbook of the International Law Commission 157-8 (1957).
82. Unfortunately no material is available in public domain that would suggest why India did not join ICSID. However, the author had the opportunity to interview persons associated with the process in the Government of India where the decision of not to join ICSID was taken. The analysis is based on those discussions.

to add the word 'socialist' in the preamble.[83] Although the ICSID Convention was prepared slightly before this time the wave of socialism was already flowing. The decade of the 1960s and thereafter was characterized by nationalization of banks. The Government of India issued an ordinance nationalizing fourteen largest commercial banks in 1969.[84] These banks contained 85% of the total bank deposits.[85] Banks were nationalized because they became an important tool to facilitate development of the economy. The banking sector was also emerging as the largest employer.[86] Nationalization was limited to banks and did not extend to other sectors. Also, the government control of the economy was much tighter. The domestic priorities of the time were against any strict regime for investment protection. The word socialism was added to enable the courts to lean more in favour of nationalization and State ownership of industry.[87] With time, the socialist fervour has waned out, and there was no support for nationalization in the economic philosophy of the Government or people, unlike the time when the ICSID Convention came into existence. Overtime the word socialist has been interpreted by the Supreme Court of India to be the basis for creation of an egalitarian society believing in equitable distribution of wealth rather than concentration of economic activity in the public sector.[88] After the reforms of 1991, the Courts have upheld privatization of the economic activity.[89]

Access to ICSID arbitration for foreign investor is based on consent. The jurisdiction of an ICSID tribunal extends only to those disputes for which the host State has submitted a consent in writing.[90] This consent may be given through a direct agreement for any existing or future disputes or a host State legislation or BITs. It is not necessary that consent of both parties be recorded in a single instrument. A host State can express its offer to arbitrate in domestic investment law or treaty which can later be accepted by an investor in writing.[91] This unilateral consent expressed in a legislation or a treaty is often called 'arbitration without privity'.[92] However once a State party consents to the ICSID Convention then consent to take each dispute to ICSID is not required. Although at the time of the making of the ICSID Convention this was not the understanding of the makers of the ICSID Convention yet it has so evolved.[93] In

---

83. Constitution (Forty-Second) Constitution Amendment Act, 1976, *supra* n. 79.
84. *See* Banking Companies (Acquisition and Transfer of Undertakings) Ordinance, 1969.
85. Granville Austin, *Working a Democratic Constitution – A History of the Indian Experience*, 215 (Oxford University Press 1999).
86. Rimple Saini and S.L. Lodha, *Banking Development in India*, 5 Journal of Economics and Sustainable Development 26-7 (2014).
87. *Excel Wear v. Union of India* 4 SCC 224, 245 (1978); *National Textiles Worker's Union v. PR Ramkrishnan* 1 SCC 228 (1983).
88. M.P. Jain, *MP Jain's Indian Constitutional Law*, Vol. I, 18-20 (6th ed., LexisNexis Butterworths Wadhwa Nagpur 2010).
89. The Supreme Court upheld privatization of telecommunication. *Delhi Science Forum vv Union of India*, 2 SCC 405 (1996).
90. ICSID Convention Regulations and Rules, *supra* n. 2, at Art. 25(1).
91. *See* the ICSID, *Report of the Executive Directors on the ICSID Convention*, *supra* n. 16, at p. 43 at para. 24.
92. Schreuer, *supra* n. 15, at 191; Jan Paulsson, *supra* n. 36, at 10.
93. Lowenfeld, *supra* n. 14, at 47, 55-7.

India, the ICSID Convention was perceived to be the one where separate consent would not be necessary.

India has resisted multilateral rules and arrangements on protection of foreign investment. The only regime that India has agreed to is under Trade Related Investment Measures (TRIMs) Agreement. TRIMs is a part of the set of WTO Agreements which India had to agree with. In any case, the TRIMs Agreement is very narrow in scope and limited to protection of investments that relate to goods. Except for TRIMs, India is not a party to any multilateral agreement on investment (MAI) protection. India objected to the negotiations for the MAIs. India has continued its opposition for further negations at the WTO for a MAI protection.[94] ICSID seeks to create a multilateral treaty providing for dispute resolution. Therefore, India possibly continued to oppose the ICSID.

§8.04 PROS AND CONS OF JOINING ICSID

The ICSID system has some benefits and drawbacks. One of the criticisms of investment arbitration is that the tribunals are ad hoc.[95] They lack any permanent institutional character and therefore are beyond the fetters that control the judicial activity in an institutional framework. ICSID does not provide for a permanent judicial body. Tribunals are created on an ad hoc basis, yet the existence of an institution has an influence of the decision-making of the tribunals. They may not be bound strictly by the rule of precedent or *stare decisis*, yet there is an element of consideration that consistency in judicial determination at least in consonance with the ethos of the ICSID Convention is maintained. Investment tribunals are expected to be careful while applying the ICSID Convention because it is an instrument of international policy for the promotion of economic development.[96] Moreover, ICSID provides an institutional bedrock. A treaty instrument like ICSID is considered to be the best method of protecting investments as it has the much needed support of hegemonic powers and balances the interests of all including the developing States.[97] Additionally, the Secretariat of ICSID presents a report every year to the Administrative Council where each Member State is represented by a representative.[98] Despite the institutional nature and the possibility of institutional control of the performance of arbitral tribunals, the impression of ICSID with the Member States has not been consistent and positive –

---

94. Ministry of Commerce, *India Opposes Multilateral Agreement on Investment*, http://pib.nic.in/archive/releases98/lyr2003/rjul2003/15072003/r150720033.html (accessed 1 Jul. 2017).
95. Gus Van Harten, *Investment Treaty Arbitration and Public Law*, 181-4 (Oxford University Press 2007).
96. Schreuer, *supra* n. 15, at 4-5, 8; UNCTAD, *Scope and Definition: UNCTAD Series on Issues in International Investment Agreements*, II 52 (2011) http://unctad.org/en/Docs/diaeia20102_en.pdf (accessed 14 Aug. 2013).
97. M. Sornarajah, *The Settlement of Foreign Investment Disputes*, 164-6 (Kluwer Law International 2000).
98. ICSID Convention Regulations and Rules, *supra* n. 2, at Art. 4(1), p. 51 at Art. 5(4).

especially with the Latin American states. Bolivia,[99] Ecuador,[100] and Venezuela[101] have all withdrawn from the Convention. Argentina has threatened to leave ICSID.[102] Mexico and Brazil are not parties to ICSID because it is not aligned with their interests.[103] An important reason for the discontent of these States is that the ICSID system is heavily inclined towards protection of interests of foreign investors and the tribunals constituted under ICSID have issued inconsistent awards.[104] This impression about the ICSID is a major obstacle for States like India from joining ICSID.

The criticisms of pro-investor bias[105] and inconsistent decision-making by investment tribunals are the general criticism of the regime of investment treaty arbitration (ITA).[106] This criticism impacts the general outlook towards the ITA per se. However, this criticism cannot be levelled exclusively against the ICSID system as such. There is nothing unique in ICSID or the Convention that would aggravate the problem of pro-investor bias and inconsistent decision-making. On the contrary, the ICSID Convention offers some benefits that favour States as compared to ad hoc arbitrations. As opposed to ICSID arbitrations, ad hoc arbitrations do not enjoy any institutional support and a strong enforcement mechanism. While awards under the ICSID convention are facilitated by the ICSID's enforcement mechanism, ad hoc arbitrations rely on the NYC on the Recognition and Enforcement of Foreign Arbitral Award for their enforcement. Another prominent feature of ICSID Convention is the assistance offered by the Centre's Secretariat to the tribunals and disputing parties. The Secretariat facilitates the arbitral process by maintaining a panel of arbitrations, screening arbitration requests and assisting in the constitution of arbitral tribunals and the conduct of proceedings. Such functions are typically carried out by the disputing parties themselves in ad hoc arbitrations.

---

99. Bolivia submitted its denunciation under Art. 71 of the ICSID Convention on 2 May 2007, taking effect on 3 Nov. 2007: Press Release, Int'l Ctr. for Settlement of Inv. Disputes [ICSID], *Bolivia Submits a Notice Under Article 71 of the ICSID Convention* (16 May 2007) http://icsidfiles.worldbank.org/icsid/ICSID/StaticFiles/Announcement3.html (accessed 1 Jul. 20 17).
100. Ecuador officially denounced the ICSID Convention under Art. 71, having effect on 7 Jan. 2010: Press Release, ICSID, *Ecuador Submits a Notice under art 71 of the ICSID Convention* (9 Jul. 2009) https://icsid.worldbank.org/en/Pages/News.aspx?CID = 87 (accessed 1 Jul. 2017).
101. Venezuela submitted its denunciation under Art. 71 of the ICSID Convention on 24 Jan. 2012, taking effect 25 Jul. 2012: Press Release, ICSID, *Venezuela Submits a Notice under Article 71 of the ICSID Convention* (26 Jan. 2012) https://icsid.worldbank.org/en/Pages/News.aspx?CID = 47 (accessed 1 Jul. 2017).
102. Argentina has yet to submit notice of withdrawal under Art. 71 of the ICSID Convention but has announced its intent to do so: *Argentina in the Process of Quitting from World Bank Investment Disputes Centre*, MERCOPRESS (31 Jan. 2013) http://en.mercopress.com/2013/01/31/argentina-in-the-process-of-quitting-from-world-bank-investment-disputes-centre (accessed 1 Jul. 2017).
103. Oscar Lopez, *Smart Move: Argentina to Leave the ICSID*, 1 Cornell International Law Journal. Online 121, 125 (2013) http://cornellilj.org/wp-content/uploads/2014/01/Lopez-Smart-Move-Argentina-to-Leave-the-ICSID-final.pdf (accessed 1 Jul. 2017).
104. *Ibid.*, at 121, 123-4.
105. Van Harten, *supra* n. 95, at 168-9, 173-4.
106. *See* Suzan Franck, The Legitimacy Crisis in Investment Treaty Arbitration: Privatizing Public International Law Through Inconsistent Decisions, 73 Fordham Law Review 1521 (2005).

Jurisdiction of an ICSID tribunal is derived from Article 25 of the ICSID Convention. It states that:

> Article 25(1): The jurisdiction of the Centre shall extend to
>
> between a Contracting State (or any constituent subdivision or agency of a Contracting State designated to the Centre by that State) and a national of another Contracting State, which the parties to the dispute to submit to the Centre. When the parties have given their consent, no party may withdraw its consent unilaterally.

Investment treaties provide a very wide definition of investment, which is normally enlisting of the types of assets that would be treated as investments.[107] In ad hoc arbitrations once it is established that the investment is one of the assets enumerated in the list then the requirement of establishing investment for the purpose of asserting jurisdiction is satisfied. This not the case with arbitral tribunals constituted under the ICSID Convention. Article 25 is important because to access ICSID, in addition to satisfying the jurisdictional requirements of the investment treaty or a contract based on which arbitration is invoked, the foreign investor has to independently satisfy the requirements of Article 25. The word 'investment' has an independent meaning under the ICSID Convention in addition to the meaning under the investment treaty based on which arbitration is invoked. Therefore, there is an additional substantive hurdle to satisfy for a foreign investor, which is that his investments satisfy the requirements of investment under the ICSID Convention as well. Investment tribunals constituted under the ICSID Convention have dutifully followed this procedure and ensured that the dual requirements of establishing the definition of investment are satisfied.[108] This dual test is called the 'double keyhole' approach[109] or the 'double barrel' test.[110]

The definition of investment as per the ICSID Convention introduces an objective element to investment. Otherwise, while defining investment, investment treaties simply set out kinds of assets that could be called investment. An investor is simply required to satisfy these categories without the need to establish any other objective element to prove that the foreign investor has made an investment in the host State. Objective test for establishing the existence of investment is very important. It is crucial because one cannot lose sight of the fact that the foreign investment should ultimately contribute towards the development in the host State economy.[111]

---

107. See Chapter 4 for a detailed discussion on jurisdictional requirements.
108. See 'The Notion of "Investment" in International Investment Arbitration' by Noah Rubins in Norbert Horn, *Arbitrating Foreign Investment Disputes: Procedural and Substantive Legal Aspects*, 289-90 (Kluwer Law International 2004). Some tribunals have not followed this approach. For example see *Lanco v. Argentina*, Decision on Jurisdiction, ICSID Case No. ARB/97/6, 48 (8 Dec. 1998); *MCI v. Ecuador*, Award, ICSID Case No. ARB/03/6, 157-60 (31 Jul. 2007).
109. *Aguas del Tunari v. Bolivia*, Decision on Jurisdiction, ICSID Case No. ARB/02/3, 278 (21 Oct. 2005).
110. *Malaysian Historical Salvors v. Malaysia*, Award, ICSID Case No. ARB/05/10, 55 (17 May 2007).
111. Aniruddha Rajput, *Defining Investment-A Developmental Perspective*, 2(1) Indian Journal of Arbitration Law 13-4 et seq. (2013).

Chapter 8: India and ICSID §8.04

The objective elements of the definition of investment under the ICSID Convention were set out in *Salini v. Morocco*. These are: (a) contribution of the investor; (b) duration; (c) operational risk; (d) contribution in host State's development. These elements constitute the 'Salini test'. Tribunals outside the ICSID Convention have been inconsistent with the application of the 'Salini test'.[112]

Although these tests have been set out, there is a tendency not to get into each of them in detail and see if they are satisfied. Tribunals often make a general statement that the requirements appear to be satisfied, and there is no need to go to each aspect.[113]

Article 25 specifies substantial requirements of jurisdiction[114] which means that these requirements are not merely procedural but are substantial and have to be satisfied before a tribunal can exercise jurisdiction. These requirements relate to the nature of the dispute (definition of investment or *ratione materiae*) and the nature of the parties (definition of investor or *ratione personae*).[115] Consent for access to ICSID is important but that by itself does not suffice for a tribunal to exercise jurisdiction. The Report of the Executive Directors makes this clear as well:

> While consent of the parties is an essential prerequisite for the jurisdiction of the Centre, consent alone will not suffice to bring a dispute within its jurisdiction. In keeping with the purpose of the Convention, the jurisdiction of the Centre is further limited by reference to the nature of the dispute and the parties thereto.[116]

The Tribunal in *CSOB v. Slovakia* stated that the additional constrains under the ICSID Convention have to be satisfied in the following words:

> 68. The Slovak Republic is correct in pointing out, however, that an agreement of the parties describing their transaction as an investment is not, as such, conclusive in resolving the question whether the dispute involves an investment under Article 25(1) of the Convention. The concept of an investment as spelled out in that provision is objective in nature in that the parties may agree on a more precise or restrictive definition of their acceptance of the Centre's jurisdiction, but they may not choose to submit disputes to the Centre that are not related to an investment. A two-fold test must therefore be applied in determining whether this Tribunal has the competence to consider the merits of the claim: whether the dispute arises out of an investment within the meaning of the Convention and, if so, whether the

---

112. Salini test has been applied even by non-ICSID arbitral tribunals such as *Romak S.A. (Switzerland) v. The Republic of Uzbekistan*, UNCITRAL, PCA Case No. AA280, 198-208 (26 Nov. 2009). However in *White and Industries v. India*, the tribunal declined to extend the Salini test to non-ICSID arbitrations, paras 7.4.8-7.4.9. For other awards, *see* Aniruddha Rajput, *Defining Investment-A Development Perspective*, *supra* n. 111.
113. *El Paso Energy International Company v. The Argentine Republic*, Award, ICSID Case No. ARB/03/15, 201-2 (31 Oct. 2011); *AES Summit Generation Limited and AES-Tisza Erömü Kft v. The Republic of Hungary*, Award, ICSID Case No. ARB/07/22, 6.4.1-6.4.2 (23 Sept. 2010).
114. Schreuer, *supra* n. 15, at 82.
115. *Ibid.*
116. ICSID Convention Regulations and Rules, *supra* n. 2, at p. 35 at para. 27.

dispute relates to an investment as defined in the Parties' consent to ICSID arbitration, in their reference to the BIT and the pertinent definitions contained in Article 1 of the BIT.[117]

The impact of the 'Salini test' is that India has incorporated it in the recently released Model BIT.[118]

The ICSID Convention provides a distinct advantage of an objective definition of investment as compared to ad hoc arbitration. Since India is suggesting that it would want to negotiate investment treaties based on an objective definition this attraction of ICSID wanes for India. There is no assurance that all tribunals would apply the 'Salini test' even if they are constituted under ICSID. Additionally, even if they apply the 'Salini test' the trend shows that they have been applying the test in a generic fashion rather than insisting on application of each element of the test. Tribunals often make a reference to the elements of the test and do not conduct a detailed analysis as to whether each of them is satisfied.[119] For example, in his commentary on the ICSID Convention, Schreuer suggests that these 'features should not necessarily be understood as jurisdictional requirements but merely as typical characteristics of investments under the Convention.'[120] Tribunals have used these criteria subject to variations to determine the existence of investment.[121] In majority of the cases, these criteria

---

117. *Ceskoslovenska Obchodni Banka, A.S. v. The Slovak Republic*, Decision on Jurisdiction, ICSID Case No. ARB/97/4, 68 (24 May 1999).
118. Ministry of Commerce and Industry, Government of India, *Model Text for the Indian Bilateral Investment Treaty*, Art. 1.4 (28 Dec. 2015) http://www.finmin.nic.in/reports/ModelTextIndia_BIT.pdf (accessed 17 Jul. 2017).
119. *Salini Costruttori S.p.A. and Italstrade S.p.A. v. Kingdom of Morocco*, Decision on Jurisdiction, ICSID Case No. ARB/00/, 5308 (23 Jul. 2001); In *Malaysian Historical Salvors v. Malaysia* the Tribunal said:

> the Tribunal agrees that this criterion [regularity of profits and return] is not always critical. Further, this has not been held to be an essential characteristic or criterion in any other case cited in this Award, and its presence or otherwise may therefore not be determinative of the question of 'investment'. *Malaysian Historical Salvors v. Malaysia*, Award, *supra* n. 110, at 108.

120. Schreuer, *supra* n. 15, at 83.
121. Noah Rubins, *The Notion of "Investment" in International Investment Arbitration*, in Arbitrating Foreign Investment Disputes: Procedural and Substantive Legal Aspects, 267-70 (Norbert Horn (ed.), Kluwer Law International, 2004).

Chapter 8: India and ICSID §8.04

were held to be satisfied.[122] Only in limited cases, tribunals held that the conditions were not satisfied.[123]

Each criterion has been attached different weight. Contribution or commitment has been interpreted in only financial terms as well as know-how, equipment, personnel and services. Contribution has been extensively interpreted, which is appropriate.[124] Contribution to economic development is an important criterion but has been declared to be subsumed in other criteria.[125] Each criterion has not been rigidly applied, and tribunals have exercised great deal of margin of appreciation in the interpretation and application of these criteria.[126]

Jurisdiction means the limits within which the facilities of ICSID are available.[127] The question of jurisdiction may arise at various stages of ICSID proceedings such as institution, jurisdiction or merits phase.[128]

---

122. *Consortium RFCC v. Royaume du Maroc*, Decision on Jurisdiction, ICSID Case No. ARB/00/6, 58-66 (16 Jul. 2001); *Consortium Groupement L.E.S.I. - DIPENTA v. République algérienne démocratique et populaire*, Award, ICSID Case No. ARB/03/08, 13-4 (10 Jan. 2005); *AES Corporation v. The Argentine Republic*, Decision on Jurisdiction, ICSID Case No. ARB/02/17, 88 (26 Apr. 2005); *Bayindir Insaat Turizm Ticaret Ve Sanayi A.S. v. Islamic Republic of Pakistan*, Decision on Jurisdiction, ICSID Case No. ARB/03/29, 130-8 (14 Nov. 2005); *Jan de Nul N.V. and Dredging International N.V. v. Arab Republic of Egypt*, Decision on Jurisdiction, ICSID Case No. ARB/04/13, 91-6 (16 Jun. 2006); *L.E.S.I. S.p.A. and ASTALDI S.p.A. v. République Algérienne Démocratique et Populaire*, Decision on Jurisdiction, ICSID Case No. ARB/05/3, 72-3 (12 Jul. 2006); *Helnan International Hotels A/S v. Arab Republic of Egypt*, Decision on Jurisdiction, ICSID Case No. ARB/05/19, 77 (17 Oct. 2006); *Saipem S.p.A. v. The People's Republic of Bangladesh*, Decision on Jurisdiction and Recommendation on Provisional Measures, ICSID Case No. ARB/05/07, 99-102, 109-11 (21 Mar. 2007); *Ioannis Kardassopoulos v. The Republic of Georgia*, Decision on Jurisdiction, ICSID Case No. ARB/05/18, 116 (6 Jul. 2007); *Noble Energy, Inc. and Machalapower Cia. Ltda. v. The Republic of Ecuador and Consejo Nacional de Electricidad*, Decision on Jurisdiction, ICSID Case No. ARB/05/12, 125-35 (5 Mar. 2008).
123. *Joy Mining Machinery Limited v. Arab Republic of Egypt*, Award, ICSID Case No. ARB/03/11, 53-63 (6 Aug. 2004). In some cases the requirement of contribution to economic development was not satisfied: *Mr. Patrick Mitchell v. Democratic Republic of the Congo*, Decision on Annulment, ICSID Case No. ARB/99/7, 23-48 (1 Nov. 2006); *Malaysian Historical Salvors v. Malaysia*, Award, *supra* n. 110, at 48-148. In *Patrick Mitchell v. DR Congo* the foreign investor was claiming that the activity of setting up a law firm amounted to investment and in *Malaysian Historical Salvors v. Malaysia* the foreign investor was claiming that the contract with the host State for location and salvage of the cargo of the 'DIANA,' a British vessel that sank off the coast of Malacca in 1817 is an investment.
124. *Consortium RFCC v. Royaume du Maroc*, Decision on Jurisdiction, *supra* n. 122, at 61; *Consortium Groupement L.E.S.I. - DIPENTA v. République algérienne démocratique et populaire*, Award, *supra* n. 122, at 14(i); *Bayindir Insaat Turizm Ticaret Ve Sanayi A.S. v. Islamic Republic of Pakistan*, Decision on Jurisdiction, *supra* n. 122, at para. 131; *L.E.S.I. S.p.A. and ASTALDI S.p.A. v. République Algérienne Démocratique et Populaire*, Decision on Jurisdiction, *supra* n. 122, at para. 73(i); *Malaysian Historical Salvors v. Malaysia*, Award, *supra* n. 110, at para. 109.
125. *Consortium Groupement L.E.S.I. - DIPENTA v. République algérienne démocratique et populaire*, Award, *supra* n. 122, at para. II. 13(iv); *L.E.S.I. S.p.A. and ASTALDI S.p.A. v. République Algérienne Démocratique et Populaire*, Decision on Jurisdiction, *supra* n. 122, at para. 72(iv).
126. Schreuer, *supra* n. 15, at 133-4.
127. ICSID, *Report of the Executive Directors on the ICSID Convention*, *supra* n. 16, at para. 22 states that: 'The term "jurisdiction of the Centre" is used in the Convention as a convenient expression to mean the limits within which the provisions of the Convention will apply and the facilities of the Centre will be available for conciliation and arbitration proceedings.'
128. Schreuer, *supra* n. 15, at 83.

There were extensive deliberations as to whether the terms 'investor' and 'investment' should be defined in the ICSID Convention. Broches was opposed to limiting or defining investments because it would be difficult to find satisfactory definition of investment was likely to lead to jurisdictional controversies.[129] Various attempts made at defining investment failed and the Report of the Executive Directors notes that there is no definition of investment under the Convention in the following words:

> No attempt was made to define the term 'investment' given the essential requirement of consent by the parties, and the mechanism through which Contracting States can make known in advance, if they so desire, the classes of disputes which they would or would not consider submitting to the Centre (Article 25(4)).

The focus in this chapter is on the definition of investor and investment because these are distinguishing features of the ICSID Convention and a major benefit of joining the ICSID system. The disputes have to arise 'directly' out of an investment. Therefore, issued that are ancillary to investment cannot be raised before ICSID.[130] It is not that the investments have to be direct, rather the dispute has to arise directly out of an investment.[131] There is no such requirement in ad hoc arbitrations. States have tried to narrow the scope of directness by arguing that general policies undertaken for restoring the health of economy and general public good cannot be said to arise directly out of investments. The tribunals have distinguished between general measures and measures that would affect investors and held that once it is found that the measures do affect the investments then their nature as general measures is not relevant and does not exclude the measures from the jurisdiction of tribunals.[132]

The jurisdictional requirement represents the unique nature of ICSID as a forum for resolving mixed disputes – i.e., disputes between foreign investor on one side and the State on another. Disputes between private parties would normally be decided before domestic courts.[133]

Another reason for dissatisfaction with the ICSID in India is the finality of ICSID awards. All Member States of ICSID are under an obligation to treat an ICSID award as binding and enforce it within their jurisdiction, and the award is to be treated as a final judgment of the highest court.[134] States are not under an obligation under customary

---

129. ICSID, *History of the ICSID Convention: Documents concerning the Origin and the Formulation of the Convention, supra* n. 43, at 22, 54, 59.
130. Schreuer, *supra* n. 15, at 106-7.
131. *Fedax N.V. v. The Republic of Venezuela*, Decision on Jurisdiction, ICSID Case No. ARB/96/3, 24 (11 Jul. 1997); *Ceskoslovenska Obchodni Banka, A.S. v. The Slovak Republic*, Decision on Jurisdiction, *supra* n. 117, at paras 71, 72; *CMS Gas Transmission Company v. The Republic of Argentina*, Decision on Jurisdiction, ICSID Case No. ARB/01/8, 52, 66, 68 (17 Jul. 2003); *Siemens A.G. v. The Argentine Republic*, Decision on Jurisdiction, ICSID Case No. ARB/02/8, 150 (3 Aug. 2004).
132. *CMS Gas Transmission Company v. The Republic of Argentina*, Decision on Jurisdiction, *supra* n. 131, at para. 33; *AES Corporation v. The Argentine Republic, supra* n. 122, at 48, 49, 57, 60; *Continental Casualty Company v. The Argentine Republic*, Decision on Jurisdiction, ICSID Case No. ARB/03/9, 72 (22 Feb. 2006).
133. Schreuer, *supra* n. 15, at 82.
134. ICSID Convention Regulations and Rules, *supra* n. 2, at Art. 54.

international law to recognize or enforce foreign judgments or foreign arbitral decisions. States can withhold recognition and enforcement or subject it to conditions that they prescribe.[135] Article 54 of the ICSID Convention makes it obligatory on all Contracting States to recognize an award rendered under the ICSID Convention and enforce pecuniary obligations imposed by the award as if that award 'were a final judgment of a court in that State'.[136] If the Contracting State has a federal constitution then it may be enforced through the federal constitution and may be treated 'as if it were a final judgment of the courts of a constituent state'.[137] By virtue of this provision, the ICSID Convention does not leave any discretion to domestic courts or any other authority to interpret, revise or annul ICSID awards.[138] This provision puts an ICSID award at the same footing as final judgment of national courts. If such a judgment can be enforced under domestic law then there is no restriction on enforcing the ICSID award.[139] The Report of the Executive Directors, which is an influential document for interpretation confirms this position in the following words:

> 43. The doctrine of sovereign immunity may prevent the forced execution in a State of judgments obtained against foreign States or against the State in which execution is sought. Article 54 requires Contracting States to equate an award rendered pursuant to the Convention with a final judgment of its own courts. It does not require them to go beyond that and to undertake forced execution of awards rendered pursuant to the Convention in cases in which final judgments could not be executed.[140]

According to Amerasinghe, Article 54 requires Contracting States to equate an award with a final judgment of a domestic court. The Convention does not require Contracting States to go beyond that equation. Therefore, there is no forced execution in situations where a final judgment could not be executed.[141] However a situation of non-enforcement of the final judgment of a State is highly unlikely.

This excludes the power of host State to review an ICSID award. Non-ICSID awards are amenable to review under the NYC. But the ICSID Convention excludes the use of NYC for enforcement of awards and makes its awards automatically enforceable. The NYC provides for grounds for interference with an award. Therefore, the ICSID system excludes all domestic and international rules and procedures for enforcement of awards.[142] States can also enforce awards against investors in cases where the host States win an arbitration.[143] The NYC contains grounds for review of an award. In the early stages of the drafting of the Convention there was a proposal to include those

---

135. Amerasinghe, *supra* n. 21, at 815.
136. ICSID Convention Regulations and Rules, *supra* n. 2, at Art. 54(1).
137. *Ibid.*
138. Schreuer, *supra* n. 15, at 1127.
139. ICSID, *History of the ICSID Convention: Documents concerning the Origin and the Formulation of the Convention*, *supra* n. 43, at pp. 242, 304.
140. ICSID, *Report of the Executive Directors on the ICSID Convention*, *supra* n. 16, at para. 43.
141. Amerasinghe, *supra* n. 21, at 816.
142. *Ibid.*, at 793, 815; Aaron Broches, *The Convention on the Settlement of Investment Disputes between States and Nationals of Other States*, 136 II Recueil des Cours 331, 401 (1972).
143. Amerasinghe, *supra* n. 141.

provisions, however, Broches resisted and prevailed.[144] Therefore, the ICSID Convention has a system of enforcement which is independent of the NYC and other international and domestic law rules dealing with the enforcement of foreign arbitral awards.[145] NYC would be relevant where a State is part to the NYC but not a party to the ICSID Convention. The operation of Article 54 is not limited only to the losing State. It starts with the words '[E]ach Contracting State...'. Therefore, an award can be enforced in any State that is a party to the ICSID Convention, including the State party to the dispute and the home State of the foreign investor.[146]

The attraction for not joining ICSID is that awards passed by ICSID are directly enforceable without the need of judicial review or the procedure under the NYC. The question is whether at present the NYC can be used to challenge investment arbitration awards in India? Article I(3) of the NYC allows the States to make reservations to the NYC that the Convention will be only applied to differences arising out of commercial relationships that are considered as commercial under the law of the State making such a declaration. India has made such a declaration.[147] Awards passed by investment tribunals are not commercial in nature. Rather disputes arising out of commercial transactions are excluded from the purview of investment tribunals and particularly ICSID.[148] Therefore the NYC is not available for challenging awards of investment tribunals. In a sense, there is no remedy available in Indian law to challenge investment awards.[149] Article 54 has been interpreted to mean that it leaves no discretion to domestic courts or other authorities to allow interpretation, revision or annulment of awards.[150] The domestic courts where enforcement of an ICSID award is sought have the limited authority to verify the authenticity of the ICSID award.[151] Even the order of

---

144. Schreuer, *supra* n. 15, at 1118.
145. Amerasinghe, *supra* n. 135.
146. Schreuer, *supra* n. 15, at 1124.
147. India's Declaration: 'In accordance with Article I of the Convention, the Government of India declare that they will apply the Convention to the recognition and enforcement of awards made only in the territory of a State, party to this Convention. They further declare that they will apply the Convention only to differences arising out of legal relationships, whether contractual or not, which are considered as commercial under the law of India.' Contracting States of the New York Convention, http://www.newyorkconvention.org/countries (accessed 1 Jul. 2017).
148. Article 1(2) of the International Convention for Settlement of Investment Disputes, 1965 limits the application of Convention to '...investment disputes between Contracting States and nationals of other Contracting States.' Tribunals have declined to entertain pure commercial disputes from time to time. See *El Paso Energy International Company v. The Argentine Republic*, Decision on Jurisdiction, ICSID Case No. ARB/03/15, paras 74,75 (27 Apr. 2006); *SGS Société Générale de Surveillance S.A. v. Islamic Republic of Pakistan*, Decision of the Tribunal on Objections to Jurisdiction, ICSID Case No. ARB/01/13, 173 (6 Aug. 2003); Van Harten, *supra* n. 95, at 45, 47, 49, 50.
149. It is possible that a petition could be filed under Art. 226 of the Constitution of India before High Courts invoking their extraordinary powers. But these powers are exercisable in cases of violation of fundamental or other legal right. It would be a challenge for the Government of India to establish that such rights have been violated and therefore the award could be challenged under Art. 226. Also see Prabhash Ranjan and Deepak Raju, *The Enigma of Enforceability of Investment Treaty Arbitration Awards in India*, 6 Asian Journal of Comparative Law 1 (2011).
150. Schreuer, *supra* n. 15, at 1127-8.
151. *Ibid.*, at 1128.

ordre public exception has been excluded in the Convention for the reason that it would have been a dangerous erosion of the binding character of the award.[152]

In the place of a challenge to award in domestic courts, the ICSID Convention provides for annulment. Therefore, ICSID provides a two-tier dispute resolution. Annulment proceedings are not an appeal. It is unlike the Appellate Body of the World Trade Organization (WTO) which performs an appellate function. The Annulment Committee does not perform a full-fledged review, but is limited only to serious errors. Annulment can take place in the following situations:

(a) that the Tribunal was not properly constituted;
(b) that the Tribunal has manifestly exceeded its powers;
(c) that there was corruption on the part of a member of the Tribunal;
(d) that there has been a serious departure from a fundamental rule of procedure; or
(e) that the award has failed to state the reasons on which it is based.[153]

Award could be executed even while annulment proceedings are pending, unless the enforcement of the award is stayed by the annulment committee.[154]

The annulment committee's scope of examination is restricted to the legitimacy of the process of a decision and does not extend to its substantive correctness.[155] It is a form of review which takes as premise 'the record before the tribunal'.[156] Therefore, the committee cannot annul an award on the ground of error of fact or law.[157] While the committee can only annul the award and not reverse or amend it,[158] the remedy of annulment is not a matter of right but tribunal's discretion. There is a growing consensus on the reasoning adopted by the 'third generation' of decisions[159] that annulment is a discretionary remedy and need not necessarily be the outcome in all

---

152. Amerasinghe, *supra* n. 21, at 815.
153. ICSID Convention Regulations and Rules, *supra* n. 2, at Art. 52.
154. Schreuer, *supra* n. 15, at 1146.
155. *CDC Group plc v. Republic of Seychelles*, Decision on Annulment, ICSID Case No. ARB/02/14, 34 (29 Jun. 2005); *Empresas Lucchetti, S.A. and Lucchetti Peru, S.A. v. The Republic of Peru*, Decision on Annulment, ICSID Case No. ARB/03/4, 97 (5 Sept. 2007); Lucy Reed, Jan Paulsson, Nigel Blackaby. *Guide to ICSID Arbitration*, 99 (Kluwer Law International 2011).
156. *CDC Group plc v. Republic of Seychelles*, Decision on Annulment, *supra* n. 155, at para. 34; *Empresas Lucchetti, S.A. and Lucchetti Peru, S.A. v. The Republic of Peru*, Decision on Annulment, *supra* n. 155, at para. 97.
157. *Amco Asia Corporation and others v. Republic of Indonesia*, Decision on Annulment, ICSID Case No. ARB/81/1, 23 (16 May 1986); *Hussein Nuaman Soufraki v. The United Arab Emirates*, Decision on Annulment, ICSID Case No. ARB/02/7, 85-7, 97 (5 Jun. 2007); *Maritime International Nominees Establishment v. Republic of Guinea*, Decision on Annulment, ICSID Case No. ARB/84/4, 4.04 (22 Dec. 1989); *CMS Gas Transmission Company v. The Republic of Argentina*, Decision on Annulment, ICSID Case No. ARB/01/8, 158 (25 Sept. 2007).
158. Schreuer, *supra* n. 15, at 901; *Maritime International Nominees Establishment v. Republic of Guinea*, Decision on Annulment, *supra* n. 157, at para. 4.04; *Amco Asia Corporation and others v. Republic of Indonesia*, Resubmitted Case: Decision on Annulment, ICSID Case No. ARB/8 1/1, 1.18 (3 Dec. 1992).
159. Christoph Schreuer, *Three Generations of ICSID Annulment Proceedings*, 17 http://www.univie.ac.at/intlaw/wordpress/pdf/69.pdf (accessed 19 Jul. 2017) in: Emmanuel Gaillard and Yas Banifatemi. *Annulment of ICSID Awards* (Juris Publishing Inc. 2004).

circumstances.[160] The committee in *CDC v. Seychelles* summarized this trend and noted, 'the ad hoc Committees operating during the last two decades have considered that a Committee has discretion to determine not to annul an Award even where a ground for annulment under Article 52(1) is found to exist.'[161] A committee may refuse to annul an award if it is unnecessary or would unjustifiably erode the finality of ICSID awards.[162]

As noted above, the review of decision of a tribunal happens on very limited grounds. The Annulment Committee may disagree with the findings and even find that the tribunal committed serious errors of law. However, whether the award should be annulled depends on whether the violation amounts to a 'substantial' one of any of the grounds in Article 52(1).[163] For example, even though the Committee in *CMS v. Argentina* found that the tribunal had committed 'a manifest error of law', it refused to annul the award citing the limited jurisdiction under Article 52 and lack of power to substitute its own view for that of the tribunal.[164]

The ICSID Convention provides the possibility of excluding certain kinds and categories of disputes from its purview. The state party to the ICSID Convention may at the time of ratification, acceptance or approval or any other time thereafter notify the class or classes of disputes which it would not submit to the ICSID.[165]

It is difficult to predict whether India may want to join the ICSID system. It may not have a lot to gain from the jurisdictional requirements while the fear of mandatory enforcement of awards without a possibility of review remains.

---

160. *Wena Hotels Ltd. v. Arab Republic of Egypt*, Decision on Annulment, ICSID Case No. ARB/98/4, 83 (5 Feb. 2002); *Compañiá de Aguas del Aconquija S.A. and Vivendi Universal S.A. v. Argentine Republic*, Decision on Annulment, ICSID Case No. ARB/97/3, 66 (3 Jul. 2002). Also see *Hussein Nuaman Soufraki v. The United Arab Emirates*, Decision on Annulment, *supra* n. 157, at para. 24; *Maritime International Nominees Establishment v. Republic of Guinea*, Decision on Annulment, *supra* n. 157, at paras 4.09-10.
161. *CDC Group plc v. Republic of Seychelles*, Decision on Annulment, *supra* n. 155, at para. 37, 65.
162. *Ibid.*, at para. 71; *Amco Asia Corporation and others v. Republic of Indonesia*, Resubmitted Case: Decision on Annulment, *supra* n. 158, at para. 1.20; *Compañiá de Aguas del Aconquija S.A. and Vivendi Universal S.A. v. Argentine Republic*, Decision on Annulment, *supra* n. 160, at para. 66; *Maritime International Nominees Establishment v. Republic of Guinea*, Decision on Annulment, *supra* n. 157, at para. 4.10; Schreuer, *supra* n. 15, at 1040.
163. *Mr. Patrick Mitchell v. Democratic Republic of the Congo*, Decision on Annulment, *supra* n. 123, at 20.
164. *CMS Gas Transmission Company v. The Republic of Argentina*, Decision on Annulment, *supra* n. 157, at paras 135-6.
165. ICSID Convention Regulations and Rules, *supra* n. 2, at Art. 25(4).

CHAPTER 9
Conclusion

Since the time of independence, approach towards protection of foreign investment has gradually changed overtime. The changes have oscillated between often irreconcilable positions. These positions were an outcome of the demands of the times. Immediately after independence, India was concerned for ensuring its economic growth. It showed readiness to protect foreign investments and did not nationalize or expropriate ownership of industries and strategic economic activities controlled by the former colonial power. But it insisted on national treatment (NT). At the international level, India led the newly independent States that were keen on taking back control of their vital natural resources and economic control. NT of foreign investment with the right of host State to expropriate foreign property and no State responsibility for violation of rights of foreign investors was supported at the international fora. Once the economy started faltering and the winds of change in economic thinking started gathering momentum world over, India embraced that change. It started protecting rights of foreign investors through investment treaties. But, yet again, once India realized the exposure it had of potential investment claims it reconsidered its changed position on investment treaties. The policy has changed as per the demands of the time. It is not just India but all the States, including the traditional capital-importing and capital-exporting countries, are adjusting their policies to the changing circumstances of investment treaty arbitration (ITA).

Even at present protection of foreign investment in India and India's relationship with ITA are in a state of transition. In this state of transition, the policy and the legal regime on the protection of foreign investment and ITA are moving, albeit, in opposite directions.

The extent of protection of foreign investment in India is increasing and getting stronger. The legal and regulatory structure for protection of foreign investment in India is fairly robust. Steps are being taken to make that structure stronger, stable and investor friendly. All branches of the State are protective of interests of foreign investors in India. The Government is taking repeated steps to reform and improve the regulatory structure and environment for foreign investors and the business environment generally. The judiciary, on the other hand, has not discriminated against foreign investors and ensured that it is available for controlling the actions of the Government wherever they fall short of the standards of treatment contained in the Constitution of India. The standards of treatment in the Constitution are higher than that provided under the investment treaties. Moreover, the time taken for enforcement of rights through the judiciary through the writ jurisdiction of high courts is considerably less than that taken otherwise in Indian courts.

On the other hand, the attitude towards ITA in India is moving in the opposite direction, as compared to the attitude towards protection of foreign investment in India. The old bilateral investment treaties (BITs) that contained liberal provisions on treatment standards and access to arbitration through broad jurisdictional and dispute resolution provisions have been cancelled. In their place, new BITs are being negotiated on the basis of 2015 Model BIT. The 2015 Model BIT reflects efforts to narrow treatment standards and reduce access to investment arbitration by limiting jurisdictional and dispute resolution provisions. The changes are inspired by the fear of expansive interpretation by investment tribunals and a large number of investment claims pending against India – in addition to the investment claims lost in past. Concerns about transparency in investment arbitration proceedings are also addressed in the 2015 Model BIT. The central concern manifest in the changes is conserving regulatory freedom. The fear of investment claims against legitimate regulations for public interests such as the protection of the health, environment, human rights, labour reforms, etc. has been generating concerns amongst States and in the literature. As economic growth takes place in India and more and more people are lifted out of poverty, simultaneous steps would have to be taken to improve the quality of life. These steps would demand for adopting of regulations in public interest. These regulations would in many situations interfere with interests of investors and inflict economic losses on private businesses. A balance between protection of investor interests and public interest through conservation of regulatory freedom is a must. This explains the movement of the policy and the legal regime in different directions in relation to the protection of investors in India and India's approach towards ITA.

This conflicting approach towards protection of foreign investment in India and ITA is justifiable at this stage since India is still a predominantly capital-importing State. The amount of investment flowing out of India has increased over the last few years, and this upward trend may continue in the future. The inflow of foreign investment into India far outpaces the outflow of investment from India. The vast gap in the ratio of inflow and outflow of investment would continue until India reaches a certain threshold of development and growth hits a plateau. This would, however, take some time. Therefore India may remain predominantly a capital-importing country. In such a situation, the exposure of investment claims is far higher than the prospect of Indian investors using investment treaties to initiate proceedings against other States. The experience shows that very few cases have been filed by Indian investors against other States. The relative number of cases filed by Indians and the gross amounts of claims of those proceedings are significantly lower than the number and gross amount of claims of cases brought against India. In the current situation, although the approach

Chapter 9: Conclusion

towards ITA may appear regressive, it is necessary and a demand of the present situation. China adopted a similar stance. While China was growing fast, it granted limited protection to foreign investors through investment treaties. For example, upon ratification of the ICSID Convention, China made a reservation to the extent that it submitted to the jurisdiction of ICSID disputes over 'compensation resulting from expropriation or nationalisation'.[1] As China grew and started exporting capital and the ratio of outflow of capital matched the inflow of capital to an optimal degree, China changed its investment treaties. It adopted a liberal model of entry and operation, liberal standards and dispute resolution clauses.[2]

The 2015 Model BIT has introduced many new provisions. Some of these provisions, such as the 'enterprise-based' definition of investment, are not to be found in BITs of any other State. One way of looking at these developments is to simply decry it by saying that India is risking by doing something that no one has done. Another way is of appreciating the innovation. The willingness to innovate and take new steps shows that India does not wish to be a silent rule taker, where the traditional exporting countries introduce some models of BITs and India, and India would simply follow them. This is a situation where India is willing to usher a new path. It would be too early to announce the path moribund even before it has played out. Sufficient reasons exist for undertaking such a path. What really needs to be seen is how other States respond. This could be a situation where India could move from being a 'rule taker' to a 'rule maker', which would be a welcome change not only to the ITA but also represent overall willingness of India to undertake a leadership role.

Thus, on the two central issues discussed in the book – protection of foreign investment in India and India's relationship with ITA – there is paradox as the attitude towards investment protection in India is progressive but ITA is regressing. It would be interesting to see how this relationship unfolds in the future.

---

1. *See* Freshfields Bruckhaus Deringer, *Resolving Disputes in China through Arbitration*, 53 (2006) http://www.freshfields.com/publications/pdfs/2006/14706.pdf (accessed 22 Jul. 2017).
2. For an analysis of the change in China's policy *see* Stephan W. Schill, *Tearing down the Great Wall: The New Generation Investment Treaties of the People's Republic of China*, 15 Cardozo Journal of International and Comparative Law 73 (2007), http://heinonline.org/HOL/LandingPage?handle = hein.journals/cjic12&div = 1.

Bibliography

9th Session of the International Law Commission (Yearbook of the International Law Commission, 1957).

A. de Lapradelle and N. Politis, *Rescuil des arbitrages internationaux* (Vol. I, 78, 21 October 1861).

Actival International SA v. Conservas El Pilar SA YB (Tribunal Supremo, Commercial Arbitration XXVII 2002).

A.F.M. Maniruzzaman, *State Contracts in Contemporary International Law: Monist v. Dualist Controversies* (12 European Journal of International Law 309, 2001).

Albert Jan van den Berg, *The New York Arbitration Convention of 1958: Towards a Uniform Judicial Interpretation* (Wolters Kluwer, 1981).

Albert van den Berg, *Enforcement of Arbitral Awards Annulled in Russia* (27(2) Journal of International Arbitration, 2010).

Albert van den Berg, *Should Setting Aside of the Arbitral Award Be Abolished?* (29(1) ICSID Review, 2014).

Alwyn Freeman, *The International Responsibility of States for Denial of Justice* (31 Longman, 1938).

Andrea Giardina, *State Contracts: National versus International* (5 Italian Yearbook of International Law 147, 1980).

Andreas Lowenfeld, *The ICSID Convention: Origins and Transformation* (38 Georgia Journal of International and Comparative Law, 2009).

Andrew Newcombe and Luis Paradell, *Law and Practice of Investment Treaties: Standards of Treatment* (Law and Business, 2009).

Aniruddha Rajput, *India's Shifting Treaty Practice: A Comparative Analysis of the 2003 and 2015 Model BITs* (7 Jindal Global Law Review, 2016).

Aniruddha Rajput, *Problems with the Jurisprudence of Iran-US Claims Tribunal on Indirect Expropriation* (30 ICSID Review 589-615, 2015).

Aniruddha Rajput, *Defining Investment - A Developmental Prospective* (2 Indian Journal of Arbitration Law 12, 2013).

Antonio Parra, *The History of ICSID* (Oxford University Press, 2012).

Asha Kaushal, *Revisiting History: How the Past Matters for the Present Backlash Against the Foreign Investment Regime* (50 Harvard International Law Journal, 2009).

Bryan A. Garner (ed.), *Black's Law Dictionary* (9th ed., West Group, 2009).

C.H. Schreuer, *The ICSID Convention: A Commentary* (Cambridge University Press, 2009).

Bibliography

Campbell McLachlan, Laurence Shore and Matthew Weiniger, *International Investment Law: Substantive Principles* (Oxford University Press, 2008).

Catherine Titi, *Investment Arbitration in Latin America: The Uncertain Veracity of Preconceived Idea* (30(2) Arbitration International: The Journal of the London Court of International Arbitration, 2014).

Charles Brower, *A Crisis of Legitimacy* (7 National Law Journal, 2002).

Charles Dupuis, *Liberte des voices de communication et le Relations internationals* (Recueil des Cours, Vol. I, 1924).

Chittaranjan Amerasinghe, *The International Centre for Settlement of Investment Disputes and Development through the Multinational Corporations* (9 Vanderbilt Journal for Transnational Law, 1976).

Chittaranjan Amerasinghe, *State Responsibility for Injuries to Aliens*, 215 (Oxford University Press: Clarendon Press, 1967).

Christoph Schreuer, et al., *ICSID Convention: A Commentary* (2nd ed., Cambridge University Press, 2009).

Durga Das Basu, *Commentary on the Constitution of India*, 5 (8th ed., LexisNexis Butterworths Wadhwa Nagpur, 2009).

Durga Das Basu, *Shorter Constitution of India*, II (14th ed., LexisNexis Butterworths Wadhwa Nagpur Reprint, 2010).

Eduardo Jimenez de Arechaga, *International Law in the Past Third of a Century* (159 Recueil des Cours, Vol. I, 1978).

Emer de Vattel (translated by Charles Fenwick), *The Law of Nations or the Principles of Natural Law (Le droit de gens, ou principles de la loi naturelle)* (350 William S. Hein & Co. Vol. II, 1995).

Eric Neumayer and Laura Spess, *Do Bilateral Investment Treaties Increase Foreign Direct Investment to Developing Countries?* (33(10) World Development October 2005).

Fali Nariman, *India's Legal System: Can It Be Saved?* (Penguin Books, 2006).

French Seller v. German Buyer, 16 December 2010, Bundesgerichtshof (36 Yearbook of Commercial Arbitration 2011).

G. Sacerdoti, *Bilateral Treaties and Multilateral Instruments on Investment Protection* (269 Recueil des Cours 1997).

Gerald Fitzmaurice, *The Meaning of the Term 'Denial of Justice'* (13 British Yearbook of International Law 93, 1932).

Grant Haessian and Kabir Duggal, *The 2015 Indian Model BIT: Is This Change the World Wishes to See?* (30 ICSID Review – FILJ 729).

Granville Austin, *Working on a Democratic Constitution – A History of the Indian Experience* (Oxford University Press, 1999).

Gus Van Harten, *Investment Treaty Arbitration and Public Law* (Oxford University Press, 2007).

K.S. Harisankar, *Annulment versus Enforcement of International Arbitral Awards: Does New York Convention Permit Issue Estoppel?* (International Arbitration Law Review, 2015).

Hazel Fox and Philippa Webb, *The Law of State Immunity* (3rd ed., Oxford University Press).

Bibliography

Hege Elisabeth Kjos, *Applicable Law in Investor-State Arbitration: The Interplay Between National and International Law* (Oxford University Press, 2013).

Hersch Lauterpacht, *Oppenheim's International Law* (Longmans, Green & Company, 1955).

History of the ICSID Convention, ICSID, Volume II.

Hop Dang, *The Applicability of International Law as Governing Law of State Contracts* (17 Australian International Law Journal 133, 2010).

Hussein Haeri, *A Tale of Two Standards: Fair and Equitable Treatment and the Minimum Standard in International Law* (27(1) Arbitration International, 2011).

Ian Brownlie, *Principles of Public International Law* (7th ed., Oxford University Press, 2008).

Ignacio Gomes-Palacio and Peter Muchlinski, *Admission and Establishment*, in Oxford Handbook of International Investment Law (Peter Muchlinski, Federico Ortino and Christoph Schreuer (ed.), Oxford University Press, 2008).

IMF, *Balance of Payments Manual* (6th ed., IMF, 2008).

International Law Commission (1958) II Yearbook of International Law Commission 82.

Iona Tudor, *The Fair and Equitable Treatment Standard in International Law of Foreign Investment* (Oxford 54-68, 2008).

IPOC International Growth Fund Ltd v. L V Finance Group Ltd., Court of Appeals, British Virgin Islands (22 Yearbook of Commercial Arbitration, 2008).

Ivar Alvik, *Contracting with Sovereignty: State Contracts and International Arbitration* (Hart Publishing, 2011).

J.F. Poudret and S. Besson, *Comparative Law of International Arbitration* (Thomson Sweet & Maxwell, 2006).

Jagdish Bhagwai and Padma Desai, *India: Planning for Industrialization* (Oxford University, 1970).

James Allsop, *The Authority of the Arbitrator* (Clayton Utz Sydney of University International Arbitration Lecture, 2013).

Jan Paulsson, *Arbitration Without Privity* (10(2) ICSID Review: Foreign Investment Law Journal, 1995).

Jan Paulsson, *Denial of Justice in International Law* 2 (Cambridge University Press, 2005).

Jason Webb Yankee, *Bilateral Investment Treaties, Credible Commitment, and the Rule of (International) Law: Do BITs Promote Foreign Direct Investment?* (42(4) Law and Society Review, 19 November 2008).

Jay M. Shafritz, *The Harper Collins Dictionary of American Government and Politics* (Harper Perennial, 1993).

Jimenez de Arechaga, *International Law in the Past Third of a Century* (I Recueil des Cours, 159, 1978).

John Jackson, *The World Trading System* (2nd ed., MIT Press, 1997).

Jose Alvarez and Gustavo Topalian, *The Paradoxical Argentina Cases* (6 World Arbitration and Mediation Review 491, 2012).

Kabir Duggal, *The Changing Landscape of Investor-State Arbitration in India* (7 Jindal Global Law Review 2016).

Bibliography

Krishnan Jayanth K and Kumar C. Raj, *Delay in Process, Denial of Justice: The Jurisprudence and Empirics of Speedy Trials in Comparative Perspective*, Paper 155 (Articles by Maurer Faculty, 2011).

Leon E. Trakman, *Investor State Arbitration or Local Courts: Will Australia Set a New Trend?* (46 Journal of World Trade 83, 2012).

Lisa Sachs and Karp Sauvant, *BITs, DTTs, and FDI Flows: An Overview, The Effect of Treaties on Foreign Direct Investment: Bilateral Investment Treaties, Double Taxation Treaties and Investment Flows* (Oxford University Press, 2009).

Live Law News Network, *The Unending Uncertainty in the Death Sentencing Policy in Indian Courts*, Livelaw.in (13 May 2015), http://www.livelaw.in/the-unending-uncertainity-in-the-death-sentencing-policy-of-indian-courts/ (accessed 10 July 2017).

Lucy Reed, Jan Paulsson and Nigel Blackaby, *Guide to ICSID Arbitration* (Kluwer Law Arbitration, 2011).

M. Hallward-Driemeier, *Do Bilateral Investment Treaties Attract FDI? Only a Bit...and They Could Bite* (World Bank Policy Research Papers, WPS 3121).

M. Sornarajah, *A Coming Crisis: Expansionary Trends in Investment; Treaty Arbitration*, in Appeals Mechanism in International Investment Disputes (Karl Sauvant (ed.), Oxford University Press 2008).

M. Sornarajah, *Portfolio Investments and Definition of Investment* (24 ICSID Review-Foreign Investment Law Journal 516, 2009).

M. Sornarajah, *The International Law on Foreign Investment* (3rd ed., Cambridge University Press, 2010).

M. Sornarajah, *Resistance and Change in the International Law on Foreign Investment* (Cambridge University Press, 2015).

M. Sornarajah, *The Settlement of Foreign Investment Disputes*, Kluwer Law International (2000).

M.P. Singh, *Securing the Independence of the Judiciary – The Indian Experience* (10 Indian International & Comparative Law Review 245, 2000).

Matthew Saunders and Claudia Solomon, *Enforcement of Arbitral Awards Against State Entities* (23(3) Arbitration International, 2007).

Michael Feit, *Responsibility of the State under International Law for the Breach of Contract Committed by a State-Owned Entity* (28 Berkeley Journal of International Law 142, 2010).

Michael Kidron, *Foreign Investment in India* (11-2 Oxford University Press, 1965).

Monique Sasson, *Substantive Law in Investment Arbitration: The Unsettled Relationship Between International Law and Municipal Law* (Kluwer Law International, 2010).

M.P. Jain, *Indian Constitutional Law* (6th ed., revised by Samaraditya Pal and Ruma Pal, Vol. 2 Lexis Nexis Buttersworths Wadhwa, 2010).

Nigel Blackaby and Others, *Redfirn and Hunter on International Arbitration* (5th ed., Oxford University Press, 2009).

Noah Rubins, *The Notion of 'Investment' in International Investment Arbitration*, in Arbitrating Foreign Investment Disputes: Procedural and Substantive Legal Aspects (Nobert horn (ed.), Kluwer Law International, 2004).

Bibliography

Oscar Lopez, *Smart Move: Argentina to Leave the ICSID* (1 Cornell International Law Journal Online 121, 2013).

P. Mayer, *Mandatory Rules of Law in International Arbitration* (2 Arbitration International 274, 1986).

P. Sanders, *New York Convention on the Recognition and Enforcement of Foreign Arbitral Awards* (Netherlands International Law Review, 1955).

Perusahaan Pertambangan Minyak Dan Gas Bumi Negara et al., US Court of Appeals, 5th Circuit, 23 March 2004 (29 Yearbook of Commercial Arbitration 1262, 2004).

Prabhash Ranjan and Deepak Raju, *The Enigma of Enforceability of Investment Treaty Arbitration Awards in India* (6 Asian Journal of Comparative Law 1, 2011).

Prabhash Ranjan and Deepak Raju, *Bilateral Investment Treaties and the Indian Judiciary* (46 George Washington International Law Review 809, 2013-2014).

Prabhash Ranjan, *India and Bilateral Investment Treaties – A Changing Landscape* (ICSID Review 2014).

Prosper Weil, *The State, the Foreign Investor, and International Law: The No Longer Stormy Relationship of a Menage A Trois* (15 ICSID Review 401, 415, 2000).

R. Jijon-Letort and J.M Marchan – Perez Bustamante & Ponce, *National and International Arbitration in Ecuador* (43 The Arbitration Review of the Americas, Global Arbitration Review, 2012).

Raghuram Rajan and Arvind Subramanian, *Aid and Growth: What Does the Cross-Country Evidence Really Show?* (NBER Working Paper No. 11513, August 2005, Revised February, 2007).

Ran Hirschl, *The Origins and Consequences of New Constitutionalism* 294 (Harvard University, 2004).

Rimple Saini and SL Lodha, *Banking Development in India* (5 Journal of Economics and Sustainable Development, 2014).

Robert Jennings and Arthur Watts (eds), *Oppenheim's International Law*, I (9th ed., Oxford University Press, 2008).

Rudolf Dolzer and Christoph Schreuer, *Principles of International Investment Law*, 104-15, 125-6 (2nd ed., Oxford University Press, 2012).

Rudolf Dolzer and Margarete Stevens, *Bilateral Investment Treaties* (Martinus Nijhoff Publishers, 1995).

S. Vasciannie, *The Fair and Equitable Treatment Standard in International Investment Law and Practice* (70 British Yearbook of International Law 99, 1990).

Sebastian Lopez Escarcena, *Indirect Expropriation in International Law* (Edgar Elgar Publishing Limited, 2014).

Shyam Divan and Armin Rosencrancz, *Environmental Law and Policy in India* (2nd ed., Oxford University Press, 18 April 2002).

Stephan Schill, *Fair and Equitable Treatment, the Rule of Law and Comparative Public Law*, in International Investment Law and Comparative Public Law 151 (Stephan Schill (ed.), Oxford University Press, 2010).

Stephan Schill, *Illegal Investment in Investment Treaty Arbitration* (11 The Law and Practice of International Courts and Tribunals 281, 2012).

Stephan Schill, *The Multilateralization of International Investment Law* (Cambridge University Press, 2009).

Stephen Schewebel, *Justice in International Law* (163 Cambridge University Press, 1994).

Stephen Vasciannie, *The Fair and Equitable Treatment Standard in International Law and Practice* (70 British Yearbook of International Law 99, 1990).

Sudhanshu Ranjan, *Justice: Judiciary and Democracy in India*, 2-3 (Taylor & Francis Group, 2012).

Susan D. Franck, *The Legitimacy Crisis in Investment Treaty Arbitration: Privatizing Public International Law Through Inconsistent Decisions* (73 Fordham Law Review 1521, 2005).

T. Baty, *The Canons of International Law* (John Murray, 1930).

Tom Moore, *Grynberg Drops World Bank Lawsuit* (5 November 2013).

Upendra Baxi, *Taking Suffering Seriously: Social Action Litigation in the Supreme Court of India* (4 (6) Third World Legal Studies 107, 1985).

Ursula Kriebaum, *Investment Arbitration – Illegal Investments* (Austrian Arbitration Yearbook 307, 2010).

V.R. Krishna Iyer, *Quality of Justice is not Strained*, Indian Express (27 November 2003).

W. Michael Reisman and Mahnoush Arsanjani, *The Question of Unilateral Governmental Statements as Applicable Law in Investment Disputes* (19(2) ICSID Review – FILJ, 328, 2004).

World Investment Report 2010: *Investment in a Low-Carbon Economy* (UN, 2010).

Electronic Sources

'Bolivia Notifies World Bank of Withdrawal from ICSID, Pursues BIT Revisions', Investment Treaty News, 4 May 2007, available at: http://www.iisd.org/pdf/2007/itn_may9_2007.pdf (last accessed 1 July 2017).

'Investor-to-State Dispute Settlement: Some Facts and Figures' (European Commission, 12 March 2015) p. 6 available at: http://trade.ec.europa.eu/doclib/docs/2015/january/tradoc_153046.pdf (last accessed 4 March 2017).

About Us, http://www.makeinindia.com/about (last accessed 1 July 2017).

Asit Ranjan Mishra, India rejects EU, Canada's bid for global investment pact, http://www.livemint.com/Politics/3mD8bKW3Q6rSiyfQVFcgSM/India-rejects-EU-Canadas-bid-for-global-investment-pact.html (last accessed 1 July 2017).

Deepakshi Sikarwar, 'India seeks fresh treaties with 47 nations', http://economictimes.indiatimes.com/news/economy/foreign-trade/india-seeks-fresh-treaties-with-47-nations/articleshow/52458524.cms?intenttarget=no (last accessed 1 July 2017).

Denunciation of the ICSID Convention and BITS: Impact on Investor-State Claims' IIA Issues Note No. 2 (December 2010, UNCTAD) available at: http://unctad.org/en/Docs/webdiaeia20106_en.pdf (last accessed 4 March 2017).

Ecuador Country Profile, UNCTAD Investment Policy Hub, available at http://investmentpolicyhub.unctad.org/IIA/CountryBits/61 (last accessed 1 July 2017).

Edwina Kwan, 'Australia's Conflicting Approach to ISDS: Where to From Here?', http://kluwerarbitrationblog.com/2015/06/04/australias-conflicting-approach-to-isds-where-to-from-here/ (last accessed 1 July 2017).

Government of India, 'Office Memorandum', available at: http://fipb.gov.in/Forms/OMabolitionFIPB.pdf (accessed 1 July 2017).

International Monetary Fund, 'For India, Strong Growth Persists Despite New Challenges', 22 February 2017, available at: http://www.imf.org/en/News/Articles/2017/02/21/NA022217-For-India-strong-growth-persists-despite-new-challenges.

Vrinda Bhandari, On trial the criminal justice system, The Indian Express (25 September 2014), http://indianexpress.com/article/opinion/columns/on-trial-the-criminal-justice-system/ (accessed 10 July 2017).

Kyla Tienhara, Patricia Ranald Investment Treaty News, 12 July 2011, http://www.iisd.org/itn/2011/07/12/australias-rejection-of-investor-state-dispute-settlement-four-potential-contributing-factors/ (last accessed 1 July 2017).

Lauge N. Skovgaard Poulsen, Jonathan Bonnitcha, Jason Webb Yackee 'Analytical Framework for analyzing Costs and Benefits of Investment Protection Treaties' LSE Enterprise (March 2013) available at http://discovery.ucl.ac.uk/1471852/1/bit%20framework.pdf (last accessed 3 March 2017).

Live Mint referring Nagesh Kumar, South & South-West Asia Office of the United Nations Economic and Social Commission for Asia and the Pacific (UNESCAP) http://www.livemint.com/Money/K1BnZ0ZQV6FhJKsZWcMHVL/India-ranks-10th-in-FDI-inflows-UNCTAD-report.html (last visited 3 March 2017, last accessed 1 July 2017).

Ministry of Micro Small and Medium Enterprises, Government of India, Industrial Policy Resolution (IPR), 1948, http://laghu-udyog.gov.in/policies/iip.htm.

Panji Prasetyo, 'Protecting the government in investor-state dispute' The Jakarta Post 27 June 2016 available at: http://www.thejakartapost.com/news/2016/06/27/protecting-government-investor-state-dispute.html (last accessed 3 March 2017).

Prime Minister's Office, 'Cabinet approves Bilateral Investment Treaty between India and Cambodia to boost investment', http://www.pmindia.gov.in/en/news_updates/cabinet-approves-bilateral-investment-treaty-between-india-and-cambodia-to-boost-investment/ (accessed 19 March 2019).

Reserve Bank of India, 'India's International Investment Position (IIP), December 2016', 31 March 2017; available at: https://www.rbi.org.in/scripts/BS_PressReleaseDisplay.aspx?prid=40023 (last accessed 1 July 2017).

Anup Surendranath, Death is entirely discriminatory, The Hindu (17 September 2012), http://www.thehindu.com/todays-paper/tp-opinion/death-is-entirely-discriminatory/article3905516.ece (accessed 10 July 2017).

The Economic Times, http://economictimes.indiatimes.com/news/economy/foreign-trade/fdi-up-40-to-29-44-bn-in-apr-dec-fy16/articleshow/51175467.cms (last accessed 1 July 2017).

The Economic Times, With $85 trillion, how India can become world's largest economy, 12 November 2011, http://economictimes.indiatimes.com/opinion/et

Bibliography

-commentary/with-85-trillion-how-india-can-become-worlds-largest-economy/ articleshow/10699821.cms. According to PwC Indian economy will be second largest, but the gap between the India and other economies will be large, PwC, 'The world in 2050', p. 2, available at: https://www.pwc.com/gx/en/issues/the-economy/assets/world-in-2050-february-2015.pdf (last accessed 1 July 2017).

The Economist, 'The Arbitration Game', The Economist 11 October 2014 available at http://www.economist.com/news/finance-and-economics/21623756-governments-are-souring-treaties-protect-foreign-investors-arbitration (last accessed 1 July 2017).

The first version of the Model BIT – Ministry of Commerce and Industry, Government of India, Model Text for Indian Bilateral Investment Treaty, https://www.mygov.in/sites/default/files/master_image/Model%20Text%20for%20the%20Indian%20Bilateral%20Investment%20Treaty.pdf (accessed on 19 March 2017).

The Sydney Morning Herald 7 October 2015 available at: http://www.smh.com.au/comment/tobacco-carveout-highlights-risks-of-tpp-20151007-gk38os.html.

UNCTAD, World Investment Report, 12, available at: http://unctad.org/en/PublicationsLibrary/wir2017_en.pdf (last accessed 1 July 2017).

UNCTAD, World Investment Report, 8, 9, available at: http://unctad.org/en/PublicationsLibrary/wir2017_en.pdf (last accessed 1 July 2017).

James Allsop, The Authority of the Arbitrator, Clayton Utz Sydney of University International Arbitration Lecture (2013) https://www.claytonutz.com/ialecture/content/previous/2013/speech_2013 (accessed on 14 July 2017).

Table of Cases

International Investment Treaty Cases

ADC Affiliate Limited and ADC & ADMC Management Limited v. Republic of Hungary, Award, ICSID Case No. ARB/03/16 (2 October 2006), **54**, **55**, **61**, **68**

ADF Group Inc. v. United States of America, Award, ICSID Case No. ARB/(AF)/00/1 (9 January 2003), **106**, **119**

AES Corporation v. The Argentine Republic, Jurisdiction, ICSID Case No. ARB/02/17 (26 April 2005), **74**, **189**

AES Summit Generation Limited v. Republic of Hungary, Award, ICSID Case No. ARB/07/22 (23 September 2010), **187**

Aguas del Tunari, S.A. v. Republic of Bolivia, Jurisdiction, ICSID Case No. ARB/02/3 (21 October 2005), **186**

Aguaytia Energy LLC v. Republic of Peru, Award, ICSID Case No. ARB/06/13 (28 November 2008), 66

Alasdair Ross Anderson et al v. Republic of Costa Rica, Award, ICSID Case No. ARB (AF)/07/3 (19 May 2010), **50**, **51**, **56**

Alpha Projektholding GmbH v. Ukraine, Award, ICSID Case No. ARB/07/16 (8 November 2010), **53**

Amco Asia Corporation and Ors. v. Republic of Indonesia, Award, ICSID Case No. ARB/81/1 (20 November 1984), **68**

American Manufacturing & Trading Inc. v. Republic of Zaire, Award, ICSID Case No. ARB/93/1 (21 February 1997), **74**

Antoine Fabiani (no 1) (France v. Venezuela) (5 Moore International Arbitrations, 31 July 1905), **163**

Antoine Goetz et consorts v. Republique du Burundi, Award, ICSID Case No. ARB/95/3 (10 February 1999), **64**

Archer Daniels Midland Company v. The United Mexican States, Award, ICSID Case No. ARB (AF)/04/5 (21 May 2005), **117**

Asian Agricultural Products Ltd. v. Republic of Sri Lanka, Award, ICSID Case No. ARB/87/3 (27 June 1990), **61**, **74**, **107**

Autopista Concesionada de Venezuela CA v. Venezuela, Award, ICSID Case No. ARB/00/5 (23 September 2003), **66**, **68**

Table of Cases

Azurix Corp. v. The Argentine Republic, Award, ICSID Case No. ARB/01/12 (14 July 2006), **68, 112–113**

Bayindir Insaat Turizm Ticaret ve Sanayi A S v. Pakistan, Award, ICSID Case No. ARB/03/29 (24 August 2009), **61, 117**

Biwater Gauff v. United Republic of Tanzania, Award, ICSID Case No. ARB/05/22 (24 July 2008), **107**

Canuzzi International S.A. v. The Republic of Argentina, ICSID Case No. ARB/03/7 (10 June 2005), **123**

CDC Group plc v. Republic of Seychelles, Decision Annulment, ICSID Case No. ARB/02/14, 34 (29 June 2005), **193, 194**

Ceskoslovenska Obchodni Banka, A.S. v. The Slovak Republic, Decision on Jurisdiction, ICSID Case No. ARB/97/4, para. 54 (1 December 2000), **73**

CMS v. Argentina, Award, ICSID Case No. ARB/01/8 (12 May 2005), **63**

CMS Gas Transmission Company v. The Republic of Argentina, supra n. 15, at para. 117, **64, 68, 74, 105, 106, 190, 193, 194**

Compania de Aguas del Aconquija S.A. and Vivendi Universal S.A. v. Argentine Republic, Award, ICSID Case No. ARB/97/3 (20 August 2007), **4, 68, 106, 107, 113**

Compania del Desarrollo de Santa Elena S.A. v. Republic of Costa Rica, Award, ICSID Case No. ARB/96/1 (8 June 2000), **66**

Consortium Group L.E.S.I.–DIPENTA v. People's Democratic Republic of Algeria, Award, ICSID Case No. ARB/03/8 (10 January 2005) **66, 189**

Consortium R.F.C.C. v. Kingdom of Morocco, Award, ICSID Case No. ARB/00/6 (16 July 2001), **189**

Continental Casualty Company v. The Argentine Republic, Award, ICSID Case No. ARB/03/9 (22 February 2006) **74, 190**

Corn Products International Incorporated v. Mexico, ICSID Case No. ARB (AF)/04/1 (15 January 2008), **117**

Czech Republic v. CME Czech Republic, Case No. T 8735-01, 9 ICSID Report 439, **140**

Duke Energy International Peru Investments No. 1 Ltd. v. Republic of Peru, Decision on Jurisdiction, ICSID Case No. ARB/03/28 (1 February 2006), **66, 73**

El Paso Energy International Company v. The Argentine Republic, ICSID Case No. ARB/03/15, Jurisdiction (27 April 2006), **151, 192**

El Paso Energy International Company v. The Argentine Republic, ICSID Case No. ARB/03/15, Award (31 October 2011), **151, 187**

El Paso Energy International Company v. The Argentine Republic, Decision on Jurisdiction, ICSID Case No. ARB/03/15, para 36 (27 April 2006), **74, 128**

Empresas Lucchetti, S.A. and Lucchetti Peru, S.A. v. The Republic of Peru, Decision on Annulment, ICSID Case No. ARB/03/4 (5 September 2007), **193***Enron Corporation and Ponderosa Assets, L.P. v. Argentine Republic*, Award on Jurisdiction, ICSID Case No. ARB/01/3(14 January 2004), **73, 131**

Fedax N.V. v. The Republic of Venezuela, Award, ICSID Case No. ARB/96/3 (11 July 1977) **77, 190**

Fraport AG Frankfurt Airport Services Worldwide v. The Republic of the Philippines, Award, ICSID Case No. ARB/03/25 (16 August 2007), **42, 47**

Table of Cases

Gas Natural SDG SA v. Argentina, ICSID Case No. ARB/03/10 (17 June 2005), **74**, **131**

Generation Ukraine v. Ukraine, Award, ICSID Case No. ARB/00/9 (16 September 2003), **62**

Genin and Ors v. Estonia, Award, ICSID Case No. ARB/99/2 (25 June 2001), **63**, **119**

Grand River Enterprises Six Nations Ltd v. United States, ICSID Case No. ARB/10/5 (12 January 2011), **119**

Great Britain v. Mexico Claims Commission, Decision No. 55 of 18 June 1931, **162**

Gustavo F W Hamester GmbH & Co KG v. Republic of Ghana, Award, ICSID Case No. ARB/07/24 (18 June 2010), **48**, **57**

Helnan International Hotels A/S v. Arab Republic of Egypt, Decision on Jurisdiction, ICSID Case No. ARB/05/19, 77 (17 October 2006), **189**

Hochtief AG v. Argentina, ICSID Case No. ARB/07/31 (24 October 2011), **74**, **124**

Impregilo S.p.A. v. Islamic Republic of Pakistan, Decision on Jurisdiction, ICSID Case No. ARB/03/3, para. 109, (22 April 2005), **128**

Impregilo S.p.A. v. Pakistan, ICSID Case No. ARB/03/3 (22 April 2005), **128**

Inceysa Vallisoletana S.L. v. Republic of El Salvador, Award, ICSID Case No. ARB/03/26 (2 August 2006), **40**, **48**, **49**, **54**, **56**, **58**, **68**

Inmaris Perestroika Sailing Maritime Services GmbH v. Ukraine, Jurisdiction, ICSID Case No. ARB/08/8 (8 March 2010), **53**, **54**

Ioan Micula, Viorel Micula, SC European Food S.A.S.C. Starmill S.R.L. and S.C. Multipack S.R.L. v. Romania, Award, ICSID Case No. ARB/05/20 (24 September 2008), **65**, **84**

Ioannis Kardassopoulos v. Georgia, Award, ICSID Case No. ARB/05/18 (6 July 2007), **47**, **56**, **63**, **189**

Jan de Nul N.V. and Dredging International N.V. v. Arab Republic of Egypt, Award, ICSID Case No. ARB/04/13 (16 June 2006), **189**

Joy Mining Machinery Limited v. Egypt, Jurisdiction, ICSID Case No. ARB/03/11 (6 August 2004), **73**, **77**, **189**

Klockner Industie-Anlagen GmbH and Ors. v. United Republic of Cameroon, Decision on Annulment, ICSID Case No. ARB/81/2 (3 May 1985), **65**

Lanco International Incorporated v. Argentina, Jurisdiction, ICSID Case No. ARB/97/6 (8 December 1998), **74**

LESI SpA and ASTALDI SpA v. Algeria, Jurisdiction, ICSID Case No. ARB/05/3 (12 July 2006), **189**

LG&E Energy Corp., LG&E Capital Corp., and LG&E International, Inc v. Argentine Republic, Decision on Jurisdiction, ICSID Case No. ARB/02/1, para 73 (30 April 2004), **74**, **128**

Liberian Eastern Timber Corporation (LETCO) v. Government of the Republic of Liberia, Award, ICSID Case No. ARB/83/2 (31 March 1986), **65**, **67**, **139**

Loewen Group, Inc. and Raymond L. Loewen v. United States of America, Award, ICSID Case No. ARB(AF)/98/3 (26 June 2003), **157**

M.C.I. Power Group L.C. and New Turbine, Inc. v. Republic of Ecuador, Award, ICSID Case No. ARB/03/6 (31 July 2007), **66**

Maffezini v. Spain, Award, ICSID Case No. ARB/97/7 (25 January 2000), **63**, **65**, **74**, **123**, **131**

Table of Cases

Malaysian Historical Salvors, SDN, BHD v. The Government of Malaysia, Award, ICSID Case No. ARB/05/10 (16 April 2009), **186, 188, 189**

Mamidoil Jetoil Greek Petroleum Products Societe Anonyme S.A. v. Republic of Albania, Award, ICSID Case No. ARB/11/24 (30 March 2001), **52, 53**

Maritime International Nominees Establishment (MINE) v. Republic of Guinea, Award, ICSID Case No. ARB/84/4 (6 January 1988), **193, 194**

Marvin Roy Feldman Karpa v. United States of Mexico, Award, ICSID Case No. ARB (AF)/99/1, (16 December 2002), **67, 84, 153**

Mihaly International Corporation v. Sri Lanka, Award, ICSID Case No. ARB/00/2 (15 March 2002), **68, 77**

Mr. Patrick Mitchell v. Democratic Republic of the Congo, Award, ICSID Award No. ARB/99/7 (9 February 2004), **73, 189, 194**

MTD v. Republic of Chile, Award, ICSID Case No. ARB/01/7 (25 May 2004), **66, 105, 124**

Noble Energy Inc. v. Republic of Ecuador, Jurisdiction, ICSID Case No. ARB/05/1 (25 March 2008), **189**

Noble Ventures v. Romania, Award, ICSID Case No. ARB/01/11 (5 October 2005), **105, 106**

Occidental Petroleum Corporation and Occidental Exploration and Production Company v. Ecuador, ICSID Case No. ARB/06/11 (24 September 2012), **64, 117**

Palma Consortium Limited v. Bulgaria, ICSID Case No. ARB/03/24 (8 February 2005), **119, 131**

Parkerings-Compagniet AS v. Lithuania, Award, ICSID Case No. ARB/05/8 (14 August 2007), **74, 117**

Phillippe Gruslin v. Malaysia, Award, ICSID Case No. ARB/99/3 (27 November 2000),**63**

Phoenix Action, Ltd. v. The Czech Republic, Award, ICSID Case No. ARB/06/5 (15 April 2009), **43, 74**

Plama Consortium Limited v. Republic of Bulgaria, Award, ICSID Case No ARB/03/24, para. 145 (27 August 2008), **45, 75**

Quiborax S.A. and Non Metallic Minerals S.A v. Plurinational State of Bolivia, Award, ICSID Case No. ARB/06/2 (16 September 2015), **57**

Robert Azinian, Kenneth Davitian & Ellen Baca v. The United Mexican States, Award, ICSID Case No. ARB (AF)/97/2, paras 105, 120 (1 November 1999), **63, 164**

Ronald S. Lauder v. The Czech Republic, Final Award, UNCITRAL, para. 292 (3 September 2001), **105**

Rumeli Telekom A.S. and Telsim Mobil Telekomunikasyon Hizmetleri A.S. v. Republic of Kazakhstan, Awar74d, ICSID Case No. ARB/05/16 (29 July 2008), **168**

Saipem SpA v. The People's Republic of Bangladesh, Award, ICSID Case No. ARB/05/07 (30 June 2009), **61, 68, 161, 189**

Salini Costruttori S.P.A. and Italstrade S.P.A. v. Kingdom of Morocco, Jurisdiction, ICSID Case No. ARB/00/4 (31 July 2001), **47, 73, 128, 188**

Salini Costruttori S.P.A. and Italstrade S.P.A. v. The Hasemite Kingdom of Jordan, Award, ICSID Case No. ARB/02/13 (29 November 2004), **123, 128, 131**

Table of Cases

Sempra Energy International v. Argentina, Award, ICSID Case No. ARB/02/16 (18 September 2007), **64, 74**

SGS Societe Generale de Surveilance S.A. v. Islamic Republic of Pakistan, ICSID Case No. ARB/01/13, Jurisdiction (6 August 2003), **63, 77, 151, 192**

SGS Societe Generale de Surveilance S.A. v. Republic of Philippines, ICSID Case No. ARB/02/6, Jurisdiction (29 January 2004), **63, 106**

Siemens A.G. v. The Argentine Republic, Award, ICSID Case No. ARB/02/8 (17 January 2007), **107, 113, 123, 131, 190**

Sistem Mubendislik Sanayi Ve Ticaret A.S. v. Kyrgyz Republic, Award, ICSID Case No. ARB(AF)/06/1 (30 September 2009), **169**

Societe Generale de Surveillance SA v. The Republic of Paraguay, ICSID Case No. ARB/07/29 (10 February 2012), **106**

Soufraki v. United Arab Emirates, ICSID Case No. ARB/02/7 (5 June 2007), **84, 193**

Southern Pacific Properties (Middle East) Limited v. Arab Republic of Egypt, Award, ICSID Case No. ARB/84/3 (20 May 1992), **54, 65**

Suez Sociedad General de Aguas de Barcelona S.A. and InterAguas Servicipus Intergrales del Agua, S.A. v. The Republic of Argentina, ICSID Case No. ARB/03/17 (16 May 2006), **74, 123**

Tecnicas Medioambientales Tecmed, S.A. v. The United Mexican States, Award, ICSID Case No. ARB (AF)/00/2 (29 May 2003), **66, 105**

Telenor Mobile Communications v. The Hungary, ICSID Case No. ARB/04/15 (13 September 2006), **123, 131**

Tokios Tokeles v. Ukraine, Jurisdiction, ICSID Case No. ARB/02/18 (28 April 2004),**41, 63, 128, 173**

Tza Yap Shum v. The Republic of Peru, ICSID Case No. ARB/07/6 (19 June 2009),**84, 123**

United Mexican States v. Metaclad, Supreme Court of British Columbia, 5 ICSID Report 236, **140**

Urbaser S.A. and Consorcio de Aguas Bilbao Biskaia, Bilbao Biskaia Ur Partzuergoa v. Argentine Republic, Jurisdiction, ICSID Case No. ARB/07/26 (19 December 2012), **57**

Waste Management Inc v. United Mexican States, ICSID Case No. ARB(AF)/00/3, Award (30 April 2004), **105, 151**

Wena Hotels Ltd. v. Arab Republic of Egypt, Award, ICSID Case No. ARB/98/4 (8 December 2000),**61, 107, 194**

Wintershall Aktiegesellschaft v. Argentine Republic, ICSID Case No. ARB/04/14 (8 December 2008), **123, 131**

World Duty Free Company Limited v. Kenya, Award, ICSID Case No. ARB (AF)/00/7 (25 September 2006), **49, 68**

PCIJ and ICJ Cases

Application of the Convention of 1902 Governing the Guardianship of Infants, Judgment, ICJ Reports (1958), **156**

Table of Cases

Barcelona Traction, Light and Power Company Limited (Belgium v. Spain), Merits, [1970] ICJ Reports 3 (5 February 1970), **62**

*Certain German Interests in Polish Upper Sil*esia, Merits, Judgment No. 7, PCIJ Series A, No. 7 (1926), **156**

Differences Relating to Immunity from Legal Process of a Special Rapporteur of the Commission on Human Rights, Advisory Opinion, ICJ. Reports, 62 (1999), **156**

Electronica Sicula S.p.A (ELSI) (United States of America v. Italy), Judgment, ICJ Reports 15 (20 July 1989), **64**

Free Zones of Upper Savoy and District of Gex, Order of 6 December 1930, PCIJ Series A/B, No. 46 (1930), **158**

Greco-Bulgarian 'Communities', Advisory Opinion, PCIJ Series B, No. 17 (1930), **158**

Jurisdiction of the Courts of Danzig, Advisory Opinion, PCIJ Series B, No. 15 (1928), **156**

LaGrand (Germany v. United States), Provisional Measures, Order of 3 March 1999, ICJ Reports 9 (1999), **158**

Pulp Mills on the River Uruguay (Argentina v. Uruguay) [2006] ICJ Reports 113, **131**

SS Lotus (France v. Turkey), Judgment, No. 9, PCIJ Series A, No. 10 (1927), **156**

SS Wimbledon (Britain v. Germany), PCIJ Series A, No. 1 (1923), **158**

The Ambatielos Claim (Greece v. United Kingdom), Merits, Judgment, ICJ Reports 10 (1953), **176**

The Oscar Chinn Case (Belgium v. United Kingdom), Judgment, PCIJ Series A/B, No. 63 (12 December 1934), **97**

Treatment of Polish Nationals and Other Persons of Polish Origin or Speech in the Danzing Territory, Advisory Opinion, PCIJ Series A/B, No. 44 (1932), **158**

UNCITRAL Cases

EnCana Corporation v. Republic of Ecuador, Award, LCIA Case No. UN3481, UNCITRAL (3 February 2006), **62**

Ethyl Corporation v. The Government of Canada, Jurisdiction, UNCITRAL (24 June 1998), **4**

*Link-Trading Joint Stock Company v. Department for Customs Control of Moldov*a, Final Award, UNCITRAL (18 April 2002), **67, 97, 153**

Merrill & Ring Forestry L.P. v. The Government of Canada, Award, UNCITRAL (9 January 2003), **68, 106, 107**

Methanex Corporation v. United States of America, Award, UNCITRAL (3 August 2005), **67, 68, 98**

Sergei Paushok, CJSC Golden East Company and CJSC Vostokneftegaz Company v. Government of Mongolia, Jurisdiction, UNCITRAL (28 April 2011), **54**

Swembalt AB, Sweden v. The Republic of Latvia, Award, UNCITRAL (23 October 2000), **63**

Vodafone International Holdings BV v. India, UNCITRAL (17 April 2014), **154**

White Industries Australia Ltd. v. Republic of India, UNCITRAL, Final Award, (Award of 30 November 2011), **73, 77, 162**

Cases from Indian Courts

ABL International Ltd. v. Export Credit Guarantee Corporation of India, 3 SCC 553 (2004), **153**
Ashok Sadarangani & Anr. v. Union of India, 11 SCC 321 (2012), **148**
Baldev Singh v. State of Punjab, AIR SC 1231 (2011), **163**
Bandhua Mukti Morcha v. Union of India (UOI) and Ors, 3 SCC 161 (1984), **159**
Bharat Aluminium Co. v. Kaiser Aluminium Technical Services Inc., 9 SCC 552 (2012), **141**
Bhim Singh v. Union of India, 4 RCR (Criminal) 234 (2014), **163**
Binny Ltd v. V Sadasivan, 6 SCC 657 (2005), **152**
Bishamber Dayal Chandra Mohan v. State of Uttar Pradesh, 1 SCC 39 (1982), **100**
Bombay Dyeing & Manufacturing Co v. State of Bombay, SCR 1122 (1958), **101**
Brijendra Singh v. State of Uttar Pradesh, 1 SCC 597 (1981), **48**
Canara Bank v. Debashish Das, AIR SC 2041 (2003), **166**
Central Inland Water Transport Corporation Ltd v. Brojo Nath Ganguly, 3 SCC 156 (1986), **143**
Centre for Public Interest Litigation v. Union of India (2G Spectrum Case), 1 CGBCLJ 209 (2012), **31, 159**
Chairman, Indore Vikas Pradhikaran v. Pure Industrial Coke & Chemicals Ltd., 8 SCC 705 (2007), **100**
Chandrakant Patil v. State, 3 SCC 38 (1998), **148**
Chiranjit Lal v. Union of India, SCR 869 (1950), **101**
Commissioner Hindu Religious Endowment v. Lakshmichandra, SCR 1005 (1954), **101**
Dallal v. Bank Mellat, X1 Yearbook of Commercial Arbitration 547, [1986] 1 QB 441, **136**
Delhi Cloth and General Mills v. Union of India, 4 SCC 166 (1983), **153**
Delhi Development Authority v. Skipper Construction Co. (P) Ltd., 4 SCC 62 (1996), **148**
Delhi Science Forum v. Union of India, 2 SCC 405 (1996), **183**
Dhakeswari Cotton Mills v. CIT, 26 ITR 775 (1954), **166**
Director of Settlements, AP and Ors. v. M.R. Apparao & Anr., 4 SCC 638 (2002), **148**
DLF Qutab Enclave Complex Educational Charitable Trust v. State of Haryana, 5 SCC 622 (2003), **101**
Dwarka Nath v. ITO, AIR SC 81 (1996), **153**
Dwarka Prasad Agarwal v. B D Agarwal, 6 SCC 230 (2003), **152**
Dwarka v. Sholapur Mills, SCR 674 (1954), **101**
Excel Wear v. Union of India, 4 SCC 224 (1978), **183**
Express Newspapers (P) Ltd. v. Union of India, 3 SCR Supl. (1985), **153**
Flamingo Duty Free Shop Ltd. v. Union of India, (110) BomLR 1730 (2008), **159**
Food Corporation of India v. Kamdhenu Cattle Feed Industries, 1 SCC 71 (1993), **111**
In Re: Inhuman Conditions in 1382 Prisons, 3 SCC 700 (2016), **163**
Indian Handicrafts Emporium v. Union of India, 7 SCC 589 (2003), **99, 101**
Jilubhai Nanbhai Khachar v. State of Gujarat, Supp (1) 596 (1995), **99**
Joshi Technologies International Inc. v. Union of India, 7 SCC 728 (2015), **151**

Table of Cases

Karaha Bodas Co LLC v. Perusahan Pertambangan Minyak Dan Gas Bumi Negara et all, 4 SLR 345 [2006], **137**
Kasturi Lal Lakshmi Reddy v. State of Jammu and Kashmir, 4 SCC 1 (1980), **109**
Keshavanandha Bharti v. State of Kerala, 4 SCC 225 (1973), **99**
Koch Navigation v. Hindustan Petroleum, Supp. 1 SCR 70 [1989], **140**
KT Plantation (P) Ltd. v. State of Kerala, 9 SCC 1 (2011), **155**
Life Insurance Corporation of India v. Escorts Ltd., 1 SCC 264 (1986), **151**
M Naga Venkata Lakshmi v. Vishakhapatnam Municipal Corporation, 8 SCC 748 (2007), **100**
Mafatlal Industries Ltd. v. Union of India, 5 SCC 536 (1997), **153**
Mahabir Auto Stores v. Indian Oil Corporation, 3 SCC 752 (1990), **150**
Maneka Gandhi v. Union of India, 1 SCC 248 (1978), **152**
Manohar Lal Sharma v. Principle Secretary (Coal Block Allocation Case), 9 SCC 5 16 (2014), **159**
Martini Case (Italy v. Venezuela), X RIAA 644 (8 July 1904), **157, 161**
Merill and Ring Frosty v. Canada, Award, IIC 427 (2010), **68, 106**
Minmetals Germany GmbH v. Ferco Steel Ltd 1 All ER (Comm) 315 (1999), **143**
MM Pathak v. Union of India, (2) SCC 50 (1978), **101**
Montano Case (Peru v. USA), 2 Moore International Arbitrations 1630 (1863), **161**
MP Oil Extraction v. State of Madhya Pradesh, 7 SCC 592 (1997), **111**
Mumbai Kamgar Sabha, Bombay v. M/S Abdulbhai Faizullabhai & Ors, AIR SC 1455 (1976), **159**
Murlidhar Aggarwal v. State of UP 2 SCC 472 (1974), **144**
National Buildings Construction Corporation v. S Raghunathan, 7 SCC 66 (1998), **111**
National Central Cooperative Bank v. Ajay Kumar, AIR SC 39 (1994), **166**
National Textiles Worker's Union v. PR Ramkrishnan, 1 SCC 228 (1983), **183**
Navjyoti Co-operative Group Housing Society v. Union of India, 4 SCC 477 (1992), **111**
Niko Resources Limited v. Union of India, 347 ITR 369 (Guj) (2015), **153**
Novratis AG and Ors v. Union of India & Ors, AIR SC 1311 (2013), **159**
Punjab Communications Ltd. v. Union of India (1999) 4 SCC 727, **110**
Purushottam Dashrath Borate & Anr. v. State of Maharashtra, 6 SCC 652 (2015), **163**
R.C. Cooper v. Union of India, 3 SCR 530 (1970), **153**
Ramachandra Rao v. State of Karnataka, 4 SCC 578 (2002), **147–148**
Re Vinay Chandra Mishra, 2 SCC 585 (1995), **148**
R. M. Investment & Trading Co. Pvt. Ltd. v. Boeing Co. and Anr., 1 SCR 837 [1994], **140**
Renusagar Power Co Ltd. v. General Electric Co, Supp (1) SCC 644 (1984), **140, 143**
Renusagar Power Co. Ltd. v. General Electric Co. and Anr. 1 SCR 432 [1985], **140**
RK Garg v. Union of India, 4 SCC 675 (1981), **109**
Rupa Ashok Hurra v. Ashok Hurra and Anr., 4 SCC 388 (2002), **148**
Sahara India Real Estate Corporation Ltd and Ors. v. Securities and Exchange Board of India and Anr, 10 SCC 603 (2012), **147**
Sakal Papers (P) Ltd. and Others v. Union of India, 3 SCR 842 (1962), **153**
Santosh Kumar Satish Bhusan Bariyar v. State of Maharashtra, 6 SCC 498 (2009), **163–164**

Shrilekha Vidyarthi (Kumari) v. State of Uttar Pradesh, 1 SCC 212 (1991), **150**
Sitaram Sugar Co. Ltd v. Union of India, 3 SCC 223 (1990), **110**
South Central Railway Employees Cooperative Credit Society Employees Union v. B. Yashodabai and Ors, 2 SCC 727 (2015), **148**
State of Madhya Pradesh v. Nandlal Jaiswal, 4 SCC 566 (1986), **109**
State of Madhya Pradesh v. Ranojirao Shinde, SCR 489 (1968), **101**
State of Mysore v. KC Adiga, (2) SCC 495 (1976), **100**
State of Punjab v. O.G.B. Syndicate, 5 SCR 387 (1964), **155**
Subhash Kumar v. State of Bihar and Ors, 1 SCR 5 (1991), **159**
Sunil Batra v. Delhi Administration, 4 SCC 494 (1978), **159**
Supreme Court Advocates on Record Association v. Union of India, 4 SCC 441 (1993), **148**
Supreme Court Bar Assn. v. Union of India, 4 SCC 409 (1994), **148**
Tata Engineering and Locomotive Co. Ltd. v. State of Bihar, 6 SCR 885 (1964), **152**
Tata Press Ltd. v. Mahanagar Telephone Nigam Ltd., 5 SCC 139 (1995), **152**
The State of Kerala v. General Manager, Southern Railways, AIR SC 2538 (1976), **155**
Timken India Limited and Ors. v. Deputy Commissioner of Income Tax and Ors., 4 TMI 592 (2016), **153**
ONGC Ltd v. Saw Pipes Ltd, 5 SCC 705, **145**
Renusagar Power Co Ltd. v. General Electric Co, **140**
Murlidhar Aggarwal v. State of UP, 2 SCC 472 (1974), **144**
Union of India v. Hindustan Development Corporation, 3 SCC 499 (1993), **109**
Vellore Citizens Welfare Forum v. Union of India & Ors, AIR SC 2715 (1986), **159**
Vincent Narain v. Union of India, 1 SCC 226 (1999), **159**
VJ Ferreira v. Bombay Muncipality, 1 SCC 70 (1972), **101**
Vodafone International Holdings BV v. Union of India, 6 SCC 613 (2012), **154**
Zaheer Mauritius v. Director of Income Tax, 7 HCC (Del) 271 (2014), **153**

Other Cases

Achmea B.V v. Slovak Republic, Award, PCA Case No. 2008-13 (7 December 2012), **53**
Actival International SA v. Conservas El Pilar SA, 27 YB Com Arb 528-532 (Tribunal Supremo (Supreme Court) Madrid 2002), **143**
AIG Capital Partners Inc and others v. Republic of Kazakhstan and others (2006) 1 All ER 284 [2006] EWHC Civ 1529, **139**
Ambatielos Claim (Greece v. UK), XII RIAA 83, 120 (6 March 1956), **165, 176**
Beschluss des VII Zicilsenats vom 4.10.2005-VII ZB 9/05. Bundesgerichtshof (German Federal Supreme Court) found at 2 (5) TDM (2005), **139**
BG Group PLC v. Republic of Argentina, US Supreme Court, 572 US I (2014) 9, **65, 140**
Chattin Case (US v. Mexico) IV (Sale No.1951, V.1) RIAA 282 (23 July 1927), **156**
Chemtura v. Canada, Award, IIC 451 (2010), **107, 67**
Council of Civil Service Unions v. Minister for the Civil Service, 3 All ER 935 (1984), **112**
Dallal v. Bank Mellat, X1 Yearbook of Commercial Arbitration, 547 at 553 (1986), **136**

Table of Cases

Disputes Concerning the Interpretation of Article 79 of the Treaty of Peace, RIAA, vol XIII (Sales No. 64.V.3) (1955), **156**
Eastern Sugar B.V. v. Czech Republic, SCC Case No. 088/2004 (2004), **4, 64**
El Oro Mining Company (Great Britain) v. Mexico, V. RIAA 191, **162**
Emanuel Too v. Greater Modesto Insurance Associates, Award, No. 460-880-2, (1989) 23 Iran-USCTR 378 (29 December 1989), **97**
French Seller v. German Buyer, (Oberlandesgericht Munich (23 November 2009), **143**
French Seller v. German Buyer, Bundesgerichtshof (16 December 2010), 36 YB Com Arb 273 (2011), **143**
Frontier Petroleum Services Ltd. v. The Czech Republic, Award, IIC 465 (2010) (12 November 2010), **107, 113**
Gami Investments v. Mexico, IIC 109 (2004) (15 November 2004), **74, 118**
Himpurna California Energy Ltd. v. Indonesia, Interim Award, (2000) XXV Yearbook of Commercial Arbitration 11 (26 September 1991), **157**
Karaha Boda Co. LLC v. Perusahaan Pcrtambangan Minyak Dan Gas Bumi Negaraetall & Perushaan Pertambangan Minyak Dan Gas Bumi Degara, 29 Yearbook of Commercial Arbitration 1262 (US Court of Appeals, 5th Circuit, 23 Mar. 2004), **137**
Liberian Eastern Timber Corporation (LETCO) v. Government of the Republic of Liberia, 659 F Supp. 73, **139, 67**
Minmetals Germany GmbH v. Ferco Steel Ltd, 1 All ER (Comm) 315, 331 (England 1999), **143**
National Grid Public Limited Company v. Argentina, Case 1:09-cv-00248-RBW (3 November 2008), **65, 74, 119, 131**
Occidental Exploration and Production Company (OEPC) v. Ecuador, Award, LCIA Case No. UN3467 (1 July 2004), **106, 64**
PT First Media TBK (formerly known as PT Broadband Multimedia TBK) v. Astro Nusantara International BV and others, SGCA 57, 90 (Singapore 2013), **143**
PT First Media TBK v. Astro Nusantara International BV, SGCA 57 (2013), **143**
Republic of Ecuador v. United States of America, PCA Case No. 2012-5, **130**
Romak S.A. v. The Republic of Uzbekistan, Award, PCA Case No. AA280 (26 November 2009), **73, 187**
RosInvestCo UK Ltd. v. The Russian Federation, Case No. 079/2005 (October 2007), **123**
Saluka Investments BV (The Netherlands) v. The Czech Republic, Partial Award, ICGJ 368 (PCA 2006) (17 March 2006), **67, 97**
Salvador Commercial Company, UNRIAA, vol XV (Sale No.55 V.3) (1902), **156**
SD Myers Incorporated v. Canada, 2004 FC 38 (13 January 2004), **117**
Sea-Land Service, Inc v. The Islamic Republic of Iran, Award, No. 135-33-1 (1984) 6 Iran-USCTR 149, 150-4 (20 June 1984), **97**
Sedelmayer v. Russian Federation (Germany/Soviet Union BIT), Decision on Jurisdiction and Final Award, 2 Stockholm Int'l Arb.Rev. 1 (7 July 1998), **139**
Societe PT Putrabali Adyamulia v. Societe Rena Holding et Societe Moguntia Est Epices, Cour de cassation, France, 05-18.053 (29 June 2007), **143**
Vladimir Berchader *and Moise Berschader v. The Russian Federation*, Case No. 080/2005 (April 2006), **123**

William Nagel v. The Czech Republic, Award, SCC Case No. 049/2002 (9 September 2003), **63**

Yaung Chi Trading Ltf v. Government of the Union of Myanmar, Award, ASEAN ID Case No. ARB/01/1 (31 March 2003), **52**

Table of Statutes

Banking Companies (Acquisition and Transfer of Undertakings) Ordinance, 1969, 183
Bolivian Constitution 2009, 170
Constitution of India, 1950, 147
Contempt of Courts Act, 1961, 154
Foreign Exchange Management Act (FEMA), 1999, 40
Foreign Exchange Regulation Act (FERA), 1973, 15, 26, 39, 45
Indian Arbitration and Conciliation Act, 1996, 139
Land Acquisition Act, 2013, 101
Right to Fair Compensation and Transparency in Land Acquisition, Rehabilitation and Resettlement Act, 2013, 101

Table of Treaties and Other Legal Instruments

Albania-Croatia BIT, 108
Argentina-Spain BIT, 115, 122, 123
ASEAN Comprehensive Investment Agreement (adopted 26 February 2009, entered into force 29 February 2012), 157
ASEAN Framework Agreement on the ASEAN Investment Area, 1998, 108
BLEU (Belgium-Luxemburg Economic Union)-India BIT
Bosnia and Herzegovinia-India BIT, 70, 78, 122, 134
Brunei Darussalam-India BIT, 135
Croatia-Ukraine BIT, 1997, 108
France-India BIT, 27, 91, 93, 121
India Model BIT (1993), 26
India Model BIT (2003), 7, 27
India Model BIT (2015), 6, 7, 27, 31, 32, 36, 38, 39, 46, 49, 61, 62, 69, 75, 83, 86, 87, 89, 91, 96–98, 104, 108, 125, 127, 129, 135, 196, 197
India Netherlands BIT, 27, 60, 78, 94, 103
India-Armenia BIT, 60, 69, 70, 80, 82, 90, 95, 102, 120, 129–132, 134, 135
India-Australia BIT, 30, 37, 38, 60, 73, 77, 81, 93, 95, 103, 104, 115, 120, 162, 163
India-Austria BIT, 37, 38, 60, 80, 83, 90, 92, 93, 96, 103, 120, 134
India-Bahrain BIT, 60, 70, 80, 82, 89, 92, 93, 95, 103, 120, 129
India-Bangladesh BIT, 27, 60, 78, 89, 92, 93, 95, 103, 121, 129, 130, 135
India-Belarus BIT, 72, 81, 92, 93, 96, 103, 121, 135
India-Bulgaria BIT, 70, 81, 89, 96, 103, 121
India-Columbia BIT, 90, 92, 94, 96, 107, 108, 117, 124
India-Congo BIT, 70, 79, 89, 95, 103, 121
India-Croatia BIT, 60, 70, 81, 95, 121
India-Cyprus BIT, 70, 78, 89, 94, 96, 103, 132, 135
India-Czech Republic BIT, 60, 72, 80, 82, 89, 94, 103, 121, 130, 134, 135
India-Denmark BIT, 27, 60, 78, 92, 96, 122
India-Djibouti BIT, 70, 78, 92, 95, 121, 132
India-Egypt BIT, 70, 78, 93, 103, 121, 135
India-Ethiopia BIT, 70, 80, 82, 95
India-Finland BIT, 60, 70, 81, 82, 94, 96, 132, 135
India-Germany BIT, 4, 27, 38, 59, 72, 79, 89, 94, 96, 103, 122

Table of Treaties and Other Legal Instruments

India-Ghana BIT, 60, 70, 80, 92, 95, 103, 121, 134
India-Hungary BIT, 79, 89, 94, 95, 103, 132
India-Iceland BIT, 70, 79, 95, 103, 121, 129, 132
India-Indonesia BIT, 16, 27, 70, 78, 92, 96, 103, 134
India-Israel BIT, 60, 70, 78, 95, 103, 121, 130, 134, 135
India-Italy BIT, 27
India-Jordan BIT, 78, 92, 103, 132
India-Kazakhstan BIT, 60, 70, 79, 121, 132, 134
India-Korea BIT, 60, 79, 89, 115, 121, 134
India-Kuwait BIT, 30, 60, 78, 89, 90, 92, 94, 96, 104, 163
India-Kyrgyzstan BIT, 67, 70, 78, 132
India-Lao PDR BIT, 60, 70, 78, 95, 121
India-Latvia BIT, 60, 70, 79, 94, 95, 104, 122, 132, 134, 135
India-Lithuania BIT, 70, 92, 93, 104, 132, 134, 135
India-Macedonia BIT, 71, 79, 82, 96, 104, 135
India-Malaysia BIT, 38, 61, 72, 93, 96, 130, 134
India-Mauritius BIT, 29, 80, 103
India-Mexico BIT, 27, 61, 75, 81, 82, 90, 107, 117, 135
India-Myanmar BIT, 71, 79, 121, 132
India-Nepal BIT, 16, 60, 71, 72, 79, 90, 91, 96, 103, 134
India-Oman BIT, 71, 78, 95, 132
India-Poland BIT, 27, 81, 103, 129, 132
India-Portugal BIT, 81, 82, 94, 130
India-Qatar BIT, 71, 81, 82, 90, 93, 96, 130
India-Russia BIT, 81, 96, 103, 135
India-Saudi Arabia BIT, 27, 81, 82, 90, 104
India-Senegal BIT, 71, 81, 82, 102
India-Singapore Comprehensive Economic Cooperation Agreement, 2005, 108
India-Singapore Free Trade Agreement, 2003, 106
India-Slovenia BIT, 71, 81, 90
India-Sudan BIT, 27, 71, 78, 132
India-Syria BIT, 71, 81, 82, 134
India-Tajikistan BIT, 71, 78, 132
India-Thailand BIT, 27, 71, 79, 82, 95, 132
India-Trinidad and Tobago BIT, 71, 79, 103, 132
India-Turkey BIT, 71, 81, 82, 90, 96
India-Turkmenistan BIT, 71, 79, 132
India-UAE BIT, 92
India-Yemen BIT, 72, 79, 90
India-Zimbabwe BIT, 72, 79, 96
Indian Model BIT, ix, 32, 39, 75, 76, 87, 129, 131
Investment Agreement for the COMESA Common Investment Area (23 May 2007), 157
New-Zealand-Singapore Free Trade Agreement, 2001, 108
New-Zealand-Thailand Closer Economic Partnership Agreement, 2005, 108
Protocol, India-China BIT, 27, 38, 60, 70, 78, 91, 93, 95, 103, 121, 134

Trans Pacific Partnership Agreement, 6, 106
Treaty Between the Government of United States of America and the Government of Rwanda Concerning the Encouragement and Reciprocal Protection of Investment (Rwanda-United States of America) (adopted 19 February 2008, entered into force 1 January 2012), 157
Treaty of Amity, Commerce and Navigation, US-Congo, 88
Treaty of Friendship, Commerce and Navigation, US-Nicaragua 1867, 88
United States-Singapore Free Trade Agreement, 106

Others

International Center for Settlement of Investment Disputes, Convention on the Settlement of Investment Disputes, Convention on the Settlement of Investment Disputes Between States and Nationals of Other States: Documents Concerning the Origin and the Formulation of the Convention (1968), 178
Agreement Establishing IFAD (1976), 180
Agreement Establishing the African Development Bank (1963), 180
Geneva Protocol, 1923, 140
ILC Draft Declaration on Rights and Duties of States, General Assembly Resolution 375 (IV), Annex, Article 13 (6 December 1949), 158
ICSID Administrative and Financial Regulations, 179
ICSID Arbitration Rules, 133, 135, 181
ICSID Convention and Conciliation and Arbitration Rules 11 (2), 189
ICSID Report 2013, 171
Preamble of UN Charter, declaration of Sixth Committee, 172
Report of the Executive Directions on the Convention on the Settlement of Investment Disputes Between States and Nationals of Other States (ICSID), 73, 171, 178, 191
Report of the Executive Directors to the Convention, 1 ICSID Reports, 173, 178,
Rome Statute of the International Criminal Court, 181
Seventy-eighth report on Congestion of Under-Trial prisoners in Jails, Law Commission of India, D.O. No. F.2(19)/78-L.C, (February 1979), 163
Statement of Object and Reasons, Constitution (Forty-Fourth) Constitutional Amendment Act, 1978, para 5, 98
Third Report on Diplomatic Protection, International Law Commission, UN Doc. A/CN. 4/523 (2002), 162
U.N. Convention on the Law of the Sea (1982), 180
UNCTAD, Admission and Establishment, UNCTAD Series on Issues in International Investment Agreements, 2002, 36
United Nations Convention on Jurisdictional Immunities of States of States and Their Property, 138
United Nations Economic and Social Council, 'The Promotion of the International Law of Private Capital: Progress Report by Secretary General, E/3325 (26 February 1960), 175
World Bank, World Development Report 2005, 5

Index

A

Administrative
  action, 87
  audi alterem partem, 166
  authorities, 111, 113
  bodies, 107
  British administrative law, 110
  cost, 130
  Council, 184
  decision, 150–151, 158
  FET, 105
  exercises of administrative power, 115
  expenses, 148
  and financial regulations, 179
  issues, 159
  law, 63, 115
  legitimate expectations, 110
  mandatory rules, 62
  Model BIT, 134
  proceedings, 77, 109
  resolution, 177
  review, administrative actions, 115
  simple administrative order, ICSID, 178
Aliens, 17, 19, 20, 35, 160, 161, 179, 182
Applicable law
  Art. 11, India-Germany BIT, 59
  Art. 38(1), Stature of the ICJ, 67–68
  BITs, 60–61
  Constitution of India, 67
  domestic law, 62–64
  international law and domestic law, 64–66
  and jurisdiction
    international tribunal, 69
    investment, 69–77
    investor, 78–86
  015 Model BIT, 69
  LCIA Rules of Arbitration, 59
  legal principles, 59
  2015 Model BIT, 61–62
  New York Convention (NYC), 66–67
  procedural law, investment treaty arbitration (ITA), 59
  UNCITRAL Rules on Arbitration, 59
  World Trade Organization, 68
Arbitrary actions, 4
Article 226 of the Constitution of India, 148–150, 153
Article 42(1) of the ICSID Convention, 47
Asset
  acquiring, host State, 3
  determination of character of, 62
  domestic law, 65
  enforcement, 137, 138
  enterprise, 73
  foreign investment, 41
  form of, 72
  German Law, 139
  ICSID Convention, 136
  immunity, 181
  investment, 37, 69, 72, 141

225

Index

neutralization, 168
open-ended, 74
ownership of, 51
procurement and transfer, 53
protection, 75
reconstruction companies, 44
transit and entry fee, 139
types of, 186
value, 94, 97
Asset based definition, 74
Automatic route, 42, 43

B

Bilateral Investment Promotion and Protection Agreements (BIPA), 6, 27
Bona fide, 48, 49, 58, 67, 86, 111, 112, 114, 154, 165
Bribery, 49–51

C

Cabinet Committee on Economic Affairs (CCEA), 42
Cap(s)
  compliance, 44
  conditions, 44
  domestic ownership, 15
  investment, 41, 43
  nature of, 42
  restrictions, 44
  sectoral, 43, 45
Central Government, 14, 28, 42, 155, 157
Charter on Economic Rights and Duties of States, 15
China
  'cooling-off' period, 130–132 (AU: The locators do not relate to China. Please advice)
  commercial, 7, 14, 16, 21, 37, 39, 63, 73, 77, 96–98, 138–140, 150, 192 (AU: The locators do not relate to China. Please advice)
  commercial arbitration, 30, 59, 77, 138–140, 144, 167, 169, 175 (AU: The locators do not relate to China. Please advice)
compensation, 197
conditions of entry, 38
confidential information, 133 (AU: The locator do not relate to China. Please advice)
Constitution of India
  Amendment, 182
  Art. 14, 151, 152
  Art. 19, 152
  Art. 19(1)(f), 98
  Art. 21, 152
  Art. 31, 98
  Art. 32, 157
  Art. 73, 40
  Art. 132, 147
  Art. 141, 67, 170
  Art. 300-A, 99
  functional independence, 148
  fundamental rights, 99
  right to property, 99
  standards of treatment, 196
Contract
  allocation of property, 140
  breach of, 151
  capacity, 181
  commercial, 139
  concession, 65, 70
  illegal, 144
  investment treaty, 186
  joint venture, 44
  MSEB, 28
  procure, 50

226

public procurement, 151
remedy of arbitration, 29
responsibility, 163
rights to money, 69
service, 49
transactions, 139
Control of property, 101
Corporate planning, 13, 22
Corporate restructuring, 85
Creeping expropriation, 169
Customary international law
   denial of justice, 160, 161, 170
   and domestic law, 61
   FET standard, 107
   foreign investment, 25
   limitation, 36
   primary responsibility, 176
   principle of, 138
   Regulatory freedom of States, 67, 97
   rule, 156
   standard of the international minimum standard, 105, 106
   State responsibility, 20
   treatment of foreigners/aliens, 17
   violation, 108

D

Dabhol Power, 28, 29
Debentures, 41, 42, 45, 69
Defence
   Constitution of India, 157
   CPC Sect. 79, 155
   enforcement proceedings, 137
   estoppel, 49
   illegality, 53–56
   industry, 44
   investment claim, 63
   manufacturing sectors, 2
   recognition, 136
   substantive, 56, 57
   violation of international law obligations, 66

Delays
   causes, 154
   denial of justice, 163
   ground of, 55
   Indian judicial system, 30, 160, 162, 163
   ruinous/equivalent to refusal, 161
Denial of benefits, 86
Denial of justice
   Art. 38(1), The Statute of the ICJ, 160
   Azinia v. Mexico, 164–166
   bona fide errors of the judiciary, 165
   customary international law, 160
   definition, 160
   elements, 169
   factors, 163
   and FET, 104, 167
   fundamental breaches of due process, 166
   grounds of, 154, 157, 161
   identification, 161
   India-Kuwait BIT, 163
   Indian courts, 163
   investment disputes, 68
   investment treaties, 161
   judicial/administrative proceedings, 109
   limitations, rules of, 169
   MFN clause, India-Australia BIT, 162–163
   procedural unfairness, 164
   remedies, 161–162
   Saipem v. Bangladesh, 160–161
   scope of, 170
   White Industries v. India, 162
Diplomatic protection
   arbitration, 25
   doctrine of, 18
   foreign investment disputes, 176
   ICSID Convention, 177
   invocation of, home State of the foreigner, 17
   State responsibility, 18, 19

Index

UN Charter, 19
Domestic courts, 3, 20, 27, 30, 62, 65, 89, 134, 136, 138, 141, 143, 149, 157, 161, 164, 165, 169, 170, 182, 190–193
Domestic law
 accommodation, 62
 analysis of, 109–110
 application of, 62
 asset, 65
 and customary international law, 61
 denial of justice, 160
 disputes, investment, 62
 effect of *renvoi*, 62
 enforcement of award, 137, 138
 expropriation, 98–102
 FPS, 104
 good faith, 48, 49
 host State, 47, 66
 ICSID award, 191, 192
 ILC Draft Articles on State Responsibility, 157
 and international law, 64–66
 investment, 44, 47
 2015 Model BIT, 38
 protection, 5, 63, 182
 quasi-judicial body constitution, 28
 requirement of compliance, 37, 46
 rules, 133
 source, 67
 Spain, 65
 standard of public policy, 144
 violations, 52–56, 63, 145, 161
Double nationality, 80

E

Effect equivalent to
 direct expropriation, 91, 97
 expropriation, 89
 India-Columbia BIT, 89, 90
 indirect expropriation and measures, 89, 90
 Mexico-India BIT, 89, 90
 nationalization, 89, 90

Enforcement
 commercial arbitration, 167
 contract, 144
 dispute resolution provisions, 127-13
 foreign awards, 141, 192
 ICSID award, 192
 investment awards, 135–140
 mechanisms, 175, 185
 place of, 142
 proceedings, Indian Arbitration Act, 139, 140
 refusal, 142, 143
 rights, 196
 and setting aside of an arbitration award, 141
 time of, 142
Enterprise based definition, 32, 75, 76, 197
Entry and operation
 conditions, 35
 consequences of violation (*see* Illegality)
 FCN treaties, 35
 foreign investment and investors, India, 9, 36
 Indian arbitral practice
  Art. 1102.1, NAFTA, 36–37
  Australia-India BIT, 37–38
  'controlled entry model', 37
  FPS, FET and NT, 38
  'liberalized entry model', 36–37
  2015 Model BIT, 38–39, 46
  patterns of, 37
 liberal model of, 197
 regulatory framework, India
  approval process, FIPB, 42–43
  authorities, 45
  capital investment, 41–42
  control, 39
  FDI Policy, 39–41, 45, 46
  FEMA Regulations, 42
  foreign investment, 42
  RBI Act, 39
  restrictions, 44
  sectoral limitations and caps, 43–45

228

Index

Erga omnes, 137
Established and acquired, 72
Estoppel
   application of, 55
   defence of, 49
   illegalities, investment, 55
   and legitimate expectations, 114
   period of limitation, 55
   principle of, 54
Exhaustion of local remedies, 31, 161–163
Expropriation
   BITs, 88
   direct, 168
   domestic law of India, 98–102
   indirect, 168–169
   investment treaties, 89–98
   judicial, 168, 169
   nationalization, 88
   NIEO, 88
   provisions, 101–102
   right to fair compensation and transparency, land acquisition, 101
   and threat of nationalization, 174
   types of, 169

F

Fair and equitable treatment (FET)
   acts of judiciary, 167–168
   and FPS
      analysis of domestic law, 109–110
      legitimate expectations, 110–115, 160
      treaty practice, 102–109
   principle, 46
   treatment standards, 32, 38
   violation, 46
FCN. *See* Friendship Commerce and Navigation Treaties (FCN)
FEMA. *See* Foreign Exchange Management Act (FEMA)
FERA. *See* Foreign Exchange Regulation Act (FERA)
FIPB. *See* Foreign Investment Promotion Board (FIPB)
Foreign direct investment (FDI), 26, 42, 45, 46, 154
Foreign Direct Investment Policy (FDI Policy), 2, 8, 36, 39–43, 45, 46
Foreign Exchange Management Act (FEMA), 26, 39, 40, 42, 45
Foreign Exchange Regulation Act (FERA), 15, 19, 26, 39, 45
Foreign Investment Promotion Board (FIPB), 26, 41–43
Fork in the road, 134
FPS. *See* Full protection and security (FPS)
Fraud, 28, 48–53, 57, 85, 142, 145, 164
Free Trade Agreements (FTA), 3, 27, 36
Friendship Commerce and Navigation Treaties (FCN), 35, 88, 176
FTA. *See* Free Trade Agreements (FTA)
Full protection and security (FPS), 8, 38, 87, 102–115
Fundamental rights, 11, 12, 99, 144, 150, 152, 159

G

General Assembly, UN
   NIEO, 24, 25
   participation, 20
   resolutions, 21–23, 88
General principles of law, 61, 63, 67, 114
Germany
   BITs, 4, 25, 27, 38, 59, 72, 79, 94, 122, 176
   The Federal Court of Justice, 139
   insurance schemes, 174
   Trade Agreements, 16
Good faith
   breach of, 54
   compliance, 129
   conditions, entry and operation, 47
   dispute resolution, 130
   effort, 131

Index

FET, 105
foreign investor, 53, 73
Gain Protection of Investment Treaties, 48–51
Indian Model BIT, 75
Intentional withholding of information, 45
investment arbitration, 46
legitimate expectations, 110
2015 Model BIT, 75
Government route, 42, 43

H

High Court, 28–30, 147–150, 154, 159, 196
Hull formula, 25

I

IBRD. *See* International Bank for Reconstruction and Development (IBRD)
ICSID. *See* International Center for Settlement of Investment Disputes (ICSID)
ILC Draft Articles on State Responsibility, 66, 152, 156, 157
Illegality
  defence of, 53–56
  domestic law, 52–53
  foreign investment, 46–47
  good faith to gain protection of investment treaties (*see* Good faith)
  investment treaties, 47
  ITA, 46
  Kardassopoulos v. Georgia, 47
  regulatory framework, host state, 47
  Salini v. Morocco, 47–48
  stage, 56–58
In accordance with the national laws, 37, 69, 72

Indian Arbitration Act, 29, 139–145
Indian Model BIT 2003, 27
Indian Model BIT 2015, 36, 38, 39, 46, 61, 62, 69, 75, 83, 87, 89, 91, 96–98, 102, 104, 108, 125, 127, 129, 135, 196, 197
Indirect expropriation, 32, 89–92, 97, 168, 169
International Bank for Reconstruction and Development (IBRD), 171, 172
International Center for Settlement of Investment Disputes (ICSID)
  Art. 42(1), 47
  India
    adoption, Model Rules on Arbitral Procedure, 175
    advantages and disadvantages, participation, 184–194
    arbitration services, 176
    BITs, 135
    capital, 173
    dispute resolution, 175
    economic development, 173
    FCN Treaties, 176
    formulation, ICSID Convention, 171–172
    IBRD, 172
    international claim, 176
    negotiating process, 172, 177–179
    non-participation, 181–184
    political risks, 174
    private capital, 173, 174
    protection of foreign investment, 172, 177
    structure and function, 179–181
    World Bank, 172, 175–176
  jurisdiction, 58, 85
  object and purpose of, 85
  purpose of, 48
  ratification, 197
  tribunal, 49, 136
International Court of Justice (ICJ), 61, 64, 67, 128, 129, 132, 160, 167

International law
  BIT, 61
  breach of, 65
  customary, 35, 36, 61
  and domestic law, 9, 48, 49, 59, 64
  general, 35
  General principles of, 61, 62
  issues of, 3
  and protection of foreign investment, 16–26
  rules, 47
International minimum standard
  breach of, 19
  Calvo doctrine, 18
  claim of, 18
  customary, 105
  FET Standard, 106, 107
  form of, 87
  host State, 17
  NT standard, 21
  treatment for foreigners back on the agenda, 25
International public policy, 55, 85, 144
Investment treaty arbitration and Indian judiciary
  protection of foreign investment, 149–155
  responsibility
    actions of judiciary, 155–156
    denial of justice, 160–166
    expropriation, 168–169
    FET, 167–168
    ILC Draft Art. 4(1), 156–157
    ILC Draft Articles on State Responsibility, Art. 3, 157
    judicial activism, 158–160
    State, 156
    Treatment of Polish Nationals case, 157–158
  structure and nature, 147–149
Investor
  British investors, 11
  foreign, 1–9, 11, 13–15, 17–21, 23, 25, 27, 28, 30, 31, 33, 35–56, 58, 62, 65–69, 73, 75, 77, 79, 84, 86–89, 97, 98, 102, 105, 106, 108, 110, 112, 115–119, 124, 134, 140, 141, 147–149, 151, 152, 154, 157, 159–163, 165–171, 174–177, 179, 182, 183, 185, 186, 190, 192, 195–197
  Indian investors, 10
  jurisdiction
    BIT, 78–79, 81–82
    compliance, 81–82
    ICSID, 85
    2015 Model BIT, 83–86
    ratione personae, 78
  pro-investors and anti-investors, 5

J

Judicial activism, 168–160
Judiciary
  enforcement of rights, 196
  Indian judiciary (*see* Investment treaty arbitration and Indian judiciary)
  investment treaty arbitration (*see* Investment treaty arbitration and Indian judiciary)
  and legislature, 87
Jurisdiction
  appellate, 164
  and applicable laws, 59–69
  award, 137
  and dispute resolution clauses, 27
  domestic, 110
  excessive, 106
  exclusive, 28, 29
  exercises, Supreme Court, 150
  host State courts, 18
  ICSID disputes, 58, 176, 183, 185–190, 194, 197

Index

illegitimate assertion, 166
international, 164
investment
    ICSID Convention, 73
    India-Czech Republic BIT, 72
    Indian-Armenia BIT, 69–70
    2015 Model BIT, 75–77
    non-ICSID case, 73–74
    UNCTAD, 75
investor, 77–86
lack of, 56
liberal, 153
national, 24
refusal of, 52
stage of, 56
tax, 154
tribunal, 57, 133
unknown jurisdiction, 174
writ, 149, 152, 154, 155

L

Land acquisition, 97, 101
Lasting interests, 3, 40
Legality, 38, 44, 46, 48–51, 55–58, 65
Legal persons, 78, 80, 82
Legitimate expectations
    FET, 105
    regulatory framework, 105–106
    treatment standards
        arbitral jurisprudence, 110
        circumstances of invocation, 114–115
        claim, 113
        defined, Supreme Court of India, 110–111
        reasonableness and natural justice, 111
        Saluka v. Czech Republic, 112
        Tecmed v. Mexico, 110
Legitimate regulations, 112, 196
Like circumstances, 36, 117, 119, 124, 125
Local bodies, 55

M

Maffezini, 65, 116, 123, 125, 131
Market rate, 95, 96
Market value, 25, 93, 94, 96, 97, 99–101
Measure (s)
    arbitrary/discriminatory, 104
    BIT, 90–91
    definition, 87
    direct/indirect, 89–90
    expropriatory, 88, 89, 169
MIGA. *See* Multilateral Investment Guarantee Agreement (MIGA)
Misrepresentation, 28, 48, 49, 54, 56
MNCs. *See* Multi-national corporations (MNCs)
Most favoured nation treatment (MFN) and NT
    BITs, 115–116
    determination of violation, 116–117
    discrimination, 118
    double taxation treaty, 124
    exceptions, 119–123
    foreign and national investors, 115
Multilateral Investment Guarantee Agreement (MIGA), 26, 178
Multi-national corporations (MNCs), 15, 24, 37, 175

N

National
    Bank, 139
    citizen, 84
    courts, 3, 21, 164, 169, 191
    development and social progress, 17
    dual, 84
    economies, 173
    foreign contractors, 119
    interest, 12
    and international law, 64, 66
    insurance, 174
    investors, 115, 118
    jurisdiction, 24

law, 62, 66, 69, 72, 81, 119, 182
NT (*see* National treatment (NT))
and regional economy, 36
Nationalization
  coal sector, 14
  definition, 88
  economic activity and natural resources, 20
  expropriation, 89, 90
National treatment (NT), 8, 12, 13, 36, 87, 152, 195
Natural persons, 81
Natural resources
  extraction and export, 11
  NIEO, 20-21
Negotiations, 7, 16, 31, 34, 69, 87, 97, 102, 130, 131, 181, 184
New International Economic Order (NIEO), 15, 23, 88, 181
Newly independent States, 13, 16, 17, 21-23, 88, 172, 195
New York Convention for Recognition and Enforcement of Foreign Arbitral Awards, 175
NIEO. *See* New International Economic Order (NIEO)
Non-discriminatory, 67, 92, 94, 98, 119
Non-resident entity, 40, 42, 44

P

Physical protection, 107, 108
Piercing of corporate veil, 85
Place of incorporation, 81
Political risks, 174
Portfolio investments, 40, 76
Preamble, 22, 32, 37, 38, 85, 144, 173, 183
Precedent, 143, 144, 147, 149, 158, 184
Pre-investment activity, 76, 77
Private capital, 173, 174
Property
  expropriation, 88, 92, 100
  foreign, 11, 13, 15, 24, 25, 92, 182, 195
  foreign investor, 17
  form of, 62
  intellectual property rights, 1, 69, 159
  investments, 62
  movable and immovable, 69, 181
  nature of, 138
  ownership of, 51
  private, 19, 20, 88, 168
  protection, 102, 178
  right to property, 12, 36, 98-100
  specific categories, 138
  value of, 94, 97
Prospective planning, 86
Protection of foreign investment
  and Indian judiciary
    Art. 14, 152
    Art. 19, 152
    Art. 21, 152
    Art. 32, 149-150
    Art. 226, 153
    Art. 298, 150
    FDI investment, 154
    writ remedies, 151
  and International law
    natural resources, 21-23
    NIEO, 24, 25
    Porter Convention, 18
    protection of foreign investment, 17
    State responsibility, 19-20
    trade agreements, 16
Public corporations, 84
Public interest
  protection, 109
  social and economic affairs, 151
Public interest litigation, 159
Public policy, 142-145

R

Rate of interest, 63, 64, 95
Ratione materiae, 56, 69, 77, 187

Index

Ratione personae, 69, 78, 187
RBI. *See* Reserve Bank of India (RBI)
Recognition of award, 136, 141
Regulatory framework, 7, 8, 10, 15, 26, 30, 35, 37, 39–47, 58, 105, 106, 167
Report of the Executive Directors, 85, 173, 190, 191
Reserve Bank of India (RBI), 2, 39–41, 45
Resident entity, 44
Right to property, 12, 36, 98–101

S

Salini test, 73, 187, 188
Saipem v. Bangladesh, 160–161
Seat of arbitration, 63, 137, 141, 143–145
Sectoral requirements, 41, 44
Sectors
  business, 118
  coal, 14
  commercial banks, 14
  economic, 118
  export of natural resources, 11
  FDI Policy, 43
  labour intensive and priority, 1
  life insurance, 14
Setting aside award, 136, 137, 139, 141, 142, 145
Shares
  FDI Policy, 41
  investment, 40
Social justice, 19, 20, 182
Sources of international law, 67, 160
Stable and predictable environment, 106
Standing, 52, 69, 73, 117, 152, 159
State immunity, 138
State responsibility, 19–21, 65, 66, 68, 155–157, 166, 182, 195
Substantial business activity, 82, 83
Supreme Court of India, 30, 40, 51, 102, 110, 111, 113, 140, 144, 159, 170, 183

T

Taxation, 13, 53, 116, 120–122, 124, 160
Technical know-how, 1, 22, 75, 174
Territory of other contracting party, 79
Transparency, 101, 105, 133, 168, 196
Treaty practice, 8, 37, 102, 108

U

UN Charter, 18, 19
United Nations, 2, 16, 23, 25, 181
Unreasonable, 3, 51, 101, 109, 110, 113, 145, 162, 163

V

Value of property, 13, 24, 25, 69, 92, 94, 97, 99–101, 168
Vienna Convention on Law of Treaties, 61, 66, 158

W

Waiver, 50, 62
White Industries v. Australia, 30, 73, 167
White Industries v. India, 9, 77, 116, 162
World Trade Organization (WTO), 68, 116, 184, 193
Writ jurisdiction, 148, 149, 151, 152, 154, 155, 196

Z

Zamindars, 20, 98